Sir Francis Drake

By the same author

FICTION

Crisis in Zanat

The Robbers Passing By

GENERAL

The Crime of Mary Stuart

Vote of Censure

The portrait of Sir Francis Drake is reproduced from the miniature by Nicholas Hilliard by kind permission of the National Portrait Gallery, London.

Sir Francis Drake

George Malcolm Thomson, 1899–

William Morrow & Company, Inc., New York, 1972

To my
English and American editors,
B.D.F. and J.C.W.

Printed in the United States of America.
Library of Congress Catalog Card Number 70-182961

Contents

List of Illustrations

List of Maps

Author's Notes

I should be most ungrateful as well as discourteous were I not to acknowledge the kindness and help I received while preparing this book from the staff of the British Museum Reading Room and particularly those in the Map Room and State Paper Room. In the Public Records Office my visits were made fruitful through the benevolent efficiency of the staff and, above all, of Mr E. K. Timings. Miss Joyce Batty has transcribed for me Elizabethan manuscripts which I should have found it very hard to read. I have also to thank the officials at the National Maritime Museum, Greenwich, and the librarians at the Municipal Library, Plymouth. At the Wasa Dockyard, Stockholm, I was able to tread the decks of a salvaged galleon belonging to a period not much after Drake's and form a personal impression of what life was like aboard ships at that time. I must express my thanks to Sybil Rang for the speed and efficiency with which she has typed a difficult manuscript. And, finally, let me say how grateful I am to Lieutenant P. Banyard, R.N., and the staff of the Hydrographic Department of the Navy for the interest they showed in the search for Port Pheasant.

G.M.T.

About Money

The relative values of the different kinds of currency in the seventeenth century are well known and may, for example, be found in Fynes Moryson's *Itinerary*. When the attempt is made, however, to relate these to modern values, complications arise for several reasons: (1) the current wave of inflation, (2) the recent adoption by Britain of a decimal coinage, and (3) the fact that the American dollar did not exist in the sixteenth century.

Nonetheless, if one uses as a base the formula $2.40= £1, the following comparative values for sixteenth-century currencies apply:

the English pound sterling = $2.40
the shilling = .12
the penny = .01
the ducat = .66
the peso = 1.08
the pistole (or pistolet) = .72
the écu (or crown) = .72

It is not easy, however, to make a meaningful relationship between the purchasing power of money then and its value now. I have assumed that a Tudor pound would buy as much as £30 ($72.00) today. This is, at best, a guess. As James A. Williamson points out in *Hawkins of Plymouth*, written in 1949, any general factor 'is entirely misleading, not only because some things have altered in price more than others, but also because a great number of things in common use now were unknown and unpriced then'.

These cautions must be borne in mind when, as in the following pages, the Elizabethan pound is taken to be the equivalent of £30 ($72.00) today. The evidence is inconclusive: Drake, for example, as Vice-Admiral of the English fleet, is paid 30*s*. a day ($3.60); a mariner gets 50 pence (50 cents) a month; to build a man-of-war costs £5 ($12.00) a ton. And so on.

As in this note, whenever dollar values are stated in the text they adhere to the formula $2.40= £1.

I

No Peace Beyond the Line

> 'Gold is the devil,' said Howard, the old man, 'it alters your character. However much you find, even if it is more than you can shift, still you think of getting more. And for the sake of getting more, you forget the difference between right and wrong.'
>
> *The Treasure of the Sierra Madre* – B. Traven

Half a century and a little more had passed since the world was divided. Divided once and for all by a shaven curialist in Rome drawing a line vertically on the globe in mid-Atlantic, north to south – so! Pope Alexander, by the authority of Almighty God, had ordained that it be done. And, for once, he had acted with the best of intentions.

Certainly, too, he could not be accused of having wasted time. It was only a few months since Christopher Columbus, sailing to the west, had discovered the New World for Spain.

Por Castilla y por Leon
Nuevo Mundo halló Colon[1]

But it was not solely a question of what Columbus had discovered. Voyaging to the south and east, a Portuguese named Bartolomeo Diaz had rounded the Cape of Good Hope. The new world lay not in one direction but in two!

If the world were not divided as plainly and authoritatively as the waters of the Red Sea had been parted for the Children of Israel, then troubles would surely come. In the general interest of Christendom, the two chief exploring nations, Spain and Portugal, should be kept apart in strictly defined areas, the limits of which should be fixed by Christ's Vicar on earth.

Acting on the advice of his Chancery, the Pope provisionally ordered that the line be drawn a hundred leagues west of the Cape Verde Islands. Later, after the King of Portugal objected that this would not allow his carracks enough sailing room as they worked southwards along the African coast on their way to the Indian Ocean, the line of demarcation was pushed another two hundred and seventy leagues farther west, so that it stood half-way between the Azores and the West Indies.

Finally, the Bull *Inter Caetera* of 25 September 1493 settled the matter, assigning to the heirs of Ferdinand and Isabella, the Spanish monarchs, the new-found regions west of the Atlantic and forbidding all persons of no matter what rank, estate, degree, order or condition, to go for the sake of trade or any other reason whatsoever to the said islands and countries.[2]

Pope Alexander's knowledge of geography was no better than that of any well-educated man of his time. Columbus had landed on a Caribbean island and believed that he was off the coast of Asia. And like Columbus, the Pope was working in the dark. For example, he cannot have foreseen that, by drawing the line of demarcation where he did, Brazil (undiscovered until 1500, seven years after his Bull) would fall into the Portuguese sector. In the autumn of 1493 this may reasonably have seemed too improbable a contingency to worry a man of sixty-two, who had just ascended the throne of Peter and had many more immediate anxieties. For example, Pope Alexander had bought the votes of the Sacred College and was haunted by the fear that, in consequence, he might be denounced for simony. He was, too, a devoted father, oppressed with family troubles.

In the circumstances Pope Alexander's demarcation can only be considered an impressive exercise of level-headed and imaginative statesmanship. And, within the limits of what he sought to achieve, was it not a triumph? 'Two peoples, neighbours and consequently enemies in Europe, sailing in two opposite courses on the globe, could not fail at last of meeting each other . . . They met and did not attack each other. This, which ought to be considered as very amazing, was owing to Pope Alexander VI, one of the worst of men.'[3] Even today, when the Spanish and Portuguese empires have all but vanished, the cultural vestiges of the Pope's edict remain: South America speaks Spanish, except for Brazil, which speaks Portuguese.

The settlement might have had a better chance of being peacefully accepted by the rest of Christendom if the Spaniards, the stronger and tougher of the Pope's two beneficiaries, had followed a liberal, tolerant commercial policy in their overseas possessions. But this was asking too much of the temperament of Spaniards. In fact, as time went on, their exclusiveness tightened and grew more jealous. Spain's claim to dominion over half the world outside Christendom had the paradoxical effect of narrowing the outlook of her rulers and deepening only their avarice. Nations that were excluded from the American trade were correspondingly resentful, and none more so than the French and English.

Very soon their resentment had more to feed on. Gold and silver, the ultimate and infinitely alluring symbols of wealth, were found in Spanish America, in quantities unheard of until then. A prospector in the Andes stumbled on the vast Potosi silver deposits. A German innovation by which the metal was treated with mercury multiplied the output tenfold.[4] Shipped eastwards across the ocean, the output of the mines brought enormous wealth up the Guadalquivir which was laid in the treasure house in Seville;* wealth which could be spent on luxuries or used by the King of Spain, who owned one-fifth of the bullion, to buy arms and hire soldiers. The gold of the Indies helped to change the balance of military power in Europe.

Was it to be supposed that this extraordinary Spanish windfall could fail to arouse diverse emotions in princes who had not been so lucky in the draw? Was it surprising that Francis I of France would formally warn the Spanish ambassador that he renounced none of France's rights in the New World? 'I have never seen a clause in the last will of Adam conceding such exclusive control to kings Manoel and Charles' – at that time the rulers of Portugal and Spain, whom – because of their monopoly

* A low estimate of its aggregate value for the years 1503–1660 is £257 million ($616 million), about £7,500 million ($18,000 million) in modern terms.

of tropical produce, he called 'the royal grocers of Europe'.[5]

Or that Henri II of France dreamed of a *coup de main* against Panama where the treasure was collected before being sent to Spain? 'At the magic word Peru a fever of gold seized on the calmest.'[6]

The English did not escape from the infection of envy which Spain's wealth and exclusiveness aroused. Refusing to recognise the papal bull of demarcation, they pointed indignantly to a treaty just six years earlier by which the Spanish monarchs, Ferdinand and Isabella, had granted full liberty of trade to the English in all their dominions. Did it not apply to the Spanish possessions in America? This judicial question might have been debated were it not a waste of time to debate such an issue with Spaniards swelling with a sense of power, achievement and God-given mission. Outsiders such as the English could do nothing but hope covetously that, one day, the luck would turn in their favour. Some twist in policy, some new discovery in geography, either might do the trick. For if the world had, in the course of a few years, turned out to be a varied and astonishing place very different from the cosy little Christendom of their fathers, a vast area of its surface was still veiled from the eyes of Western man, half a century after the discovery by Columbus.

Intelligent guesses were made and wild surmises were confidently trusted. It was thought that it should be possible to sail eastwards round the north rim of the world to the silk and pepper of the East. It was believed that a channel, known to geographers as the Strait of Anian, would allow ships to sail round the north of America to the Far East. The width of North America was not known. The expanse of the Pacific was under-estimated. Australia had not been discovered, although its existence was suspected. Magellan's Strait was believed to divide the American continent not from a modest group of islands but from a vast southern land circling the earth and extending as far north as New Guinea. This was variously known as Beach and Terra Australis Incognita and was predicted to be rich in gold.[7] The thought that beyond the horizons there were still discoveries to be made and prizes to be won produced a rare ferment among seafaring men on the Atlantic shores of Europe. And the idea that a papal edict or a Spanish whim could impose a veto on the questing spirit of men who were as good as any at sea seemed to many of them preposterous. Seamen in the Atlantic ports were invaded by gleaming visions. And after all, if their hands itched to seize the riches which Spain was extracting from her American mines, their eagerness was no baser than the impulse of the original Spanish colonisers. Bernal Diaz, historian of the conquest of Mexico, acknowledged that his fellow-countrymen went there 'to serve God and His Majesty, to give light to those in darkness and also to get rich'.[8] They had got very rich indeed.

Strange and ironical was the destiny that, in the years after the Reformation, overtook the militant nation dwelling in the poor land south of the Pyrenees. Spain was the last of the Western countries to throw off the Islamic yoke. She was still, all through the sixteenth century, a prey to Moslem pirates and the fear of Turkish galleys. It was natural, then, that she should be the most faithful, severe and intransigent champion of the Catholic cause. The role was one which conformed to the Spanish temperament and consorted with the national interest. The Inquisition operated in Spain as a national institution, free of papal supervision and serving political as well as religious purposes. It conducted ceaseless doctrinal warfare against heretics, Jews and *conversos*. Had these latter suspects truly seen the light? Were they really sincere Christians?

The Inquisition had the means at hand to determine such theological questions and, in that great popular institution, the *auto-da-fé*, a method of penalising those who could neither flee nor be 'reconciled'. In the end, then, the Inquisition became an instrument of racial 'purity' and cultural unity, which was what popular sentiment in Spain wished it to be.

That sentiment was inflamed by a just pride in national accomplishment: Spaniards had driven the Moors back to Africa and had won for the Faith vast new territories in America. Theirs was essentially an aristocratic society of soldiers and conquerors. At the apex (under the King) were the nobles, sixty in all, growing in numbers to three hundred as the century advanced, leaders of the aristocracy that had been given the Moorish lands in Spain when the Moslem ebbed sadly back to Africa. There was Mendoza, Duke of Infantado, who had 90,000 vassals; Guzman, Duke of Medina Sidonia, who was able to offer Philip of Austria 2,000 horse; Enriquez, Admiral of Castile, owner of most of Valladolid province – all, with many more, members of a close-knit, closely intermarried society of magnates who owned more than ninety-five per cent of the land surface of Spain, although they accounted for less than two per cent of its people.

Was it any wonder that Spaniards, wherever they were, admired and sought to imitate those vastly rich, vastly privileged, tax-free noblemen on whom the Crown rained pensions and other favours in compensation for having deprived them of real political power? When a merchant or a professional man (provided that he was not a suspect Jew, as he often was) became rich enough to put the whole matter of commerce behind him, he invested his money in real estate and began to fish for a title.*

Inevitably the Spanish emigrants to America shared the outlook of their brothers in the homeland. Seventy thousand of them had left home by 1570 and had multiplied and prospered by enslaving the native people in Mexico, Peru and on the Caribbean shores. How many millions of these Indians had died of overwork, starvation or mere heartbreak it is impossible to say. In one year of epidemic in Mexico (1576) forty or fifty per cent of the Indians perished. For all concerned, this was a calamity. For the Indians were the working population and the Spanish settlers had come to America to escape from that ultimate disgrace, *el deshonor de trabajo*, the dishonour of work. But when the conquered Indians faded away under the lash or in the

* 'Au xvie siècle, pas un état, pas un prince qui ne vende contre argent comptant, des titres de noblesse.' (In the sixteenth century, not a state, not a prince who did not sell titles of nobility for ready money) – Braudel, *La Méditerranée*, p. 620.

'no peace beyond the line'. So Captains Bontemps, Bras de Fer, Jambe de Bois and other picturesque corsairs sailed to the Caribbean with a good conscience and high hopes.[10]

When a party of French Huguenots established a settlement on the coast of Florida, the Spaniards regarded it as a direct threat to their position in the Indies. This it certainly was. The homeward-bound treasure fleets sailed, perforce, through the Florida Channel and crossed the Atlantic between 30° and 40°, taking care not to fall south of the Azores lest they lose the wind for Spain. They were therefore vulnerable to attack from any hostile base which might be established on the Florida shore. Accordingly, when the Spanish admiral whom King Philip put in charge of operations, a ruthless sailor named Pero Menendez de Aviles, captured the settlement, he flayed the leader alive and hanged the rest. And he put up a notice explaining that he had done so not because they were Frenchmen but because they were Lutherans. The King of Spain minuted the dispatch in which this atrocity was reported, 'As for those he has killed, he has done well.' The explanation given by Menendez was not, however, accepted by the French, who in due course wiped out the settlement which the Spaniards had established on the site of the French one. The French avengers, led by a Gascon, Dominique de Gorgues, put up a notice testifying that they had not been inspired by animosity against the Spaniards as such, but against treacherous thieves and murderers. A French poem of the time took a more nonchalant view of the business:

Qui veut aller à la Floride
Qu'il aille – j'y ai esté.
(Whoever wishes to go to Florida,
let him go – I've been there.)[11]

What John Hawkins launched was something subtler than the French privateering and, on the face of it, more respectable, more in conformity with his position as one well-established in the shipping business and married to a daughter of the Treasurer of the Navy. After consulting with a Spanish associate in Tenerife, a merchant named Pedro de Ponte, Hawkins travelled up to London one day in 1560, or thereabouts.[12]

He talked to the money-bags of the City as one who was himself a man of substance since his share of the family business was, just then, valued at £10,000 ($24,000). In various richly panelled offices in the labyrinth of alleys between St Paul's and the Tower, he explained to magnates like Sir Lionel Duckett and Sir Thomas Lodge what he had in mind. Merchants like these knew him already as one who was bold but reputable, a man of his word as well as one who could weave the thread of an idea into a dazzling fabric promising certain adventure and possible profit. John Hawkins had the qualities of a company promoter of genius.

From his talks in the City there emerged a syndicate to exploit the West Indian slave trade. Hawkins sailed to Sierra Leone, where he bought four hundred slaves from the local authorities of this Portuguese trading post. These officials were nervous about the light in which the transaction might appear to their government in Lisbon. They insisted, therefore, that Hawkins make a show of force so that they could convincingly clear themselves with their own people. Hawkins, who obviously had foreseen this possible development in the plot, was just the man to oblige. He played to perfection and with success the part of a truculent and menacing corsair and departed for Hispaniola with his shiploads of Negroes. Thus, at any rate, he described the incident.

The Portuguese version of events was somewhat more circumstantial. Hawkins, they said, had captured six of their ships in which were more than nine hundred Negroes in addition to ivory and other cargoes. He had overwhelmed the Portuguese owners with insults and tortures. Whatever the truth of the matter, Hawkins had reason to think that he could count on the support of his government. Already Whitehall had heard about Portuguese grievances. They had complained of the trading activities of the English sea captain Martin Frobisher, who had retorted that their sovereignty in Africa did not reach farther than their guns could fire. When the Portuguese ambassador argued in reply that culverin range could not be the only test of sovereign rights, Queen Elizabeth put in her oar: If the Africans, out of the obedience they owed to the King of Portugual, did not wish to sell their slaves, nobody on earth could force them to do so.

In Hispaniola, Hawkins faced the same sort of problem as in Sierra Leone. The Spanish official, Licenciate Lorenzo Bernaldez would not trade unless the business appeared to be done under duress. Hawkins had the guns, the muskets and the pikes – to say nothing of the fierce-looking crews – to satisfy that condition. He sold the slaves for whom, he knew, there would be no lack of eager customers in the sugar plantations of the island. He paid the legal seven and a half per cent duty on the deal and he was granted, by Bernaldez, a trading licence which was as valid as Bernaldez could make it.

Hawkins knew perfectly well that the licence had no validity at all. But, true to his role of lawful, if resolute, trader he invested the proceeds of his slave deal in gold, pearls, sugar and hides. Whatever else it might be, then, this was not an act of piracy. From the Spanish point of view, it was an outrageous breach of their law, an affront to their sovereignty, a commercial transaction carried out under the threat of violence. But value had been given for value. Hawkins had asked the fixed price for his slaves, and had paid at the ruling rate for the commodities he bought. Acting as a legitimate merchant would do he sent two of his ships (loaded with sugar and hides) to Lisbon and San Lucar, at the mouth of the Guadalquivir. Their arrival there came to the ears of the Casa de Contratacion, the office in Seville which was the headquarters of the Spanish colonial monopoly. This audacious testing of the Spanish reaction produced a clear but hostile response. Both cargoes were confiscated and the merchants in whose names they had been shipped (one English and one Spanish) were thrown into prison. Bernaldez, who was in the weak position of being a convert from

Jewry, was ordered to return to Spain to account for his activities. Yet, in spite of the loss of these two ships with their cargoes, the voyage was a commercial success. Hawkins and his City backers made a handsome profit, out of which Hawkins bought a house in the City, near the Tower.

Next time he ventured to the Caribbean he would be more heavily capitalised and more impressively backed. The Highest in the land herself would be one of his shareholders. Yet surely the warning from Seville – the seized ships and the gaoled merchants – must have been understood in London and Plymouth. The Spanish government was not going to play the part which Hawkins had assigned to it. Why, then, go on with the business? Because Hawkins thought he could demonstrate to the Spanish king that it would be less expensive, more profitable, wiser, to accept the reasonable proposals which he, Hawkins, would put to him – and, in the meantime, there was the hope of further good dividends for Hawkins Brothers and their business associates.

And now – some time in the course of 1561, in all probability – the business engaged a young relative of Hawkins', a ship's officer with a precocious experience of the sea. He was called Francis Drake.

II

A Permit to Trade

'Better to abide the jutt of the uncertainty.'
John Hawkins at San Juan de Ulua

Like most families that have come up in the world, the Hawkins clan did not lack poor relations. Their Drake kinsmen, for example, a family of the highest respectability, had been one of the victims of the religious upheavals of the age. John and Margery Drake were living at Crowndale, in the parish of Tavistock in Devon, in the reign of Henry VII. Comfortably off, it seems, for they paid a rent of £4 a year for the land they farmed on Lord Bedford's estate, and well thought of in the neighbourhood. Their son, Edmund, had in his turn a son, born in his grandparents' cottage one day in 1542 (the exact year is hedged about with doubts, but this seems the likeliest). Francis Russell, later Earl of Bedford, stood godfather at the christening, thus marking the good standing of the Drakes in the district.

Edmund Drake had been to sea as a young man, so it is said. And certainly nothing could be more likely at that time and in that place, when a boy, turning his back on Dartmoor, splendid but inhospitable, had only to walk a few miles southwards along the Tavy to reach one of the most beautiful harbours in the world, Plymouth Sound. As a sailor, Edmund was liable to be more quickly infected by the Protestant wind that blew along the seaways and into the ports of Western Europe. As an outspoken Protestant, he found it wise to flee when the Cornish peasants rose against the Prayer Book of Edward VI and marched on Plymouth and Exeter in 1549. A refugee in Plymouth Castle along with his family, Edmund Drake was rescued by a ship named *The English Galley*, whose captain, Richard Drake, may have been a relative. He sought safety farther east and took his growing brood of boys to live in a hulk in the Medway near Chatham Dockyard, England's main naval base. There the cannon of Upnor Castle and a chain across the estuary guarded the royal warships at their moorings.

Somewhere on those muddy waters, between those marshy banks, Edmund Drake reared his family of twelve sons. He was, during the reign of Mary Tudor, a 'reader of prayers to the Navy' and when the Protestant wind blew again and Elizabeth followed Mary to the throne, Edmund became vicar of Upchurch in Kent. Life on the Medway had, however, left its mark on the family. Three at least of the Drake boys became sailors.

In short, the family grew up beside the sea and surrounded by the fleet. The boys were educated – how well? On the Bible and, lest there be any backsliding in their Protestantism, on Foxe's Book of Martyrs which, with its crude and horrific woodcuts, was likely to reawaken to a proper anti-popish zeal any theological sluggard. There was no sign whatever of anything of the kind in Francis. Almost the earliest personal glimpse we have of him is on his first voyage to the West Indies in 1566 when, by his proselytising fervour, he converted to Protestantism a Cardiff shipmate named Morgan Gilbert, who may have lived to regret that he yielded to these persuasions. Six years later, he was caught by the Spaniards and sentenced to two hundred lashes and twenty years in the galleys by the Inquisition. If ever he returned to Wales, there is no record of it in history.

Francis was a sturdy boy, rather under the average height, with bold bright eyes and reddish hair, who had brought with him to the Thames the broad vowels of his native Devon.[1] The hulk on the Medway – or the Vicarage at Upchurch – must soon have been intolerably crowded with twelve boisterous little Drakes aboard. Accordingly, Francis took service with a skipper who owned a boat trading out of the Thames to the cross-Channel ports. What age was he then? Twelve? Ten? He need not have been more. In those days ten was quite a normal age for a boy to go to sea.

The skipper was elderly, the vessel was barely seaworthy, but Francis learnt some of the secrets of the sailor's trade from both of them. And when the old man died, he left the tub to his apprentice, whom plainly he regarded as a boy of exceptional promise. Drake kept it for a while and then sold it for what it would fetch. He was going on to other things. At the dawn of his twenties he found himself trained in the profession which was at that time the most exciting and, to those willing to accept its dangers, the most profitable in the world: he was a mariner.

He was not the sort of mariner who would be content with the small risks and modest profits of trips across to Flushing or Brill or Le Havre – or even down to La Rochelle. The known world, which had once been confined to the Mediterranean and the seas immediately around it, was expanding. The oceans were opening their horizons and whispering their enchantments. 'The drama of the sixteenth century is that around this universe which could be spanned in sixty days, the vast, the immense world was just revealing itself.'[2] The blue-eyed, burly young skipper with his leaky craft and his evangelical background had an imagination which would take fire at such a drama and ambition which craved a part in it.

Besides, he had good connections in the business: he was a relative, as we have seen, of John Hawkins of Plymouth, who had by now built up a substantial merchant fleet, and had acquired influential friends in London. Had not the Lord Treasurer and the Earl of Leicester recommended him to the heralds for a coat of arms? By that time, Hawkins had made his second voyage to Africa and the Indies with four vessels, one of them a ship of the Queen's, the *Jesus of Lubeck*. This was an imposing old dowager of the seas which, many years before, Elizabeth's father had bought from the Germans. Did Elizabeth know what was projected at the time she allowed Hawkins to sail it and to display the royal standard as if he were her admiral? If the question was asked in the City counting-houses or along the quays at Plymouth, it would be answered by a shrug or a wink.

But Francis Drake, as quick-witted a young man as ever came out of the coastal trade, would not doubt for a moment that his Hawkins kinsman, who addressed his sovereign in high-toned language ('I have always been a help to all Spaniards and Portugals that have come in my way without any harm or prejudice by me offered to any of them'), was, nevertheless, a master of the more unconventional forms of business.

Could not he, Francis Drake, find a place beside his cousin in the glittering structure of business – if business was the proper word – in the Indies? The question carried its own answer to a young man of Drake's temperament. In 1563, when he was barely of age, he sailed as third officer in a Hawkins ship calling at ports in the Gulf of Gascony and going on to the Guinea Coast. There was the sailors' dream-world of adventure, of easy money, of profits big enough to make a young man forget that the coast had its nightmare side. Fever. Three years later, in November 1566, Drake made his first visit to the Caribbean in an expedition mounted by the Hawkins firm and commanded by Captain John Lovell.

Drake was twenty-three, perhaps twenty-four, when the four ships of the flotilla, total tonnage 350, sailed south-west out of Plymouth for the Cape Verde Islands, where they could catch the trade winds to blow them to the west. What Drake's duties were on the voyage is not certainly known: he did not command one of the ships; he was not master; perhaps he was master's mate. In any case, he received an intensive course in trade and navigation as it was practised by English captains once they were out of sight of Plymouth Hoe and out of earshot of the Privy Council and the Court of Admiralty. He was likely to be a diligent student who did not spend all his time at sea converting his Welsh shipmate to Protestantism. There was a strong practical streak in the young man's religion.

What happened on the voyage can be learned from Portuguese sources. According to these, Lovell captured five of their ships off the Cape Verde Islands, sending the plundered goods to England and carrying off to the Spanish Main the Negro slaves which, by chance, he found in their holds. To trade in these slaves was a form of business utterly forbidden in the Spanish colonies. The slave trade was a strict monopoly. But if an English captain like Lovell had the good fortune to meet two Spanish merchants who chanced to have 1,500 pesos in their purse, and if he relieved them of this burden and, honest man, gave them twenty-six slaves in return, who could say that he was robbing them? The usual price of a slave being £25 ($60) a head, Lovell was giving the Spaniards about 2,000 pesos' worth for the 1,500 pesos he had taken from them. In other words, by this impudent subterfuge he and his Spanish friends had found a way of circumventing the prohibitions on colonial trade. It seems, too, that in delivering slaves Lovell was completing contracts which Hawkins, the head of the firm, had made on the previous voyage. It was, in fact, a repeat performance of Hawkins's earlier exploits.

Continuing his cruise along the Spanish Main on the heels of a French squadron commanded by that well-known corsair Captain Jean Bontemps, Lovell arrived off Rio de la Hacha, a small coastal settlement at the mouth of a river. What happened there we can guess from the account which a local Spanish official, Treasurer Castellanos, sent to King Philip of the victories which 'we in this little city have won over two very large corsair armadas, one French and the other English'. Both of these marauders had, it seemed, been driven off by the valour of a mere sixty local people, inexperienced and ill-equipped. This success was to be attributed solely to God and 'the skill of our Captain-general', the writer's brother Miguel, 'another Horatius'![3]

Frustrated in his efforts to do business in the slaves, the Englishman Lovell had been compelled by hunger and thirst to leave ninety slaves on the river bank opposite the town and had 'sailed away in very great desperation and grief'. Would the King agree that these slaves should be divided among the people of Rio de la Hacha – who had, said the Treasurer, earned the reward by their bravery? And would His Majesty be good enough to withdraw the judges who had come from Santo Domingo, who were – at such a time! – to investigate the town's dealings with John Hawkins two years earlier? It is not known whether King Philip called off his watchdogs, and doubtful whether he believed the story of how the ninety Negroes came to be left on the river bank. What is certain is that he forced Rio de la Hacha to pay for its slaves, and that Hawkins wrote to Castellanos bitterly complaining that he had not been given the purchase money for the slaves who, by agreement or otherwise, were left behind.

In spite of this setback, it seems that the voyage brought a reasonable return to those who had invested money in it. These shareholders might be privy councillors or City financiers, or perhaps the Queen herself, all of whom had piously looked down their noses when, before the venture was launched, John Hawkins had given his bond for £500 ($1,200) that his ships would not be sailing to the Indies. The Spanish ambassador had been satisfied. King Philip had sent his thanks to his cousin Elizabeth. And John Hawkins had transferred the ownership of the vessels to his brother, William. Thus, the letter of the law had been observed, as well as the niceties of international decorum. And Hawkins Brothers had chalked up another commercial success.

Their next venture opened in circumstances in which farce and fantasy were mingled with big business and power politics. Charlatans and confidence men, forgers of imaginative maps and tellers of fabulous tales abound in an age of discovery, as natural to its climate as the explorers and conquistadores whom they deceive and inflame. A readiness to believe, going along with an insouciant gaiety of invention, lends a quality of irresponsible inspiration to the era. The world is a fairy kingdom which may at any moment come true. 'What is that island?' asked Sir Walter Raleigh of a Spanish cartographer. 'It is called the Painter's Wife's Island. Why? Because she wanted an island of her own. He put it in to oblige her.'[4] Gold – that word above all had power to summon up the legions of credulity.

One day in 1567, two Portuguese rogues named Antonio Luis and Andre Homem told a remarkable story to William Wynter of the Navy Board in London. They reported that in a part of Africa, still unoccupied by any of the European powers, there was a gold mine fantastically rich and within convenient reach of a good harbour. Wynter was impressed by what he had heard. Burghley* was impressed. The Queen herself, Tudor cupidity overcoming Tudor caution, was impressed. Planning and preparation followed. And John Hawkins was chosen as commander of an expedition which would sail to Africa to find out whether there was any substance in this Portuguese story. The Queen contributed two naval vessels and conferred on the expedition the right to fly the royal standard. Various privy councillors put money in. The City invested. Admiral Wynter of the Navy Board became a shareholder. Hawkins lent four ships of his own. The Tower of London supplied cannon and gunpowder. And the suspicions of the Spanish ambassador, rekindled every now and again by some new turn in events, were damped down if not extinguished. In July 1567, while Lovell – and Drake with him – were still on their way home from the Caribbean after their brush with Castellanos, Hawkins sailed the Queen's ships out of the Thames to Plymouth.

While he waited in that home port, making up his crews to full strength and ensuring that they were all at church on Sunday as God-fearing seamen should be, Lovell's ships came round Rame Head from the sea and cast anchor in the harbour. Hawkins, who had perhaps been loitering in Plymouth for that very purpose, invited young Drake and some others to come along with him on the new voyage. They were not reluctant. In the meantime there occurred one of those half-sinister incidents typical of the time. Seven armed ships, flying the Spanish royal standard, entered the Sound.

Their commander, a Flemish admiral, Alphonse de Bourgogne, Baron de Wachen, omitted to dip his flag and strike his topsails to the Queen's ships at their deep-water anchorage in

* Lord Treasurer, Elizabeth's most powerful minister.

the Cattewater. It was either a flagrant discourtesy or a deliberate testing of the state of English nerves. In either case, the correct answer was not in doubt. Hawkins fired his culverins and went on firing until, with the English shot thumping on the Spanish hulls, the customary salutes were made. Explanations followed. Beer and chickens were sent over to the Baron's flagship. Report went up to Her Majesty in London; reproof came back to her too faithful, too truculent commanding officer, reproof as sincere, no doubt, as the Baron's protestations of innocence were. And with that the business ended? Not quite.

A Spanish ship, lying off the town, had some Flemish prisoners aboard, unfortunates condemned to a living death in King Philip's galleys. One day, masked men swarmed aboard her, overcame the crew and set the prisoners free. A monstrous act of violence! And one for which Hawkins was responsible, as Baron de Wachen swore. 'Not so,' retorted Hawkins. 'It is more likely to have been done by Flemings from one of your own ships.' But, on the whole, the Privy Council when they considered the business decided to believe the Flemish baron. It was no moment to pick a quarrel with Spain and no doubt they had a fair idea of Hawkins's histrionic talents.

Now a fresh crisis arose. The two Portuguese, Homem and Luis, were nowhere to be found. Their usual drinking places were searched in vain. Then it turned out that they had last been seen in a small boat heading for the French coast. Which proved that they were a pair of swindlers? Everybody thought so and most people confessed that, from the beginning, they had suspected as much. The Lord Admiral had foreseen what would happen. Lord Burghley reprimanded Hawkins for not keeping a sharper eye on the missing pair. And the Queen, when apprised that 'the Portugals who should have directed us in this pretended enterprise have fled', ordered that instead of its original objective the fleet should pick up Negroes on the Guinea Coast and sell them in the Indies. It is, of course, deeply shocking to find an English queen and her chief advisers taking part in the slave trade. Nor is it any less shocking because she was only a modest and belated participant in a business in which the Kings of Spain and Portugal were already operating on a grand scale.

But if we read back our moral attitudes into history we may gain in self-esteem but hardly in understanding of the past. The truth is that, in the sixteenth century, only France among the Christian powers rejected slavery. The institution has now earned an additional odium because of its racial associations: because it has been a subjection of black men by white. In the sixteenth century, it was nothing of the kind. No Algerian lady of rank but had her retinue of Christian (i.e. European) slaves. In a single raid, a few years before the Hawkins voyages, Algerian corsairs carried off four thousand slaves from Granada. Regular centres existed for the exchange of captives. Pious societies raised money for their release. Slaves were simply unfortunate people, usually prisoners of war. They might be of any race.[5] This does not, of course, justify Elizabeth, Hawkins, Philip or any of the others.

The new expedition from Plymouth followed the customary pattern which Elizabeth and her chief minister had, with exceptional solemnity, sworn would not be repeated this time. On 2 October 1567 the *Jesus of Lubeck*, painted in the green and white colours of a Queen's ship, led the flotilla out of Plymouth Sound into the favouring wind that swept them southwards towards Tenerife and, as it chanced, into an alarming gale. The old ship was marvellously given to rolling in anything of a sea, groaning and shuddering and leaking copiously as her timbers worked one against the other. Very soon, as wind and waves pounded remorselessly on, Hawkins was advising his crew to seek safety in prayer for, alas, they were beyond mortal aid. To Francis Drake, who sailed in the *Jesus* as an officer, the admonition may have come with something less than its full power to comfort. For, if he believed passionately in the Lord's care for His own, in this world and the next, he had at that moment good reason to give priority to the things of this world. Between his homecoming with Lovell and his departure with

Hawkins he had spent about three weeks ashore. In that time he had met a Plymouth girl whom, if the *Jesus* ever entered Plymouth Sound again, he intended to marry.

However, against all reasonable expectations, the *Jesus* was still afloat when she dropped anchor at Santa Cruz in Tenerife, where the fleet reassembled as had been planned. After circumventing the local Spaniards, who barely concealed their intention to sink the English ships, Hawkins fired a polite salute and set sail for the African coast. He meant to go looking for slaves as far south as Sierra Leone. This time, however, the Portuguese authorities refused to co-operate and the African chiefs resisted. Worse, they rained poisoned arrows on the English traders. Hawkins himself was hit by one of these missiles and would probably have died had an African not given him an antidote.

On the whole, it was an arduous and unrewarding trip until the good news came that a local king in Sierra Leone wanted help with the besieging of a walled town named Conga. Hawkins committed his entire force to the operation. Cannon were brought up and incendiaries were fired into the town. At last, Conga, burning fiercely, fell to the English and their African allies, who allotted Hawkins two hundred and sixty of the vanquished – the luckier survivors of the battle – and butchered the rest for dinner. The time had now come for the English ships to catch the trade winds for the westward crossing. It had been hard work, with heavy casualties. But they had close on five hundred Negroes below decks – enough to bring a good return when exchanged for the pearls, silver, cochineal, indigo, hides and other products of the Indies. But the question arose: could the business be done this time? Hawkins thought it could, although he can hardly have overlooked the signs of sharpened hostility which he had so far encountered from Spaniards and Portuguese alike. The men who managed the Spanish colonial monopoly were particularly worried over foreign interlopers in the Negro business.

They might bring in more profitable goods in their slave-ships. For slaves were not the most valuable of commodities. After all, a slave had to be kept alive during an Atlantic crossing that would last from six to eight weeks. His food, however simple, cost money which must be set against the price he would fetch in the labour market in Hispaniola or the Spanish Main. There was therefore a temptation for a trader who had a permit for a hundred slaves to bring in, say, eighty only and fill up the ship-room thus made available with manufactured articles, which might not even be Spanish. He might pay the import duty on slaves and cheat the authorities of the higher customs revenue to which they were entitled on manufactures. Concerned as it was about the opportunities for fraud that lurked in fairly honest trade, what was Seville likely to think of the bland English captain who had not even the shadow of a permit to trade? What was likely to be the opinion of his Catholic Majesty?

Hawkins can hardly have doubted that the cold welcome he had received in Africa was in obedience to some edict emanating from Lisbon, that it was probably the result of Spanish pressure on the Portuguese government and that he could expect the same greeting in the Indies. But with tact, luck and a show of force he was sure that he would win through. Force he possessed in ample measure. His flotilla, by methods more or less respectable, had swelled to ten ships. One, the *Judith*, was under the orders of Francis Drake. It was Drake's first ship. Another, *The Grace of God*, was commanded by a Frenchman, Captain Bland (or Planes), whom the English had met when he was prowling to no good purpose along the African coast. Thus it was quite a formidable fleet – Spaniards would have called it an Armada – that bore down on the islands which guarded the Caribbean, the Lesser Antilles, Trinidad and Margarita. At the last-named, darkness was closing in when a group of mounted Spaniards, alarmed by the approach of an unknown fleet, saw a boat coming towards the beach. 'Who are you?' they called out. The answer came, 'Englishmen, and the worshipful Master

John Hawkins is our general. We have a letter for your Governor.'

Margarita was a poor little island with an inordinate appetite for slaves. The reason was a simple one. They were worked to death in the pearl fisheries which were the main industry of the place. Hawkins had an equally pressing need for fresh food, his ships having been at sea for six months. And, whatever might be the views of the Governor and his colleagues, they were not likely to resist the powerful fleet that Hawkins brought into their little harbour. All the ingredients of a profitable commerce existed. It went on for eight days during which a substantial amount of English cloth was exchanged for meat and maize while Hawkins and the Spanish officials exchanged hospitality and amiable sentiments. On the ninth day the English fleet resumed its course westwards along the coast. Hawkins was going to Borburata, a mainland port three hundred miles away. There he meant to cast anchor and arrange to have a letter sent on to the Governor of the province.

Don Diego Ponce de Leon, Governor of New Andalusia, as that portion of the Venezuelan coast was called, was put in something of a quandary by the proposition which John Hawkins made to him. The Governor was a mature man of some distinction, belonging to one of the four great landowning families who, apart from substantial estates which were the property of the Archbishop of Toledo, divided the province of Andalusia among them.[6] As a well-educated gentleman of long experience in the Colonial service, Ponce de Leon was as capable as the next man of recognising casuistry when he saw it. And here it was unblushingly displayed in the polite letter of this extraordinary Englishman. Trade, said Hawkins, was forbidden by the King, so he would not even mention it. On the other hand, if he were allowed to sell sixty Negroes and some English goods he had brought along, it would help him to pay his soldiers and would in no sense be a breach of the King of

Spain's orders. Would not the Governor come and call on him to discuss matters?

The Governor did not miss the mention of 'soldiers'. His officials had already counted the guns carried by the English fleet. And, when this Hawkins referred to 'diverse inconveniences which befall those who are too precise in observing precepts', Ponce de Leon thought he knew just what was meant. Besides, the Englishman said, 'If you come, you should not find me ungrateful.' A significant phrase. On the other hand, the Governor had strict instructions from the King to put down the illicit traffic in the Indies which had grown up under his slack and possibly corrupt predecessor, Bernaldez.

The letter from Hawkins reached the Governor at a time when he was making a tour of inspection of country where, lying to the east, was a new city recently founded, later known as Caracas. While waiting on an answer Hawkins opened shop on the shore at Borburata and awaited customers with all the confident amiability of a regular merchant; he also took the opportunity to exercise his slaves so that their health and physique could be admired by potential buyers. The customers duly arrived; business was done until word came from Ponce de Leon regretfully informing the 'right worshipful' John Hawkins that he was not allowed to trade. However, this proved to be only the first move in the game as Hawkins had expected it to be.

The English ships remained at anchor at Borburata, their cannon frightened off any pirates who might be lurking about and their shops did a roaring business in good English cloth and strong West African Negroes without any interference from the Governor. Ponce de Leon may even have collected a commission on the trade in some indirect but dignified way. After all, grandees of Spain did not forsake their vast latifundia for the boredom, worries and fevers of the New World without expecting to enrich themselves in one way or another.

No doubt there would be a rebuke from Madrid in due course. But when would it come? How soon? Ponce de Leon knew that he could count on the double voyage to Spain and back taking two hundred days or more. True, an *aviso* (dispatch boat) could beat this time. But that was an expensive mode of communication to be used only in a dire military emergency. The Governor was prepared to risk a royal thunderbolt which was at least seven months off.

Meanwhile Hawkins shut up shop in Borburata and sailed farther west along the coast. He had done a great deal of trade and took with him testimonials from the local bishop (to whom he had presented two slaves) and other worthies. It was time to move on. In advance of the main squadron he sent Drake with the *Judith* (50 tons) and the *Angel* (33 tons). It was Drake's first independent command. His task was to reconnoitre Rio de la Hacha, which he had last seen on his visit with Lovell on Whit Monday of the previous year. On that occasion the English had been cheated, as they saw it, of the price of ninety Negroes by de Castellanos, the Spanish King's Treasurer. This time, Drake asked for water for his ship. Castellanos replied with gunfire. Thereupon, Drake's gunners, on their captain's orders, put two shot through the Treasurer's house. After that, there was nothing for Drake to do but wait for the rest of the flotilla to come up. While he waited, he entertained himself by carrying off a Spanish captain under arquebus fire. Hawkins, on arrival, demanded leave to sell sixty Negroes and told Castellanos reassuringly that if he should chance to see any armed men ashore he had no need to worry. He had only to order them to leave and they would forthwith return to their ships. The Treasurer replied that he was armed and ready to fight.

After that, Hawkins landed about two miles from the town under cover of a heavy bombardment from the ships. There was a fight or, at any rate, a brief exchange of fire in the course of which the Spaniards, who were heavily outnumbered, lost their ensign. They retired into the woods and Hawkins marched into Rio de la Hacha at the head of his troops. He found the town deserted. Negotiations with the Treasurer were now opened. They went forward slowly at first and more briskly when, by what may have been a mischance, part of the town was set alight, including Government House. When Castellanos sent an obstinate message saying he did not care if Hawkins destroyed the whole place, the Englishman cunningly drove a wedge into the enemy front. He told the Spaniards who brought him the message that it was all very well for the Treasurer to talk defiantly. *He* had sent his belongings into safety! The argument impressed the Spaniards who were tired of sitting in discomfort in the woods outside their own town. Just then, Hawkins had the good fortune to be led, by disloyal slaves, to where the Treasurer had hidden the government bullion.

In the end, Castellanos, deserted by his compatriots, agreed to spend 4,000 pesos of the government's money on sixty slaves, and another 1,000 pesos on twenty for himself. These preliminaries at an end, the local planters were allowed to come into the market as purchasers of a hundred and fifty Negroes, plus a great deal of English cloth. Then, with a ceremonial exchange of presents between the two protagonists, Hawkins moved on. His call at Rio de la Hacha had brought him about £7,000 in gold for the Negroes alone and an unknown additional sum for the cargo he had brought out from England. He left Castellanos to explain to his royal master how it had all happened. To this task the Treasurer proved equal.

Two royal officials in the town, Lazaro de Vallejo Aldrete and Hernando Costilla, writing to the King, described the Treasurer's military conduct in glowing terms: 'All were astonished at his great valour (both his adversaries and also the residents) for certainly it was a business that today, on looking back at it, fills with fear those who were present.' Castellanos, in his missive, told the King that he had paid 4,000 gold pesos as ransom for prisoners the English corsairs had taken and also for the section of the town which had not yet been burnt down.[7]

Before leaving, Hawkins had put ashore a number of Negroes, some of them children not more than six years old, some of them over a hundred. Castellanos explained to the King that he was fattening them up so that they would be worth something and was selling them off a few at a time, although the inhabitants thought they should get the slaves for nothing, in compensation for the damage done to the town. He concluded, 'Unless Your Majesty sends an armada to patrol, it is impossible for Your Majesty's vassals to live and maintain themselves . . . We entreat Your Majesty to deign to remedy all this with speed.'

At Santa Marta, a village farther along the coast, Hawkins, by agreement with the Governor, made an imposing demonstration of force, after which both sides settled down to trade and a hundred and ten Negroes were disposed of.

However, by this time, the whole of New Andalusia was thoroughly alerted. Not only were Hawkins and his fleet of ten ships on the coast but a corsair had seized a gold-laden frigate out of Nicaragua, and another had seized two frigates at San Bernaldo. Cartagena, chief commercial port in the region, put itself in a state of defence. It had a determined governor, a garrison of five hundred foot, some cavalry and a few thousand armed Indians. Hawkins cautiously tested the town's fighting spirit. The results were discouraging. Cartagena returned shot for shot. The Governor refused to trade or even to allow the English ships to take on water and victuals. Reluctantly, Hawkins decided that an assault on the fortified port would be too dangerous a venture. While it would have been convenient to sell the residue of his slaves, his fighting strength was down below the four hundred mark. The time had come to sail for home.

But home was farther off than he or any of his company realised.

With any reasonable luck, Hawkins and his companions should have sighted Rame Head at the entrance to Plymouth Sound in a matter of eight weeks. Instead of that, the ships were still trying to work their way out of the Caribbean against adverse winds when bad weather hit them and, especially, hit the elderly and feeble *Jesus of Lubeck*. As one wrote who sailed in her on that voyage, 'On either side of the stern-post, the planks did open and shut with every sea, the seas without number and the leak so big as the thickness of a man's arm, the living fish did swim upon the ballast as in the sea.'[8] Running before the wind, Hawkins was driven towards dangerous shoals in the Gulf of Mexico, somewhere on the Florida coast. Then the wind veered round to the north and carried the ships (all but one, the *William and John*, which beat to windward and made for England) across six hundred miles of sea to the Yucatan Peninsula.

By this time it was just two months since Hawkins had weighed anchor at Cartagena. He should have been home. But the victuals were running short and the *Jesus* was in no state to face an Atlantic crossing. This was a problem complicated by the financial agreement governing the enterprise. If the ship needed repair, the cost would fall proportionately on all the members of the syndicate. But if she were wrecked or abandoned, the whole loss would be the Queen's. These were the terms on which voyages of that kind were financed. It would be easy and sensible to transfer the treasure from the *Jesus* to the other ships and send her gracefully to the bottom of the Gulf of Mexico. But 'she was the Queen's Majesty's ship and . . . should not perish under his hand'. Hawkins did not relish the thought of an audience with her at which he had to tell her how it befell that *her* ship was the only unit of the fleet not to return.

In his dilemma, he sought advice from a Spanish ship he encountered. The Spanish skipper told him that his best plan would be to cross the Bay of Campeche and moor at San Juan de Ulua, a roadstead which served as the seaport of Vera Cruz and starting point for the land journey to Mexico City, capital of New Spain. It was at Vera Cruz that the bullion and produce of the country was assembled for the long sea voyage back to Spain. The only trouble was that the plate fleet – the treasure fleet – was expected to arrive at San Juan from Spain about the end of September. Very soon! Then, after taking on board the year's output of the Mexican mines, it would return to Seville. Obviously, an encounter with a Spanish force of such importance could raise the possibility of grave diplomatic and military consequences. It would, in effect, be a head-on collision with King Philip himself.

Hawkins decided he must risk the meeting and thought that, given luck and speed, he might avoid it. As a precaution, he insisted that two other Spanish ships he fell in with later should remain in his company. In one of them, travelling as a passenger, was a man from Mexico City named Villa Nueva. And so, showing the royal standard only, 'so dim through the foul wearing in foul weather that [the local officials] never perceived the lions and flower de luces till they were hard aboard the *Jesus*', Hawkins led his battered ships into the port of San Juan de Ulua, on 15 September 1568.

III

Echo Beyond the Mexique Bay

'Courage my hearts for a fresh charge. Sound Drums
and Trumpets, and St George for England.'
Seaman's Grammar – Captain John Smith 1627

Two days after the arrival of the English fleet, the situation at San Juan de Ulua was as delicate as it could be. In the harbour – if the roadstead could be called a harbour – were John Hawkins' battered ships with their hungry crews. Outside, in an ugly cross sea, waiting for the norther to die down so that he might force an entry, was Don Martin Enriquez, newly appointed Viceroy and Captain-General of New Spain (Mexico), voyaging in a fleet of galleons (the Flota) commanded by Don Francisco de Luxan. The encounter which Hawkins had hoped to avoid when he took the risk of entering the roadstead had occurred. This particular fleet had left San Lucar in Andalusia about two months earlier bringing, among other goods, 873 quintals of mercury, a consignment of critical importance for the silver mines of Mexico which, unlike Peru, had no domestic output of this metal. More important still, however, was the presence in the fleet of a Viceroy-designate.

San Juan de Ulua, an unprepossessing spot, was the handiwork of men with only a little help from nature. About half a mile off-shore, a low island, hardly more than a sandbank, and about a bow-shot across, rose out of the Gallega Reefs, providing some shelter from wind and waves. Approaching from the east, through dangerous shoals, vessels came to an anchorage where the water was four fathoms deep and where the island shore facing the mainland had been built up into a quay with freestone and gravel. Quite large ships could approach so close to the island that their beak heads projected over the land. The

King of Spain employed twenty strongly-built Negroes to keep the island in good repair. On it there was a small chapel, a building called the House of Lies and a platform with a few cannon. It was as desolate a stretch of the Mexican coast as could be found in the Bay of Campeche. Inland, the country was flat and unhealthy, much afflicted by wind-blown sand.

Hawkins had not bargained for a meeting with King Philip's

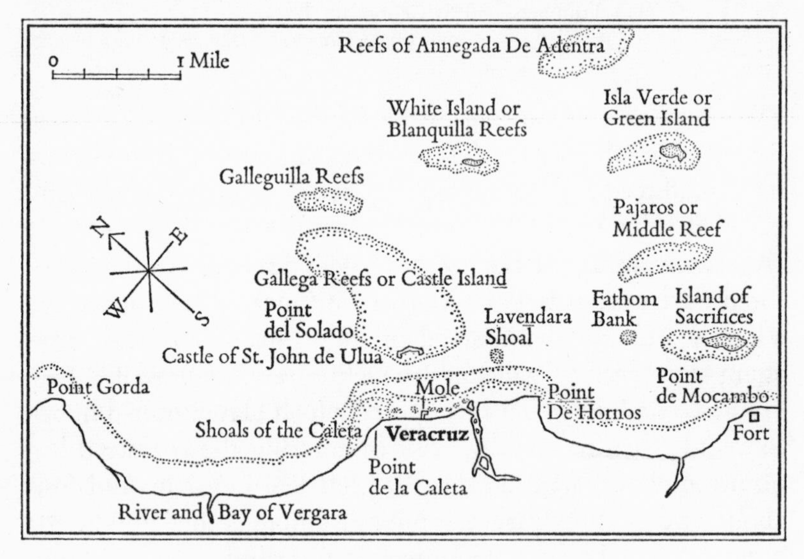

1 Chart of San Juan de Ulua
From a chart of 1841 drawn by Captain R. F. Cobb

own representative in Mexico, invested with all the semi-regal pomp with which Spanish protocol surrounded such an exalted personage. He was faced by a grave dilemma. To deny Don Martin entry to a protected anchorage on his own coast at the opening of the hurricane season would be an inconceivable act of defiance. To use force to prevent that entry would be an affront to which his Catholic Majesty would almost certainly retaliate with a declaration of war on Queen Elizabeth. This was a responsibility which a serious-minded merchant like John Hawkins could not take. He had two ships of the Queen's in his fleet and he had been warned before leaving England that the

Queen thought it was no time to push the controversy with Spain to the point of open rupture.

On the other hand, while he probably had the gun-power to prevent Don Martin's royal galleon from reaching the anchorage through the difficult navigation channel, it would be quite a different matter dealing with him once he had tied up alongside the English ships. Hawkins did what was probably the best he could do in the circumstances. Having strengthened the five-gun battery on the island with six cannon taken from a carrack in the harbour, he opened negotiations with the Viceroy. Meanwhile, Don Martin was fretting and fuming on the open sea while he waited for his vice-admiral, Captain Juan de Ubilla, to join him. A north wind threatened at any moment to drive his galleon ashore either on the ill-omened Island of Sacrifices or on the reef of La Lavandara (The Washerwoman) which, hidden by the sea in any kind of weather, and only betrayed by the broken water above it, was even more sinister. In his predicament, Hawkins decided to send a Spanish intermediary, Captain Antonio Delgadillo, to negotiate with the Viceroy terms on which the two fleets could make joint use of the port.

Don Martin was in almost as great a quandary as Hawkins: if he remained outside the roadstead the heavily laden merchantmen his armed vessels were escorting might be wrecked; if, on the other hand, he parleyed with the Englishman, he would risk a stern rebuke from the King for entering into an agreement with an interloper who was little better than a pirate. In this difficulty, the Viceroy decided that he would make an agreement and, simultaneously, that he would break it. Part of the bargain was that ten hostages were to be exchanged. The Viceroy dressed some seamen as their social betters and invited them to draw lots which of them was to go. When they showed some reluctance to fall in with this plan, Ubilla, who had in the meantime appeared on the scene, offered himself as one of the hostages in which he was followed by his nephew and four other gentlemen. The Viceroy was moved to admiration by something which, in view of what he had in mind, was certainly no empty gesture. Here is what he planned: after they had all arrived safely in the anchorage, he would introduce a hundred and fifty soldiers from Vera Cruz secretly into one of the merchantmen. Then, on an agreed signal, the English ships would be overrun and their crews slaughtered. That was the simple project as the Viceroy unfolded it. The negotiations with the English were now swiftly concluded. The business of the hostages was satisfactorily arranged, and Hawkins 'bearing a godly and Christian mind', as his gunner, Job Hortop, piously says, 'void of deceit and fraud, judged the Spaniards to have done the like'. It may be doubted whether Hawkins was quite so trustful as that but, at all events, a trumpet blew as a sign that agreement had been reached and on 21 September the Viceroy with his thirteen ships entered the roadstead and made fast. Salutes were exchanged between the two fleets.

San Juan de Ulua was now overcrowded with ships moored side by side, and the English were considerably outnumbered. But Hawkins, commanding the roadstead with his shore cannon which he had protected with ramparts of shingle, believed that, with any ordinary degree of vigilance, he had little to fear. Yet he can scarcely have been easy in his mind, for he had ample reason to suppose that some treachery was being planned. In one of the merchantmen, he noticed, additional gun-ports were being cut. When Hawkins complained of this, he was promised that anything he disliked would be removed. When no action was taken, he sent his ship's master, Robert Barrett, who spoke Spanish, to renew his protest to the Viceroy. Barrett came from Saltash just across the Tamar from Plymouth and was a cousin of Drake's. As soon as he arrived on the Spanish ship about half past nine in the morning, Don Martin, the Viceroy, threw him below hatches.

During the hours of darkness, he had started to implement his plan by introducing two hundred armed men into a dismantled hulk in the harbour. On an agreed signal, these would emerge, board the English ships, rush the shore guns and slaughter the Protestant corsairs. Nervously waiting for the return of his skipper, Hawkins sat down to dinner. During what must have been a tense meal one of his guests, Villa Nueva, the man from Mexico City who had been captured just before Hawkins arrived at San Juan, was found by an observant young steward named John Chamberlain to have a dagger hidden in his sleeve. Hawkins sprang to his feet and, ordering the Spaniards to be arrested, went quickly out on deck, snatching up a cross-bow on his way. He leapt from the deck of the *Jesus* on to the *Minion*, which was moored on the outside of the row of English ships. He was in time to see Ubilla in the bow of a cargo ship strenuously pulling on a hawser in the attempt to bring the vessel alongside the *Minion*.

'You are not behaving like a gentleman,' he shouted, which in the circumstances was surely a mild enough reproof.

'I am following my vocation as a fighter,' retorted Ubilla.

'You are right,' said Hawkins – or so at least Ubilla thought – and fired a bolt at him. An English sailor, levelling an arquebus, killed a man standing beside Ubilla. At this moment Ubilla waved the white cloth which was the signal for action by the Spaniards. On the Spanish flagship, Don Luis Zegri, Mayor of Vera Cruz, blew his trumpet and shouted the war-cry, 'Santiago!' The Spaniards scrambled for their weapons and the fight was on.

Later, Ubilla was criticised for having given the signal an hour too soon. Had he not done so, the surprise would have been complete. No Englishmen would have escaped and none of their ships would have been saved. Ubilla's defence was that already Hawkins had discovered what was afoot.

On the island, things went well for the Spaniards. There they had been drinking with the gullible English – and no doubt encouraging them to take too much. When the trumpet blew, the Spaniards pulled out the daggers they had been hiding and leapt on their drinking-companions. Very soon the island was cleared of English, all of whom were killed, except three who swam to the *Jesus*. After that the shore cannon were turned on the English ships by Don Francisco de Luxan, the Spanish admiral.

On the ships moored in the harbour fighting was more even. The *Minion* was taken by Spaniards and retaken by Hawkins. Shouting: 'God and Saint George! Upon those traitorous villains! I trust in God the day shall be ours!' he led a counter-attack of seamen and soldiers who scrambled down from the deck of the *Jesus*. The *Minion*, recaptured, was cut loose from her moorings. As it chanced, the Spanish *almirante* now came into the sights of the *Minion*'s cannon. A grapeshot set fire to a powder barrel on the Spaniard, which blew up with an immense explosion that littered the roadstead with dead bodies and wreckage. Immediately afterwards, the Spanish flagship was hit and burst into flames. For a few minutes it seemed she would follow her consort and be totally destroyed. Sink she did, but it was in such shallow water that she was able to continue the fight. The crowded harbour was now full of the reek and bellow of gunfire.

Ubilla, whose ship had been sunk in his absence and who had failed to seize either the *Minion* or the *Jesus*, leapt ashore and ordered a mulatto to put two barrels of powder on to a ship and let her loose in the harbour with a slow match at the powder. While he was waiting for the fire to take, Ubilla was alarmed by a shout from the flagship. There, on his knees, was the navigating officer crouching so as to keep under cover from the English small-arms fire and calling out that the Viceroy was on board, with only four or five men to guard him. Ordering some reluctant soldiers to follow him, Ubilla boarded the stricken ship in search of Don Martin, whom he found with his back to the mainmast, armed at all points and full of fight. The Viceroy demanded to be told what Admiral Luxan was doing.

The answer was quickly supplied by the shore batteries which Luxan had brought into play. They were already making things uncomfortable on the *Jesus*. There were five cannon shot in her mainmast, her foremast was broken in half by a chain shot and her hull badly holed. In this crisis, the *Jesus* and the *Minion* drew off two ships' length from the Spanish fleet.

In a momentary lull in the fighting, Hawkins called to his Negro page, Sam, for a cup of beer – a silver cup – and drank to all of them, bidding the powder-blackened gunners stand to their pieces like men. He had no sooner put the cup down than a ball from a demi-culverin carried it overboard. 'Fear nothing,' said Hawkins. 'God who has preserved me from this shot will also deliver us from those villains.'

Juan de Ubilla, having made his report to the Viceroy, went ashore once more. The first attempt to use fireships having failed, he now offered money to a shipowner named Felipe Boquin for the use of his vessel. Set on fire in four places, this ship was sent against the English fleet, which by this time was reduced to four ships. Seeing the fireship bear down on them the crew of the *Minion*, in alarm, cut their cables and tried to work out to sea. And now Captain Bland, the Frenchman, was in trouble. He tried to work to windward of the Spanish ships, meaning to use his vessel as a fireship against the enemy. But alas, his ship had lost its mainmast over the side by a hit from a chainshot; he set the vessel alight and took to his pinnaces. Only the *Jesus*, with the St George's Cross flying from the stump of her mast, the *Minion* and Drake's little barque, the *Judith*, were left. But at this moment Hawkins decided that the *Jesus* must be sacrificed.

He was already annoyed with the *Minion*, which had panicked when the fireships attacked. Now he ordered both it and the *Judith* to come alongside his flagship, using her as cover from the Spanish cannon. In that way the crew, the supplies and the treasure in the *Jesus* were transferred to the other ships, although a trunk filled with four hundredweight of pearls and silver was left behind. Night having fallen, the two surviving vessels sailed out of the roadstead. Hawkins, on the testimony of a French eye-witness, stayed on the *Jesus* until it was almost too late to leave. He sprang aboard the *Minion* when she had already begun to sheer off. Thus the Queen, if she read the account of the fight, would not doubt that her admiral had done all he could to save her ship. Of one thing Hawkins was unaware. In the confusion of the battle, his eleven-year-old nephew, Paul, who served as his page, had been at his uncle's side, holding a richly jewelled plate. Seeing an Englishman killed, the boy in terror stayed on the *Jesus* until it was too late to jump. He was captured, and many years afterwards he married a well-to-do half-caste woman in Mexico. What explanation John Hawkins gave to the boy's father is not recorded.

The battle at San Juan de Ulua, which had begun at ten in the morning and raged all through the day – twenty ships side by side in a stretch of water about half a mile long – at last died away. The fireships guttered out. The culverins ceased to clamour. Darkness and silence fell upon San Juan de Ulua.

The *Jesus* was abandoned. The *Angel* had been sunk and the *Swallow* captured. The men who were able to leave the *Jesus* had been divided between the *Minion* and the *Judith*. With the new day came a strong north wind which put the *Minion* in grave danger of being driven ashore. Hawkins lost three anchors and two cables in his struggle against the storm. By that time Drake and the *Judith* had vanished. As Hawkins said later, 'They forsook us in our great misery.'

It was a somewhat severe reproach, although it seems to have done Drake's reputation more harm with later historians than it did at the time. It is possible Drake thought that when Hawkins ordered him to clear off he was announcing a general *sauve qui peut*. This is a conjecture. What is certain is that the *Judith* was a mere barque of 50 tons, the *Minion*, a Queen's ship, at least six times bigger. In the storm that blew, Drake would have enough to do keeping his little vessel off the rocks without sparing thought for his bigger companion. In any case, what could he have done? He had, on the face of it, a better case for accusing Hawkins of forsaking him. As events show, Hawkins bore no grudge against Drake afterwards.

The *Minion* had a tragic homeward trip. There were two hundred men on board her when she fled from San Juan de Ulua. One hundred of them elected to be put ashore when it became obvious that there would not be food for all of them during an Atlantic crossing. Rather risk the mercy of the Indians or – more unkind – that of the Spaniards than face a slow death by starvation at sea. As it was, the hundred that were left aboard ate dogs, cats, rats and parrots during the crossing. They stewed hides to keep alive. One by one they died. Many who had survived the crossing succumbed to over-indulgence when at last they were driven to the Galician coast near Vigo, for ill-luck with the wind prevented them from sailing directly back to England.

In the end, when the *Minion* dropped anchor in Mounts Bay, Cornwall, fifteen men were alive on board. It was 25 January 1568, four months after the departure from San Juan de Ulua. Drake had arrived at Plymouth just five days before. It may be asked why, in a fast-sailing 50-ton barque, he had taken so long to make the crossing. The possibility arises that, on the way home, Drake had been up to some mischief. He was a hot-tempered young man, as the two hits on the Treasurer's house at Rio de la Hacha had already shown; he was quite capable of seeking to square accounts with the Spaniards by methods which his more diplomatic relative, Hawkins, would not approve.

For Hawkins, the voyage had ended in an almost unredeemed disaster. He had squandered the lives of some hundreds of men: the ten hostages, Barrett, master of the *Jesus*, men killed in the fighting, men captured, men marooned at their own insistence and men who starved. Many had died horrible deaths. Four hundred had left Plymouth with Hawkins; in all, seventy came back. Even in that age when life was cheap, especially the lives of men who went to sea and knew they would be lucky to reach middle age, this casualty rate was on the high side. There would be wives and mothers in Devon asking whether John Hawkins need have been so simple as to trust the word of Don Martin Enriquez.

The Viceroy's conduct calls for some explanation. He was a Spanish gentleman, the son of a Marquis, member of a distinguished family. The Enriquez were Admirals of Castille and owned most of the provinces of Valladolid and Valencia.

But, as Don Martin saw it, the surprise at San Juan de Ulua was a matter of domestic concern, an operation of internal security, rather than an incident of war. He was dealing with law-breakers, trespassers, men who were little better than pirates and who made their crimes worse by an incredible insolence. He felt no more bound in conscience or honour to keep his word to them than a police officer feels obliged to respect his bargain with a blackmailer. This, however, was a point of view which neither Drake, posting angrily up to London to demand a commission of reprisals from the Privy Council, nor Hawkins, staggering ashore on a Cornish beach from a ship that was half-way between a mortuary and a hospital, could be expected to share. They had lost three ships (one of them a vessel of the Queen's) and many shipmates. They consoled themselves as well as they could with the gold, silver and pearls rescued from the *Jesus* in those frenzied last minutes of the fight. Four pack-horses were needed to take the proceeds up to London – estimated value £13,500.

All things considered, it was a reasonable return if the English dead are not put in the balance against it. But it was unlikely to seem adequate to a boy like Paul Hawkins, or a man like Job Hortop. Hortop, a gunner in the *Jesus*, was one of those put ashore on the Mexican coast when Hawkins divided his crew. Lincolnshire-born and London-bred, he spent the next twenty-three years in Spanish dungeons or chained to a bench on one of King Philip's galleys. He had ample time to regret the day when the call of the sea and the lure of treasure tempted him to quit his trade as a gunpowder-maker to the Queen. At the end of 1590, Hortop found his way back to London. He had been one of the losers in the game of chance played in the Caribbean. There were many less fortunate than he.

IV

The Duke of Alva's Silver

'Il y a dans le jeu anglais beaucoup de souplesse et pas mal d'hypocrisie.'
('There was a good deal of flexibility in English policy and not a little hypocrisy.')

Fernand Braudel

While John Hawkins, Francis Drake and their companions were absent on the business which ended so disastrously at San Juan de Ulua, events in Europe had taken a decisive turn for the worse.

Decisive? It is hard to apply such an adjective to the relations of two human beings who showed such an extraordinary dislike of finality as Elizabeth Tudor and Philip Hapsburg. They were as different as they could be. The one twisted, flirted and teased until at last an open quarrel could no longer be averted. The other heavily pounded on, with God breathing down his neck. But each of them hesitated a long time on the brink of the irreversible.

At what moment it became clear to each that a collision was after all inevitable, who can say? It is likely that Elizabeth, being the weaker, the woman, the more nervous of the two, with the more penetrating intelligence, had a deeper insight into what was happening. Her mind leapt more quickly from an inkling to its deductions. And she hid her understanding well. Hers was a policy spun out of a hundred strands of silky irresolution, in which endless waverings in purpose were at length resolved in an ultimate consistency. From the first years of her reign, when she was a mere girl, she displayed a terrifying vehemence of temperament coupled with a cold, alarming penetration of mind. 'She seems to me incomparably more feared than her sister,' reported the Spanish Count of Feria in the first year of her reign. Four months later, he called her 'the daughter of the Devil'. As unjust as a spoilt child, as unreasonable as a god,

Elizabeth drove her ministers over and over again to the brink of hysterical breakdowns, without ever losing their devotion. What was the secret of the hold this extraordinary woman had over those who served her in love and suffering? One can only guess that it was sheer brilliance of intellect wedded to a personality of volcanic force. Men felt that they were in the presence of a genius.

She detested war and not only because it was wasteful. Too much can be made of her parsimony which was, after all, not a personal avarice. She was not simply the head of state but the State itself, embodied in a thin girl who grew into a bony woman. The Treasury was her purse and there was nothing in it to begin with and little enough at the end. But the cost of war, hateful as it was, was not the reason she loathed it. War was the final gamble of princes and Elizabeth preferred to play her own games in which she made the rules and kept the score. There were, however, circumstances in which war must be faced and, if there was no escape, must be fought. Annoying as it might be this was a matter on which she would find herself in agreement with the 'Puritans', the anti-Spaniards, the war party which was growing up in England. And Elizabeth hated Puritans. She did not even regard Spain as the natural enemy. For what of France, always nearer and only temporarily weaker? But if the security of England were plainly and immediately threatened, then all her prejudices would be put aside, resentfully – but promptly. She had come to the throne in evil days: 'The Queen poor; the realm exhausted; good captains and soldiers wanting; the people out of order.'[1] By cunning and patience, she had remedied all that. And by cunning and patience, at the least possible cost in money, she would safeguard what she had built.

In the autumn of 1567, on Philip's orders, the troops of his general, the Duke of Alva, arrived in the Netherlands. They were made up of three *tercios*, or brigades, of the highly trained Spanish professional soldiers who, so long as they were paid, were the most formidable military force in Europe. They were also the most expensive. A Spanish *tercio*, consisting of about three thousand fighting men, cost 1,200,000 ducats for a campaign. That was a great deal of money even to a monarch as rich as Philip of Spain. It was more than his total subsidy from the Spanish clergy plus the allowance – the *cruzado* – which the Pope gave him on condition that he used it to defend the Catholic faith. Fortunately for Philip these were not his only sources of income.

Alva's regiments settled down in their new quarters. The Naples *tercio* was in Ghent, the Lombardy *tercio* in Liège, the Sicilian in Brussels. Nor was the purpose for which Philip had sent them there in any doubt. 'I neither expect nor wish,' he had explained to the Pope, 'to be a lord of heretics.'[2] The Low Countries were rich, unruly and a prey to the subversive teachings of Luther and Calvin. He was determined to make them like Spain, his beloved Spain, a fortified camp of the Catholic Church.

Philip was the willing prisoner of Spain, that beautiful, empty, desolate land which had held the front of Christendom against the Moors and which lay between the Mediterranean and the Ocean Sea. And the Spaniards, knowing love when they saw it, rewarded him with their devotion. This remote, repressed bureaucrat king – 'the best of his secretaries',[3] as the Bishop of Limoges had sneered – chained by duty to his desk in the Escorial, was a highly popular Spanish monarch. He might be 'hard, haughty and intransigent'. So were they. He might be cruel. The nation that had driven out the Moslem were not the gentlest of human kind. They loved Philip for the same reason that the English loved Elizabeth. They were returning an affection.

There was a psychological flaw in his family, wherever it may have come from, the Burgundian or the Portuguese blood or simply from an undue devotion to in-breeding.* It was a zest for withdrawal from the world more suitable to monks than kings. His forebear, Prince Henry the Navigator, had shut

* Philip's nephew, Sebastian of Portugal, had six great-great-grandparents instead of sixteen.

himself up in his clifftop house at Sagres with his oceanic dreams. Rudolph, the Emperor, Philip's nephew, became a recluse living on top of the castle hill at Prague, fascinated by astronomy and plunged in morbid gloom. The Emperor Charles, Philip's father, had given up his greatness to retreat into the monastery at Yuste.[4] And Philip, who ruled a great portion of the Christian world from the desk where he sat ceaselessly reading, minuting and dictating to secretaries – this slave to his kingship – was building in the Guadarrama mountains the vast palace–monastery–mausoleum which he called San Lorenzo, and others have called the Escorial.

Yet his life was not simply a flight into the chilly realms of denial. His character was more complex than that. He assembled a wonderful collection of paintings and laid the foundations of a magnificent library. While he appears in history almost as a monster, how charming are the letters he wrote to his little daughters during his stay in Lisbon: 'Do the clocks keep time at San Lorenzo? How much have you grown since I saw you last? Let me have the measurements exactly.' How lucky they had been to hear the song of the nightingale at Aranjuez! (where he had a little palace). This year he must deny himself that music . . . Strange to meet in such letters the casual remark that he had been at an *auto-da-fé*. It is easier to understand the near-cynical tolerance of Elizabeth, so much nearer the temper of our own time.[5]

In Spain, people understood the conscientious, devout man who brought so much misery into the world. But with the Netherlands, it was different. There, the people were given to display, drink and disorder. They loved splendour but lacked dignity. Philip disliked them; could not understand them; worse still, did not live among them. There was, too, an inescapable, fatal weakness of centralised monarchy in the sixteenth century: time and space. To send a letter from Madrid to Brussels took Philip's excellent postal system fifteen days.[6] It is true that the Genoese bankers in Spain usually had news forty-eight hours before the King. But bankers – it was their business –

had means of persuading official couriers to dally on the way. 'I have had nothing from the King on the affairs of the Netherlands since 20 November,' wrote a Spanish official in Antwerp one day in February 1575. As the years passed, and pirates on the sea and Huguenots on the French roads grew bolder, Philip's problem of communications with his Netherlands dominion became more severe. And when, in 1567, he sent that harsh sergeant-major, the Duke of Alva, to impose his will on the Low Countries, he had made a disastrous mistake. He had alarmed the English queen.

Elizabeth might be reluctant to face military realities, but she could read a map as well as anyone. She did not need to be told that the mouth of the Scheldt was only ninety miles from the mouth of the Thames and that Antwerp in Spanish hands would make an excellent naval base. There was only one possibility more disagreeable than that – Antwerp might fall into French hands. If she doubted that Philip's policy towards her had hardened, she could reflect on another pointer that became visible just then. An agreeable Spanish ambassador in London was replaced by an altogether more unfriendly one.

So if the Dutch would fight, whether for religious freedom or against oppressive taxation, that might be a convenient turn in events in so far as a rebellion by subjects against their prince could ever be excusable. She might even help them with a little money, with some arms. But cautiously and always with an ear open for any peace whispers that might be carried from Philip along the winding passages of the diplomatic labyrinth.

He was not, after all, a monarch to be challenged lightly, lord of Spain, Naples, Milan, Sicily and the Netherlands. Beyond the seas, where seventy thousand of his subjects had settled, he had possessions whose fabulous wealth was only in its golden dawn, as men prophesied. Before long, Philip's revenue from the Indies, his royal fifth of the output of the mines, the tributes laid annually at his feet by Indians and Negroes, the proceeds of the Alcabala (sales tax) in the Indies – taken together they would amount to a fifth of the Spanish government's total income. Better still, the revenue from America was a *net addition* to the funds in the Spanish treasury. Before reaching Europe, it had paid all the costs of administration in the Indies.

And that was not the end of the story. There was also the residual four-fifths of the production of the American mines which belonged to individual Spanish entrepreneurs who, from the wealth they were accumulating, would augment the total of tax money.[7] It is true that there was another side to this golden coin: the inflow of precious metals to Spain with no corresponding growth of industrial production at home brought about an inflation of prices. If the cost-of-living index in Spain had been 100 in 1500, it had risen to 400 a century later. But who understood the word inflation or recognised its danger in the year 1568? All that people knew was that in Madrid there ruled a monarch who could afford to keep a hundred thousand men under arms and could spend on a single campaign by one of his infantry brigades more than the entire ordinary annual revenue of the English state.*[8]

Even if Elizabeth had been warlike and not a pacifist, a spendthrift instead of a frugal housekeeper, she would have hesitated many times before challenging Philip. Indeed, what is hard to understand is that she went as far as she did to bait him. To risk the war she did not want; to struggle by every diplomatic means to avoid a collision which, by stroke after stroke of policy or connivance, she brought nearer! How can it be explained? Except on the hypothesis that, from the beginning, Elizabeth, in some secret involution of her brain, had believed war to be inevitable. Perhaps she was right from the beginning, for can one imagine that a man as devout and doctrinaire as Philip should under any circumstances abandon his heaven-sent mission of extirpating from his realms heresy, Jewry and Islam?

It was certainly inevitable from the moment the Duke of Alva and his *tercios* arrived in the Netherlands. From that day, the danger became more manifest; it was nearer, more probable, although it might not be more immediate. Philip had under-

* £260,000, roughly 1,000,000 ducats.

taken a police operation in the Netherlands which would cost him a vast amount of money and might ruin his richest province. He had other troubles too. A bitter revolt of the Moriscoes to quell in the mountains of Granada. A naval war threatening in the Mediterranean where the Sultan was massing his galleys against the Venetian island of Cyprus. This, if it came to war, would be an attack on Christendom itself and already the Pope was calling for a crusade. And, at home in the very heart of his family, Philip was afflicted by a poignant and dreadful tragedy: his heir, Don Carlos, had inherited insanity from his grandmother and was doomed to die, in captivity, before many months had passed.

Two at least of these circumstances gave England a breathing-space. Philip would seek to postpone the clash with Turkey until he had crushed the Moriscoes. And until he settled with the Sultan, he would be unwilling to turn on England. 'God grant,' cried Frances de Alava, anxiously watching the Turkish preparations, 'that before that dog the Sultan can arm, the Albujarra rebels – the Moriscoes – have been chastised.'[9] The civil war in Spain was all the more dangerous because Philip had stripped Southern Spain of men to fill up Alva's regiments in the Low Countries. It was not likely either that he would wage one war in the Mediterranean and another, simultaneously, in the Atlantic. It was true that the first war would be fought with galleys and the second, as Elizabeth's admirals would be sure to tell her, with sailing-ships able to operate in Atlantic weather. They were different kinds of war; but in respect of each of them, Spain had troublesome deficiencies.

She had enough galleys to fight in the Central Sea and, at Barcelona, the facilities to build more. But all over the Mediterranean there was a shortage of manpower for the oars. If the Christian and Moslem galley fleets are taken together, they needed as many as two hundred thousand men on the benches. These men were hard to come by, and especially for the Christian states. Spain enslaved her gipsies, and Venice sent her recruiting agents as far off as Bohemia in search of volunteers willing to share with slaves and convicts the brutal life on the rowing benches. But the shortage persisted.

As for the Atlantic war, Spain had no ocean-going warships, apart from the galleons ear-marked to convoy the plate fleets which brought treasure from the Indies. And all through this period of history, the number of her seamen declined, nibbled at by corsairs, French, British, Algerine and Dutch. Many men who might have crewed the Spanish merchantmen or ships of war were lured away to the easier life which American wealth brought to the Spanish mainland. A few years after Philip's death, Tomé Cano, a shipbuilder, shook his head over the fact that Spain's mercantile fleet, which a quarter of a century before had numbered a thousand sea-going ships plus four hundred from Portugal, was practically swept from the seas. Only the ships of the Flota were left, sailing under armed convoy. Could a colonial empire thrive while its shipping dwindled? Could it survive?

Amid the pressing problems of 1568 the questions had only an academic interest. The Spanish king was scraping about in the villages of Galicia for men to meet Alva's endless demands for reinforcements. More seamen were wanted for the treasure fleets? Then, at a pinch, enlist foreigners. But no more than six in a ship. And no Frenchmen, no English, no Portuguese, unreliable even although they were not heretics. Money, too, was short? Then let it be borrowed from the Genoese at ten or twenty per cent until, with the mercy of Providence, the next Flota sailed up the Guadalquivir. And then when the gold was safely in the Treasury there was still the problem of making sure that it reached the military paymasters in Brussels.

Spain suffered from one grave geographical weakness, which Antonio Perez, Philip's secretary, his counsellor, eventually his enemy, explained to the King. His empire was the wrong shape. Leaving the Indies aside, consider the problem in Europe. 'It is also necessary to remember,' wrote Perez to the King, 'that the long arm of France borders on all the states belonging to Your Majesty, such as the crown of Aragon, Navarre, Guipizcoa, the provinces of Milan and Flanders. They are the head, the arms and the feet of your monarchy. And if we wish to make a body out of all these members, it happens that France, by her position, holds the place of heart . . . In addition, she dominates the sea route to Italy.'[10] It was true. Where the nerve centre and strategic cross-roads of Philip's empire should have been, there was instead a foreign power, part Calvinist, traditionally hostile, wholly unreliable, ruled in the name of her wretched sons by the slippery Italian woman who had been his mother-in-law, Catherine de' Medici.

Only a few weeks before Drake and Hawkins came back from their unhappy expedition, there had been an incident in the English Channel which brought home to the King of Spain how inconvenient a neighbour he had north of the Pyrenees. Having raised a loan in silver coin from Genoese bankers, he sent off the money by sea to Antwerp to pay Alva's troops. It did not reach its destination. Huguenot privateers were sailing out of La Rochelle with commissions from the Prince of Condé or Coligny, Admiral of France and head of the Protestant party. There were English ships among them as well as French. The Cardinal de Châtillon, Coligny's brother and like him a Huguenot, was in London distributing commissions, conferring the right to capture at sea 'all the enemies of God otherwise called papists'.

As it chanced it was French privateers who encountered the Spanish treasure ships and hunted them into English ports. The French lurked threateningly offshore while the English authorities, shaking their heads, professed to be alarmed at the temptation which this was putting before the French who, being rough and lawless men, might force their way in and seize the Spanish ships where they lay, silver and all. In everybody's interest, the English argued, it was better to bring the coins ashore and lock them up in some safe place. The Spaniards were, however, unconvinced by this reasoning, especially as they saw that the English harbours were crowded with craft discharging cargoes taken from Catholic ships and that, in Plymouth, the Mayor himself was busily engaged in unloading and selling the stolen goods! But what could the Spaniards do but agree?

In London, the news of the mishap to Alva's pay chests was received with well-simulated embarrassment by the Queen and Lord Burghley, the Lord Treasurer. These two were, of course, delighted by any opportunity to cripple Alva if only – and here was the problem – it could be arranged in conformity with international law and the correct relations that should exist between two states not openly at war. To that question much anxious thought was devoted in Whitehall. In the middle of all this pondering, Burghley learned to his relief that the money, which amounted to £85,000, did not after all belong to the King of Spain, the borrower. It remained the property of his bankers, the Genoese firm of Spinola, until it should arrive in Antwerp.

This discovery altered the situation considerably and was held to justify the English government in detaining the money while they made up their minds what to do with it. At this point, the Spanish Ambassador, de Spes de Gurau, lost his temper. He wrote to Alva suggesting that he should seize all the English property he could lay his hands on in the Netherlands. Surrounded as he was by mutinous soldiers clamouring for their back pay, Alva did as de Spes suggested. Between them, those two hot-tempered Spaniards had made a major blunder.

About this time, the tension was given an extra turn of the screw. News arrived at the London offices of the Spinola bank that a great disaster had befallen the Hawkins expedition in the Indies. This was either an early rumour of the San Juan de Ulua affair, or it was an independent story without foundation. More likely it was the former. Although Drake and Hawkins were still on the sea homeward bound and no certain knowledge of their fate existed, the fight at San Juan had occurred eight weeks before. There was time for the news to cross the Atlantic in a fast dispatch boat such as might be employed by a banking house with a financial interest in the Hawkins venture, as the Spinola firm probably had. The bad news was sent from Bernardino Spinola in London to William Hawkins in Plymouth, who promptly demanded that Burghley should seize Alva's money as compensation for the injury done to his brother. This was the atmosphere about the time Alva laid his hands on the English property in Flanders. It ensured that public opinion would be likely to support any measures of retaliation the English government might take.

A general seizure of English goods before England had denied the redress of a grievance was a direct breach of a century-old treaty between England and the Netherlands. Furthermore, the official English story was that, at that very time, the Queen had been considering sending Alva's silver to Antwerp under escort. If this were indeed the case, then apparently there had been no denial of redress. By the ill-tempered and precipitate action of de Spes and Alva, Spain had put herself morally in the wrong. More important, and more welcome to the directors of English policy, she had given the Queen a heaven-sent excuse to pounce on Spanish goods in England. As they chanced to be much more valuable than all the English goods in Flanders, the exchange was not unsatisfactory from Elizabeth's point of view. This was the moment when Drake returned to England and Hawkins followed him.

Both were burning with indignation over the ungentlemanly conduct of the Viceroy of New Spain. Both demanded reprisals. To the Spanish ambassador, already sufficiently annoyed by the 'miscarriage' of his policy over Alva's silver, their demands seemed the mere insolence of two pirates. But worse was to come. Hawkins brought to London for sale the treasure which he had won by illegal trade in the Indies and had saved from the *Jesus* at San Juan. Hawkins, member of a firm which was deep in the privateering war against Spanish trade in the Channel, which was hand in glove with the Huguenots, which was becoming richer almost every day through its auctions of goods stolen on the high seas! Could English impertinence go farther? Even if His Excellency of Spain had been a broad-minded man, capable of seeing some merit in the other side's case, it would have been natural that he was irritated by English statesmen and seamen in the early days of 1569. What is more remarkable is that Hawkins, whose personal charm must have been as great as his duplicity, quickly won the confidence of that dour Catalan, de Spes de Gurau, whom he persuaded of his secret devotion to the Spanish cause.

Meanwhile, a far-reaching and dangerous conspiracy was being prepared in England at the heart of which was an Italian banker named Ridolfi who was an agent of the Pope. This was the plan: Mary Stuart was to be released and set on the English throne after Elizabeth had been assassinated. Alva was to invade England with an army. The Duke of Medina Coeli was to come over with a fleet from Spain to which Hawkins declared that he was ready to add ships of his own. Spanish money and titles of nobility were to reward the Plymouth shipowner, who in fact was keeping Lord Burghley fully informed of the developments. One day, to his amazement, de Spes de Gurau was summoned to appear before the Council and was told to leave the country. This, after a last-minute attempt to murder Burghley, he did. And probably he never knew to whom he owed the collapse of his plans.

These events lay two years ahead at the time of the seizure of the Duke of Alva's silver. And how did *that* affair end? Very sensibly, as might have been expected. Elizabeth took over Philip's debt to the Genoese bankers, who were delighted by the transfer. And Philip decided that in future he would send money to Flanders overland. It was a slow method and it was expensive; it was not even safe. To convey 100,000 crowns from Florence to Paris on one occasion required seventeen wagons, five companies of horse and two hundred infantry.[11] But better so than incur the perils from storm and human malice in the Bay of Biscay and the Channel. And the money must go through. The troops must, alas, be paid! For Philip, a Catholic king – *the* Catholic King – must discharge the duty which heaven had laid upon him. He must crush the Lutherans in the Low Countries. 'God and His Majesty' – the two ideas were joined indissolubly in the mind of every Spanish official. They were hardly distinct in Philip's. His Majesty would carry out God's will at whatever cost to himself in treasure or to Spain in lives.

As for the unofficial, undeclared war at sea, so profitable to those who were lucky, so deadly to those who were not, it was going on with mounting fury and with new methods. Hawkins' tactics had been a mixture of bland threats and unscrupulous negotiations. He had been wont to appear from nowhere in overwhelming force and inveigle the Spanish colonists into a conspiracy with himself against their home government. Now the rules were about to change. No doubt the old game would go on. Fires would be lit at selected points on the coast of Hispaniola; boats would row in stealthily at night from ships lying off shore; rendezvous would be kept; goods would be delivered. Transactions of this kind were described to Philip. 'I believe this,' wrote the King in the margin of the dispatch.[12] Diego Ruiz de Vallejo (1568) wrote from New Segovia to the King, complaining that no punishments could prevent the colonists from trading with the corsairs: 'They buy at night and cover each other. We [the officials] have conscientious scruples about putting them on oath. All we succeed in doing is to make them perjure themselves.' But these contraband activities, annoying as they might be for the Spanish authorities, were on a petty scale. The time had come for bolder tactics and, possibly, for younger men. From now on, John Hawkins stayed at home, tending his far-spread commercial interests, fishing with some skill in troubled political waters, increasingly drawn into the business of the Navy Board. And Francis Drake elbowed his way to the front as a leader in the new phase of the conflict, the undeclared war on Spain.

Between his policy and that of Hawkins there was a difference not simply of degree but of kind. Hawkins had hoped to work in collaboration with the King of Spain, policing the Caribbean with his galleons and pinnaces so that the Spanish settlements, ships and, above all, treasure would be protected against corsairs of whatever nationality. There was no doubt at all that he could have done the job. He had ships enough of his own, a fleet of sixteen armed vessels of various sizes, based on Plymouth, and fifteen hundred seamen on the payroll. Naturally, he would expect to be rewarded: a recognised share in the Indian trade, a privileged position for himself above all foreign traders; all this to be duly sanctioned by King Philip over his royal seal. It was to be a partnership between the King and Hawkins, with the latter assuming a naval protectorate over the former's American domains. This, broadly speaking, was the proposition, at once logical and impudent, which Hawkins put forward and which Philip rejected for reasons which are surely not hard to guess.

At a time when the religious conflict in Europe was growing more bitter, was he to give special rights in his own sea to one breed of Protestants? These patrols which Hawkins proposed to set up would need local bases, which before long the English would want to fortify and arm with cannon manned by English gunners! With his own merchant marine dwindling while that of England swelled and broadened, fed by a thousand rivulets of enterprise, Philip could envisage a day when he would be sharing the mastery of the house – *his* house – with a handsome, dandified English merchant. And no doubt the Englishman had exactly the same picture of the future.

Drake's approach was radically different. He saw that Spain was not to be lured into a consortium of interests. It was therefore necessary that she should be challenged, plundered, humiliated and brought to battle. It was to be a trial of strength fought out and decided at sea where Drake did not doubt that the superior seamanship and gunnery of the English would prevail. This may seem an ambitious programme for a young officer of modest means who had served only a few months earlier during a serious naval defeat. But Drake was resourceful, imaginative and boundlessly self-confident. Modesty was not among his weaknesses.

He nourished, too, in his bosom, something that Hawkins

1 Sir John Hawkins
(*National Maritime Museum*)

2 Lord Burghley
(*National Portrait Gallery*)

3 Prospect of Plymouth: a portion of a large coloured chart of the southern coast of England from Land's End to Exmouth, drawn in the reign of Henry VIII *c.* 1536 (*British Museum*)

did not have and which made Elizabeth profoundly uncomfortable: a burning Protestant zeal. The covert struggle with Spain was to him not simply a tangle of business deals, as it was to Hawkins, or an intricate game of skill, as the Queen played it. It was a passage of arms, in a holy war, the preliminary skirmishes of an inevitable decisive battle. 'He was a man,' as one critical observer wrote after his death, 'not only sufficient in the trivial parts of navigation but even large beyond his profession in undertaking that vast empire of Spain, a mass so far above him in council, wealth and disciplined armies.'[13] Drake thought he had found the tender area in that mass, where a few ships with a handful of desperadoes on board could do damage out of all proportion to their strength and spread terror out of all proportion to the damage. But he did not emerge as a leader at once.

During the months immediately following his return to England in the *Judith*, the only certain thing known of him is that on 4 July 1569, five months later, he married Mary Newman, his Plymouth sweetheart, in the village church at St Budeaux on the Tamar estuary a few miles north of Plymouth. Apart from that little is known with certainty of his career although a great deal can be surmised. It is said that he went with Sir William Wynter on an expedition that took supplies and arms to the beleaguered Huguenots in La Rochelle. It is said that he served in one of the Queen's ships in Irish waters. This is very likely true. It has been conjectured – but it seems less probable – that, between his return to Plymouth in January and his marriage in July, he took part with French corsairs in attacks on Spanish settlements in the Caribbean.

It was a time of stirring activity on the nearer and farther seas and who can doubt that Drake, young, daring, enthusiastic and already an experienced sea officer, was somehow and somewhere engaged in it. The year after he married he was certainly in the Caribbean where he fell in with a French captain named Leyerre and laid plans for later voyages. From which of the two main privateering camps, English or French, the general conception of the future campaigns emerged is a matter of speculation. Certainly, only a spark of imagination was needed to tell resourceful and acquisitive seamen of either nation that in the Caribbean Sea and the islands around it, above all, in the isthmus which divided that sea from another ocean and its unimaginable wealth, lay a truly marvellous opportunity where a small number of desperate men might enrich themselves while inflicting a disproportionate amount of damage on Spanish power.

It seems that the French were first to explore the possibilities of the Chagre River, which runs into the Caribbean almost due north of the Pacific city of Panama. They found it could be navigated for some distance inland. To Drake this was of great interest. For already, it seemed, he was dreaming, not simply of plundering the Spaniards but of making a permanent settlement in their golden isthmus. Meanwhile, he went here and there in the Caribbean, observing and sketching – for he was, like many captains of that time, an assiduous painter – stopping Spanish ships, and probably addressing them in the plainest terms. One ultimatum from English corsairs to a Spanish ship has survived in the Archives of the Indies: 'Captain and crew of this frigate: We are surprised that you ran from us in that fashion and later refused to talk with us under our flag of truce . . . To any who courteously may come to talk with us, we will do no harm. Who does not come, his be the blame . . . Done by English who are well-disposed, if there be no cause to the contrary. If there be cause, we will be devils rather than men.'[14]

This 'audacious letter', as an outraged Spanish official called it, when complaining to King Philip ('being most beneficent and most Christian, Your Majesty will be pleased to apply a remedy to all this'), was delivered from a pinnace belonging to an English ship at Cativa Headland. Drake in his ship, the *Swan*, was anchored there at that time. The letter is very much in his style of veiled truculence, but there is, of course, no evidence that he wrote it.

Some time in the course of his voyage, Drake found a concealed cove on the coast of the Main, perfectly designed to serve his purpose. There he set up a base and left ships' stores. He evaded the attempts of Diego Flores de Valdes, Captain-general of the Tierra Firme fleet, which guarded the coast, to lay him by the heels. The Spanish officer could not risk his galleons too near the shore, which is rocky in that area of the coast. After a time Drake sailed for home, with every intention of returning next year to plague the Spaniards. He had a great many ideas in his head.

V

The Treasure House of the World

'Lo, here, my sons, are all the golden mines,
Inestimable drugs and precious stones,
More worth than Asia and the world beside.'
Tamburlaine the Great – Christopher Marlowe

Considering what Drake had in mind, the force he took out of Plymouth Sound on the eve of Whit Sunday, 24 May 1572, was none too great. He was the commander of a fleet of two vessels, one small and the other tiny. His flagship was the *Pasche* (or *Pasco*) which perhaps belonged to that well-known firm of ship-owners, Hawkins Brothers, although one of Drake's brothers had a £25 share in her. The *Pasco* was of 70 tons; her consort, the *Swan*, 25 tons, belonged to Drake himself and her captain, the second-in-command of the expedition, was his brother John Drake. The *Pasco* had a crew of 47; the *Swan*, 26; all of the sailors were under thirty except one. The two ships carried enough provisions for a year and bristled with artillery to a degree surprising in insignificant trading vessels. More than that, they bore carefully stowed away in casks below decks, where prying eyes could not see nor salt water invade, an impressive assortment of lesser weapons.

With this modest but well-found squadron, Francis Drake proposed to cause trouble in the Spanish empire of King Philip II, which had at that time reached a new peak of prestige. Although Spanish galleys were only one component of the Christian fleet at Lepanto, that victory over the Turks seemed to have established Spain as the first naval, as she was already recognised as the first military, power.

Drake's project was therefore sufficiently audacious in all conscience, but it was neither crazy nor ill-considered. On the contrary. A great deal of planning had gone into it and at least one long voyage of reconnaissance and preparation. When the

Pasco cleared Rame Head that May afternoon, her captain had a clear idea of where he was going and a fair notion what he would do when he arrived there. He set his course south-west by south.

Five weeks later, having been sighted in the interval by no inquisitive stranger, the two ships sailed into the Caribbean Sea between Dominica and Guadeloupe and anchored off a rocky uninhabited island, nine miles from Dominica. There the fishing was good and the ships' water-butts could be replenished from sparkling mountain streams. On 1 July they weighed anchor and steered into the afternoon sun, working their way to the west towards the Spanish Main and, after five days, glimpsing the snowy peaks of the Sierra Nevada behind Santa Marta, a small Spanish settlement on the coast known to Drake from earlier visits. But, having no intention of warning anyone of his arrival, Drake kept a good thirty miles' distance between him and the coast. He was making for that same cove which, a year before almost to a day, he had prepared for his return. He called it Port Pheasant.* After four centuries, this lost Elysian harbour has still power over the imagination of those who read of it. How it must have lifted the hearts of those sunburnt, ship-weary English sailors when, just forty-nine days out of Plymouth, the *Pasco* followed by the *Swan* threaded the gateway to what seemed an earthly paradise! What they saw was this:

Between two high points was a channel, just a hundred yards across, half a cable's length, giving entrance to a harbour a mile in extent, with a depth of ten fathoms of translucent water, swarming with brilliant fish. All round this inlet the land rose, ravishingly beautiful, luxuriantly covered with trees, some of them tall and some so large that four men touching hands were needed to girdle them. One at least, which must have been the composite growth of a main stem and 'buttresses', as the wondering English called them, measured thirty-nine yards in circumference. Its timber was heavier than lignum vitae, they swore. These woods, as the name which Drake gave to the place

* See Appendix II.

implies, were alive with pheasant and other wildfowl. Eden? It seemed to be so. But there were traces of the serpent.

Drake had just dropped into the *Pasco*'s longboat to be rowed ashore when he caught sight of a thin column of smoke rising out of the trees. At once he ordered the *Swan*'s boat to be manned and armed. Plainly, all was not as it should be. When he went cautiously ashore he found, nailed to a tree, a lead plate with this message scratched on its surface:

> 'Captain Drake, if you fortune to come to this port make haste away, for the Spaniards which you had with you here last year have bewrayed the place and taken away all that you left here. I departed from hence this present 7 of July, 1572. Your very loving friend, John Garret.'

Garret, a Plymouth skipper known to Drake and his companions, had evidently been brought to the place by seamen who had been members of Drake's crew on the expedition of the previous year. And having found that the Spaniards had surprised the secret harbour he had set a big tree alight as a warning signal. Then he had sailed away just five days before Drake arrived on the scene. Now what was to be done? Obviously, the prudent course was to take Garret's advice and leave at once, but Drake, pacing to and fro on the shore, trying in vain to trace the paths he had cleared through the trees twelve months earlier and which a year of tropical rain and sun had obliterated, decided to do nothing of the sort.

After all, the nearest Spanish settlement was a hundred miles along the coast. It was not likely that he would be detected and, even if he were, he had no need to fear an early disturbance. It would be difficult to find another harbour as idyllic and as convenient for his purpose as Port Pheasant. Stowed away in the holds of his two ships were three pinnaces which had been taken apart and were all ready to reassemble. These boats were an essential element in the operations Drake had planned. Port Pheasant was an ideal place to work on them.

He ordered the *Pasco* and the *Swan* to be anchored in the harbour. Then he set the carpenters to work. Meanwhile, he and the crews cleared a quarter of an acre of land at the water's edge where he planned to build a fort. It would have five equal sides, one of which, looking over the harbour, would be left open so that the pinnaces could be quickly launched. Trees were felled and man-handled into position until a stockade thirty feet high was built. Outside, the ground was cleared of vegetation for a space of fifty feet.

Next day there came a surprise which, although not so dangerous as it might have been, was nevertheless disturbing. An English ship nosed its way into the cove. It turned out to be an Isle of Wight barque owned by Sir Edward Horsey and commanded by James Ranse. The barque had a crew of thirty aboard, some of whom may have visited Port Pheasant with Drake on a previous voyage and subsequently talked about it. Whatever Drake's private thoughts were about the unexpected visitors, he received them cordially and agreed that Ranse, who had already taken two Spanish prizes, a shallop and a Spanish advice boat carrying official messages from Seville to Nombre de Dios, should join in the venture he had planned.

This was ambitious enough in all conscience, being no less than an attack on Nombre de Dios itself, one of the main keys to the Spanish colonial system. The port, situated on the Caribbean shore of the Isthmus of Panama, was the northern Atlantic terminus of the land route from Panama, on the Pacific coast. By this trail mule-trains brought the gold and silver from the mines of Peru, as the Mexican treasure came on the trail from Mexico City to Vera Cruz to meet the fleets which carried it to Seville. With this metal, King Philip paid his army of officials, his satraps, his client princes and above all, his soldiers, who kept the Netherlands in subjection, France in awe, half of Italy at heel and England in a state of nervous apprehension. Without the bullion Spain would shrink to her natural dimensions. She would no longer be mistress of the world but would become a land with a decaying industry and a population of nine millions,

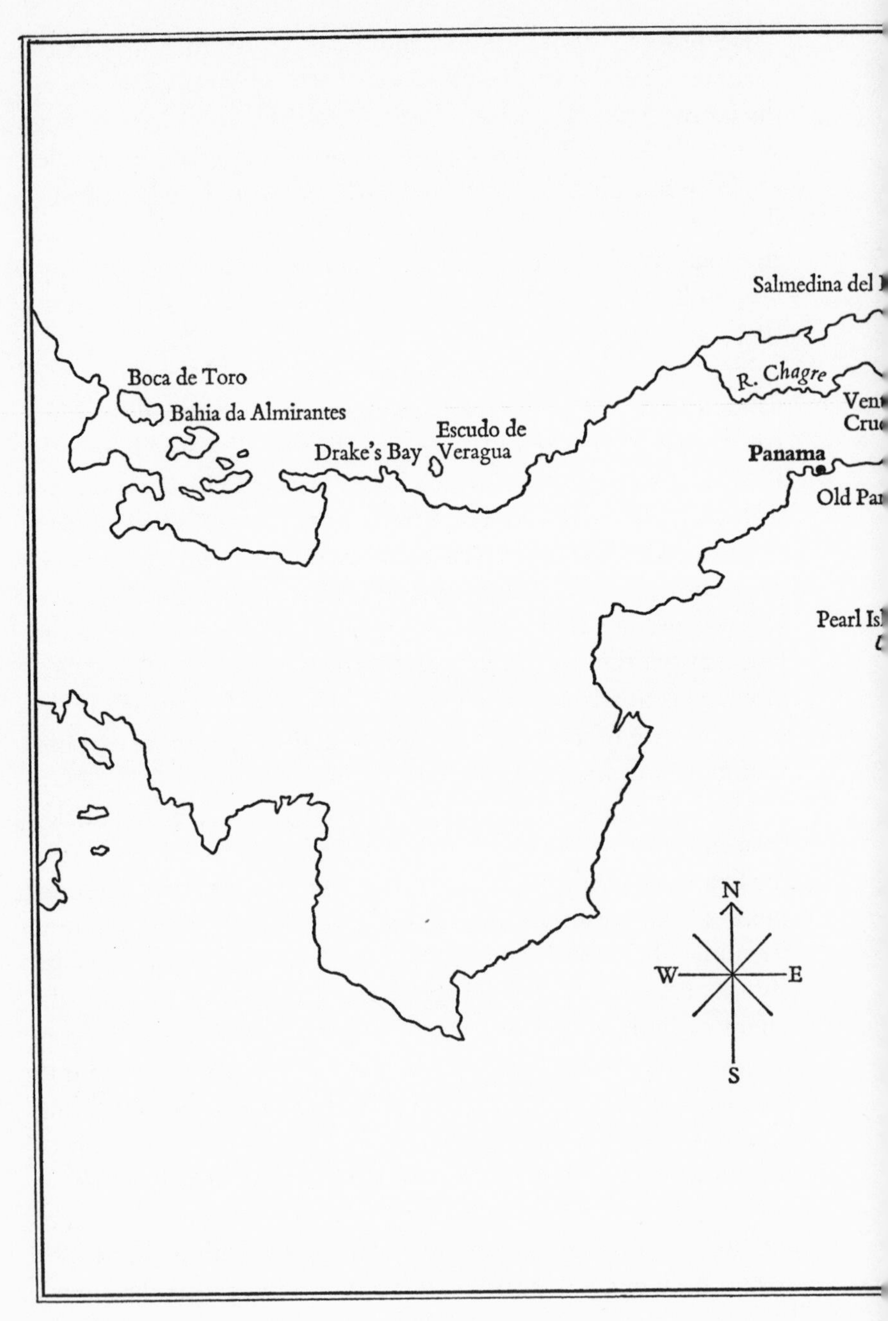

2 Isthmus of Panama

Nombre de Dios
Isla de Mona
Rio de San Francisco
Punta de San Blas
Islas Mulatas
Islas de las Palmas
PANAMA
Punta de los Boquerones
Isla de Pinas
Acla
PROVINCIA DEL DARIEN
Gulf of Darien
Rio Grande de San Juan

only two-thirds that of France (although twice that of England), and falling steadily as a result of emigration.

The mines of Peru, added to the mines of Mexico and the pearl fisheries, made all the difference. By the end of the King's life, the American colonies were sending 670,000 gold ducats a year to Spain.*

Every year the arrival of the two treasure convoys from Havana and Nombre de Dios, the Flota and the Galeones, seventy ships on an average, was awaited with anxiety in Spain. Upon their safe crossing of the Atlantic depended King Philip's power to raise money in the market at Genoa. When they failed to come, Spanish credit collapsed.

In short, a firm grip on the Isthmus of Panama would throttle the Spanish empire. Drake had probably no such ambitious project in mind when he set sail from Plymouth with his two little ships. But he thought of the gold, as others had thought of it before him. If Englishmen had been alive to their interests, Richard Eden, a clerk in Philip's English Chancery during the Spanish king's marriage to Mary Tudor, had written 'that rich treasury called Perularia' (the bullion warehouse in Seville) 'might long since have been in the Tower of London'.[1] Through Drake's doing, some small fraction of that treasure would one day find its way to just that repository. But not yet awhile.

A week after arriving at Port Pheasant, Drake sailed westwards with the pinnaces in tow on which his carpenters had finished their work. He cast anchor at the Isle of Pines, which rises out of the water into twin peaks and is covered with fine tall trees. There, three days later, he fell in with two frigates which blacks were loading with timber for Nombre de Dios. What they told him was of the highest interest.

The power of Spain in that region was not threatened by European corsairs alone. Eighty years before, black slaves had fled into the mountains from their Spanish masters. They had

* Equal, roughly, to £170,000 in English money at that time; or £5,000,000 in modern values.

carried off Negro and Indian women and established themselves under chieftains in three communities, one on each side of the trail from Panama to Nombre de Dios and a third in the south part of the Isthmus. These mountain people were the Cimarrons – later known to the English as Maroons. They received many recruits. The Bishop of Panama, writing to the King of Spain in 1570, bewailed the fact that, of every thousand Negroes landed, three hundred escaped to the wilds.[2] And by the following year the Cimarrons had grown so bold that they carried off thirteen Negro women from the place where they washed clothes at Nombre de Dios. Six weeks before Drake's arrival the Cimarrons had all but taken Nombre de Dios by a surprise attack. In consequence, the town expected the Governor of Panama to send reinforcements any day.

Drake listened to the story and put the Negroes ashore on the mainland. He reflected that either they would join the Cimarrons or they would go to Nombre de Dios, taking with them the news that he was in the neighbourhood. Neither way made much difference. He meant to be in the town before them! For, as he pointed out in a phrase which is stamped with his personal brand of humour, 'He was loath to put the town to too much expense – which he knew they would willingly bestow – in providing beforehand for his entertainment!' The moment for action had arrived.

Leaving the ships behind, he put fifty of his crew and twenty of Ranse's into the pinnaces (three of his and one of Ranse's) and fitted them out from the ships' armoury with targets, fire-pikes, muskets and calivers, bows, partisans and finally two drums and two trumpets. At an island seventy miles nearer Nombre de Dios, he put the party ashore for training in their weapons. After that was over, he delivered a rousing speech, emphasising the weakness of the town and his confidence in victory. How could he fail with companions like-minded with himself! What had they to fear when their coming would be a complete surprise! The seamen raised a cheer and scrambled aboard the pinnaces. Drake set sail.

By sunset, the four little craft, clinging close to the rocky shore so as to keep out of sight of the Spanish coastguards, had run cautiously aground six miles from Nombre de Dios Bay. Grapnels were out to keep them from drifting. There they waited until the night was black about them. Then, rowing hard, they rounded the headland and entered the Bay, waiting in stillness for the moment to attack.

It had been Drake's original idea that the landing should be made at dawn but, hearing some nervous murmurs from the crew (the town was big and strong and so forth – in fact it was about the size of Plymouth) he changed his mind. Action was the best cure for such poor-spirited talk, which might be infectious. When the moon began to show its light on the horizon, he announced, 'The sun is rising. Daybreak is here. The time has come.' So the attack on Nombre de Dios opened at three o'clock in the morning, a full hour before it had been planned.

A few minutes before, a Spanish ship – which later proved to be a caravel belonging to Juan Maria, laden with Canary wine – had come into the bay. Indeed, it had not yet furled its spritsail. But its master was evidently an alert seaman, with a suspicious nature. When he saw four pinnaces making at speed for the town, he had no doubt that something unusual was happening. He sent off his ship's boat to warn the town. Drake, realising the danger in time, steered his pinnaces between the boat and the shore. Thus, the English raiders landed without opposition on the glimmering sand of a little bay just twenty yards from the first houses of the town. On a platform above the bay stood six cannon, but only one gunner was on duty, and he ran off. While the attackers were busily engaged in tipping the guns off their mountings, they could hear church bells pealing, drums beating and outcries from the town. Someone – perhaps the gunner – had raised the alarm.

Leaving twelve men to guard the pinnaces, Drake led the way to the top of a hill on the east side of the town. There, he had been told, was a battery of guns which covered Nombre de Dios. But it was not so. Although a site had been prepared, no guns were in position. Drake issued his orders for the attack on the town. His brother John, along with a tall, serious, thick-spoken Devon man named John Oxenham, would lead eighteen men behind the King's Treasure House and would enter the market-place by one end while he with the others, numbering forty, would march up the street with drums beating and trumpets blaring. Each party would have three of the fire-pikes, on which Drake relied to spread alarm among the enemy.

There was no time to lose, for Nombre de Dios was now in a state of alarm. Lines of lighted match were strung across the market-place from the church to the Cross to simulate a rank of musketeers. This was a form of deception which had proved useful on previous occasions in frightening Negro assailants. But by this time day was approaching and already there was light enough to see by. Soon the Spaniards would realise how derisory was the force that was attacking them.

The fight for the market-place, which was at the centre of Nombre de Dios, was short and sharp. The Spaniards fired 'a jolly hot volley' and Drake felt a sudden heavy blow on the leg. The English answered with muskets and a flight of arrows, 'fine roving shafts', as one who was present called them. Then they went in for the hand-to-hand scuffle, in which the fire-pikes – flame-bearing spears used in close naval action – were particularly effective.

The Spaniards fought back hard until in their rear they heard men shouting the English war-cry, 'St George!' Drake's brother had burst in at the far end of the market-place. Hearing this tumult behind them, the main Spanish force broke and ran. Drake was master of the place. Cost: one man killed. The trumpeter lay stretched out on the sand. Drake shouted: 'Stop that bell ringing!'

But the church was strong; the door was fast. Someone proposed to shoot his way into the steeple. Drake would not have it. After all, the treasure was the most important thing and, with luck, he would reach it before the Spaniards rallied, before the sun was up. Two or three prisoners had been taken. He had them brought before him: 'Where is the Governor's house?' That was the place where the mule-trains were unloaded and the silver bars – but not the gold – were stored. Faced by a fierce-eyed, imperious little man who shook a weapon in their faces, the Spaniards told him what he wanted to know.

Now came a moment which, even in the terse narrative of an eye-witness who was, maybe, Drake himself, is beautiful and dramatic. The Governor's house stood open and, apparently, empty. At the top of the stairs, a candle threw a quivering yellow light on the walls. Below, at the door stood a fine riding pony, patient and saddled, ready to take its master or mistress on a journey which the sudden onset of the attack had interrupted. A scene that was likely to stay in a man's memory even if, in the rush of more pressing affairs, he could not pause to savour it.

The treasure! The silver! There it was, neatly stacked behind bars in the ground floor of the Governor's house. A sight to fill men's hearts with wonder and greed. Silver bars one on top of the other, one beside the other, one behind the other – seven feet by ten feet by twelve feet high – that was what they guessed, those cut-throats from England, peering in at the gently gleaming, infinitely enticing metal in the gloom of the Governor's cellar. How much was there? How many tons of silver? They could count it after they had taken it back to the ships. Partisans and pikes went to work on the iron grill. It was open!

They were about to lay hands on the treasure they had come so far to seek when Drake, that extraordinary young man, shouted 'No!' They must stand to their weapons. The town was full of people, angry, vengeful and armed. Besides, he argued, this was only silver. The real treasure, the gold, was locked in the King's Treasure House near the waterside. He would order men to break in and there they would find more gold than their four pinnaces could carry and stay afloat. If there was anyone present, staring at all that silver and tempted to utter words about a bird in the hand, he spoke to them under his breath. Drake at that moment was not a man to be crossed.

In any case, a new crisis arose. Word came from the beach that the pinnaces were in danger. They must be clear of the shore by daybreak. A Negro named Diego had shouted to the men guarding the boats, 'Are these Captain Drake's boats? Then take me aboard.' A week earlier, he said, the King (meaning, no doubt, the Governor of Panama) had sent in a hundred and fifty troops to guard the town. The news agreed in a sinister way with the warning they had been given by the Negroes at the Isle of Pines.

When the news reached Drake he sent his brother John and Oxenham to the pinnaces. There they found the guards in a state of alarm. Men had been running up and down on the shore with the matches of their muskets alight, calling out '*Qué gente? Qué gente?*' and firing at random. Later on, when there was time to reflect, it was decided that these were men from outlying parts of the town who had come to see what all the uproar was about.

No sooner had this news been brought back to Drake from the pinnaces than a tropical storm of the utmost violence broke over the town – thunder, lightning and torrential rain, ruining bowstrings and damaging match and powder. The English ran for shelter under a penthouse at one end of the Treasure House where, while they waited, muttering broke out among them. What, men wanted to know, were the odds against them in a town of such strength?

Drake was furious at such craven talk. 'I have brought you to the treasure house of the world,' he cried, with that gift he had for the inflammatory phrase. 'If you leave without it, you may henceforth blame nobody but yourselves.' Half an hour later, the storm ended as suddenly as it had begun and Drake understood clearly that his men must have no more leisure to grumble and the enemy no more chance to recover. 'Break into the treasure house,' he told his brother and Oxenham. 'The rest of you – follow me to hold the market-place until the job is done.'

At that moment disaster struck. Francis Drake fell in a faint.

In the first minutes of the attack on the town, a musket ball had struck his leg. He had kept it secret but now his boot was full of blood and he was leaving crimson footprints on the sand.

They gave him a drink to restore him, tied his scarf round his leg and begged him to go to the pinnace. They refused to risk his life – for all the gold in the Indies. He argued, weak but vehement: better risk life than leave so high an enterprise unfinished. In the end they cut the dispute short. Using force they carried their protesting captain to the shore, leaving the dead body of the trumpeter stretched on the market-place. Perhaps some of them were glad enough to have so respectable an excuse for retreat from the town. What is certain is that none of them had the resolution and spirit to fill Drake's place.

So the attack on Nombre de Dios had, through a stroke of ill-luck, ended in failure. No gold, no silver, no pearls – only the wine-ship from the Canaries which they seized as they left the bay in their pinnaces. It was not much, but it was better than nothing. The Alcalde of the town was told at High Mass next morning that Juan Maria, owner of the ship, offered a reward of 2,000 pesos if it was recovered. But when he tried to assemble a force to pursue the English, a quarrel broke out among the officers, and the troops disembarked in disgust.[3]

The English raiders did not go far in their retreat. A few miles to the west of the town they found a pleasant island which served as a kind of market garden for Nombre de Dios. There they went ashore and lived in plenty for a couple of days while the surgeons tended the wounded. There, too, they were visited by an envoy from the Governor, an affable little man with a notable gift of flattery – a spy, as Drake decided. The Spanish visitor was chiefly interested in knowing whether the English arrows had been poisoned, which he would find it hard to believe of a man like Captain Drake who had behaved so well during his visits to the Main in the last two years. Reassured on this point, he asked Drake if he needed any provisions.

'We have plenty here,' Drake told him. 'I want only that special commodity which the country yields. Tell the Governor

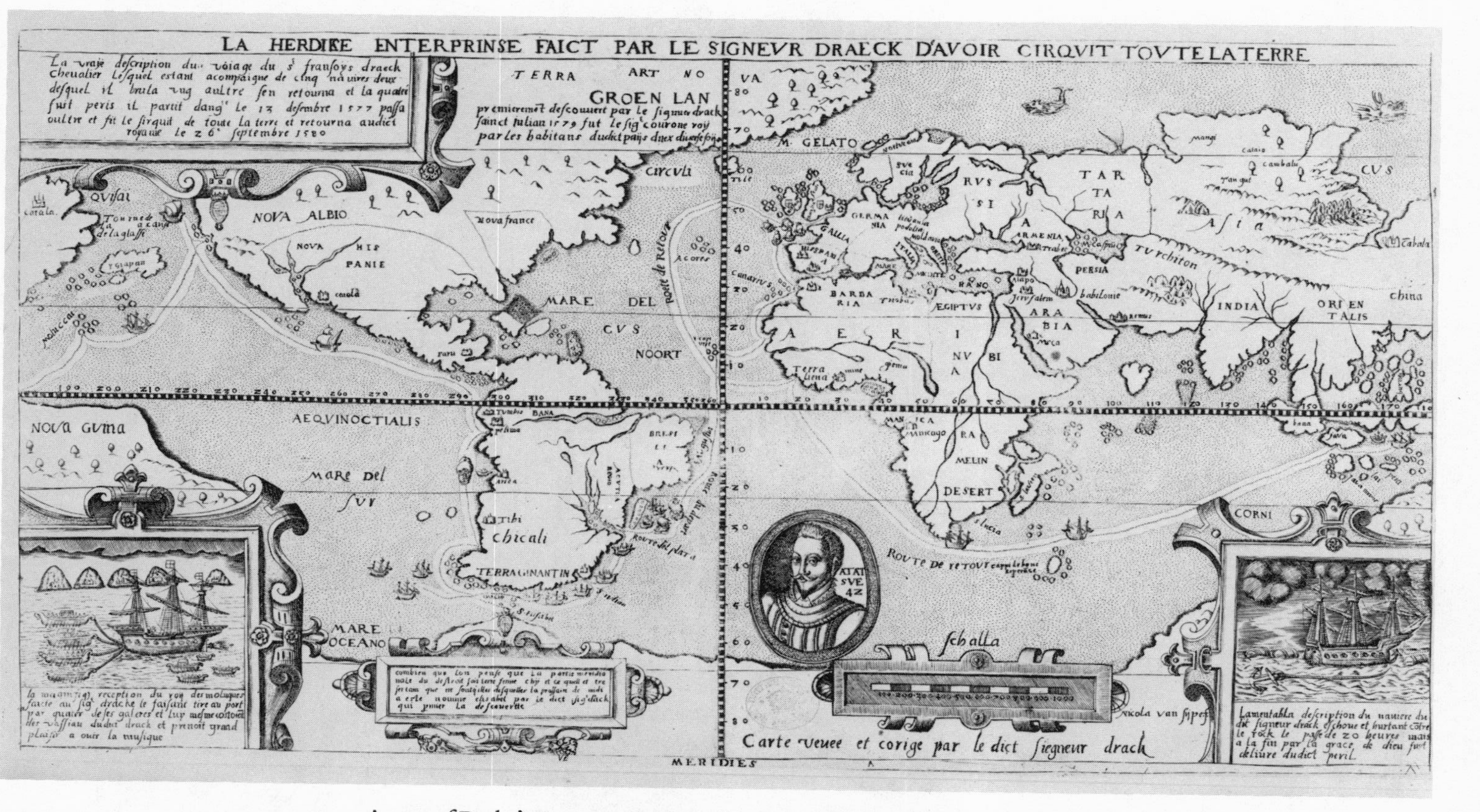

4 A map of Drake's circumnavigation of the world, engraved by Nicola van Sype, after the French original approved by Drake himself (*British Museum*)

5 A Dutch engraving of the Spanish treasure ship plundered by Drake in the Pacific (*National Maritime Museum*)

to keep his eyes open for, if God lends me life and leave, I mean to reap some of the harvest you get out of the ground and send to Spain to trouble all the earth.' 'Without offence,' answered the Spaniard, 'why did you go away, leaving three hundred and sixty tons of silver and a much greater value of gold in iron chests in the King's Treasure House?' Drake grimaced and pointed to his wound.

Next day the four pinnaces sailed to rejoin the ships at the Isle of Pines. When Captain Ranse had heard their story, he announced that, now they had been detected, the project had become too dangerous. He proposed, therefore, to sail for home. It was a prudent decision which Drake seems to have accepted with composure. But he himself had other plans. He would not go back to Plymouth without making the Spaniards pay the cost of his voyage. Having failed once to take the treasure, he would make another attempt. He had sent his brother John and a seaman named Ellis Hixon to explore the Chagre River which he himself had visited on his last trip. By three days' rowing upstream, a pinnace would reach Venta Cruces, where the mule trail from Panama – the Camino Real, the royal road – came down to the river and there was a wharf at the river bank and a warehouse. The road can still be seen. It can even be used by a careful horseman, although fallen trees obstruct the way. Drake listened carefully to his brother's report when he returned from the reconnaissance. No doubt John had been charged to get in touch with the Cimarrons. And no doubt he had done so.

Turning his back on Nombre de Dios, Drake sailed along the coast to the east. He dropped anchor in calm water between two islands and led his three pinnaces into the harbour of Cartagena, the biggest seaport on that part of the Spanish Main.

Meeting an old Spanish sailor who was sitting alone on a frigate deserted by his shipmates – who had gone ashore as sailors will to fight about a woman – Drake asked for news. Two hours before, said the old man, a Spanish pinnace had passed making all the speed it could to the town with oars and sail. As it went by, it had asked the old man: 'Have any English or French been about lately?' 'No,' he told them. 'Look out!' warned the pinnace and passed on. Later, heavy gunfire was heard from Cartagena. The smaller craft could be seen crowding together under the shelter of the castle's guns. Obviously Drake's presence had now been detected. The guns were being fired as a warning to shipping.

The old man had some further news for his English visitors: round the next point was a cargo ship from Seville, unladen, and bound for Santo Domingo next day. A ship with an empty hold. Drake thought that she might be useful! They sailed on to inspect her, swarming aboard her on the starboard side. No easy task, for she was all of 240 tons – and for Drake, with his wound unhealed, it must have been a difficult climb. Once on deck, they thrust the crew below hatches. Then they towed the vessel out of range of the town's cannon. Obviously, after so outrageous a defiance of Spanish authority in an important colonial seaport, there was no chance of surprising Cartagena.

What was to be done? Drake retired with his prize to an island where he knew there were fish in plenty. On the way, he seized two Spanish dispatch-boats bound for Cartagena with the news that Drake would have sacked Nombre de Dios had he not been wounded. But now he was in a predicament: he had too many ships and too few men. He burnt one of the prizes and turned the other into a storeship: even so, he had one ship more than he could properly man. Yet if he sacrificed one of the ships he had brought out from Plymouth he would certainly anger its crew. It was a delicate situation calling for all his inventive powers.

He had a word in private with Thomas Moone, the ship's carpenter in the *Swan* who came from Saltash just across the Tamar from Plymouth. With Moone, Drake could be completely frank. What he proposed was this: Moone was to go down into the well of the ship in the middle of the second watch. With a big spike gimlet he was to bore three holes as near the keel as he could manage, putting something in place to deaden the sound of the inrushing water. When the puzzled but devoted Moone protested that the *Swan* was not only a fine new ship but was Drake's own property, the captain told him that in due course everybody would be glad it had been done. Moone did as he was told and kept his mouth shut. Next morning, when Drake was about to go fishing with his brother, he remarked casually how low the *Swan* was riding in the water. John Drake sent a steward to find out what the matter was. The steward went down the scuttle and came up faster than he went: he had found himself up to his waist in water. 'I have not pumped twice in six weeks,' said John Drake. 'Now I have six feet of water in the hold. Excuse me if I don't go fishing with you.'

'I'll come and help you.'

But John would not have it. 'I have enough men on board. Go on with your fishing so that we may have something for dinner.'

When Drake returned at three in the afternoon he found that, with all the crew's work at the pumps, they had only succeeded in lowering the water level by a foot and a half.

'The best thing,' said Drake, 'is for you to command the *Pasco* and the pinnaces. As for the *Swan*, let it be burned.' And so, in the face of anguished protests, Drake sacrificed the little ship in which a great part of his capital must have been invested.

After this exhibition of the way in which the slyness in his character was allied to a desperate streak, he led his diminished fleet westwards once more to the Gulf of Darien to hide in some out-of-the-way place until the alarm among the Spaniards had died down. A suitable spot was found, ground was cleared, and huts were built, including a large house for their meetings. The smiths set up their forge with the anvil, iron and coals they had brought from England. And while one half of the company were at work, the other half played bowls, quoits, skittles. They practised archery at the butts or went hunting. There was no lack of game about.

On the same day as this busy, pleasant life began, a woebegone Portuguese arrived in a dispatch boat at Nombre de Dios to report that he had been captured by English corsairs – by Captain Ranse in all probability – and held prisoner at Port Pheasant, of which he gave an accurate account. The Audiencia of Panama reported the incident to the King in the prescribed form: under a cross, the document opened with the words 'Sacred Catholic Royal Majesty' and finished, 'Humble servants of Your Majesty who kiss Your Majesty's royal hands and feet.' It was one of a series of nervous, obsequious dispatches that acquainted Philip of the terror that was growing up in his Caribbean possessions. In six months the news would be worse.

VI

Thank God, Our Voyage is Made!

'These startling developments have agitated and alarmed this kingdom.'

Colonial dispatch to the King of Spain

Drake continued to prowl about the Spanish Main. Meanwhile, he collected provisions, robbing some settlers' larders, and pillaging hogs, hens and maize from unfortunate frigates. He built and filled four storehouses, thirty or forty miles apart, so that if one was discovered and its contents carried off, there would still be enough food left for his company. He had at one time supplies for two thousand men. Meanwhile, cruising farther to the west, John Drake had found a satisfactory base of operations, a harbour set among rocky islands* too dangerous to enter by night.

But, more important than that, John had made contact with the Cimarrons, and had brought two of them back with him. A conference followed between the two parties in a wood by a river's side. The Cimarrons, whose sole thought was one of revenge on their Spanish oppressors, learned with surprise that Drake's chief interest was in that bright but useless metal, gold. They had hidden in a river bed a great amount of it which they had stolen from the Spaniards not because it interested them but because by doing so they would annoy the people who had enslaved them. But the trouble, as they explained in the course of the discussion, was that the rainy season had come, and the flow of water in the river was too high for them to retrieve the buried metal. Moreover, in wet weather, the Spaniards did not bring their gold overland.

In short, the disconcerting truth was that Drake must wait five months before he could attempt a new coup. Drake hid his

* The Mulatas archipelago.

chagrin as best he could. He ordered his artillery to be brought ashore and, with the help of his Cimarron friends, decided to build a triangular fort from timber brought from the mainland near by and boards and planks from a prize he had taken. Leaving the humdrum work of construction to his brother, John, he then set off with two pinnaces on a new descent on Cartagena, two hundred miles away.

There, after taking a few unimportant prizes, he was invited to go ashore and talk under a flag of truce. He stepped on land alone, but would go no farther than that. 'I have not enough strength to conquer you,' he said, 'but I have enough judgment to beware of you.' He had not forgotten the lesson of San Juan de Ulua. He explained that he wanted to trade and had any amount of the kind of merchandise that they needed in Cartagena. The Spaniards excused themselves saying, how regretfully one does not know, that they were permitted to buy only powder and shot from foreigners. No other form of commerce was permissible. Drake heard the news with displeasure. 'You are likely to have little rest,' he warned them, 'if you will not trade with me on fair terms.'

Next morning, the wind having changed from west to east, two well-manned frigates put out from Cartagena, meaning to prevent the raiders from making off with one of the small vessels they had captured. While John Oxenham stayed to fight off these newcomers, Drake went with all possible speed towards the prizes. There he found that some of his Spanish prisoners had got into a canoe and were hoping to tow the captured vessels within range of Spanish guns. Other Spaniards were swimming to the shore. Drake dealt with the situation in his usual summary style: he ordered that one prize should be sunk and the other set on fire. Then he went back to help his friend Oxenham. At that moment, however, the wind was blowing in from the sea with such force that the English pinnaces were driven into Cartagena harbour ahead of the Spaniards who cheered loudly, thinking that the enemy had been delivered into their hands. But things did not turn out like that.

In the smooth harbour water, Drake and Oxenham were able to make to windward of the enemy who, after a few shots, did not press the matter further but retired to the town. A long pause followed. For ten days of strong wind, high seas and heavy rain, Cartagena awaited a new attack, and the English shivered in their open boats outside the harbour. Once they made a bid to capture a frigate coming into port but it was run ashore to avoid them. An infantry captain, Martin de Mendoza, led some horsemen down to the mole; there was an exchange of fire, and both parties withdrew. The frigate was saved. Although Drake did not know it, this was a fresh disappointment of his hopes, for the vessel had gold and silver aboard. On another day, the Spaniards tried to entice the English into an ambush ashore, but had somewhat the worse of the engagement mainly because a frigate they brought up could not get within range of Drake's pinnaces.

By this time the English were short of food and, the wind abating somewhat, set out eastwards along the coast in search of it. They were out of luck. The Spanish officials, aware that marauders were about, had ordered the farmers to drive their cattle into the hills. A frigate was seen and boarded but it carried neither meat nor money, and after another week of short commons and near-famine, they anchored off the entrance to the little port of Santa Marta, of which Drake had disagreeable memories. They hoped to find ships to plunder or, failing that, sheep or shellfish on the rocks. What, in fact, greeted them was thirty or forty rounds of gunfire.

The officers of the pinnaces held a council the business of which was pursued all the more urgently because of a culverin ball that fell into the sea between the boats during their deliberations. 'Let's go a little farther east,' said the crew of one pinnace, 'and hope that the peasants will sell us food.' Rather than remain at sea in a terrible storm and a leaky boat, Drake wanted to go much farther east, a hundred miles or even four hundred. The crew of the other pinnace were firm.

'We will willingly follow you through the world,' they said, 'but we do not see how either our boat will live in this sea without being eaten up by the storm or how we ourselves will be able to endure so long on the food we have – a gammon of bacon and thirty pounds of biscuits for eighteen men.' 'You are better provided than I am,' Drake pointed out, 'who have only a gammon of bacon and forty pounds of biscuit for twenty-four! I do not doubt that you will take the same chance as I do, and willingly depend upon God's almighty providence which never fails them that trust in Him.'

After that, he hoisted his foresail and set course for Curaçao, five hundred miles farther east. Shaking their heads over their captain's headstrong behaviour, the crew followed his lead.

God's almighty providence was not slow in rewarding those who trusted in Him. A Spanish ship of 90 tons, plying westwards, had the impertinence to shoot off its guns at the English pinnaces. Drake put over his helm and followed it. He waited until a shower had settled the sea then he went in with his guns blazing. He found food aboard the Spanish vessel in good condition which 'we received as sent us of God's great mercy'. Next day, when they had put their Spanish prisoners ashore, Drake set sail to the west with his two ships. He was a great deal worried by a mysterious disease which had broken out among the crews and which now carried off one of his quartermasters, Charles Glubb, 'a very tall man and a right good mariner'. However, other members of the crew, touched by the same infection, recovered. Drake ordered the smaller and faster of the two boats to sail ahead to Fort Diego, to carry to his brother and the rest of the company the news of his coming. They were warned, too, that the time had come to make ready for the 'land journey'. This was a projected expedition, the idea of which had emerged from the conference with the Cimarrons seven weeks before. The main party arrived back at their ship on 27 November, bringing with them a dozen demijohns of Madeira. These they had found where they had been buried after the wine ship was captured in Nombre de Dios Bay during the abortive attack on the port.

Bad news greeted Drake on his return. His brother John had been killed. He had made a rash attack on a Spanish frigate, armed only with a broken rapier, an old fish spear and a rusty caliver. John had the rapier in one hand and his pillow over the other when he boarded the Spaniard at the head of a storming party. He was shot, fatally, in the stomach and 'within the hour, this young man of great hope ended his days, greatly lamented'. But worse tidings were to come.

They lay low, waiting for the news, which was the whole point of their long, hazardous stay in these waters, that the fleet had come from Spain to collect the treasure. But to linger there was to take a terrible risk. The English sailors were struck by a virulent infection.* Ten of them fell ill, and most of the sick died within a few days. One of them was Joseph Drake, who died in his brother's arms.

An extraordinary incident followed. Drake, who had lost two brothers in a matter of days, ordered the surgeon to dissect his brother's body so that the nature of the disease should be clearly established and others might benefit from the knowledge gained. The verdict was, 'A swollen liver, a sodden heart and guts all fair.' The narrator adds, 'This was the first and last experiment that our captain made of anatomy on this voyage.' It spoke of a spirit of vehement, not to say ruthless, enquiry in the man.

All this time the Cimarrons had been acting as intelligence agents for Drake. Now, in the first week of January 1573, they brought in news that the Flota commanded by Don Diego Flores de Valdes had arrived from Spain in Nombre de Dios. The time for action by the raiders was at hand. Drake sent out one of his pinnaces, the *Lion*, to verify the story. It was not a difficult mission. If the Flota had come into the Bay, all the local frigates would be converging on the port with provisions. The *Lion* had the good luck to fall in with a frigate from Tolu, laden with maize, hens and pumpkins and carrying thirteen Spaniards, one of whom was the Secretary of Tolu. With great

* Yellow fever.

difficulty, Drake dissuaded his allies, the Cimarrons, from cutting the throats of these prisoners. Then he consulted with the head men among the Cimarrons about what kind of weapons, food and clothes would be needed for the arduous journey which he was determined to make into the mountains of the Isthmus, the Cordilleras. Shoes, shoes. Any amount of spare shoes. That was the earnest advice of the Cimarrons. There would be many rivers to cross, they said, with stones and gravel in their beds. Drake listened with grave attention.

When, at length, he set off on his journey into the wild interior, southwards, towards Panama and the great South Sea, the Pacific, he had eighteen Englishmen in his party. Twenty-eight of the original band had died of fever or were sick, and five were left to guard the Spanish prisoners. He had recruited thirty Cimarrons, who not only carried their own weapons but also acted as bearers for the party. More than that, they provided food for the cooking-pots with their skill as hunters. An observant Englishman noticed that they carried several kinds of arrows. Those for battle were like the Scottish arrows, but rather longer, tipped with iron, wood or fishbone. For shooting big game, they relied on an arrow with an iron head weighing a pound and a half, razor-sharp and shaped like that of a javelin; for smaller quarry, the arrow-head was half as heavy; for birds, it weighed only an ounce, but the iron was highly tempered and would keep a good edge for a long time.

The journey over the successive ridges of mountain, covered with a dense mass of tropical vegetation, was extraordinarily arduous. At sunrise every morning the travellers started on their way; at ten o'clock they rested for two hours and trudged on until four. Then it was time to camp for the night, always near a river. If no huts had been prepared on previous journeys, the Cimarrons ran up shelters quickly for them, thatched with palmito boughs or plantain leaves, and with ventilation cunningly adapted to the steamy heat of the river valleys or the piercing cold of the mountains. There was abundance of fruit near the rivers – too much, in fact, unless they ate sparingly –

and plantains and potatoes which they roasted. Their Cimarron hunters brought in wild pigs and, once, an otter. When Drake baulked at this last delicacy, Pedro, the Cimarron chief, rebuked him: 'Are you a soldier and hungry and yet doubt whether this be meat?'

On the third day of the trek they arrived at a Cimarron town. This, in its way, was quite a substantial settlement, sited near a river, with an eight-foot ditch around it and a mud wall ten feet high. The town was traversed by one broad street and several narrower cross streets. It was clean and pleasant and consisted of something over fifty households. The inhabitants changed their clothes, which were rather in the Spanish style, to welcome the English guests. They kept patrols out, at a distance of three miles round, lest their enemy came, although in fact the village was more than a hundred miles from either Nombre de Dios or Panama. To Drake's delight, they showed themselves quite ready to drop their adoration of the Cross and learn the Lord's Prayer instead. But he recognised that this was no time for proselytism, or indeed to heed those beguiling Cimarron voices which promised that, if he stayed only two or three days longer, he would be twice as strong.

At noon on the second day of the visit, he resumed the march. Four Cimarrons kept a mile in advance of the main party, moving silently through the forest and breaking branches to show the way. Twelve Cimarrons acted as a rearguard. The trees were high and in their shade the air was cool. At ten o'clock on the morning of the fourth day, they reached the summit of a ridge running east and west. Here, in the branches of an exceptionally tall tree, the Cimarrons had built a wooden platform. Now occurred what is the real climax of the whole remarkable journey. From this observation post Drake – sight of sights! – saw the two oceans simultaneously: the blue of the Caribbean on the one hand and the yellow of the Great South Sea on the other. It was a moving, unforgettable revelation of the wonder, the scale, the emptiness of the world. To clap eyes on it thus, suddenly, after that long, weary trek through the forests, was to have the imagination stirred. And to be young, pious, patriotic, a sailor, was to have ambition explode. Standing on that crow's nest which the Cimarrons had built in that tree, Drake besought Almighty God of His goodness to give him life and leave to sail once an English ship on that sea. And John Oxenham, who was with him on the platform and who shared the excitement of that high moment in adventure, swore that, if Drake did not forcibly prevent him, he would follow, by God's grace.

After that, the travellers resumed their way southwards and downhill, through forests which after a time opened into champaign country bearing a grass which to their wonder grew faster than the cattle could eat it. They were now within a day's march of Panama and it was necessary to walk warily, for the country was liable to be scoured by fowlers supplying the Panama market with game. Within three miles of the town was a wood near the Royal Road which led towards Nombre de Dios. This wood they approached along the dry bed of a river and there they rested in the shelter of the trees while one of the Cimarrons went forward on a scouting expedition, dressed like a Panama Negro. It was important to find out at what time the *recuas* (the mule-trains) were loaded for their night journey over the eighteen miles of open country between the town and Venta Cruces where the forest begins. The spy brought back good news. The Treasurer of Lima, who meant to take the first advice boat for Spain, was going to travel that night to Nombre de Dios with his daughter and family. There would be fourteen mules in the train, eight of which would be carrying gold and one jewels. This train would be followed by two others of fifty mules each, mostly carrying food but some with a little silver too. On hearing this, the raiding party marched twelve miles in the direction of Venta Cruces.

On the way, two of the Cimarron scouts smelt a match burning and, creeping nearer, came upon a Spaniard fast asleep and snoring. They leapt on him – tied him up and gagged him so thoroughly that he was almost strangled. He proved to be a soldier belonging to a party hired by the Treasurer to guard the bullion. He begged Drake to save him from the Cimarrons, who would certainly take his life and, in addition, suggested that if that night they seized – as he swore they would – more gold and jewels than they could carry, Captain Francisco, as he called Drake, should let him have enough of the loot for himself and his mistress to live on. Whether this impudent request was granted is unknown. Probably Drake answered that the matter might wait until the gold was in his hands.

He divided the party into two – one half under himself lay in the long grass fifty yards to one side of the trail, while the other half, led by John Oxenham and Pedro, the chief Cimarron, hid on the other side somewhat nearer to Panama. Each man had donned his white shirt over his doublet so that in the darkness he would be recognised by his friends. When the moment came to spring the trap, Drake's party were to attack the leading mules in the nose-to-tail procession, while Oxenham's made for the animals in the rear.

It was just thirty-five weeks since they had slipped out of Plymouth Sound, thirty-five weeks during which they had trespassed on Spanish soil, robbed Spanish ships but failed to lay their hands on Spanish gold. Now, it seemed, the moment of achievement was at hand.

After an hour, lying in ambush, they heard through the stillness of that tropical night the deep, inexpressibly exciting sound of the mule bells of two *recuas* that were approaching, one travelling northwards from Panama, the other on the way south from Venta Cruces. The latter they would let pass – it would have no treasure in its pack saddles. It was the first, the mule-train from Panama, that interested them. And now, softer than the bells and even more thrilling, came the light patter of hoofs on the road. They were only a few hundred yards from the treasure from Peru. And at that moment, when everything seemed most promising, the whole enterprise was brought to ruin. Robert Pike, who had been applying himself too freely to the brandy bottle – and without water – rose from his hiding-place and ran towards the mules coming from Venta Cruces. A Cimarron threw the foolish man to the ground and fell on top of him. Too late! A horseman who was riding from Venta Cruces, with a page running at his stirrup, had seen the apparition in the white shirt. He spurred his horse to a gallop. Drake, head down, ears straining, heard a change in the rhythm of the hoofs on the hard ground. He feared that they had been detected although he did not know how it had happened. Perhaps it was simply that this was a place favourable for an ambush, and travellers were accustomed to hurry past. He waited for the Treasurer of Lima.

But the Treasurer met the galloping horseman about a mile farther on. From him he heard of the man in white suddenly appearing and suddenly suppressed. Perhaps it was some manifestation of the infamous Captain Drake, cheated of success at Nombre de Dios all those months ago, but believed still to be skulking about the coast! The Treasurer pulled his mule-train to the side of the track and let the other trains, mere carriers of provisions with no more than two loads of silver among them, go through. And thus, through folly, a haul worth at least 80,000 pesos* was lost.

Drake was beside himself with vexation, especially when he found out how the disaster had occurred. It was some minutes before he could take the philosophical view that God had evidently meant the gold to be preserved from him – and that probably the Treasurer had come by it honestly.

These consoling reflections did not, however, prevent him from marching on to Venta Cruces where, a mile short of the village, the track plunged into a dense wood through which a path had been cleared for the mules, just ten or twelve feet across. The Cimarron scouts came back to say that they had heard the noise of Spaniards – there were soldiers and a party of Dominican friars in the woods – and had smelt the burning of their matches. 'Get your arms ready,' said Drake, 'but don't fire until they do.' Out of the dark came a Spanish call which Drake answered.

* Worth, then, £36,000.

'*Qué gente?*' asked the Spanish captain.

'Englishmen.'

'Surrender in the name of King Philip. On the word of a gentleman and a soldier, I will use you with all courtesy.'

'For the honour of the Queen of England, my mistress,' replied Drake, 'I must pass this way.' And he fired his pistol at the captain.

The Spaniards replied with a volley which slightly wounded Drake and others of the party. John Harris was so badly hurt that his life could not be saved. Then Drake, with a blast on his captain's whistle, brought the muskets and the bows into play and ordered the advance, first at a walk, then at a run. The Cimarrons joined in the mêlée, leaping, shooting their arrows and shouting their war-song, '*Yó peho. Yó peho.*'

And so, the English running and the Cimarrons capering, the raiders drove the Spaniards before them into Venta Cruces, where in a monastery they found upwards of a thousand pardons, newly arrived from Rome and, in other houses, three ladies who had come up there to be delivered of their babies, safe from the yellow fever that laid Nombre de Dios waste. Drake ordered the Cimarrons on no account to molest these women – or any Spaniard without arms. Even so, they did not feel really safe in his absence. The Cimarrons, dark-skinned and scowling, were not the most soothing company for Spanish ladies in the mountains of Panama and, perhaps, some of their English allies did not look much more reassuring.

But now it was time to go back to the coast. Drake had been nearly a fortnight absent from his ship. Speaking encouraging words to his companions – 'before we leave this coast we shall all be bountifully rewarded for these pains' – he led the way at speed and with no thought given to empty stomachs. Nine miles from the harbour where the ship lay, the Cimarrons had built a little town where they insisted Drake should rest. He was quite willing to do so, having some trouble with his feet, like the rest of his company. In the meantime, he sent off a Cimarron with a message to Hixon on the ship, authenticated by his gold toothpick on which the words had been scratched, 'By me Francis Drake.' And so, at three o'clock that afternoon, they met a pinnace from the ship at the mouth of the Tortuga River. They were worn, wasted and downcast, having failed a second time to win the great prize. Their shipmates found them much changed – all except Captain Francis who was as ebullient as ever.

Next day, everybody began to feel better when the word went round that Drake ('knowing right well that no sickness was more noisome to impeach any enterprise than delay and idleness') was contemplating a new adventure. Oxenham was to take one of the pinnaces, the *Bear*, to the east in search of food; Drake, with the other, the *Minion*, would sail to the west in the hope of picking up some of the gold which had been mined at Veragua and likely to be on its way to join the Flota waiting at Nombre de Dios. The *Minion* was lucky enough to intercept a frigate with a Genoese pilot – one of the many of his kind on that coast – who had been in Veragua only a week before. He had no lack of interesting matters to report: a frigate would be leaving Veragua harbour in a few days with a load of gold worth millions aboard her and he was quite willing to guide them at night through the shoals and sandbanks into the port. They could do their business and be off before the alarm was given in the town. For although Drake was known to be lurking about and the population was in a state of acute anxiety, no special defence measures had been taken. But speed was essential.

Drake recruited the Genoese, sent off his frigate lighter by some of its gold, and made for Verugua harbour with all possible speed. Again he was out of luck. When the *Minion* reached the harbour mouth, two shots were fired ashore, answered by two others some miles farther inland. Contrary to the opinion of the Genoese, a warning system had been set up, paid for by a rich mine-owner of the district, Señor Pezoro. At the same time the wind swung round to the west, confirming to the devout marauders from Plymouth that God did not intend them to enter Veragua harbour just then. They sailed back to the base ship to find that in their absence John Oxenham had captured a frigate carrying maize, fat hogs and hens. Drake inspected the prize and finding her a new, well-found craft, decided to fit her out as a man-of-war.

On Easter Day, to lift the spirits of the crew, there was great feasting and jollity. Three days later they fell in with a French vessel which made signs of friendship and readiness to talk. It proved to be an 80-ton ship out of Havre commanded by Captain Têtu, a celebrated Huguenot privateer, and a cartographer of eminence. Têtu declared that he was in desperate straits for water. He came aboard bringing gifts, a case of pistols and a gilt scimitar which he said had been the property of Henri II of France. He also brought news which was none the less appalling because by this time it was months old. There had been a terrible massacre of Protestants in Paris on St Bartholomew's Eve. Coligny, Admiral of France, and leader of the Huguenot party, had been murdered. Thousands of others had perished that night. Grimly listening to the frightful story, Drake recognised the religious war was taking a more ferocious turn.

He can hardly have doubted that this was likely to happen. Before he left England, the Pope's Bull of Excommunication against Queen Elizabeth had been fastened to the door of St Paul's Cathedral in London. Nobody was likely to underrate the reality of that anathema. Only one man was likely to rate it lightly. Philip, who forbade the Bull to be published in his dominions, had himself been the target of a similar papal condemnation. Pope Paul IV in 1556 had excommunicated 'the son of iniquity Philip of Austria, offspring of the so-called Emperor Charles, who passes himself off as King of Spain'.[1] But the Bull of 1570 against Elizabeth had a sharper edge of practical menace. It contributed to an age of extraordinary tension.

Now Têtu proposed to Drake that they should join forces. The Englishman hesitated. He had only twenty men with him, against seventy seamen in the French ship. However, he agreed, on condition that the number of those who took part in the joint venture should be equal, twenty of each nation, and that any plunder should likewise be divided equally. Five or six days later, the joint party, fifteen English, twenty French and five Cimarrons, left the ships at a safe anchorage and landed at the Rio Francisco, twenty miles from Nombre de Dios by the route that they were about to take through the forest. Their object was another attempt to intercept one of the mule-trains now passing frequently on the trail between Panama and Nombre de Dios.

An English mile from the trail they rested for the night. From where they lay, they could hear the carpenters hammering and sawing as they worked on two new galleys in the harbour and then suddenly, a blessed sound fell on their ears – the mule bells of the King of Spain's *recuas*, faint at first but growing louder. The Cimarrons, listening and calculating, spread the good news among the English that they would soon have more gold and silver than they could carry away. It seemed there were three trains, one of fifty mules and two of seventy, each animal carrying 300 pounds of silver – in all, about 25 tons of the metal. The forty thieves crept cautiously forward and prepared their ambush.

On a signal they rushed the train, seizing the foremost and hindmost mules by the head. The other mules came to a halt and lay down as they had been trained to do. Forty-five Spanish soldiers who were on escort duty put up a fight for a short while and then decided to go in search of reinforcements. In the exchange of fire, Captain Têtu fell shot in the stomach by a Negro arquebusier, and lay writhing in pain. The raiders picked the mules that seemed to be most heavily burdened and relieved them of 'a few bars and quoits of gold' and 15 tons of silver, which they buried in the ground. This occupied two hours. Then, hearing some noise of approaching troops they decided to resume their march to the sea, leaving behind the badly wounded French captain.

Another Frenchman had drunk too much wine and was

trying to carry too heavy a burden of loot; as a result he lost his way and fell into the hands of the Spaniards, with what outcome can be imagined.

Two days later, the party, after travelling through the bush with all possible speed, reached the coast where they had a rendezvous with their pinnaces. There a disagreeable surprise awaited them. Seven Spanish pinnaces were cruising off the shore, sent there by the Captain-General as soon as he heard of the new attack on the mule-train.

By this time, the Spanish authorities were thoroughly alarmed. As the Council of Panama had written to the King only a week before this new attack: 'These English have so shamelessly opened the door and a way by which, with impunity, whenever they wish, they will attack the mule-trains travelling overland . . . by which must necessarily come and go the gold and silver, belonging to Your Majesty and private persons.'

'I found this coast in a pitiable condition,' reported Diego de Flores Valdes.[2] And Pedro de Ortega Valencia agreed, 'This place is as good as lost.' The most ominous feature of all, in the unanimous opinion of these Spanish officials, was the unholy alliance between the English and the Cimarrons: 'most lamentable, for the blacks are numerous'. Now, with this disastrous new raid in which English, French and Cimarron marauders worked together, the Spaniards feared that they were faced by a serious attempt to seize Panama, settle in the city and build ships on the Pacific.

No doubt, the writers of these dispatches to Madrid were concerned to paint the blackest possible picture so that the administration in Spain would be stirred to action. Even so, there is a note of genuine alarm in the messages which fell one after another on King Philip's desk. It was the alarm of men who knew that a revolt of the slaves, armed and directed by European minds, could swiftly bring the fabric of their golden empire down about their ears. They had wives, families – and while El Capitan Francisco had an eccentric reputation for chivalry, could one be so sure of his French allies, those grey-eyed Calvinists from Normandy with so many grim scores to pay off? Already they were reported (according to the horrifying rumours that floated about among the Spanish settlers) to have promised the Cimarrons that the Spaniards would be their slaves.

When Diego Calderon, alcalde mayor of Nombre de Dios, heard from the fleeing *recua* guards about Drake's successful attack on the mule-train, he ordered the drum to be beaten in the square and the standard displayed. Then he led a party of soldiers through the darkness to the scene of outrage where he found the mules unpacked and scattered, and Captain Têtu lying wounded. An indignant Spanish soldier impulsively beheaded the Frenchman, an act which was later deplored by his superiors. They thought that Têtu could probably have been persuaded to betray Drake's escape route.[3]

It was a black night of violent rain. The main party of raiders had escaped but the drunk Frenchman was found before he had shaken off the fumes of wine and ill-treated until he revealed where the stolen silver was buried. After that, he was executed. The authorities were able therefore to recover a good deal of the silver but the gold, worth 100,000 pesos* or more (for estimates differ), including 18,363 pesos consigned to the King, had gone with Drake to the sea. 'It is a sad thing,' lamented the officials in Panama, 'to contemplate the men who have been ruined by this attack. Many of them were retiring to Spain with their fortunes made by the labour of many years, some from very remote and distant provinces, to be robbed by corsairs only a league and a half from Nombre de Dios and left destroyed, ruined.'[4]

Gravest of all was the thought of those Negroes 'who have run away from their masters and advertise that they have allied and confederated themselves with the English and French (infidels and Lutherans) to destroy this realm'.

Meanwhile, down on the coast at the mouth of the Rio Francisco, Drake was troubled by the fear that the Spaniards

* £45,000.

might have captured his pinnaces and persuaded some of the crew to disclose the anchorage where the ships were hidden. How else could he explain the presence of those Spanish vessels and the absence of his own? His companions had exactly the same anxiety. It was a situation in which the buoyancy and resource of Drake's temperament showed at its most admirable. Even if the enemy had (which God forbid) taken the pinnaces, they would not have had time to reach the ships. So – 'Let us make a raft with these trees brought down by the storm and put ourselves to sea. I shall be one. Who will be the other?' A man named John Smith volunteered. Two Frenchmen who were good swimmers followed suit as also did the Cimarrons, including Pedro, their leader, although he could not row. So a raft was built, firmly tied together; a sail was made from a biscuit sack, and a young tree was shaped into an oar that could be used as a rudder. 'If it pleases God that I should put my foot aboard my frigate . . .' said Drake to his faithful, trusting followers, 'by one means or another I will get you all aboard too, in spite of all the Spaniards in the Indies.' Then he pushed off from the shore.

For the next six hours, he, Smith, the two Frenchmen and the Cimarrons sailed in their crazy craft under a blazing sun. Sometimes they were up to the waist in water, sometimes up to the armpits. But the sail held and the wind was with them. More remarkable still, they were not observed by the cruising Spanish frigates. And at last Drake sighted two pinnaces and, helped by the eyes of faith, swore that they were his. They were. The crews of the pinnaces were alarmed when they saw how few of their comrades had come back. They did not recover their spirits until Drake pulled a gold plate out of his shirt and announced, 'Thank God, our voyage is made . . .' In other words, the enterprise was showing a profit. That night they rowed back to pick up the rest of the company and retrieve the treasure they had hidden at the shore. By daybreak they were on their way to the ships where the gold and silver was equally divided between the French and the English.

A mixed party of English and Cimarrons were sent to look for the French captain and the silver which had been buried beside the Nombre de Dios trail. They found only one Frenchman, who had given up hope of being rescued, and learnt from him that Têtu was dead and that the buried silver had been dug up by the Spaniards. All they brought back was thirteen bars of silver and a few gold plates.

The hour of departure had struck. It was time to wish the French a good voyage back to Normandy and to say farewell to the Cimarrons. Drake asked Pedro to take anything he fancied as a souvenir of their alliance and Pedro's eye fell on the gilt scimitar that Têtu had given to Drake. However, he did not dare to ask for anything so precious but instead offered a gold plate to a seaman named Frank Tucker to be his spokesman with the Captain. The bargain Pedro proposed was that, in exchange for four gold plates, Drake should give him the sword. Drake refused to take the gold but was very willing to part with the scimitar. However, Pedro insisted on paying, and Drake added the gold pieces to the general fund. Thus, Henri II's scimitar was carried off to be presented to the King of the Cimarrons.

And so homewards at last, sailing past Cartagena with a large wind and, to annoy Don Diego's fleet in the harbour, with St George's flag flying at the maintop and silk streamers and ensigns floating down to the water.

The voyage home was uneventful. God Almighty sent a good supply of rainwater, a passing Spanish barque provided a pump which the frigate badly needed and a captured frigate yielded them all the provisions they required. Just twenty-three days after passing Cape Canaveral, they sighted the Scillies. They arrived in Plymouth Harbour in time to interrupt the Sunday morning sermon in St Andrew's Church with the tangible 'evidence of God's love and blessing towards our gracious Queen and country'. It was 9 August 1573, four hundred and forty-two days after they had set sail.

VII

To the Great South Sea

'Bring upon the King of Spain every imaginable outrage and disgrace.'

The Grand Signior to Queen Elizabeth.[1]

What rewards did the voyage bring to those who survived it? Probably – for no certain figures exist – there were about forty left out of the seventy-four who set forth. If that was so, casualties after the fourteen months' round trip had not been excessive in comparison with the losses which were normal on these expeditions. After all, John Hawkins had lost almost the whole of his crew three years earlier. Young Englishmen had a fair idea of the risks they were running when they set out on these escapades. They expected a commensurate return. What did Drake's voyage of 1572–3 yield?

On the assumption that the gold and silver taken from the mule-trains was all they had stolen, they had brought back 100,000 gold pesos, of which 50,000 went to their French confederates. That would be equivalent to £20,000 to divide among the English or, say, £600,000, in modern values. It was a good amount to divide among forty seamen, even if allowance is made for the fact that Drake, the commander and owner of one of the two ships adventured, would claim by right a much larger portion than the others. Among the French, wild stories were rife: it was said that each of the seamen had been given £10,000 (30,000 écus). What is likely is that the total of the prize money, as it was admitted in England, fell a good deal short of the true figure. Drake was not a man to pay the Customs searchers more than he needed, or to cause the Queen's government more embarrassment with the Spaniards than was necessary. What is certain is that the return to Plymouth in 1573 marked a definite upward step in Drake's fortunes and that, from that moment, he ceased to be a dependant of his Hawkins relations. He was henceforth a man of substance, a shipowner in his own right. And his fame, or notoriety, was spreading from the Caribbean into England and Europe. After all, he had brought off an astonishing feat. With a handful of men he had spread terror along hundreds of miles of the Spanish-American coastline. He had teased the Spanish fleet with a flotilla of pinnaces, had seized, pillaged and, in some cases, burnt an untold number of coastal craft. He had put Spanish troops to flight and evaded their pursuit. And all this had taken place in the regions of the New World, those few mountainous, fever-stricken, beautiful miles hemmed between two oceans, which were vital to King Philip's power and prestige. No wonder that the messages from Panama and Nombre de Dios to His Catholic Majesty had something of the throb and plangency of the old monastic supplication, *a furore Normannorum, libera nos, Domine.*

No doubt, Drake can claim only part of the credit for the business which alarmed the Spaniards most, the league with the fugitive slaves, for it seems that the Huguenot privateers thought of it first. But Drake had, to an extraordinary degree, captured the affection of the Cimarrons and, hardest of all, had imposed on them his ideas of discipline. He had kept their knives from Spanish throats! Bearing in mind all that the slaves had suffered from their masters, it was an impressive demonstration of personality and moral authority.

Without the help of the Cimarrons as scouts, bearers and guerrilla fighters, Drake's pertinacity could not have been crowned, as it was, with dazzling success. That event, so kindling to the imagination, so important in history, the breath-taking vision of the Great South Sea was only granted to Drake because a Cimarron had led him to a crow's-nest in a tree-top on Panama. As it was, he and his companions had brought home to Devon not simply travellers' tales of strange beasts, beautiful fish, delicious fruits, islands where pearls – and turtle eggs – could be picked up by the bucketful, streams where the Spaniards washed gold from the gravel and mines where they –

or their slaves – dug it from the earth. They had seen something else, a new world beyond the New World, a universe of water, pouring majestic, rhythmic and imperturbable on to the beaches of San Miguel. On the far side of that tremendous surge were Cathay and its silk, the marvellous Spice Islands and, somewhere lost in those oceanic spaces, the mysterious land of Beach of which the geographers had spoken, but which, it seemed, no sailor's eye had seen. Drake had seen enough during those few minutes to be sure that his next expedition would be in the Great South Sea.

Meanwhile, he bought a house in Plymouth, at the top of Looe Street just opposite the Guildhall; he acquired three ships and put them to good use. Then a hint came from London that he would be well-advised to disappear for a while. He obeyed as philosophically as he could be expected to do. It was inopportune to boast too much about the raid on the mule-trains at Nombre de Dios. Drake's return to England had coincided with one of those delusive periods when England and Spain seemed to be moving towards reconciliation.

There is some doubt about his movements during the next two years. He may quite likely have helped to escort a vast convoy to Hamburg. But certainly he found employment for himself and his ships in ferrying the Queen's soldiers to places in Ireland, 'the last of the daughters of Europe . . . to be reclaimed from desolation',* where they were badly needed.

That kingdom was afflicted just then by one of its periodic outbreaks of tribal warfare, which, if it showed any signs of dying down, was instantly rekindled by a new incursion of Redshanks from the Hebrides or Argyll, Gaelic-speaking descendants of Vikings or Celts, hungry warriors, who thought not only that fighting was the most agreeable form of commerce but also that it was the only form permissible to men of gentle blood who combined in themselves the proclivities of these two warlike stocks. The Redshanks were not always lucky. The Queen's government in Dublin was notably blind to the

* Francis Bacon.

distinction between those well-born mercenaries from Scotland and the native Irish peasants.[2] The one, like the other, should be suitably punished in the names of good order, civilisation, military necessity and so forth. Thus, one day in July 1575, a dreadful massacre occurred on Rathlin Island, where a Scottish force had taken refuge. An English force of frigates put a party of troops ashore. The Scots surrendered and were massacred to a man, woman and child. An unpleasant episode, although characteristic of the warfare of the age, and worthy of note here because, it seems, Drake was in command of the escorting flotilla. The massacre itself was directed by John Norreys, a competent commander in an age when the military genius of the English was temporarily somewhat in abeyance. A glowing picture of this cruel event was conveyed to the Queen by the Earl of Essex, a nobleman to whom she had farmed out the task and profits of the Irish 'purification'. In the end, the Irish business broke her heart.

Drake's name was put forward for this service by John Hawkins. His technical efficiency as a seaman in the Irish operations caught the eye of Thomas Doughty, an astute, well-educated young lawyer who acted as the trusted secretary of Essex until the latter found that the young man was playing him false. Not long after the Rathlin massacre, the needle of Anglo-Spanish relations swung back towards hostility and the government began to look round for an adventurous young man who could be counted on to badger the Spaniards with the least possible embarrassment to Whitehall. Drake who had caused all that commotion on the Spanish Main a year or two before? He seemed just the man for the job, Doughty thought, so Essex agreed, and recommended him to Walsingham as one well-equipped by temperament and experience to annoy King Philip. He was summoned to London and drawn into the counsels of the party of aggression. Far-reaching projects were afoot of which the inspiring genius was Master John Dee, one of the most interesting men of his time. Intelligent, imaginative and credulous, Dee[3] was a Welshman, one of a race who, in the words of his fellow-countryman, Humphrey Lhuyd, 'be somewhat impatient of labour and overmuch boasting of the nobility of their stock . . . applying themselves rather to the service of noblemen than giving themselves to the learning of handicrafts'. His interests extended from mathematics, in which he was brilliant, to the allied arts of geography and astrology. Like many other of the most distinguished men of the period, Leicester for example, Dee dabbled in the occult. His portrait shows a peering, austere, anxious man in a black skull-cap and a white beard. Only the steaming cauldron, the retort and the pentacle are needed to complete the perfect image of the warlock.

Needless to say, Dee traced his descent from Welsh kings and, indeed, claimed that the coast of America (which he called Atlantis) from Florida northwards, was his in virtue of its discovery by Owen Madoc in the twelfth century. Eventually, he fell under the spell of a medium named Edward Kelly who held seances in Dee's house at Mortlake. After a time, he and Kelly left for the Continent on a wild-goose chase in search of the philosopher's stone. No sooner had the pair departed than the mob, with indignant outcries against witchcraft, ransacked his house and destroyed many of his books. But in 1577, Dee was still mainly interested in cosmography, a science almost as shrouded in ignorance and almost as exciting to the imagination as astrology itself.

Through Edward Dyer, the poet and student of the occult, Dee had important friends at Court, Leicester and Christopher Hatton, for example. Leicester was the Queen's favourite. Hatton, Captain of her Guard, was tall, handsome and socially accomplished, the sort of man Elizabeth liked to see at Court. And he was rich enough to own a fine ship which he was willing to contribute to a voyage of exploration, all the more readily since he was an enthusiast for the idea of maritime power, the British thalassocracy of which John Dee was a prophet. Dee's book *The Perfect Art of Navigation* was dedicated to Hatton. Another follower of Dee's was that outspoken young paladin,

Sir Philip Sidney. And finally there was Mr Secretary himself, Francis Walsingham. Through Richard Hakluyt, of the Inner Temple, a fellow-Welshman with a flair for propaganda even more sensitive than his own, Dee's influence reached into the City. If it was Dee who invented the term British empire, Hakluyt was the first to celebrate the exploits of the men who founded it. These two Welshmen were at the heart of an intellectual ferment from which in time came the colonial explosion, which Hakluyt believed to be forced on England by overpopulation: 'Our prisons are festered and filled with able men to serve their country which for small robberies are daily hanged, even twenty at a clap out of one gaol.'[4]

Guessing as best he could from the evidence before him, Dee laid down one or two general principles of cosmography. He believed that gold, silver and spices – almost as precious as the metals themselves – were generated by the heat of the sun. It was useless therefore to look for gold in the Arctic regions. On the other hand, Cathay, that dream kingdom of exotic luxury, could, he deduced, be reached by sailing west-about round North America through the Straits of Anian, the entrance to which had so far eluded all the explorers. Finally there was Beach – Terra Australis Incognita – where gold lay waiting to be picked up by the pioneer who was lucky enough to sight its coast.

Beach. The name was first used by Marco Polo, who applied it to a land of gold and elephants lying to the south of Cathay. Probably he had Indo-China in mind. In the opinion of John Dee, the existence of a vast southern continent could be deduced from the proposition or, rather, the axiom, as he regarded it, that there must be as much land south of the equator as north of it. The only problem was to find it.

In the early weeks of 1577 it seemed to some men in Britain that the time had come to put these theories to the test. There was a series of conferences in John Dee's house at Mortlake. Men who were prominent in what might be called the forward school of political thinking at Court came to talk and listen to the great idealogue. In May of that year, Dee published a discourse in which he spoke of an attempt 'by a British subject presently interested in God's glory'.[5] This unnamed hero had 'secretly offered up to God and his natural sovereign the employing of all his skill to that place, being the very ends of the world', to discover that which had defeated so many valiant captains. In its context, this seemed to hint that a fresh attempt was about to be made to solve the problem of the Straits of Anian.

What, in fact, was in the minds of the promoters? An approach to the Pacific by the Straits of Magellan and a return by the same route. But was there nothing else? For instance, an attempt to open up trade with the Spice Islands, the Moluccas? That was something which would annoy the King of Portugal, who had a monopoly of the trade. If it was contemplated at all, it was best referred to by hints and in whispers. Colonisation in South America, south of the bounds of Spanish or Portuguese influence? That had been an idea of Sir Richard Grenville's, a member of one of those West Country families of Protestant gentry and shipowners from which came so much of the impulse of English expansion. Grenville, Gilbert, Raleigh, Champernowne, Drake, Hawkins and the like – many of them were linked by family ties. Without those sons of a comparatively few square miles of English soil, how different would have been the Elizabethan story! It may have been that Sir Richard's project for a colony was embedded in this new design? Or, perhaps, a search for the Pacific entrance to the Straits of Anian? Since that would involve a voyage northwards along the western coast of Spanish America, its dangers were obvious. Spanish settlements were strung out along hundreds of miles of that coast and the Spaniards were inordinately sensitive to anything that might disturb the peace of the Great South Sea. Perhaps, then, it was best to talk of a search for Terra Australis and its wealth and leave it at that.

And who should be chosen to lead the expedition? This question was not easily settled. Martin Frobisher, an excellent mariner and a man of courage, was already fully committed to exploration in the north-west of America. John Hawkins was by this time ear-marked to rebuild the Queen's Navy. Sir Richard Grenville was too notorious an anti-Spaniard. To choose him would be to ring the alarm bells in Madrid.

Another man whose name might have been considered was Walter Raleigh. But his ambition was fixed on the seaboard of North America. Besides, he was only twenty-three years old. That left Drake. As commander he would be every bit as likely as Grenville to annoy the Spaniards but he was more manageable, readier to lend himself to devious practices and more easily expendable. That aspect was important because it was necessary that the Spaniards should be put off their guard. This was easy enough to an expert in deception like Walsingham. 'There is a suspicion,' writes a Spanish agent in London* in September 1577, 'that Drake the pirate is to go to Scotland with some little vessels for the purpose of getting possession of the Prince of Scotland.'[6] Important people were to board the ships, so as to give the impression that it was bound for the Indies. Nearer the time of sailing, the rumour spread that the ships were bound for Alexandria.

It seems, too, that on the English side there was a variety of ideas about what was afoot and that those who favoured one project were not frank with the others. Burghley, the Lord Treasurer, the wariest and most influential of Elizabeth's ministers, 'of all men of genius the most a drudge; of all men of business, the most a genius',[7] would be likely to disapprove of any unnecessary provocation of the Spaniards. In the 'forward' party, a man like Walsingham regarded war as inevitable and any damage done to Spain in the meantime as so much gain for England. Walsingham was one of those who initiated the expedition, and it was he who put forward Drake's name to the Queen.

That is, at any rate, Drake's story, although it is quite possible

* Antonio de Guaras, a Spanish merchant in London, who acted as an informal representative of his country in the absence of a regular Ambassador.

that the original impetus came from Drake himself. He knew that his comrade John Oxenham, who had stood at his side that marvellous day in Panama, had already left for the Isthmus with collapsible pinnaces stowed in the hold of his ship. Even if envy and ambition had not been part of Drake's nature, which they certainly were, the thought that Oxenham was a step ahead of him would be a cause for impatience, for an irritated tugging at his red beard and a frown above his round blue eyes.

Most important and, naturally, most obscure of all were the knowledge and intentions of the Queen. She was, as in so many ventures of the time, the great anonymous capitalist. Lincoln, Leicester, Hatton, Walsingham, were all subscribers to the venture; so were two members of the famous naval family of Wynter (two other members of which were to sail with the ships) and John Hawkins. Drake himself was down for £1,000. This was a substantial investment, showing that the young marauder of Nombre de Dios had not spent all his winnings in the intervening four years, and had probably even added to them. How much money the Queen put in is not known for certain. Drake said it was 1,000 crowns. But, in any case, she was taking the greatest risk, the risk of war if some impetuous aggression on Drake's part proved to be more than King Philip could stomach.

How much did Elizabeth know about what was intended? A draft plan of the project, prepared some time in the first half of 1577, leaves it conveniently doubtful whether Drake was to seek trade and employment for English shipping in South America or in the conjectured Terra Australis.[8] It says, however, that the secret, true purpose of the voyage was to be disclosed to the Queen's Majesty. Why need it be secret if it was something quite innocent like the finding of an unknown continent? And why employ a man with Drake's reputation as a fire-eater on a mission where there was danger of a clash with Spain, unless that danger had been faced and discounted?

Drake gave his own account of the business. At the crisis of the voyage, he told his assembled ships' companies that the Earl of Essex had recommended him as one suited to serve against the Spaniards. Walsingham had asked him to suggest where the King of Spain might most effectively be damaged. Drake had put forward some ideas, but had refused to put anything in writing – 'affirming that Her Majesty was mortal and that if it should please God to take Her Majesty away it might be that some prince might reign who might be in league with the King of Spain and then will my own hand be a witness against myself'.

He went on to tell of an interview he had had with the Queen who had said, more or less, 'Drake, I would gladly be revenged on the King of Spain for injuries I have received. You are the only man who may do this exploit. What is your advice?' He had told her that the only way the King could be hurt was in the Indies. The Queen then swore by her crown that if anyone in England told the King of Spain that she was a party to the venture, she would have his head. In particular, Burghley was not to be told about it.

There is a possibility that Drake was romancing when he gave this account of the interview. He did so at a moment when he needed to muster all the authority he could over his officers and men. And somehow, the inflammatory language put into the Queen's mouth does not ring true. He was the last man in the world to need incitement of that sort. And she knew perfectly the kind of man he was.

But it does seem likely that they met, the spidery Queen and the talkative little corsair, and that they reached an understanding. Each heard – or thought he heard – from the other what he wanted to hear. Perhaps Elizabeth was infected by the wild adventure presented to her in a rush of slurred West Country English. She may well have approved it to an extent beyond what was prudent in a statesman or seemly in a queen. She was in some respects a susceptible woman and there was in her make-up a vein of pure mischief . . . Above all, do not tell my Lord Treasurer! How true it rings! To hoodwink the grey image of wisdom who sat at her council table! It was not the smallest pleasure in life. But how far was Burghley deceived? That is another question.

Drake went off to make his ships ready for a voyage of a year or more. To explore? To trade? To make a profit? Intuition told him that the shareholders, including the one who must remain unnamed, would not look with too censorious an eye on the manner in which their dividends were earned. One result only would be despised – failure. He had seen the rollers of the Great South Sea breaking on a distant beach. Now he was going to that sea.

VIII

The Bay of Crisis

'The ship was cheered, the harbour cleared,
Merrily did we drop
Below the kirk, below the hill,
Below the lighthouse top.'

The Ancient Mariner – Coleridge

There was no time to lose. There were five ships to be fitted out. Four pinnaces to be taken apart and stowed below decks. The perfumed waters and sweetmeats sent by the Queen to be put away until a suitable time came to use them. Drake had, from the same august source, an embroidered sea-cap with a green silk scarf with red bands on which the words were picked out in gold, 'The Lord guide and preserve thee until the end.' Gifts of that kind were very much to the adventurer's taste. He had an eye for splendour and, like Hawkins, an understanding of how it could build up the prestige of the man who displayed it. Now he, Francis Drake, once the penniless younker on a half-derelict coaster, was going to play the part of an admiral of the Queen! He had her commission or, at any rate, an imposing parchment which at appropriate times he flourished, declaring that it was his brief of authority given by the sovereign. It was fitting, then, that he should have fine furniture in his cabin and silver dishes to eat from, musicians to play trumpets and viols during the long days of sailing. And that, on the bronze cannon, his arms were engraved, a globe and a star.

Drake had not forgotten the practical side of the voyage. His ship, the *Pelican*, later and better known by another name, carried eighteen guns (demi-culverins firing a 9-pound shot) lined up behind their portholes and a multitude of lesser weapons, arquebuses, calivers, bows, as well as armour of various patterns. There was a forge and everything a smith might need for his craft; there were implements to dig with and cut down trees. All this and a great deal more – food for eighteen months, beer, water – was packed into a formidable little ship, something between a merchant vessel and a ship of war, of a hundred tons or maybe a little more. The other ships of the fleet were smaller. The *Elizabeth* of 80 tons sailed from the Thames on 19 September 1577 under her captain, John Wynter, and joined the others at Plymouth. These were the *Marigold* (Captain John Thomas), 30; the *Swan* (John Chester), a supply ship, 50; the *Christopher* (Thomas Moone), 15.

Moone had been promoted since the time when, as ship's carpenter, he had sent the *Swan* to the bottom at Cartagena.

All told, there were probably a hundred and sixty-four men aboard the ships when, after a false start, they worked their way out of Sutton Pool and the Cattewater at Plymouth. Most of them were seamen; a few were ship's boys; there were an apothecary, a shoemaker, a tailor and a preacher. There was a complement of soldiers. And finally ten gentlemen adventurers had come along to share in the dangers, the glory, the expenses and it might be, the profits of the expedition. Among them were Thomas Doughty, formerly secretary to the Earl of Essex in Ireland, and his brother, John.

The fleet's departure from England went unnoticed by the Spaniards, whose espionage service was less vigilant than usual. The ships headed for the west coast of Morocco, picking up various Portuguese prizes on the way and helping themselves to any provisions that tempted them. When they fell in with a 40-ton Portuguese smack they exchanged it for Thomas Moone's 15-ton pinnace. Turning westwards to the Cape Verde Islands they took a more valuable prey off Santiago. This was a big Portuguese cargo boat laden with fine fabrics and excellent sherry and madeira. Two pipes of wine were lifted out of its hold.

More important still, it carried on board a small dark man of about sixty, with a long beard. This was Nuñez da Silva, citizen of Oporto, son of a sailor and brought up to the sea from boyhood. He was a pilot with considerable experience in Brazilian coastal waters, just the man Drake needed for the next stage of the voyage. The rich, ransom-worthy passengers were allowed to go free, but Drake kept the pilot with him when he led his flotilla south-east by south. Nuñez had sharp eyes and a retentive memory for all that happened in this strange vessel in which he was, for the next fifteen months, an enforced passenger. He was impressed by what he saw. The ship had two sheathings and double sails; she was a good sailer, admirably answering the helm, watertight when sailing with the wind astern but inclined to leak when the sea was high. She was carrying meat and fish for a month and a hundred boxes of biscuit.

Drake fascinated him. In appearance the Englishman was short and burly, sunburnt, ruddy-bearded and troubled with a musket ball in the leg, relic of that wild night at Nombre de Dios when, suddenly, everything had gone wrong. Probably he limped at times; otherwise the Portuguese can hardly have come to know about the wound. In manner, he was genial, although crisp and imperious when he gave orders, and insistent that they were promptly carried out. He was looked on with immense respect by his crew. In short, an admirable captain for a ship bound on an ill-defined and, probably, unavowable mission. Above all, a superb seaman, a serious professional.

He had brought three navigation books with him and, every time he took a prize, Nuñez noticed that the first thing he did was to look at the charts, the astrolabes, the compasses and needles. What he wanted, he took. Charts in particular. He had set off across the world with a map bought in Lisbon, the best he could find but not good enough. He spent a great deal of time drawing and painting with his young cousin John Drake, son of his uncle Robert. John was the more accomplished artist of the two. All this painting was not, of course, done simply as a diversion but had a serious practical purpose – to show how an important landfall looked as it was approached from the sea. If a captain had no talent with the brush, he took a painter along with him.

The astonished Portuguese observed how Drake dined in state, to the sound of trumpets and viols, from silver plates rimmed with gold, and garlanded with his arms. No one, whatever his rank, sat down until Drake was seated. Was so much ceremonial purely a matter of policy or did it hint at an inner lack of assurance? If so, it would not have been surprising. In that era class distinctions were still sharply drawn and firmly maintained. It was difficult for the ablest upstart to insist on the command, the deference which any young fop with an ancient name took as his God-given right. The Drakes were not Grenvilles any more than the Grenvilles were Howards. The day of the *arrivistes* was at hand but they had not yet arrived.

In the routine of the ship, religion played a notable part. Drake read the lessons, led the prayers; his voice was heard with the others' when the psalms were sung. He even preached the sermon at times, although the fleet had a chaplain aboard named Francis Fletcher. But Drake had always plenty to say on any subject and, no doubt, his pious homilies did not lack advice which could be applied to the task in hand. The evangelical sailor, master of a simple, egocentric theology, is a type that has gone out of fashion but he was the backbone of the English, Huguenot and Dutch fleets which carried on, over the years, a desultory and sometimes gainful war against King Philip's galleons.

A month after the Portuguese was kidnapped Drake sailed 'below the line' as the jargon of the day put it. And on 1 April, he sighted the coast of Brazil. By this time, his fleet, owing to various captures and exchanges, numbered six ships.

A strange and macabre incident[1] which occurred in June 1578, six months after the ships had left England, brought to the surface social and psychological stresses which had lain beneath. Thomas Doughty was tried and executed at Port St Julian, a natural harbour on the South American coast two hundred miles north of the entrance to the Strait of Magellan.

Neither the season nor the inhabitants in that region were friendly. The Indians, men of great stature clad in skins, greeted the English with a shower of arrows which killed two of the company. It seemed prudent, then, to anchor at a sandy island off the mainland where three of the ships were careened and tarred and two were broken up for firewood, the stores they carried being transferred to other ships. It was mid-winter and the weather was bitterly cold. It snowed a great deal and the sun rarely appeared. Those were days for roaring fires, for storm coats and the conical thrum (woollen) caps that were the usual headgear of the English seamen at that time.

At the time Nuñez da Silva's vessel was captured, Drake had made Doughty her captain. There was a dispute over the disposal of the cargo, and Doughty was accused of pilfering goods – wine, probably – and seems to have made a countercharge against Drake's brother, Thomas. Doughty was next appointed captain of Drake's ship, the *Pelican*. When that, too, was not a success, he was banished to the store-ship, the *Swan*. We are given an inkling of what lay behind all this. The master of the *Swan* left the mess where Doughty and other gentlemen adventurers were eating and took his meals with the sailors. And Doughty appealed to Captain Chester to assert his authority against 'these knaves' – 'We will put the sword again into your hands and you shall have the government.'

This, then, seems to have been the real issue. Doughty was putting himself at the head of a party of 'the gentlemen' against 'the knaves'. On no subject was Drake more likely to be sensitive. In spite of his coat of arms and his claim to gentle birth he was, in the eyes of some others, himself 'a knave', in command of gentlemen, the natural, accepted leaders of English society. He was conscious of the precarious ascendancy of the parvenu. Now he saw the unity and morale of the expedition being threatened at its weakest point and on the eve of the most dangerous phase of the operation. An ordeal lay ahead, although Drake can hardly have foreseen how severe it was going to be. And England was half a world away.

A jury of forty men was empanelled, with Wynter, vice-admiral of the fleet, as its foreman. Drake was judge and had, as his assessor, Captain Thomas, who was Sir Christopher Hatton's representative with the expedition. When the proceedings were opened, Drake charged Doughty with seeking to discredit him and 'overthrow' the voyage – 'besides other great matters where I have to charge you withal'. He then asked Doughty how he would be tried. 'Why, good General,' the accused man replied, 'let me live to come to my own country. I will there be tried by Her Majesty's laws.' When this was refused, Doughty asked to see Drake's commission. At this point Drake lost his temper: 'My masters, this fellow is full of prating. Bind me his arms for I will be safe of my life.' Which suggests that Doughty had made threatening gestures, as he might well have done.

The trial went on quietly enough until one of the witnesses, Edward Bright, a partisan of Drake's said that in Drake's garden at Plymouth he had heard Doughty say that the Queen and the Council could be corrupted with money; in other words, there was no need to be too squeamish about taking prizes. While this charge was being debated, Doughty let fall that the Lord Treasurer, Burghley, had a plan of the voyage. On hearing this, Drake flew into a fine state of rage. Here was an admission that Doughty had betrayed the secret purpose of the expedition to the man who, above all others, the Queen had sworn must not have it. Drake's indignation seems somewhat overdone. For one thing, he can hardly have been surprised by Bright's account of a discussion in the garden at Plymouth. He, Drake, was probably there at the time. The disclosure to Burghley was, no doubt, more serious, but only if Drake had repeated the Queen's warning to those who shared with him the secret of the voyage.

Another accusation brought against Doughty was that he used magical arts to conjure up adverse winds, unwelcome storms and even less welcome calms ('being as it were in the bosom of the burning zone'). There had come a moment when suddenly, in the midst of clear weather, the ships were lost in a palpable darkness of Egypt and struck by a furious storm. When it cleared away, one of the ships had vanished. In the sixteenth century such phenomena could either be explained naturally or by agencies of a different order.

> *Her husband's to Aleppo gone, master o' the Tiger:*
> *But in a sieve I'll hither sail*
> *And, like a rat, without a tail,*
> *I'll do, I'll do, and I'll do!*

The charge of witchcraft, then, was probably effective propaganda. It is even possible that Drake himself believed it. After all, he was a man of his age. And it was true that for thirty-six days the ship Drake was then sailing in had been separated by a storm from the rest of the fleet which had been reassembled only about fifteen miles from Port St Julian. It might have been a relief to have so alarming an incident explained by witchcraft, a phenomenon they could all understand.

Drake now asked the jury to deliver their verdict. At that one of the members, a friend of Doughty's named Vicary, protested that the proceedings were illegal. 'I don't care about the law,' the judge retorted, 'but I know what I am going to do.' Vicary persisted, arguing that they could not be responsible for taking the prisoner's life. 'You will have nothing to do with taking his life,' said Drake. 'Leave me to deal with that. You have only to see whether he is guilty.'

Thus admonished, the jury brought in a verdict of guilty on all counts while at the same time saying that they did not trust Bright to give fair testimony against Doughty who had once said that Mrs Bright had a bad name in Cambridge. Even in that modest respect they had no luck. Drake brushed the objection scornfully aside: 'I dare swear that what Ned Bright said is very true.' Whereupon he walked down to the shore with everybody except the Doughty brothers and displayed a bundle of documents to show that he was not in Doughty's debt for the position he had reached, but – 'God's will, I have left in my cabin what I especially wanted to have.' His commission from the Queen? That mysterious document, so much sought for, remained invisible. Drake then asked for the death sentence and nobody opposed him. The execution was fixed for two days later. When the time came Doughty received communion, Drake kneeling beside him at the altar. After that, they dined cheerfully together and said their farewells by drinking a toast.

Kneeling beside the block, Doughty prayed for the Queen and the happy outcome of the voyage and asked to be remembered to his friends, especially that good knight, Sir William Wynter. 'All this day,' reports an eye witness, 'he altered not one jot of his countenance, but kept it as staid and firm as if he had had some message to deliver to some nobleman.' He joked with the executioner. 'Truly, I may say, as did Sir Thomas More, that he that cuts off my head shall have little honesty; my neck is so short.' It was not quite what Sir Thomas had said, but it was near enough. When the axe had fallen, Drake ordered the head to be held up, calling out, 'Lo, there is the end of traitors!' He had preserved the forms of justice.

A three-fold veil hangs between us and understanding of those extraordinary events: we lack a trustworthy report of what happened in that bleak little island in Port St Julian; we do not know enough about the political preliminaries to the voyage; above all, it is impossible for us, in our secular age when we hold human life as sacred, to enter into the mind of a man who could exact a friend's life, then feast with him pleasantly and, a few hours later, greet his dripping upheld head with the prescribed last salute to traitors. It might make it seem more sensible to us if Drake had been a notably bloodthirsty or brutal man. But he was not. On the contrary.

Explanations may, of course, be made for him. At that time, his responsibilities were weighing heavily on him. He who had been a dashing marauder, playing a solitary game, was now the admiral of a fleet carrying out a mission of great strategic moment. As he said to a Spanish captive not long after, 'I do not know how I can go on carrying my burdens.' The decision to execute Doughty, a man whose fine qualities he recognised, had been a terrible one to take. But, as it seemed to him, there was nothing else he could do. This was the opinion of a man whose nerves were stretched to the limit, whose conscience was troubled but who believed he had been forced to act as he did.

It is easy enough to argue that Doughty's execution was a judicial murder. But that would be to assume that conditions were normal and that the regular machinery of justice was available. Nothing could be farther from the case. This was an acute emergency occurring in the course of a desperate enterprise. Here was the case of a captain-general faced with evidence, which seemed to him conclusive, of an attempt by a man of high ability and superior social standing to subvert morale and discipline in his fleet – 'the very overthrow of the voyage'. Given the time, the place and the conditions in which the emergency arose, the summary justice dealt out to Doughty was not in any way unusual. In that very bay, sixty years earlier, the great Magellan had assassinated one member of his crew, executed another and marooned two more. What was held at Port St Julian during that bitter sub-Antarctic winter was, in fact, a field general court-martial. By the standards of martial law it should be judged.

A month later, while the ships were still wintering at St Julian, there occurred a strange sequel to the Doughty affair. Drake ordered every man to confess and take communion. Then, he mustered them on shore. The chaplain, Francis Fletcher, offered to preach. Drake said, 'No. Today I must preach myself.' He began, 'I am a very bad orator for my upbringing was not in learning, but what I say now let every man take good note. Let him write it down, for I will say nothing I am not prepared to answer for to England. Yes, and before Her Majesty.' He went on to disclose what, in his judgment, had really been at stake in the crisis. Although the words he used are reported by a man who was no friend of Drake's, they are surely authentic, with the peremptory vehemence, the fresh-hewn phrases which bear his signature, and with the flair and cunning sense of an audience which he shares with greater orators.

'Wherefore,' he told them, 'we must have these mutinies and

discords that are grown amongst us, redressed . . . Here is such controversy betwixt the sailors and the gentlemen and such stomaching between the gentlemen and sailors, that it doth even make me mad to hear it. But my masters, I must have it left, for I must have the gentleman to haul and draw with the mariner, and the mariner with the gentleman. What, let us show ourselves all to be of one company . . .!

'As gentlemen are very necessary for government's sake in the voyage, so I have shipped them for that . . . and yet, though I know sailors to be the most envious people of the world and unruly without government – yet may I not be without them.'

This was plain sea-sense, shaped in the form of words that have lived, and uttered with the accents of honest passion. If any of them wanted to go home, he told them, he would put the *Marigold* at their disposal but, in that case, they had better sail for England, for if he found them in his way he would surely sink them. They would have until the next day to make up their minds. 'By my troth, I must needs be plain with you. I have taken in hand something I do not know how in the world to carry through. It passes my capacity. Even to think of it deprives me of my wits!'

Then, when every man had agreed to follow him, he turned to his captains, John Wynter and John Thomas, and relieved them of their commands. 'Why?' they expostulated. 'Why not?' he retorted, and they said no more. He went on in his vehement way: 'some of those who were there deserved the same fate as Doughty but no more would die. Those who were most guilty were admonished. They repented on their knees. Finally, he said, 'Consider what we have done, my masters. We have set by the ears three mighty princes, Her Majesty and the Kings of Spain and Portugal. If this voyage does not succeed, we should not only be a scorning and a scoffing stock to our enemies but also a great blot to our whole country for ever.' By means so dramatic and extreme Drake asserted his authority over the crew – without which a voyage, testing to the souls as well as the bodies of men, would have ended in disaster.[2]

A week later, after another service, the three remaining ships – for the vessel in which Nuñez was taken had by this time been destroyed – set sail southwards. In three days they reached the entrance to the Strait of Magellan, where he ordered them to strike their topsails on the bunt in homage to the Queen. At the same time he changed the name of his flagship from *Pelican* to The *Golden Hind* in honour of Hatton, whose crest it was. If there was any trouble on his return, which seemed probable, it would be just as well to have some claim on the gratitude of so influential a figure at Court as the Captain of the Guard.

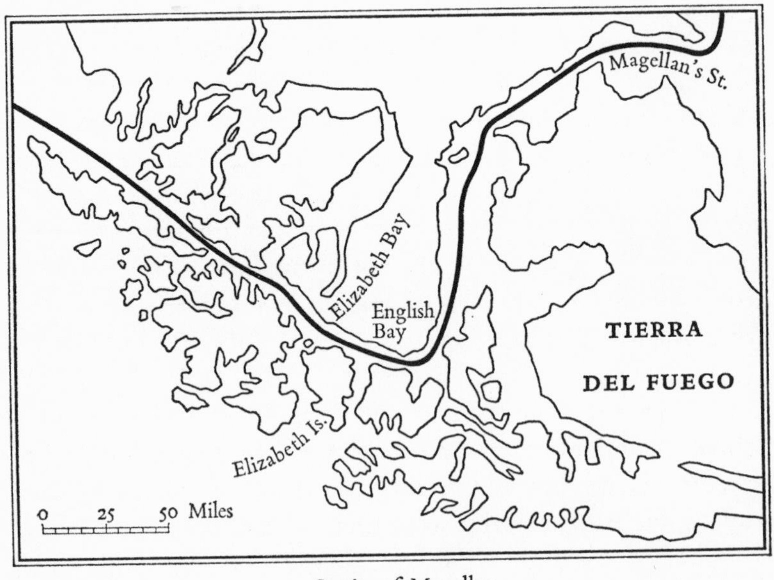

3 Straits of Magellan

The passage of the Strait, uncharted, intricate and dangerous, was accomplished in a fortnight without accident. At one group of islands they caught two thousand penguins for the larder: at another they cut down a tree so big that it required two men with arms outstretched to encircle it. This was put in the hold as ballast. Drake was taking it back to England as a gift to the Queen. Then, three days after they emerged into the Pacific, trouble struck. They were sailing north-west at the time. A storm sprang up and blew ceaselessly for three weeks from that quarter. Before it abated, the ships had been driven six hundred miles to the south-west and at last scattered. There was snow, there was darkness, and a gale that was most ferocious, stronger than anything they had ever experienced. At some time during the ordeal, the fears of the superstitious – and most of those English seamen were that – were aroused by what seemed to be a new manifestation of divine displeasure, an eclipse of the moon. And one night, the *Marigold*, Bright's ship, went down with all hands. Francis Fletcher, the chaplain, was on watch at the time in the *Golden Hind* and heard, or thought he heard, the despairing cries of the seamen drowned in 'the mountains of the sea'. None of them was seen again.

A time came when it seemed that the weather was improving. The two surviving ships, Drake's and Wynter's, were able to drop anchor off some islands not far from the point at which they had made their way out of the Straits into the open sea just a month earlier. For weary and, probably, frightened men a little peace at last? Not so. The anchors were no sooner down than a fierce squall hit the ships. The *Golden Hind*'s cable snapped. Wynter in the *Elizabeth* slipped his. Both ships sought the open sea and almost at once lost sight of one another.

Drake had fixed a rendezvous for his fleet at 30° S on the coast of Peru. But for the *Elizabeth* the question was not so easy.

Wynter waited three weeks for his admiral at a good anchorage inside the Strait of Magellan. In vain. Then he came to the conclusion that Drake must be somewhere to the leeward of him, farther east. As there seemed no prospect of getting a wind that would take them to Peru, he proposed to his crew that they should make for the Moluccas, which Drake had said he meant to reconnoitre during the voyage. But Wynter's men would have none of it. They had endured enough on this dreadful voyage commanded by a madman and, as it seemed, cursed by God. They would sail for England. Wynter gave in.

His account was later contested by two of his crew, one of

whom, a man named Cooke, said that the decision to return to England was Wynter's, while another, Edward Cliffe, maintained that it was quite against the wishes of the seamen. There is, however, evidence that men in Drake's ship thought that the Moluccas was an area in which they would be likely to find Wynter. This suggests that there was some truth in Wynter's story that Drake had mentioned these islands as a part of the world he meant to explore. It is possible, too, that Wynter, separated from his admiral and faced with a company of weary and disheartened sailors, did not state the case for a voyage to the Moluccas with much vigour. But on the question of whether or not he deserted Drake, he should surely be given the benefit of the doubt.

But where *was* Drake all this while?

Driving southwards before the gale under bare poles day after harried day, into ever colder seas, until at last he found shelter in the lee of an island far to the south of the Strait. So far as could be seen, there was then no land to the south of them. In other words, Drake had discovered that there was an alternative route round the south of the American continent. The Strait of Magellan was not a channel between America and a vast continent lying to the south of America. It separated America from a mere group of islands and beyond these at some incalculable distance lay the polar ice-cap. Terra Australis, if it existed at all, must lie far off to the west.

At last, after a final outburst of fury in which the *Golden Hind* lost another anchor, the storm died out. The like of it 'no traveller hath felt, neither hath there been such a tempest so violent and of such continuance since Noah's flood, for it lasted full fifty-two days'. Drake explained it to the crew as all part of God's purpose for, without the storm, they would not have reached the farthest point of land towards the Pole. Chaplain Fletcher went ashore and, at the southernmost point of the most southerly island, set up a stone engraved with the Queen's name and the date.

IX

The Boldness of this Low Man

'Well did thy Queen know thy great valour, which might cause the depths of the sea to tremble, when she gave thee the three vessels, the only ones ever to sight, in a single voyage, both poles.'

Dragontea – Lope de Vega

They had left Plymouth almost a year before; so far, they had accomplished nothing of what they had set out to do; the discovery of Cape Horn,* although of great geographical importance, was contested by others and was not certainly established until many years later. Now it was time to carry out the next part of the project, the reconnaissance of the west coast of South America. They had suffered incredible hardships and misfortune. Only one vessel of the fleet was left under Drake's command. Of the original company of a hundred and sixty-four, only eighty were left when the *Golden Hind* turned her beak head to the north. Soon they were fewer by four.

Making its way cautiously north along the coast of Chile, the flagship cast anchor at the island of Mocha. Here Drake went ashore with a party of reliable men. He found that the local Indians were apparently friendly, and returned with supplies of fresh food. The island was 'most rich in gold and silver and many good things necessary for the maintenance of God's good people', as Francis Fletcher noted. But 'God's good people' were due for a disappointment. Next morning, Drake went back for water and ran into an ambush. When he and his boat's crew of eleven stepped ashore at a rocky creek in which the surf ran high, more than a hundred Indians came suddenly into view. Their intentions were soon apparent. They grabbed the painter and hauled at it; they seized the oars and rained arrows on the English. Every man was hit. Drake was struck by three arrows,

* Said by Drake to be latitude 56°. Actually, 55° 58′.

one under the right eye, and narrowly escaped with his life. His Danish gunner, Big Niels, was badly wounded. Diego, the Negro who had been in his service ever since the Nombre de Dios affair in 1573, had twenty wounds, and John Brewer, the trumpeter, had seventeen. Just when it seemed that the party would be massacred to a man like so many St Sebastians, for their round targes were no protection against the Indian shafts at close range, someone had the wit to sever the painter.

Those who could, scrambled aboard, and with only two oars, the blood-dabbled sailors rowed hastily towards the *Golden Hind*. They left with the Indians two of their number, Tom Flood and Tom Brewer, who had been captured when they stepped ashore with water-butts which they meant to fill. The Dane and the Negro died of their wounds. The rest recovered in time, without much help from science. For the surgeon in the *Golden Hind* had died by this time and his assistant was in Wynter's ship, the *Elizabeth*, which had vanished. A ship's boy with more good intentions than skill was the only help they could rely on in the emergency, plus the practical medical sense of Drake.

As she worked her way northwards along the coast, the ship was now approaching the southern limits of Spanish colonisation. Conquest? Settlement? If these notions had ever figured in the plan, they were now clearly impossible. One ship, with fewer than eighty men on board, could hardly be expected to discharge the task that had been given to a squadron of five ships with a complement of more than a hundred and sixty men. The expedition would have to be content with lesser objectives.

A fortnight after the brush with the Indians, Drake found an important Spanish ship, called the *Grand Captain of the South*, lying off Valparaiso. The port was insignificant, a wretched little huddle of no more than nine houses serving as the outlet for Santiago. The vessel was more distinguished. Eleven years before it had been the *capitana* (flagship) of a Spanish expedition which, under Alvaro de Mendano, had set out to discover the fabled Isles of Ophir from which it was supposed King Solomon had brought immense treasure countless centuries before. The *Grand Captain* had then sailed under the orders of Pedro Sarmiento de Gamboa, a Spanish captain of high distinction and chequered repute. Two years before the Solomon Islands voyage, he had been tried for witchcraft by the Inquisition and had appeared as a penitent at the *auto-da-fé* at Lima in 1565. In 1571 he took a hand in the murder by torture of the last of the Incas. After that atrocity, Sarmiento devoted himself to writing a history of the Incas. However, he could not rid himself of the suspicion of the Inquisitors, who sentenced him to imprisonment. From this the Viceroy, Don Francisco de Toledo, released him so that he was a free man enjoying viceregal esteem in Lima at the moment when Drake arrived off Valparaiso, thirteen hundred miles farther south, and sighted the ship which Sarmiento had made famous.

The crew of the *Grand Captain* did not dream that any vessel entering the harbour from the open sea could be anything but a friend. They ordered up some wine and beat the drum. Next thing they knew was that Tom Moone, at the head of an English boarding party, was brandishing his sword on their deck and bawling in his best Spanish, 'Down dog!' (*Abajo perro*). Thus was the *Grand Captain* taken. One of her crew dived overboard and swam to the shore, warning the inhabitants of Valparaiso who fled to the hills behind, appalled by this unexpected incursion. Drake took possession of the village, piously donating to Chaplain Fletcher the altar cloth and plate he found in the local chapel. In the warehouses his foragers found wine and provisions, while in the captured vessel, now that they had leisure to examine her, they came on 25,000 pesos of gold worth 37,000 ducats and a large crucifix set with emeralds. After that they departed.

Unhurriedly, Drake made his way farther north along the Chilean coast so that the ship might keep the rendezvous with their lost consorts at latitude 30°. On the way, he reconnoitred any rivers and inlets that seemed promising. At one point a landing party ran into a strong force of Spanish horsemen and

Indians and lost a man in the clash. Richard Minivy was shot while retreating too slowly. Next day, at Salada Bay, a suitable place was found to clean the ship, which was foul beyond description after all these months at sea. Now it was careened and greased. The ballast was thrown out and the heavy guns were brought up from the hold and mounted in readiness for what might lie ahead. A pinnace, the last of those they had brought out in sections from Plymouth, was put together by the carpenters. The *Golden Hind* was now in a state to fight any antagonist she was likely to meet in that ocean.

Chile, a thinly settled province of King Philip's dominions, was by this time in an uproar. Somehow, the English had found their way through the Straits and were at large in the Great South Sea, 'a thing never heard of or imagined', as one horrified commentator wrote. The Governor, Don Rodrigo de Quiroga, an elderly man, was so upset by the incident that he took to his bed and, soon afterwards, died.

Disappointed by his companions at the rendezvous, Drake pressed on to the north. He bought fish from Indians and, a week after the ship had been cleaned and made ready for business, he and his companions entered the Pisagua River in search of water. They were luckier than they could have hoped, for they surprised a Spaniard who had fallen asleep on a hillside beside his mules. He was on his way from the Potosi mines three hundred miles inland and his mules were laden with thirteen bars of silver worth 4,000 ducats.

Later they came upon another Spaniard who had just come down from the Andes with a train of eight llama, each burdened with 100 pounds' weight of silver. The official narrative of the expedition describes this incident in terms that have a sly humour which can only have come from one source: 'We could not endure to see a Spanish gentleman turned carrier. So, without waiting to be asked, we offered our services and became drovers. But his directions were not so perfect that we could take the way that he indicated. As soon as he parted from us, we came to our boats.' These are, beyond doubt, the authentic words of Drake himself. That is the manner, jovial and ironical, in which he described his exploits, the outrages which caused the Spanish colonial officials so much annoyance.

After relieving the hidalgo of his silver, he went a little farther up the coast to the port of Arica, ocean terminus of the Potosi silver mines, which were the greatest single asset of the Spanish empire. It was vesper time when Drake blustered his way into the harbour and looked around for booty. The bag was disappointing, however – only two small ships, with only one Negro watchman on duty. The news of the arrival of the terrible English pirate had apparently not yet reached this important seaport. One of the vessels belonged to a man named Felipe Corco; the other to a Fleming named Nicolas Jorje. Drake put off in a pinnace and boarded the Fleming's ship in which he found a hundredweight of silver. The other ship had no cargo and was in due course set on fire by two of the English seamen who, as the story was told later, acted against Drake's wishes. It was a rowdy night in Arica. The tocsin rang, the people rushed to arms, while the visiting English, safe in their well-armed ship, passed the night by playing viols and trumpets and, as the fancy took them, firing off their cannon.

Then, hearing that a treasure ship was on the coast somewhere ahead, they set off in a hurry, taking the Flemish captain with them. Afterwards, Jorje claimed that Drake frequently threatened to kill him, annoyed by his failure to mention the treasure ship. After a long chase, they overtook the vessel at Chule, port of Arequipa, only to find that the news of their coming had gone before them. The treasure had been unloaded and was buried somewhere inland with a strong guard to protect it. Drake had missed snatching five hundred bars of His Catholic Majesty's silver on its way to Lima. In his irritation, he set sail on the captured vessel, and left it to drift out to sea and be lost. Then he headed for Callao, the port of Lima, capital of Peru, and chief city of the Spanish empire in South America.

Lima had been founded by Don Francisco Pizarro just half a century before Drake's arrival at Callao and was known officially as the Great City of the Kings with nine thousand Spanish inhabitants, fifty thousand Negro slaves and an unnumbered horde of Indians. In its Plaza Principal stood fine buildings, while in the middle a fountain played. On one corner was the Viceregal Palace, seat of a dignitary so exalted that even an Infante of Spain could hold the office without loss of prestige. Of all the prizes at King Philip's disposal with which he could tempt the grandees, few were more alluring than the Lima Viceroyalty. At this moment it was held by a Toledo, Don Francisco. By even approaching so near to this famous city, Drake was inflicting an intolerable affront on Spanish pride.

He knew that a laden treasure ship had just arrived at Callao. He had been told by Gaspar Martin, captain of a vessel whom he fell in with, that Miguel Angel's ship was expected in Callao from Panama carrying a rich cargo of silver. So, too, it was reported, was a vessel belonging to one Andres Murial. With any luck, Drake would reach those ships before their treasure was put ashore.

Callao was an anchorage set in a shallow bay which a nearby island protected from the ocean surf. The harbour was deep and, thanks to the chill of its water, free from shipworm (*teredo navalis*). Beyond a pebble beach stood the town, with a few hundred Spanish inhabitants. It was crowded with shipping when Drake stole in at ten o'clock at night on 13 February 1578, and cast anchor. The capital of Peru was six miles away, across an arid plain. In a situation fraught with opportunity and peril, abnormal quick-wittedness would be needed, as well as a degree of discipline unusual in English seamen at that time. Above all, he would require abundant good luck. As it turned out, he did not get it.

Discreet questions in Spanish revealed that the silver from the treasure ship had already been landed. While Drake was making these enquiries, a vessel put in from Panama and dropped its anchor near him. At the same time a boat rowed towards him from the shore. The port authorities at Callao had finally awakened to the fact that something strange was happening in their harbour. There was a ship that had not explained itself. When a man approaching in the boat shouted a challenge, Drake told one of his Spanish prisoners to answer by saying that this was Miguel Angel's ship arrived from Chile, the vessel Drake was hoping to overtake in his northward progress along the coast. The inquisitive man from Callao was scrambling up the side of the *Golden Hind* to verify the claim when suddenly he became aware that he was looking into the mouth of a cannon. Without pressing his enquiries further, he dropped back into the boat and rowed off with all speed to the shore. A flight of English arrows sped soundlessly after him in the night. Missed!

The ship newly arrived from Panama was the next to realise that there was something wrong. It cut its cable and stood out to sea. Drake's pinnace followed it and demanded its surrender. A well-aimed arquebus shot from the Spaniard brought down one of the pinnace's crew. At that point, Drake decided it was time to bring his uninvited call at Callao to an end. While there he had gleaned some news from Europe: the King of Portugal and the Kings of Morocco and Fez had all been killed in battle in one day. The Pope had died; so had the King of France. Nearer and more poignant, twenty-six Protestant prisoners had recently been burnt at the stake at Lima only a few miles away. Before leaving the port, he thoughtfully cut the cables of every ship in the harbour and chopped down the masts of the bigger vessels so that the whole harbourful of shipping was at the mercy of winds and waves. Then he made off after the ship that had come from Panama. When young John Drake fell into the hands of the Inquisition later on, he explained the destruction of the shipping on the ground that it had been done because Drake had hoped to capture the drifting vessels afterwards and use them in bargaining for the life and liberty of some English captives then in the dungeons of the Inquisition at Lima. One of them was his friend, John Oxenham.[2] But obviously there is a simpler explanation. If he left Callao stripped of seaworthy vessels, he could not be immediately pursued.

The ship from Panama proved to be another disappointment. When Drake fired a shot across her bows, her crew promptly deserted her and rowed back to Callao with the news. But, alas, she was carrying no treasure, only some Castilian cloth of no interest whatsoever. Drake wasted little time on her. He had heard of a vastly more tempting prey.

Meanwhile, in Lima the alarm had been raised by the arrival of a dispatch from the Governor of Callao to the Viceroy. The Viceroy put on his armour and sword and called on his gentlemen to do the same. Church bells rang out the alarm. From door to door through the town the criers ran, summoning the citizens to gather in the public square. And there on horseback, in the full panoply of war, appeared the Viceroy, bearing on his lance the royal standard of Spain. It was a time for stern and martial action worthy of the men whose fathers had, in the last of the Crusades, driven the Moslem back to Africa.

The Viceroy unlocked the armoury and distributed arquebuses, pikes and ammunition to the people. Then he ordered General Diego de Frias Trejo to defend the port while he put a guard over the King's bullion, 200,000 pesos in silver bars. By the time the General reached the harbour, however, Drake was already far out to sea. He must be pursued. Spanish honour and the safety of Peru alike demanded it. The difficulty was that the pirate had made havoc of the shipping. At last, two vessels were found fit to sail and three hundred armed citizens of Lima were put aboard them. Then troubles began.

The flagship came under the lee of an island and lost the wind. The second-in-command (the *almirante*) went on alone and, in due course, sighted the *Golden Hind*. But at that point Drake spread his top-gallant sails and lengthened the distance between him and the pursuit. The *Golden Hind* had a turn of speed which the ships from Callao could not match. After a chase that lasted most of the night, the Spaniards held a council of war and decided to return to port. Many of the gentlemen aboard were seasick and unable to stand, much less fight. When they reached Callao, the Viceroy was furious over their failure to catch the robber and ordered nobody to land on pain of death. The leading officers were sentenced to exile and heavy fines. So far as the Viceroy was concerned, the crisis was by no means at an end. In fact, Drake had a narrow escape.

No sooner was he out of sight of Callao than he ran into a dead calm. The sails hung still; the ship was motionless. Not a ripple broke the surface of the water across which he could hear the bells of a town sounding the alarm, and the shouts of the citizens, crying, 'The French, the French,' as they rushed for their arms. However, the wind freshened in time for him to escape.

As Viceroy, Don Francisco de Tolédo was responsible to the King for the safety of the whole coast of Peru. He was desperately short of artillery; indeed his plight was so grave that he even sent an officer to the Inquisition to find out if Oxenham or any of his fellow-captives had any skill in casting cannon. Oxenham could not help. John Butler, another English prisoner, said that although he could not make artillery he could supply the Viceroy with devices which, when attached to arrows or lances, would set ships on fire. He also offered 'fire wings', concocted from powder, pitch, oil and sulphur and studded with nails so that they stuck to woodwork. Such engines, proof as they might be of the diabolical ingenuity of the heretics, were not, however, what the Viceroy had in mind. He was short of cannon. In the meantime he sent a fast sailing boat to warn all the ports between Callao and Panama that an English corsair was at large. All treasure ships should at once make for port and be unloaded. And fifteen days after Drake's departure, the Viceroy dispatched two ships with a hundred and twenty soldiers aboard, to find and punish the pirates. It was, he said, the gravest crisis the kingdom had ever faced. The punitive expedition left Callao, burning to fight the enemy but with small hopes of overtaking him even if one knew which way he had gone. They had heard his boastful speeches that he would overtake the treasure ship which belonged to San Juan de Anton. But how were they to intercept him? A sharp debate broke out among the leaders of the pursuit.

Don Luis de Toledo, who was in command, thought that Drake would make for Panama. The second-in-command, Diego de Frias Trejo, thought that the pursuers should sail direct to Nicaragua; this would be the likeliest way to head off the corsair. After the matter had been endlessly argued, the General decided that they would follow the coast to Panama. In consequence, a day or two later, when they reached the Pearl Islands, they heard bad news.

Drake had concentrated on overtaking San Juan de Anton's ship, *Nuestra Señora de la Concepcion*. This was a real treasure ship, bound for Panama, with a heavy lading of bullion belonging to the King of Spain. Gradually, he gained on the prize, until, at Paita, he learned from a captured vessel that it was only two days ahead of him on the way to Panama. He divided his forces so as to broaden the sweep of the search. Sailing in the pinnace, he kept the shore in sight. The *Golden Hind* was four miles farther out to sea. The first man to sight the quarry was promised a golden chain.

Another day came and another prize was taken, a ship belonging to Benito Bravo on its way to Panama with two friars aboard her as passengers and some silver – about 18,000 pesos according to the ship's manifest. However, the Negro crew said that more of the metal was hidden away somewhere aboard and was not mentioned in the papers. Hoping to verify the story, Drake strung up a half-breed clerk, Francisco Jacome, by the neck and dropped him into the sea. But the clerk steadfastly denied all knowledge of any hidden bullion and Drake let the young man go. Rummaging about in the ship, the English sailors came upon a large gold crucifix and some emeralds almost as long as a man's finger. These eventually decorated a crown for Queen Elizabeth. Although Drake was now anxious to rid himself of Bravo's ship, there was a complication about this. It was a faster sailer than the *Golden Hind* and, if left at liberty, would catch up with the *Nuestra Señora* and would warn it of his coming. Drake solved the problem by wrapping the ship's sails round its anchor and throwing them overboard.

Having contrived this drag on Bravo's progress, he pressed on.

A week later, after he had crossed the Line and was approaching Cape San Francisco, he took a fourth prize – 15,000 pesos in gold but, more important, the good news that the *Nuestra Señora* must be almost in sight. In five hours' time, when the the Cape was in sight, a cry came from the mast-head, 'Sail-ho.' Everyone looked up. There was the excited face of young John Drake, the General's cousin, his arm flung out to seaward, where, on the horizon, nine miles away, a ship was sailing which could only be the one they sought. It would be about noon on 1 March for at that time San Juan de Anton made a note in his log that he observed a strange ship sailing close to the land, keeping the same general course that he did. Thinking no evil, he did not alter the direction of his celebrated and precious vessel.

Drake, for his part, was in no hurry. He meant to wait until darkness fell – that would be the time for him to attack the Spaniard. The problem was, however, that if he kept his present speed the *Golden Hind* would soon overtake the *Nuestra Señora* – popularly known among Pacific sailors as the '*Cacafuego*'* – while, if he were to shorten sail, the Spanish captain might notice the change and suspect some mischief.

Accordingly he made use of an old corsair's trick and dropped astern a tail of empty wine jars, thus cutting down the speed of the *Golden Hind*. By eight o'clock San Juan de Anton, watching from the poop of his ship, realised that the stranger was bent on making contact with him. He thought that probably it was bringing him a message from the Viceroy. So San Juan went about towards the *Golden Hind* and Drake, who by this time was ready to fight, cut the ropes holding the wine jars . . . The *Golden Hind* leapt forward in the water and by nine o'clock was alongside the Spaniard.

The Spanish captain hailed the *Golden Hind*. No answer. He repeated the challenge. 'Who are you?' 'A ship of Chile,' came the reply. On hearing that, San Juan de Anton came to the

* Politely, 'spitfire'.

ship's side. He knew that down in Chile there had been a rebellion. Who was to say what the newcomer was doing? By this time, the English were grappling his ship and shouting, 'English! Strike sail! Strike sail, Master Juan de Anton, or you'll be sent to the bottom!' San Juan replied, 'Who gives me orders to strike sail? Come aboard and strike sail yourselves!'

At this point, a whistle blew on the *Golden Hind.* A blast from the Spanish trumpet answered it. The English fired arquebuses and loosed a flight of arrows. Chain shot from a culverin broke the Spaniard's mizzen mast. Into the sea it crashed, carrying sail and lateen yard with it. San Juan was wounded by an arrow. Another English culverin blared out and, simultaneously, the *Nuestra Señora* was overrun by boarders from the *Golden Hind* on one side and from its pinnace on the other. Suddenly, the Spaniard's deck was crowded with armed Englishmen who had climbed up the shrouds and now stood menacingly about, brandishing their weapons and demanding that San Juan should tell them where the ship's captain and pilot were. As he refused to answer, they bundled him and the bosun into their pinnace and rowed them away. Thus, on the deck of the *Golden Hind*, San Juan saw Francis Drake. He arrived just at the moment when the Englishman was taking off his helmet and armour.

'Have patience,' said Drake affably to the Spanish captain, 'for this is the usage of war.' He ordered San Juan to be locked in a cabin in the poop with a guard of twelve to see that he did not escape. Given the exceptional circumstances, Drake behaved with the most distinguished courtesy to his guest. But he did not ignore the realities of the situation and spent three hours next morning examining his prize which, to his satisfaction, contained 400,000 pesos of silver and gold. It was a magnificent haul. It would pay all the costs of the expedition and leave enough over to give the shareholders a rich return on their money.

When San Juan was melancholy at the thought of all the King's property for the loss of which he would be blamed, Drake cheered him up: 'You shall have my receipt in full.'

Ten years ago, he explained to San Juan, the Viceroy of Mexico had broken his pledged word to his uncle, John Hawkins, in consequence of which he, Francis Drake, had lost 7,000 pesos. Since the King of Spain had been looking after his money all that time, it was clearly right that he should look after the King's. 'I have now something on account, for which, small as it is, I am grateful.'

As for the Viceroy of Peru, he cared not a jot for him, but he charged San Juan to warn the Viceroy not to kill his English prisoners or he would be sent two thousand Spanish heads. At this point in the conversation Drake, remembering the bad news he had heard at Callao, scowled and appeared to lose his temper. San Juan replied soothingly that if the Englishmen had not been killed up to then, they were hardly likely to be killed later on. What, then, would happen to them? asked Drake. In all likelihood, thought San Juan, they would be sent to serve against the Indians in Chile. On hearing this, Drake calmed down.

After three days of sailing with a fair wind on the course for Nicaragua, Drake thought that it was time to transfer the cargo from the *Nuestra Señora* – thirteen chests of pieces of eight, 80 pounds' weight in gold, 26 tons of silver, besides jewels and plate. A Spanish boy, watching the transfer, said that the ship should be called not *Spitfire*, but '*Spitsilver*', a joke which appealed to the English sense of humour.

In the hour of triumph, Drake was a generous as well as a jovial victor. San Juan was given a gilt corselet, a German firelock and a silver-gilt bowl with the name 'Franciscus Drake' inscribed on it. San Juan's officers were not forgotten, while each member of the crew was given clothes and money. Domingo de Lizarza, the ship's clerk, was given a steel shield and a sword, so that he might have the appearance of a man-at-arms, as Drake said. To San Juan, Drake handed a safe conduct lest he should fall in with any of the lost ships of the fleet: 'Master Wynter,' he wrote, 'if it pleaseth God that you should chance to meet with this ship of Saint John de Anton, I pray you use him well, according to my word and promise given unto him, and if you want anything that is in this ship of Saint John de Anton I pray you pay double the value for it, which I will satisfy again. And command your men not to do any hurt.' After that, all the prisoners from all the prizes he had taken in the Pacific were put on board the *Nuestra Señora*. A Negro slave, captured at Arica, begged on his knees to be allowed to return to his master, who was a very old man. 'You can go with God's blessing,' said Drake, 'for I don't want to take anyone with me against his will.'

Then he took his farewell cheerfully of San Juan. 'We will henceforward keep your saint's day once a year. Take your ship and go with God's blessing to Panama. Tell them that what they call Magellan's Strait is open sea through which I shall come back to visit them.'

The two ships, the laden and the looted, then parted company, San Juan sailing north-east to carry to Panama the story of his meeting with this extraordinary English freebooter, Drake to resume his leisurely way north-north-west. For two days San Juan, curious to know what Drake meant to do next, kept the English ship in sight. To the Spaniard, he had spoken as if his only thought was how to return to England as quickly as possible. He hoped to be there in six months. The Spaniard said he would be lucky to reach it in a year. For he was in a cul-de-sac: there was no way home round the north of America. Spreading before his guest a chart for which he had paid 800 ducats in Lisbon, Drake said that there were four possible routes – by the Cape of Good Hope, by the Strait of Magellan, by Norway (i.e. the passage round the north of Asia) and by a fourth way which he kept secret. Was he hinting at the mysterious straits of Anian – the north-west passage – or the way he had discovered round Cape Horn? When San Juan reached Perico, the port of Panama, he made a deposition to the president of the court, the Illustrious Alonso Criade de Castilla, recounting all he remembered of his stay on the *Golden Hind* and his talks with her commander. And Drake sailed for Coronado Bay, where on the island of Cano he found what he was seeking, a secluded inlet where he could clean and trim his ship.

In the meantime, the search party from Peru had reached Cape San Francisco just three weeks after the *Nuestra Señora* had been captured there. The debate between intuition and caution came to a head. Intuition, supported by the best maritime experience, said, 'Sail direct to Nicaragua. That is where you are most likely to find the rascal!' Caution, reinforced by some alarming new information about the corsair's gun-power, suggested that it would be wiser to plod methodically along the coast and search every bay and inlet. And caution won, although Sarmiento, chief advocate of the Nicaragua project, staked his head that he could lead the ships across the bay on the direct route, so alarming to a landsman like his commander-in-chief, Don Luis de Toledo. The search party reached Santa Elena where they found that not one ship was left in the harbour and not a person remained in the village. In the inn, displayed for all to see, was a letter from the innkeeper explaining that he had fled because of news that the Englishman was coming. Farther along the coast, they heard reports confirming the arrogance of this 'shameless robber who fears not God nor man'. But of the corsair himself, they saw not a trace, to the growing discontent of Sarmiento.

Thus Drake remained unmolested in his island retreat until he was ready to sail on. He had not wasted the time at Cano, for by chance his pinnace had captured a frigate with two China pilots aboard. These experts had brought their charts and sailing directions with them in readiness for a crossing to the Philippines. For Drake to find them was a magnificent stroke of luck. One of the pilots, Colchero, was offered 1,000 ducats to take the *Golden Hind* across the Ocean; when he refused, he was told that he had to go anyhow. When the cleaning of the ship was completed, Drake sailed to the north and west, seizing on the way (Saturday, 4 April), a ship with a cargo of Chinese silk and porcelain bound from Acapulco for Peru.

The ship's owner, Don Francisco de Zarate, described the

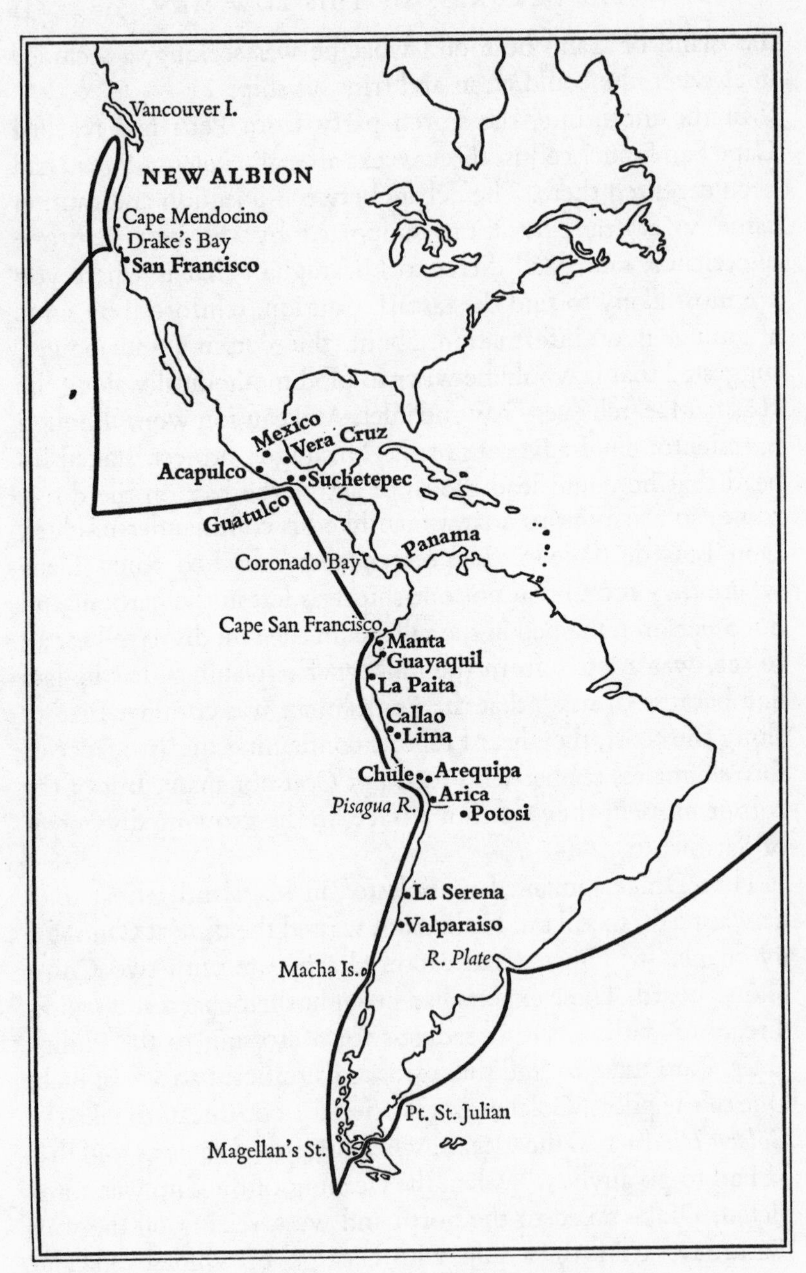

4 South America and Circumnavigation

capture later on. Zarate was a person of some consequence, a cousin of the Duke of Medina Sidonia. He was a Knight of Santiago, the red-enamelled cross of which he wore. As Don Francisco told the story, by moonlight his helmsman saw a strange vessel bearing down on them. He gave a warning shout, thinking that the men aboard the unknown vessel must be asleep. No answer. After a second enquiry, a voice said in Spanish that it was the vessel of Miguel Angel. At this moment, a pinnace swung against the quarter of Zarate's ship and before he, the helmsman or anyone else could act, arquebus bullets were whizzing over their heads and savage-looking raga-muffins armed with pikes and swords were swinging over the deck rails and demanding the surrender of the ship. A fantastic joke? At first, Zarate thought so. On that peaceful sea, under that benevolent moon, how could it be anything serious?

Thus, another Spanish ship was taken without a fight, with plenty of threatening play of weapons but no violence. The passengers were deprived of their rapiers and keys and Don Francisco was invited aboard the *Golden Hind* to meet her captain. Drake, a short, sturdy man whose red beard showed streaks of a lighter colour, was pacing to and fro on his deck. The Spaniard politely kissed his hand and was invited into his cabin. Drake came to the point at once: 'I am a good friend to those who deal with me honestly but with those who don't, I get out of humour. Tell me what silver or gold is in that ship?'

'None,' answered Don Francisco. 'Only one or two plates, one or two cups. That's all.'

After a silence during which Drake was obviously estimating how much trust he could put in the Spaniard's word, he changed the subject.

'Do you know Don Martin Enriquez (Viceroy of Mexico)?'

'I do.'

'Is any relation of his with you or anything belonging to him?'

There was not.

'Because,' said Drake, 'I would rather meet him than all the gold and silver in the Indies so that I might show him how to keep the word of a gentleman.'

Drake then led his prisoner to a cabin below deck where an old man was sitting. 'Who is this man?' said Drake. Zarate said he had no idea. 'That,' said Drake, 'is the pilot Colchero whom the Viceroy was sending to Panama to take Don Gonzalvo to China.' Whereupon he invited both Spaniards to dine with him. It was a stately meal, accompanied by music and, in the course of it, Zarate heard, to his relief and amazement, that his life and property were safe. In admiration at such magnanimity, Zarate kissed Drake's hand again. The next day being Sunday, the *Golden Hind* put out all her flags and banners and Drake appeared in splendid array. He spent most of the day in the captured ship going over the silk and porcelain she carried and picking out what took his fancy. In the friendliest way imaginable he relieved Zarate of some of his personal belongings, saying that he wanted them for his wife. In return he gave the Spaniard a falchion and a silver brazier. Zarate remarked later that Drake did not lose by the exchange.

Next day the two ships parted, after Drake had transferred all his captives, Colchero among them, to the Spanish vessel and distributed largesse to her crew. So ended an encounter between corsair and victim that is surely one of the most pleasant in the history of the sea. Zarate left, puzzled and fascinated by his host, so eccentric a mixture of menace and bonhomie, of truculent talk and impulsive kindness. One who was adored by his men, who was affable and imperious, above all else, a born commander, conscious of his gifts and filled with a blazing fire of mission, obtaining the same reverence from the gentleman adventurers as from the mariners. (The lesson of St Julian's Bay had gone home!) But how was one to place such a man in any of the recognised human categories?

A week later (Monday, 13 April) the alcalde mayor of the Mexican seaport of Guatulco – a small but important place of transhipment for Spanish merchants sending goods to Peru and Honduras, was told by some sailors who had been loitering at the water's edge that they had seen two sail just outside the harbour. Two hours later the *Golden Hind* nodded its way into port, followed by its pinnace. At that moment a party of local people, Spanish and Indian, were decorating the church for Holy Week. The alcalde (Gaspar de Vargas) at first took the new arrivals to be friendly visitors: a ship that was expected from Peru and, probably, a pearl-fishing smack. Then a sailor, who had been watching the bigger of the two ships as it dropped its anchor, raised the alarm, 'The English, The English!'

The alcalde mobilised some resistance, enough to compel the intruders to open fire with their culverins. When this happened, the alcalde decided that honour had been satisfied. He abandoned the town for a wooded hill from which he had a good view of the English ship and decided gloomily that, since she was so low in the water, she must be laden with gold and silver. He watched warehouses and bodegas being plundered and observed that the marauders were particularly interested in the heavy cotton cloth with ornamental borders which Indian women wore as petticoats. A tall hunchbacked heretic, wearing a stolen chasuble, was seen to seize the bell from the church. Later, it was used to summon the crew to man the pumps on the *Golden Hind*. Three hostages were carried off, the vicar, a visiting alcalde and a factor. The factor was dragged to the ship by a small bosun with a pock-marked face, who took the gold image of Our Lady from his rosary, saying: 'Why do you wear this? It's no good,' and bit the image hard.

The vicar, in particular, had an uncomfortable time in captivity. Not only was he compelled to watch Spaniards, fellow-Catholics, eating pork during Holy Week but he was subjected to a stream of Protestant propaganda in Drake's fluent and vigorous Spanish:[3] 'How can it be endured that kings and princes must kiss the Pope's foot? What a swindle!' And so forth. Then he showed the priest Foxe's Book of Martyrs, with its pictures of heretics being burnt at the stake in Spain. It is hardly surprising that the vicar after his release broke the promise he had given that he would return to the ship. After all, these were heretics to whom he need not keep his word.

Later on, the factor was present at prayers on the ship when Drake knelt on a cushion and recited the psalms in English for about an hour, after which four men played viols as an accompaniment to hymns. When the service was over, Drake ordered a page to dance 'in the English fashion'. At the end of the psalm-reading Drake turned to the factor. 'You will be saying now this man is a devil who robs by day and prays by night. That's what I do. But as King Philip gives a commission to your Viceroy telling him what to do and how to govern, so the Queen, my sovereign lady, has ordered me to come to these parts. I am sorry to take anything that does not belong exclusively to King Philip or Don Martin Enriquez, for it grieves me that their vassals should be paying for them. But I am not going to stop until I have collected the two millions that my cousin John Hawkins lost.'

When Drake had finished watering his ship, the hostages were released. The factor begged for a hundredweight of biscuit and a jar of wine for there was nothing left to eat in the town and the Indians had all fled to the woods. Drake laughed. He would do better than that. He would give him two bags of flour, two jars of wine, one of oil and two sugar loaves. At nightfall, when the English had withdrawn from the town, the alcalde returned to the port and inspected the damage. In the church he saw profanation that horrified him – the altarpiece of the Madonna broken in pieces, many images of St Francis defaced and unconsecrated wafers strewn on the floor and trampled on.

On the Wednesday of Holy Week, he led a small deputation of citizens who begged Drake not to take away the Spanish ship that was in the harbour. These emissaries took the precaution of dining before they stepped on board the *Golden Hind*, lest the corsair should offer them meat. This precaution was justified. For sure enough, Drake hospitably invited them to a meal. 'We kiss your lordship's hand,' they replied, 'but we have already dined on shore.' On the matter of the ship Drake was prepared to listen to reason. If the pilot came and spoke to him, all would be well. If not, he drew a finger across his throat.

The alcalde sent off a dispatch with all possible speed to the Viceroy of Mexico, Drake's old enemy, Don Martin de Enriquez. Don Martin, a gloomy proconsul with a jet-black beard, can hardly have been made more cheerful by what he read, especially as Drake lost no opportunity of justifying all his depredations by the Viceroy's breach of faith at San Juan de Ulua. Don Martin wrote at once to the King, the first of a stream of letters making clear the terror that Drake's arrival had stirred up over Central America and the fear that was widespread of still worse calamities to come. Drake was in a position where he could do the gravest damage to Mexico's trade with China. But one question was even more important for the Spanish officials: Where would Drake go next? Would he voyage back to England and, if so, by which of the routes available to him?

With all possible haste, the Viceroy organised the pursuit and capture of the marauder, a task which had already baffled his colleague, the Viceroy of Peru. He called to arms all the citizens of Mexico capable of bearing them. At the same time, the bishop of Guatemala offered the bells of his cathedral to be melted down and used for making cannon. Dr Robles, a judge of the Mexican High Court was appointed to lead the punitive expedition and enlisted three hundred 'very splendid men' to attend him. Within fifteen days he arrived at Guatulco. Among others, he took two Englishmen with him, Miles Philips and Paul Horsewell, who had been prisoners in Mexico ever since the disastrous affair at San Juan de Ulua eleven years before. Philips, who was to act as interpreter to the expedition, was a witness of the Viceroy's burst of energy – 200 men to the Caribbean, 200 to Guatemala, 200 to Guatulco and 200 to Acapulco.

Philips went with the fourth party which, finding that Drake had come and gone, put to sea after him in a small sloop of 60 tons. 'All the time I was at sea with them I was a glad man, for I hoped that if we met with Master Drake we should all be taken so that I should then be freed out of that danger and misery where I lived and should return to my own country of England again.' The appointment of Dr Robles to lead the pursuit was countermanded at the last minute owing to a serious shortage of judges on the Mexican bench. Dr Robles saw the pursuers depart with a favouring wind before he turned his horse's head towards Mexico City. But once again, sea-sickness proved too much for the pursuit. They returned to port without making contact with the corsair who, by this time, had a two months' start. So it was years before poor Miles Philips saw England again.

By the month of May the alarm had spread from the Pacific coast to the Caribbean and Don Miguel de Eraso, member of a distinguished Spanish colonial family, wrote to tell his sovereign the news that had spread much melancholy throughout these realms. 'It is a thing which terrifies me, this voyage and the boldness of this low man' – but Don Miguel was not well informed; for example, he believed that Drake was French – 'the son of vile parents (for it is said that his father was a shoemaker)'. Great confidence existed among the Spanish officials, especially those who were not engaged in the hunt, that Drake could not escape, his ship being too foul with weed to make the crossing to the Moluccas and, besides, the winds would be against him for six months. In so grave a crisis, the general of the Indies Guard, Don Christobal de Eraso himself, volunteered to cross from Nombre de Dios to the Pacific with captains and veterans, cannon and arquebuses from his fleet, and seek the pirate out.

One of the last things Drake did before leaving Guatulco was to release the Portuguese pilot, Nuñez da Silva, whom he had kidnapped all these months ago and who now faced a long spell of unpleasant interrogation by the Inquisition before at last he was allowed to go free. Since he had fallen into Drake's hands King Philip had seized Portugal. This did not make matters easier for the pilot.

The first news of these disorderly happenings in the Pacific kingdoms of the Spanish crown reached the Escorial early in August 1579 at a time when Portugal was still separate from Spain. The Council of the Indies met and resolved that the King of Portugal should be asked to order his officials in the Moluccas to intercept the pirate. At the same time, the Council suggested to Philip that his Ambassador in London, Bernardino de Mendoza, be instructed to obtain a restitution of the property Drake had stolen in view of the fact that, before leaving on the voyage, he had deposited securities as a pledge that he would not rob any subject of a kingdom with which his Queen was at peace. Philip wrote to London to ask if any information could be obtained about this 'very strange affair'.[4]

X

Spill or Save

'What English ships did heretofore ever anchor in the mighty river of Plate? Pass and repass the unpassable (in former opinion) Strait of Magellan, range along the coast of Chile, Peru and all the backside of Nova Hispania, further than any Christian ever passed, traverse the mighty breadth of the South Sea . . .?'

Richard Hakluyt

The raid was at an end. What lay ahead was something that Drake regarded as more exciting if less immediately profitable than the plundering of Spanish ships and seaports. He was passing beyond the area of European settlement and geographical knowledge. Now he was going on a voyage of exploration which might have revolutionary consequences. After leaving Guatulco, he set sail to the west, traversing fifteen hundred miles of the ocean in a long reconnaissance, before he swung north once more. By June, the *Golden Hind* was at 42° N which, if the observation was exact, as Drake's usually was, meant that the ship was just opposite the state-line dividing Oregon from California, where the Smith River runs into the sea. Already they were farther north on the American coast than any European had ever reached before. The northernmost point of any previous recorded navigation was Cape Mendocino (40°) in California, where Juan Rodriguez Cabrillo had turned south in 1542.

At that point in the voyage the weather changed abruptly for the worse. The thermometer fell sharply, hail came; ropes grew stiff with frost, and after three days of wild north-west winds they anchored close to land and rode out a succession of bitter squalls, interspersed with thick fog. They were, they believed, at 48°, which would mean that they were just south of Vancouver Island. It is possible, as the description of the weather would suggest, that they had reached some point closer to the Arctic Circle. At any rate, Drake now gave up the attempt to make further progress to the north. The voyage had lasted twenty months. The strain had been constant and terrible. The ship was a floating gold mine, using bullion as ballast. And where he had hoped to find the coastline trending towards the east it seemed to be setting in a north-westerly direction. The Strait of Anian, if it existed at all, lay somewhere farther on in seas as cold as any in north Russia. It was time to think of home. He found shelter for his ship after a fortnight, seven hundred miles to the south in 38° 30′ N, in other words on the Californian coast a little to the north of San Francisco. Today a lagoon inside Point Reynes is named Drake's Bay. It was probably there that Drake paused. The *Golden Hind* had sprung a leak and her precious cargo must be put ashore and a fort built for its protection.

While this was being done, the Indians of the region provided a diversion which both pleased and embarrassed the pious sailors Drake had brought along with him. For it was very soon apparent to them that these aborigines regarded their visitors as divine beings to be worshipped. How else could the sailors account for the strange and disconcerting behaviour with which they were greeted: weeping and adulation in which the shrill voices of the women were particularly audible. Two days after the arrival of the ship the Indians gathered in a dense mass on the hill above the fortified camp which had been built. A man among them with a voice which had great carrying power addressed the English visitors. Then, the men came forward with gifts, while the women tore their breasts until the blood ran. In order to clear up the misunderstanding which he thought existed, Drake made use of some ingenuity. All hands were summoned to prayer and, so that there could be no mistake, they were told to raise their eyes to heaven, thus indicating that they were human and that God was above. The Bible was read and psalms were sung.[2]

Deeply impressed but, probably, somewhat mystified by

these rites, the Indians departed. They returned three days later, with an important chief who had a bodyguard of a hundred skin-clad warriors. A long oration by the chief was followed by a ceremonial dance begun by a medicine-man and taken up by the others. Drake was at first cautious and watched from within his fort; later, he allowed the dancers to come inside the defences.

They crowned him with a head-dress of feathers and hailed him with a cry, 'Hioh.' Drake accepted the crown of the country in Her Majesty's name and nailed a metal plate to a post, announcing – with an English sixpence to prove it – that it was a dominion of Queen Elizabeth's. The Indians searched the faces of the seamen for those, 'which commonly were the youngest of us', that particularly pleased them, whereupon they were thrown into frenzies of adoration. Sick Indians poured in to be healed by the breath of the blond divinities and, to Drake's displeasure, sacrifices were offered. This collision between Europe and the pre-Columbian savages was strange, innocent and disturbing. Almost certainly it would have ended badly had it gone on for very long. One of the gods would have forgotten his divinity. The crew of the *Golden Hind* were, after all, the same men who had behaved so boisterously at Guatulco just two months before.

Fortunately, after a stay of four weeks, Drake decided to leave. He had inspected the Queen's kingdom of 'New Albion' as he had named it, had seen the herds of fat deer, the abundance of good soil and the strength and energy of the people. But the summer was passing. He was sixteen thousand miles from Plymouth. It was time to go home. Drake resolved to sail back to England by the Moluccas and the Cape of Good Hope. Perhaps he had always meant to do so. The parting was poignant. The Indians, plunged in despair, sought by magic rites, such as the burning of a bunch of feathers, to prevent their visitors from leaving them. The English replied with prayers and psalms, thus encouraging the heathen to forget their magic and lift their eyes and hands to heaven. From the poop of the

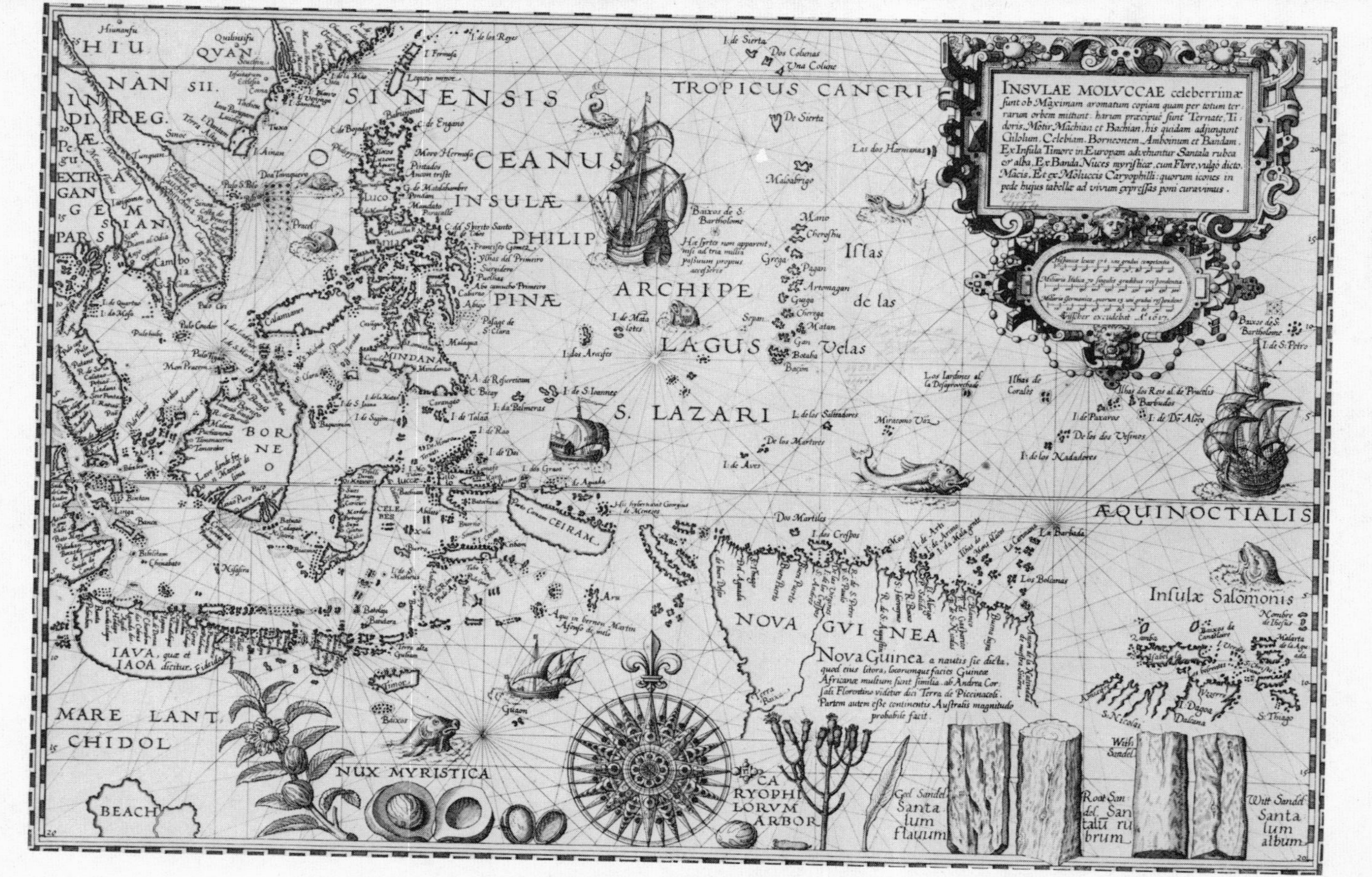

6 A map of the Spice Islands, by Petrus Plancius, originally engraved by Johannes à Doetechum *c.* 1594 (*British Museum*)

7 A map of Santo Domingo by Baptista Boazio, from Walter Bigges' *A Summary and True Discourse of Sir Francis Drake's West India Voyage*, published simultaneously in London, Leyden and Cologne in 1589 (*British Museum*)

NEC SPE NEC METV
AA
BB
EE
DD
GG
MM
Z

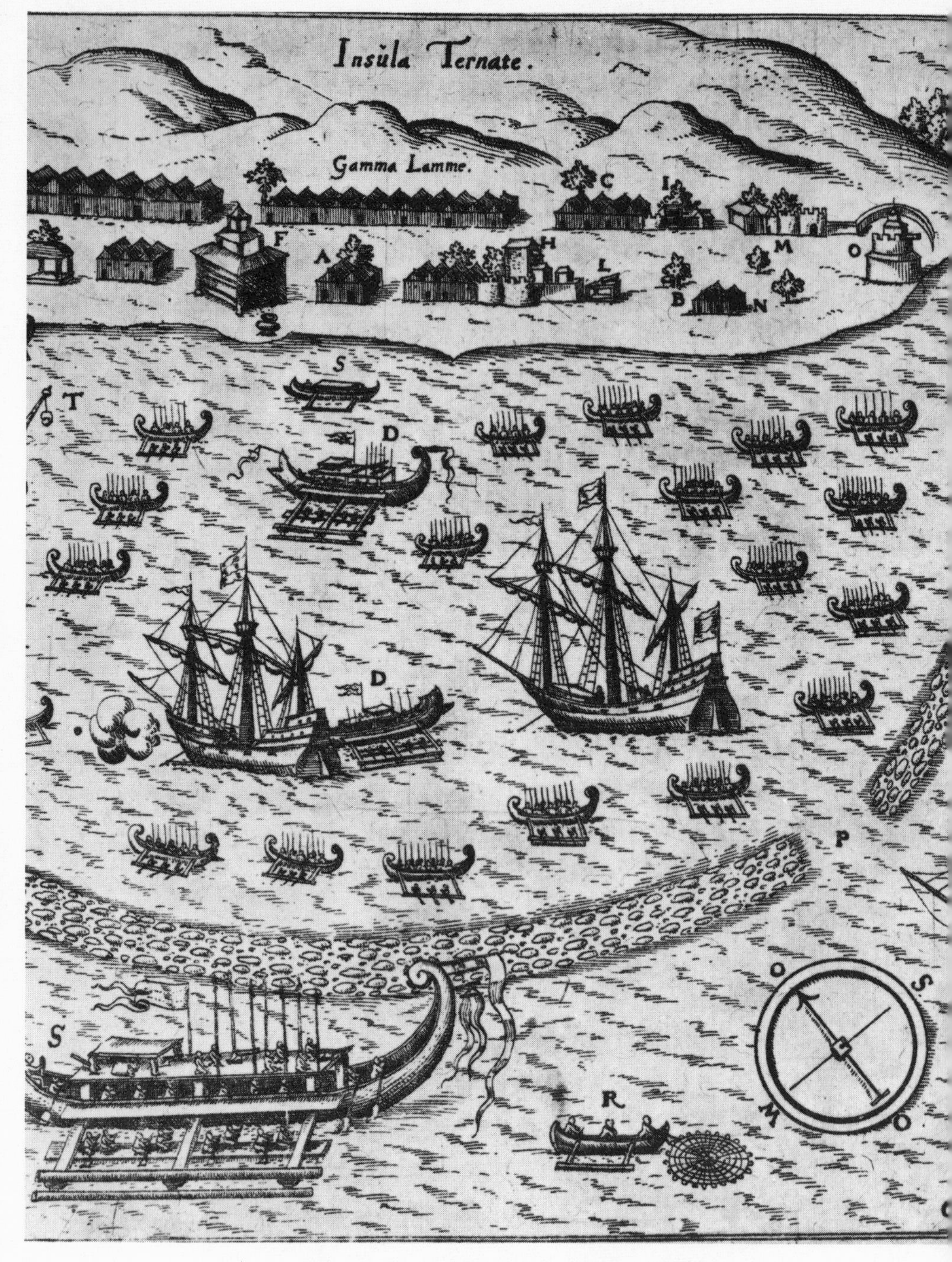

8 The ceremonial barge of the Sultan of Ternate
(*National Maritime Museum*)

Golden Hind as she sailed to the west, Drake saw Queen Elizabeth's new subjects lighting fires on the hilltops. Was it a last salute or a propitiating sacrifice?

So ended the first contact of Englishmen and the Indians of Western America as the visitors saw and remembered it. As might be expected, the record is a mixture of exact observation, very creditable to the explorers, and wild misunderstanding of what was going on. The houses, sleeping arrangements, costumes and money which Drake and his companions found all survive among the Coast Miwok of California, tribes of whom a scattered handful survives.* The King is described as wearing a coney-skin blanket and a knit-woven caul (a net cap). These, too, are found among the Californian Indians. The wailings and lacerations with which the white men were greeted were probably not the salutations to gods that the visitors supposed them to be. It is much more likely that the Indians thought that the men who had come from the sea were their own dead come back to them. Hence the painful searching of the faces of the younger and, presumably, beardless seamen. Hence, too, the extraordinary sorrow at the moment of parting.

One feature of Drake's stay on the north-west coast remains puzzling. The account of frightful cold, of snow-clad mountains and skin-clad Indians is hard to reconcile with the climate of California or Oregon in the months of early summer. But Drake was celebrated for his exact observations. He was, after all, one of the most renowned navigators of his time. On the other hand, it is unlikely that a false account of the weather off the Californian coast would be given. It is, however, possible that Drake pushed his search for the Strait of Anian farther north than Vancouver Island and that he was forbidden to disclose the exact truth about what he had discovered.[3]

After leaving the American coast, the ship was out of sight of land for sixty-eight days, running before the north-east trade winds until it came to a group of islands† about 9° N where the

* Or did until 1925.

† The Palau Islands, about six hundred miles east of the Philippines.

inhabitants were such audacious thieves that Drake paused there for one day only. Then he made for the Mindanao in the Philippines where he filled up his empty water-butts; after that, due south in the direction of the Moluccas. One day, he saw a ship which, by her sails and general trim, was European. He hailed her, asking for food and offering goods in exchange. If there was a refusal to do business, he said, he would be compelled to seize her. The stranger, which was, in fact, a Portuguese royal galleon, fled, and when pursued, ran into the shoal water where the *Golden Hind* could not follow her. At last Drake saw a line of conical mountains on the horizon ahead. A heavy perfume was borne on the wind. He had arrived at the fabled Spice Islands, the source of Portugal's most profitable trade monopoly.

Here a political situation existed of which he determined to take advantage. Although the islands were nominally under the Portuguese sovereignty, the Portuguese, by an act of treacherous atrocity, had stirred up the inappeasable hatred of one of the local potentates, the Sultan of Ternate, Baber. Almost as soon as he arrived in these waters, Drake picked up news of this feud, first from a man of mixed blood, and then from a stately Malay gentleman who hailed the ship and came aboard. He was one of Sultan Baber's rajahs. Next day, the *Golden Hind* dropped anchor off Ternate.

Drake was royally received. Four magnificent war canoes came towards his ship, rowed by men who kept time with their paddles to the sound of music. The canoes were hung with costly mats. Brass guns pointed from the bows. Aboard were important officials who announced that His Highness the Sultan was himself on the way to greet the Queen of England's emissary. Arriving in full ceremonial splendour, Sultan Baber was greeted by a salute from the *Golden Hind*'s cannon, by the blaring of trumpets and the firing of a *feu de joie* by her arquebusiers. Drake, in full dress, was on his quarterdeck, with his officers about him. The English galleon was towed into harbour by the war canoes. It was followed by the Sultan in his state barge, beating time in rapture to the music of the ship's band performing in a boat alongside him. Baber had, it seemed, formed an immediate and passionate attachment to English music.

Four days of hospitable entertainment ashore followed, even if Ramadan imposed its discipline upon the Moslem hosts. But Drake was persuaded by his crew not to venture ashore and the Sultan did not board the galleon – which, indeed, he could hardly have been expected to do since it was Drake's duty to pay the first call. Beneath the surface of cordiality, then, there was some uneasiness. The Malays were agreeable, the signs of high civilisation in the island were impressive – but it was in these waters that Magellan had been murdered sixty years before. However, all passed off well. Sultan Baber proposed an alliance against the Portuguese: in return for Queen Elizabeth's naval help he would grant English merchants a monopoly of his spice trade. While the details of the treaty were being worked out, the *Golden Hind* was loading 6 tons of cloves, as much as she had room for. When she set sail again, she travelled six hundred miles to a beautiful deserted island somewhere south of Celebes. There a fort was built and the ship was made ready for the homeward voyage.

After a month in what proved to be a place of idyllic beauty and abundance, the *Golden Hind* set off for England on 12 December. It was just two years since she had left home. She had on board fifty-nine, all that were left of the eighty men who had been in her when she emerged from Magellan's Strait and ran into that tremendous ocean storm. Considering all that had been ventured and accomplished in the crowded months which had followed – gales, explorations, plundered vessels and impudent flouting of Spanish authority in a dozen ports – the casualties had not been excessive. Now, ahead of the wanderers lay the hope of more peaceful days, an easy, uneventful journey home, through waters which might not be friendly but were at least one of the main highways of international traffic. Never was hope more bitterly or more swiftly dashed.

On 9 January, at eight o'clock in the evening when the *Golden*

Hind was running southwards before the trade wind, there was a tremendous crash and the whole company were thrown violently forward. One of the most dreaded emergencies in the seaman's life had occurred. The ship had struck hard on a reef, invisible to the eye of the look-out and unmarked on the charts of the captain. In so desperate a crisis – for it seemed to be only a matter of minutes before the galleon broke up and her crew and treasure went to the bottom of the sea – Drake did what might have been expected of him. He followed the example of John Hawkins in the *Jesus* all those years ago, and adjured his men to take to their knees and implore assistance from the Almighty. After that, he became the practical seaman once more, inspected the ship and found that, surprisingly enough, it had suffered no great damage from the rock.

The trouble was, however, that to windward the water was so deep that they found no ground where an anchor could hold. Without a purchase there, a fixed point to which a cable could be attached and a pull could be exerted, what hope was there that the *Golden Hind* would be drawn out of the teeth of the shoal? But left where she was, with the wind holding her against the reef and the waves for ever driving, she would sooner or later disintegrate. Nothing was more certain. True, they had a pinnace; but it held only twenty men and they numbered fifty-nine. A third of their number might be saved. At most. And the nearest land was twenty miles away – against a strong wind! In their predicament, Drake and his crew fell once more to their prayers. God alone could 'spill or save them', a point which Parson Fletcher stressed in a sermon he preached before giving the sacrament to his apparently doomed shipmates. At last, death in his heart, Drake brought himself to sacrifice the cargo. Eight cannon went overboard. The gold and silver were spared. But – had enough been discarded to bring release? Half the cargo of cloves followed and a great quantity of provisions went. Enough – as one chronicler said, 'to break the heart of a miser to think on't'.[4]

The situation at low tide was gloomy indeed. To port, the

water was a fathom deep. The *Golden Hind* drew more than two fathoms. And to starboard they could find no bottom with a line. Only the wind, blowing towards the reef, kept the ship upright. Then, on the afternoon of the second day, the ultimate disaster threatened. The wind died and the *Golden Hind* began slowly, inexorably, to heel over, towards the deep water. It was the moment for final petitions to the Almighty, abject confessions of past transgressions and loud outcries and then – oh miracle! – the *Golden Hind* righted herself and slipped into the deep water outside the reef.

The hilarious scene that followed proved how frightened they had all been. Francis Fletcher, the chaplain, whom Drake suspected of having been one of Doughty's supporters at St Julian, was made the butt of a schoolboy farce. He was fastened to the forehatch by padlock. The ship's company were assembled. And Drake, sitting cross-legged with a pair of slippers in his hand, cast the chaplain out of the church of God. He was not to go before the mast on pain of death and he was to wear, bound to his arm, a notice saying, 'Francis Fletcher, the falsest knave that lives.' What was the meaning of all this nonsense? An intolerable tension had been lifted. That the crew and, above all, the captain of the *Golden Hind* were in a state verging on hysteria after all these months of lonely voyaging, stress and danger, seems to be certain. And the captain took the lead in the revels. A gift for simple comedy can, as Julius Caesar knew, be part of the art of leadership.

Though the ship had been saved from the peril of the sub-marine rock, Drake's troubles were not at an end. For more than a month he sought to find a way out of the labyrinth of shoals and islands around Celebes before, at last, friendly Malays put him on the course that would take the ship to the open sea. Somewhere to the south of Java, he and his men were enjoying the hospitality of a jovial rajah when news came that several ships as big as his own were in the neighbourhood. It was no time, at this stage in his voyage, with a cargo as valuable as the one he had below hatches, to risk a clash with the Portuguese fleet. Victualled, cleaned and filled with all the spices she could carry, the *Golden Hind* set sail on 26 March for the Cape of Good Hope and, after that, with more than fifty parched and famished sailors aboard, put in at Sierra Leone for food and water. Thenceforth, it was a straight run home to Plymouth.

XI

New Year's Day at Court

'About the world he hath been and rich he is returned.'

Sir Philip Sidney to his brother, Robert[1]

'La piraterie est dans les mœurs, dans la vie quotidienne, au plus profond de l'histoire de la mer.'
('Piracy is embedded in the manners, in the daily life, in the farthest depths of the history of the sea.')

Fernand Braudel

The news of Drake's return was spreading over England like an enormous complacent smile, all the more swiftly because discreetly. For discretion there were powerful political reasons. 'Rich he is returned.' But rich at whose expense? Rich certainly, although it is difficult to reckon the exact value of the cargo that was stowed away in the *Golden Hind* when, on 26 September 1580, she came into sight round Rame Head and, while a tremor of excitement ran round the shore, she put into Plymouth Sound.

Her sails were furled and her anchor chain rattled through the hawser at some distance from the quay. Outside the Sound Drake had hailed a fishing boat and had asked the question on which his next action and, maybe, his life depended – Was the Queen alive and well? She was! Magnificent news as far as it went. But plague was raging in the town. He and his crew should not go ashore. So the *Golden Hind* kept her distance.

In his cabin, Drake wrote to the Queen a letter which Tom Brewer took to the quay by the ship's boat. There he called for a horse. He was on his way to Ashburton, to Exeter – and all the thirteen change points on the way to London.[2] Ordinary mail between the two cities took just over three days, although once, in a moment of urgent political need, a courier of Lord Burghley's had cut the time by half. One can believe that Drake, with momentous news to impart to his mistress and all the money in the world to spend, was not content with the three-miles-an-hour pace of the ordinary post. Meanwhile, he worked his galleon out of the harbour again and anchored unobtrusively behind St Nicholas Island, now called Drake's Island. There he awaited the Queen's reply.

In the meantime, his wife Mary was rowed over to the ship along with the Mayor of Plymouth. Talking to them, Drake began to pick up his bearings in an altered world.

From the news he heard, he would have no doubts that the sun of Spain was still rising and had not yet reached its zenith. The Duke of Parma, Philip's nephew and his commander in the Netherlands, was whittling away the tree of rebellion in the Protestant north of that country. In France, the Duke of Guise, Philip's pensioner, was more powerful than the degenerate king. Since July of the previous year, papal volunteers, put ashore at Smerwick on the south coast of Ireland, had been giving support to the rebels there. Most important change of all – Portugal was about to fall into Philip's grasp on the death of her King, a senile cardinal. Philip's claim to the succession was perhaps better than anyone else's. It was still more important, however, that the claim was asserted by the Duke of Alva at the head of a redoubtable Spanish invasion force. By taking over Portugal, Philip would acquire all its colonial rights and possessions on the African coast, in the Far East and in Brazil. More than that, he would now be master of the Portuguese fleet of armed galleons and capable of carrying on a naval war in the Atlantic. Nobody would doubt, least of all Drake, that this was an important change in the balance of power. He awaited in some trepidation the reply from London which would give him a hint about how the Queen thought that these events in Europe affected her personal dealings with the Spanish king. He had not long to wait.

In London, Drake's return had been anxiously expected for many months. English merchants in Seville picked up a rumour that Drake had stolen 600,000 ducats. They sent it home by express courier. John Wynter, who had parted from Drake in the storm off Magellan's Strait, had brought the *Elizabeth* safely into Ilfracombe in June 1579. About that time, strong rumours were current in Spain that Drake had landed in France and had buried some treasure there. This may have related to some provident act of Wynter's. More likely, the name of Drake was attached to the doings of some French corsair. The news of his return reached Court at a time when the Queen was putting the finishing touches to a letter to Spain complaining that Philip had prohibited all exports from Spanish ports in foreign ships (salt alone being excepted).

A crisis of policy arose among the Queen's councillors.[3] The weightiest and most experienced of them – Burghley, Crofts, the Admiral, Sussex and Secretary Wilson – drew up an order that Drake's plunder should be restored to its owners and, in the meantime, that it should be lodged in the Tower. Three councillors refused to sign, Leicester, Hatton and Walsingham, all of whom had invested money in the venture. And what of the great secret member of the syndicate? What of the Queen, with whom the final decision rested? Her reply to Drake's letter arrived in Plymouth; he tore open the missive in the cabin of the *Golden Hind* and read its contents with feverish haste. They laid most of his anxieties to rest. The Queen's orders were that he was to come to Court without delay, bringing with him samples of the interesting objects he had found on his travels. And Edmund Tremayne, his neighbour and friend, was to see that the treasure was brought ashore and lodged in a place of safety. Drake had no doubt what the summons meant. He loaded several horses with gold, silver and his choicest jewels, and hurried up to London.

Meanwhile, the dispute about English policy went on bitterly. Burghley considered that this was no time to provoke King Philip.[4] The important City interests whose money was tied up in trade with Spain and the Low Countries were appalled at the thought of further Spanish reprisals. And, popular as he might be with ordinary people, Drake was not looked on with favour in some influential quarters. Some noblemen regarded him as a swaggering upstart who dressed with all the bravery of a gentleman and, alas, could afford to do so. English Catholics detested him as a Protestant. Drake was both a Protestant and an upstart.

Don Bernardino de Mendoza, the Spanish ambassador, a soldier turned diplomat and with more of the soldier's courage than the diplomat's suppleness, a poor aristocrat with one blind eye, kept the other fiercely and distrustfully fixed on the interests of his master. He dwelt resentfully in a heretic capital under an excommunicate Queen. He worked assiduously to ruin the Queen and overturn the heresy. Mendoza lived for the day when Elizabeth would be burned at the stake in St Peter's Square in Rome, the punishment reserved for her in imagination by the more implacable of Catholics. A network of spies – English Catholics, Flemish merchants and mere hired informers – lent him ears in places where men whispered and women chattered. He had eyes in every Western port. And what he learned he passed on to his King in dispatches composed in stately Spanish. He was a single-minded patriot and, as patriots are apt to do, underrated both the sincerity and the subtlety of his opponents.

The return of the corsair, Drake, filled Don Bernardino with a rage which every rumour from Whitehall made harder to contain. The thief was posting up to London with his swag. Imagine! A year earlier, the Spaniard had reported that 'the people here are talking of nothing else but going out to plunder'.[5] Now, with this example of triumphant crime before them, what was to be expected? Unless, of course, Drake was suitably punished – and for that the omens were none too good. The Queen – 'this woman' – had certainly been a party to the whole criminal enterprise and would share in its profits. Mendoza demanded that the robber should not be received at Court. Had not the Queen promised that he would be punished if he showed his face in England again?

Elizabeth asked with a maddening show of reason how she was to punish Drake if she did not question him. And how was she to question him without seeing him? Mendoza thought he could see how it would go – as the affair of Alva's silver had gone, with cunning procrastinations, tedious legal arguments and, in the end, no satisfaction of Spain's just demands. The only difference would be that, this time, Burghley would probably not abet his mistress. Already he had vowed he would not touch a ducat of the pirate's gold and, when the time came, he kept his word. But what of the Queen herself? Would she be able to resist temptation? The matter was soon decided.

The master thief of the unknown world,[6] as some unfriendly voice had named him, arrived at Richmond Palace in his showiest clothes, his jutting beard bleached by the sun and an arrow scar showing on one of his cheeks, which were shining with the gold and carmine of the tropical seas.

The pack saddles were undone; the packages assigned to the bearers, the doors of the audience chamber were flung open. And, at the head of his procession of plunder, Francis Drake fell on his knees before the woman with the piercing gaze, the satiric mouth and the white prehensile fingers ablaze with rings. The woman who could have his head struck from his shoulders as he had struck Tom Doughty's in that bleak harbour at the other end of the world. And perhaps she would do so yet. But he thought he had brought powerful arguments against anything of that kind.

The diamonds. The crown of emeralds which, no doubt, some smith on the galleon had fashioned out of the crucifix stolen from the *Grand Captain of the South* off Valparaiso all those months ago. Gold ducats which streamed through the fingers of the acquisitive lady, painted, bewigged, brocaded, when he unlocked the chests – samples of the far greater wealth which at that moment Edmund Tremayne was stowing away in Trematon Castle. And a great map, decorated in glowing colours and showing where the ship had touched as she crawled across the wrinkled surface of the ocean.

They talked in secret for six hours, those two, Queen and robber, principal and agent. Six hours behind closed doors, during which time it is safe to say that Drake did most of the talking. It had been, after all, an extraordinary journey, a wonderful achievement, a periplus beyond compare. True, the world had been encompassed before but he, Drake, was the first captain who had made the voyage and come back with his ship. It was a theme to which he, with the gift he had of catching a mood and conveying its excitement, could do justice.

So the voyage lived again, more wonderful than the jewels and bullion in the room, since it lived in the deep colours of memory and imagination. One by one people and events rose: the worst storm since Noah, the giant Indians, the flying fish which the dolphins had hunted, the impertinences committed in Chile, Peru and Mexico, the Spaniard asleep beside his silver, Nuñez da Silva, the reluctant pilot, San Juan de Anton, the crestfallen captain of the treasure ship, the pathetic Indians of New Albion and the sophisticated rajahs of the Spice Islands – the wonders and the perils of the world, its seas so much wider than the great Columbus had believed, its lands so rich in the surprising inventions of the Almighty. All this was unrolled by the voluble little man with the scarred, weather-beaten face, to one of the most intelligent audiences in the world.

The outcome of the long interview fulfilled the worst forebodings of Mendoza. When he was given an audience at the Palace, with only two courtiers in the Chamber (the Lord Admiral and the Lord Chamberlain), and they out of earshot, he pressed the Queen for restitution of the stolen goods. And, sitting alone on the dais, she rounded on him, screaming, 'You are to blame for everything.' She recited the list of her grievances; the Irish affair, the ill-treatment of her Protestant subjects by Spanish officials and all the rest. In particular, she demanded a written apology from King Philip for his interference in Ireland. How was one to deal with a Jezebel who could, with such impudence, seize the upper ground in debate and stand the moral order on its head? While she was lecturing Don Bernardino on the law of nations, he lost his temper: he said he would replace words with cannon. In an instant, Elizabeth was all ice and calm. 'If you talk to me like that,' she said quietly. 'I will put you in a place where you cannot talk at all.' Mendoza, furious, thought that she meant it. In all the high and dangerous comedy of Elizabethan diplomacy, there is no more brilliantly acted scene than this one.[7]

Drake was sent posting back to Plymouth to take part in the registration of the treasure, a necessary formality if restitution was to be made. But with him went a private letter to Tremayne, the meaning of which was clear to the least cynical of mortals. The task of registration was not to begin until Drake had been left alone with the treasure . . . He was allowed to abstract £10,000 for himself and distribute a similar sum among his crew.[8] These tasks were faithfully performed. Drake entrusted his share to his friend, Christopher Harris of Radford, who hid the bullion in an old house at the head of Hooe Lake just outside Plymouth. The rest of the treasure of the *Golden Hind* was lodged in the Tower of London until its fate should be decided. And that fate was to be – what? To be spirited away by the complex processes of Elizabethan accounting and never, never to find its way to the coffers of King Philip (who was the rightful owner of at least a fifth of it), or to those of any other Spanish claimant.

Burghley was offered ten bars of fine gold; Sussex was tempted with salvers and vases of silver. Both refused the bribes. But others were not so scrupulous. Leicester, for example, was thought to have taken most of all. But, after all, he was a shareholder. An attempt was made on the probity of Mendoza himself with 50,000 crowns.[9] A poor man, he would gladly pay as much, he said, to see the pirate hanged! When London merchants in the Spanish trade complained of the danger that Drake was bringing on their business, he offered to buy their best ships. His arrogance at this time was offensive to many, although not to the Queen or the people.

What, in fact, was the value of the treasure Drake had brought home?[10] A million and a half ducats, said Mendoza when he was trying to alarm the English public with the enormity of the crime that had been committed. There are several ways in which the estimate can be checked. The total cost of sending out four ships with crews numbering a hundred and sixty would be in the region of £5,000. It is known that each investor received £47 for every £1 he ventured. In other words, the shareholders divided a quarter of a million, a sum that corresponds reasonably well with the records of bullion declared to the customs (£307,000). But this, of course, does not take account of the Queen's share which, it seems, was probably as much again. In April 1581, six months after the return of the *Golden Hind*, it was reported that the total value of the treasure was £600,000* and that there was £263,000 in Spanish coin in the Tower of London. Finally, there were the jewels which Elizabeth took and which she could wear or sell or pawn as was convenient. For the Queen, then, the adventure had been exceptionally profitable.

Let it be supposed that she got £300,000 out of the adventure. How did that compare with the current costs of government and war? It was more than the total of Exchequer receipts for a year. It was nearly twice the cost of fighting the Spanish Armada in 1588. It was, in all likelihood, the reason why the Crown was free of debt in the year after Drake's return. In short it was, by any reckoning, a great deal of money.

'Indeed,' writes J. M. Keynes, 'the booty brought back by Drake may fairly be considered an origin of British Foreign Investment. Elizabeth paid off out of the proceeds the whole of her foreign debt and invested a part of the balance (about £42,000) in the Levant Company; largely out of the profits of the Levant Company there was formed the East India Company, the profits of which during the seventeenth and eighteenth centuries were the main foundation of England's foreign connections; and so on.'[11]

The treasure gave Drake enormous prestige in London. 'Anyone who goes adventuring with me,' he boasted, 'will have his money back six or seven times over!'[12] Among the young seagoing men he was adored. They knew the truth about the

* About £18 million in the values of the 1970s.

Golden Hind, and that the crew had enjoyed, as was their right, the pillage of twenty prizes between the Cape Verde Islands and the Mexican coast.

The treasure was not, however, the only remarkable feature of the voyage. The *Golden Hind* had sailed with more than eighty men aboard; she had come back nearly three years later with fifty-nine. By the standards of that time these figures were highly satisfactory. After one voyage to the Caribbean, casualties of fifty or sixty per cent were not unknown. One fact is even more extraordinary. Drake could also claim that, although his exploits had cost some English lives, not one Spaniard had been killed.* All these ships boarded, with cutlasses waving in the hands of excited sailors, culverins and arquebuses firing and arrows flying, Englishmen falling dead or wounded, and not a Spanish life lost and only one Spaniard hurt by a stray arrow. What a triumph for the discipline that Drake had imposed on his men! What a tribute to the histrionic gifts of seamen to put on a convincing show of savage violence – and hurt nobody! It was in a way the most spectacular achievement of this freebooter whom the Spaniards were at that time depicting as little better than a cannibal. For it happened at a time when the normal fate of prisoners of war who had no ransom worth collecting was to be butchered. This was true in Ireland, in France or in the Netherlands. If men had the misfortune to fall into the clutches of the Inquisition, their lot was even more cruel.

Drake was now the most famous private citizen in the Western world. Princes like the Duke of Florence sought his portrait to hang beside other great captains of the age. The King of Navarre asked for copies of his charts.[13] Poets wrote bad verse about him like Nicholas Breton's:

> *Let Captains crouch and cowards leave to crake*
> *And give the fame to little Captain Drake.*[14]

Little in stature and belonging to the little people of the realm, boastful and swaggering in his glory, rousing the disapproval of

* San Juan de Anton was slightly wounded, a matter of real concern to Drake.

the gentry and the frowns of the statesmen, but all the more adorable to the people! They had picked Drake as their special hero and it is easy to see why. He had defied and insulted the Establishment – and there has never been an establishment so secure and monolithic as the Spanish monarchy in the year 1580. It was a monster; silver ran in its veins, the *tercios* were its fists and, like antibodies ready to fight disease before it was visible, the familiars of the Inquisition were on the watch against the corroding rebellions of the mind. One did not need to be a Protestant to detest the Inquisition. One might, for instance, be a Venetian or a Frenchman. Hearing of Drake's momentous voyage, millions of people realised that the world was more hopeful and the monolith not so strong as it had seemed.

He was a hero – a folk hero – and one reason was that he was a pirate.

A pirate? The title is one which Drake always rejected with indignation. Yet it is difficult to see what else at this stage in his career to call him. As he saw it, he was harassing the Queen's enemies in a period of undeclared but active war when, in countless Spanish diplomatic messages, the English were called 'the enemy'. He did not plunder indiscriminately but he was a thorn in the flesh to those, like the Spaniards and the Portuguese, who had established a monopoly and called it law. He was a man ahead of his time, and he was forcing the pace of events. So Burghley, for instance, declined to share in the proceeds of his most successful coup – although he had been quite prepared to invest in Hawkins' slaving venture a few years earlier. The Queen's first minister was, at a time when he still hoped to save the peace, not only more straitlaced than Drake but also than the Queen, his mistress.

Nothing is more absurd than to read back into the past the moral standards that came later. Piracy? An intolerable breach of the moral code? Countless English gentlemen of the highest respectability were financially interested in privateering, a business which, in practice, was with difficulty distinguished from piracy. No doubt there was a difference. A privateer waged war at his own expense and risk against the enemies of his country. But when Drake went out plundering, England and Spain were not at war. And in that case he was a pirate? No doubt. In the sixteenth century, peace passed imperceptibly into war, and what was robbery one day might on the next, even before the voyage was over, become a patriotic feat for which the church bells would be rung.

One thing more. A pirate is, by definition, the enemy of the human race. Drake was selective in his enmity. To the graver sort of naval historian he has been an embarrassment, as, in his own day, he was to the graver kind of statesman. But most of his contemporaries heartily approved what he was doing. And some of them were fired by his example. Sir Christopher Hatton, Captain of the Guard, had dealings with a pirate named John Callis. And Sir George Carey, kinsman of the Queen and Captain-General of the Isle of Wight, begged leave to take a financial interest in the depredations of a friend of his, the pirate Flud.[14] So in this respect, as in others, where today there is a firm border between the permissible and the criminal, there was then a wide area of debatable land. Privateering, in the broadest sense of the term, was becoming an English business as well as an English sport. Before long, hundreds of ships were dabbling in it. Profits were good and strict conventions governed how they were distributed. William Ivey, master of the *Tiger*, that famous ship that went to Aleppo, quarrelled with the captain, a hard-drinking Dutchman. The captain said that the crew (Thames-siders like so many of these privateering crews) were 'breaking bulk and spoiling the cargo' which was forbidden by his commission. 'Shit on thy commission,' retorted Ivey.[15] To this, the crew added some remarks about the captain's drinking habits. In the end, the dispute went to the Admiralty Court. Piracy appealed to the poaching, gaming, easy-money instincts of the English. It had, too, an educational value. Practising it or talking about it, they were brought the wind from a wider world. In all this social transformation, the example and the success of Francis Drake were crucial.

Why was he picked out from among all the daring captains of the age for a special measure of popular fame so that, eight years later, the battle with the Armada was spoken of in England and abroad as if it were a personal duel between Drake and the King of Spain? Because he was one with whom a whole mass of ordinary people, coarse, brutal, unlettered, could identify their secret talents and their unspoken aspirations. The great folk heroes have nearly all been bandits. Robin Hood, Rob Roy, Stenka Razin, Rolf the Ganger, Billy the Kid, Ned Kelly. The people are not so strict in their morals as is sometimes supposed. Especially people under the heel of a despot or the thumb of a bureaucrat. 'This people, so intelligent, so sceptical, who mock at everything published under their master's censorship, find their favourite reading in little poems which describe, with feeling, the lives of the most renowned brigands. The heroism they find in those stories delights the artistic instinct which is always alive in the masses.'[16] And the adventure, the freedom, the plunder – these delights too, attain their zenith in the form of brigandage known as piracy.

At some moment after Drake's return Elizabeth had decided that she could risk offending the King of Spain. For a time, her councillors had talked of a compromise: if Spain gave up her intervention in Ireland, the syndicate which had financed Drake's voyage would be content with a mere hundred per cent profit. At that moment the Spanish troops in Ireland were massacred and the notion was forgotten. Perhaps the Queen calculated that, while Philip was occupied in digesting his new Portuguese realm, he would not be likely to push a quarrel with England to the point of war. Nor would he wish to throw England into the arms of France. Then there was the treasure itself, a powerful argument and one of which she could make good use.

England was a small country when measured against the power of Spain. The state was poor. 'The rental of Seville alone is greater than all the revenues of this crown.' So Antonio de Guaras had told Elizabeth's Chancellor of the Exchequer, Sir

Walter Mildmay, one day in 1578.[17] No doubt the Queen could have taken more out of the pockets of her subjects. As the conflict with Spain grew fiercer and more costly her government was, in fact, driven to do just that. But how reluctant she was to increase the tax burden! Rather live on capital by selling Crown lands. Rather borrow in Amsterdam and postpone the day of reckoning.

The war, which was a reality long before it was acknowledged, was intensely popular, but Elizabeth, whose supreme asset as a statesman lay in her intuitive understanding of her people, knew that its popularity – and her own – would wane as soon as it began to hit the price of beer, the export of cloth and the primitive tax-structure of England. Besides, if Parliament were asked too often to vote extra money, Parliament might insist on a right to interfere in policy – and this, to a great political artist like Elizabeth, was a thought unspeakably odious. So her Navy must, if possible, earn its keep in trade. The war at sea should pay for itself. In the Crown's financial embarrassments, the treasure of the *Golden Hind* was something more than a modest windfall.

On New Year's Day, 1581, Queen Elizabeth wore her new emerald crown at Court. Five emeralds, Mendoza counted, grinding his teeth with rage, three of them as long as a little finger, and two round stones worth 20,000 crowns. The jewels were of the finest quality, as well they might be, coming as they did from the mines of Peru.[18]

XII

War for the Atlantic

'The wealth of both Indies seems in great part but an accessory to the command of the sea.'

Francis Bacon

The Queen's visit to Deptford that April day in 1581, coincided with a bizarre turn in English policy.[1] There she was in all her magnificence. And there was the battered historic little ship which had encompassed the world and now lay in the river, freshly painted and thoroughly cleaned, with all her flags and streamers flying. Above them, the moment the lady stepped aboard, the royal standard, with its leopards and lilies, was broken. The lilies were, perhaps, a shade tactless in the circumstances. For they were a reassertion, however unreal, of the old claim of English monarchs to sovereignty over France. And who was the Queen's guest on this occasion but a French envoy, the Sieur de Marchaumont, sent to prepare the way for the Duc d'Alençon, the French king's brother, with whom, after forty-eight years of famous if disputed virginity, Elizabeth seemed to be contemplating wedlock. Marchaumont was the forerunner of an imposing delegation which would soon come from Paris, two hundred strong, headed by the Duc himself, to discuss the final details of the marriage treaty. The thought of this union filled many of the Queen's advisers with dismay. The public took ill to it. But the greater the opposition, the more determined she appeared to be. Such was the nature of the woman.

Meanwhile, entertainment on a lavish scale was being prepared for the amorous French prince and his retinue. It was said that £10,000 of the silver Drake had brought home with him was being coined to defray these extraordinary expenses. A report like this was calculated to add to the mortification of

Bernardino de Mendoza, who had no doubt that the Queen's marriage negotiations could only be designed as an act of policy hostile to his master. For did not Alençon claim sovereignty over the Netherlands, which indisputably belonged to the King of Spain? Philip was the most sceptical of all those who watched the development of this matrimonial farce. From the beginning, he said that the marriage would not take place and that Elizabeth would be the one who broke off the negotiations.

But only the faintest shadow of doubt hung over the scene at Deptford when the Queen, who had recently spent a vast sum of money on renewing her wardrobe, arrived at the *Golden Hind*. There had been a disagreeable incident just before. A wooden bridge made for the Queen to pass over had collapsed and a hundred men had been pitched into the mud. Fortunately none of them was hurt. And now the trumpets blew; the drums beat. The burly little seaman who had lately poured such a deluge of coin into the royal till bent over the long, thin fingers. After that there was a banquet, the most splendid England had seen since the spendthrift days of Henry VIII. And after that – the Queen had promised it, and she carried out her promise with a sly, equivocal edge of insult. The King of Spain had asked for Drake's head. Now she would strike it off with a gilded sword. Saying so, she handed the sword to the Frenchman and bade him knight Francis Drake.

So it was done. The circumnavigation of the world was fittingly recognised. And by knighting the pirate, Elizabeth implicitly acknowledged that the piracies had been actions in an undeclared war. She had passed a royal sanctifying hand over the whole picturesque chapter of lawlessness, and in doing so she had defied the most powerful monarch in Christendom.

It should have meant that, from that time onwards, Elizabeth was dedicated to war with Spain. But that would have been much too simple a deduction. The Queen had a mind which could work on two levels at once, or three, for that matter. And she had a temperament which sometimes seemed to operate on a fourth level, resenting on behalf of some secret source of unreason the policy to which logic drove her. So that her ministers, having persuaded her to accept a wise course of action, had reason to fear her rage, her curses or – as happened at least once – her slipper launched at their heads.[2]

It is possible that, in the emotional, spice-laden atmosphere on the crowded deck of the *Golden Hind*, with all the glory it reflected on her reign, hearing the captain at her side, so confident and so voluble, she really thought she would defy King Philip, her ex-brother-in-law, between whom and herself there was, in spite of everything, a strange sympathy. After all, like this clever, repulsive little Valois prince, he had once wanted to marry her! It is possible, too, that at times she thought seriously of carrying through the mad escapade of this late marriage to the Frenchman. At least, it would annoy the English Puritans. It might even disturb the King of Spain. But, before long, it is likely that Elizabeth's natural caution returned. Thus, all that remained of the hour of defiance was the uncomfortable knowledge that, among the chilly stars which Dr Dee could read, a war between Philip and herself was written. One day. Inevitably. But if she had this intuition, as is likely, she hid it from everyone.

So Elizabeth continued to bamboozle friend and foe alike. They could not understand how one who was so timid could also be so bold. She was a woman. And a woman in the business of state, like a left-handed player in tennis, enforces a change in the pattern of the game, disconcerting to others. She was a woman who could not resist playing with fire.

That spring was a time of immense restlessness in English seaports. One project after another was conjured up by sailors anxious to prove that they were as bold as Drake and by geographers with theories to test. One expedition went round the North Cape to seek a way to Cathay up the Siberian rivers or round the Siberian coast. Cold and ice floes beat it back. Another expedition, in which Drake invested some money, set off for the Spice Islands planning to go by way of the Cape of Good Hope. It was mismanaged by Edward Fenton, who sailed for Brazil instead and ran into a Spanish fleet which he defeated. However, having annoyed the Spaniards, he could do no business with the local Portuguese. He came back without profit and also without young John Drake, cousin of Sir Francis, the boy who had sighted the treasure ship in the Pacific. He was wrecked off the River Plate and caught by the Spaniards. John never saw England again.[3]

The old dream of the North-West Passage had still power over certain believers. Gerard Mercator, the cartographer, wrote to his friend Abraham Ortelius, ten weeks after Drake's arrival in Plymouth, refusing to believe either that he had returned across the Pacific or that the treasure he had brought back was the fruit of plunder. 'They must have found very wealthy regions never yet discovered by Europeans.'[4] He thought they had probably found the Strait of Anian and were keeping the discovery secret.

Drake himself was involved in a scheme for drawing some advantage for England out of the collapse of Portuguese independence. A pretender to the Portuguese throne, Dom Antonio, who had been called the Prior of Crato, but had not taken a vow of celibacy, arrived in England. He was a swarthy little man with a long black beard, green eyes and a morose expression. For this latter there was some excuse. Dom Antonio had escaped from the Spaniards by the skin of his teeth. He was generally supposed to be a bastard. On the other hand, he had a casket full of magnificent jewels and a burning faith that he embodied the national tradition of Portugal. The jewels would buy him ships and cannon. His name would rally a people to his standard. And if ever, for a moment, his confidence flagged, he had friends in England to restore it. Men whose antipathy to Spain equalled his own and who were eager to support his cause.

The plan as it emerged from the discussion between the Portuguese claimant and his English associates was, in outline, that Dom Antonio should establish himself in Terceira, one of the Azores and the only possession of the Portuguese crown which remained true to him. An English fleet of eight ships and a thousand men would, under Drake's command, take possession of the island which would henceforth serve a two-fold purpose as a naval base: against the fleet bringing the treasure from the Indies and against the Portuguese carracks bringing the spices from the Moluccas.

The day before the Queen knighted Drake at Deptford, Sir Francis Walsingham put the final touches to a plan for the Terceira enterprise and to an alternative project which involved the seizure of Portugal's trading settlements in Asia. In the end, the Terceira operation was preferred. The plan indeed was so obviously advantageous that it seemed only quarrels among the participants could wreck it. These quarrels duly occurred. Dom Antonio wanted to enlarge the scale of the affair – which meant finding more money for it. The Queen refused to help unless the French came in. Drake's adherents squabbled with Frobisher's. All the investors worried about the safety of their money. And Dom Antonio, who had left one particularly magnificent diamond ring with Walsingham as security for a loan, demanded its return.

A squalid altercation broke out, the most discreditable version of which was duly reported by Mendoza to King Philip. According to this account, the Queen was suspected of detaining the jewel for no good purpose. It was nonsense. The Pretender was, with greater reason, accused of spending far more money on military preparations than had been agreed. He flounced off to France, leaving his diamond in settlement of all claims against him. With a French volunteer fleet under Filippo Strozzi, he sailed to the Azores in 1582. There he was utterly defeated by the Spaniards under the Marquis de Santa Cruz. Strozzi was killed and Dom Antonio, once more, became a fugitive. Thus was ingloriously quashed, for a time at least, a strategic conception of brilliant promise. And what became of Dom Antonio's diamond? It found its way through many dealers and owners until at last it glittered, as did so many illustrious stones, among the Russian crown jewels. Then it was called the Sancy diamond.[5]

But neither England nor Drake had heard the last of Dom Antonio.

The moment the Queen's sword in the Frenchman's hand had touched Drake's shoulder, he had gone up several steps on the social, that is to say, the political staircase of Elizabethan England.[6] There were three hundred knights in the land; usually they owed their rank to distinguished service in the field, men of proved executive talent and sufficient wealth. Above them was another, smaller and more prestigious layer, the sixty peers of the realm, whose numbers were grudgingly augmented and who, for the most part, belonged to an England that was older than the Tudors. At the very peak of power there was, of course, the Queen herself, with her frightening intellect, her appalling manners, her genius and the shrewd, humbling knowledge, which never left her, that she was the queen of the English.

Round her circled a whole solar system owing its power and momentum to her favour or her perception, bureaucrats of ability like Burghley and Walsingham, men of spirit and action like Hatton, Raleigh and Sidney. Her court afforded food and lodgings for a hundred and thirty gentlemen and their servants. More important, of course, it had in gift, through the ramifications of crown patronage, twelve hundred places which an English gentleman might accept without loss of dignity. All this court-centred radiance of office and income was independent of the old feudal England, which the Queen's grandfather and father had disrupted. It was the new England which was in those years opening like a door, a door in which Francis Drake, that afternoon at Deptford, had thrust his foot.

Famous, wealthy, the idol of the people, the new knight settled down to enjoy the rewards of his extraordinary achievement. He became a landed proprietor in Devon, buying Buckland Abbey, once a Cistercian monastery, later the country home of Sir Richard Grenville. It is beautifully situated in the shelter of a fold of the hills above the Tavy just six miles south of the farmhouse in which Drake had been born. If the restless spirit of the rover was seeking peace, here was where he could find it, within the warm pink walls set among the yew trees. Here he could watch over his farms, tend his gardens and enjoy the revenues that flowed in from the manors the Queen had given him at Sherford in Devon and elsewhere.[7] His wife, Mary, whom he had married twelve years before, died in January 1582 and was buried in St Budeaux churchyard just outside Plymouth. Three years later, Drake married Elizabeth, daughter of Sir George Sydenham, a landed gentleman in the county. It was, as they say, a good marriage. Elizabeth was a good-looking young woman of gentle birth and ample property.

There may not have been enough in the life of a country gentleman of South Devon to occupy a busy spirit. But there was also the mayoralty of Plymouth, a post in which he followed his Hawkins relatives. There was the Royal Commission on the state of the Navy in which he served after 1583 as one of its inspectors. And there were defence questions to be dealt with, like the efficiency of the county militia in Devon. In due course there was the House of Commons in which he sat (1584) as member for Bossiney.

Trips down to Plymouth; journeys up to London; business in the committee rooms of the House (bills for the more reverent observing of the Sabbath day, for the import of fish, etc.); conversations with the Queen – enough dignified, responsible public work to prevent a man with an active mind, and a tendency to put on weight, from going to sleep in his pleasant corner of England. And all the time news was blowing in from the world outside to remind him that, if he was enjoying his ease, it was not likely to last long.

The strategic crux of the Western world was no longer where it had been.[8] After Lepanto, the Turks turned their eyes eastwards to face the Persians, and the naval war in the Mediterranean died away. The battleground and the booty alike lay to the west of the Pillars of Hercules. The new war which nobody announced and which everybody entered with open eyes was a war for the Atlantic. Would the ocean and the wealth that lay on its farther shores remain a Spanish monopoly, or would the Protestant powers, England to begin with, Holland afterwards, break in and wrest the mastery from the Catholic king? Already in 1574, Don Luis de Requesens, the Grand Commander of Castile, had warned Philip, 'We can only win the war when Your Majesty becomes lord of the sea.' He was writing about the war which was being waged among the waterways and islands of the Low Countries against the Protestant rebels and their English allies. But the truth he had uttered could be applied with even greater force to the struggle which Spain, as a world-spanning empire, was obliged to wage on the high seas. It was not enough to escort the treasure fleets twice a year home to the Guadalquivir through the pirate-haunted waters north of Cuba. The naval challenge to the Spanish empire must be stifled in the harbours that nursed it.

Part of the trouble was that, in Spain, as wealth grew, the sinews of sea-power continued to wither. There was a drift of population from the coast to the interior. Andalusia was too fertile, as Bernardino de Mendoza complained to Philip; its people grew wine, oil and fruit and left seafaring to the English. He suggested that the English ships should be banned from the Spanish ports, but the King rejected the advice: Andalusia needed the exports. Mendoza's warnings of English activity grated in his master's ear: 'They are building ships without ceasing and making themselves masters of the sea.'[9] With a merchant fleet dwindling in ships and men, Philip was handicapped in meeting a sea-power as strong as the English or as desperate as the Dutch. But meet them in the end he must, separately or together.

To her disgust, Elizabeth was driven to support the Dutch, who were not merely Calvinists, which was bad enough, but also rebels against their lawful king, which was worse. With what reluctance, then, was good English money sent to Flushing and good – or, as they sometimes were, indifferent – English soldiers shipped across the North Sea to Holland. The war against Spain in the Low Countries went on, under Norreys, who quarrelled with the Dutch, and Leicester, who quarrelled with everyone. In spite of it all, Spain advanced her paw farther and farther.

The Duke of Parma, the first professional soldier in Europe, King Philip's nephew, took over command from the Duke of Alva, a violent man although one persuaded of 'the need for peace between Spain and England'. In July 1584 William the Silent, leader of the Protestant party, outlawed by Philip, was murdered in Delft. The significance of the murder was not likely to be lost on Elizabeth, who had a few months before expelled the Spanish ambassador, Bernardino de Mendoza, because he had become implicated in a plot against her, ineptly contrived by Francis Throgmorton.

In Europe, the political weather, under religious, national and commercial pressures, was becoming more stormy and more dangerous. And, in May 1585, Philip did something which lost him the support of his best friends in England, the London merchants whose prosperity was bound up with the carrying trade to Spain. At a time when there was an unusually large number of English ships in Spanish ports to relieve the famine prevailing there, he seized the ships. Looking about him, observing how France was slipping more deeply into civil war and, therefore, into impotence, how his own cause had triumphed in the Azores and was prospering in the Netherlands, he concluded that the time had come to give the English a sharp lesson in political and economic realities. It was, as it turned out, a mistake.

The *Primrose*, a London merchant ship, sailed into the Thames with a horrific story, and an important prisoner. She had been discharging her cargo in Bilbao when she was visited by the Corregidor (Sheriff) of Biscay with a party of soldiers, all disguised as merchants. At a signal, they had called on the master to surrender. But the crew of the *Primrose* fought back, threw the Spaniards into the water and made off, taking the Corregidor with them. On him they found King Philip's writ, ordering the seizure of the English ship.

The City of London, main source of shipping and finance, burned with indignation and longing for revenge. The war party at Elizabeth's Court did not miss the chance which this act of Philip's gave them to urge their point of view. But, what was more important, the adventurers and the extremists, such as Leicester and Walsingham, were now joined by the statesmen. Burghley, whose ear was always close to the City, acknowledged that the time had come for a counter-stroke, more massive than the privateering forays of the past, more dignified than mere plundering raids – for some act which would not simply be a tactical response to the danger which threatened from the Netherlands.

Letters of reprisal were issued to merchants who could show that they had suffered loss. The privateering war went on, with a slightly greater degree of respectability than before. In fact, it had never stopped. For instance, in November 1583, William Hawkins, who had left Plymouth with seven ships, intending to oust Spain from the Azores, returned laden with treasure. He had gone to the West Indies instead. Understandably, his crews refused to go ashore until they were assured of the Queen's pardon for any misdeed they might have committed. Elizabeth was more concerned with a practical aspect of the business. She dispatched the Secretary of her council to the port to make sure that she received her share of the loot. But the time for such tip-and-run tactics had passed. A strategy of ampler scope was called for.

England did not have the staying power required for a prolonged war of attrition but she was not without resources. She had a merchant marine consisting of two hundred and fifty-eight ships of 80 tons or more. These vessels were either armed already or could quickly be equipped with artillery. She had a seafaring population, hardy, patriotic and undisciplined. They numbered many thousands and, between voyages, they were apt to loiter hungrily about the ports. By laying his hands on the English ships, Philip had confirmed the Protestant suspicions of these mariners. If it was decided to launch a naval operation against the Spaniards, the skilled manpower for the business was at hand.

Early in 1585, Walsingham drew up a plan for 'the annoying of the King of Spain',[10] proposing an attack on the Spanish fishing fleets on their way to Newfoundland. The Queen approved. In the end, four distinct operations emerged from the planning in Whitehall. In June, Bernard Drake captured six hundred Spanish fishermen at sea, while Sir Walter Raleigh's patent for the colonisation of Virginia was confirmed by Parliament, and Sir Richard Grenville set out to establish a naval base on the American coast from which attacks could be launched on the Spanish Indies. Drake was chosen to lead a new expedition into the Caribbean – commission signed Christmas Eve, 1584 – on a more ambitious scale than anything that had so far been attempted.

From the Queen's point of view the advantage of enterprises like these was twofold: they were jointstock adventures, in which she was one among many shareholders, the least conspicuous but not the least grasping. And, while she waged war with one hand, she could conduct diplomacy with the other. Elizabeth's purpose was not, however, so grandiose as that of certain of her subjects. It was not to expand her dominions either east or west. She was content to be Queen of England. It was not to win a glorious victory. It was not to advance the Protestant cause. It was to persuade Philip of Spain to grant his Dutch subjects civil and religious liberties which would ensure that their country could not be used as a base of attack against England. That was why the King was to be 'annoyed'.[11]

The early months of 1585 were a time of intense naval preparation. Sir Francis Walsingham, Burghley's successor as Secretary of State, was the central flame of war. He had witnessed and survived the Massacre of St Bartholomew. He was a brilliant chief of Elizabeth's counter-espionage. Now he called back from Ireland his soldier stepson, Captain Christopher Carleill,[12] to act as Drake's lieutenant-general in the Caribbean operation. Carleill was the son of a London vintner and about

33 years of age. He had served the Huguenot cause at sea, had convoyed English merchants to Russia at a time when Denmark and Russia were at war and now hankered after colonising the American coast south-west of Cape Breton.

Drake's fleet assembled at Plymouth in July and August 1585. Two of his ships belonged to the Queen. The others were powerful armed merchantmen, one of which, the *Primrose*, the ship of the Bilbao exploit, sailed round from the Thames, having been seen off at Woolwich by a boisterous crowd.[13] In all, there were twenty-one ships and eight pinnaces, with crews totalling a thousand seamen and carrying twelve companies of soldiers under the command of Christopher Carleill.

In Plymouth Sound during the summer days there was a stirring demonstration of what a mercantile country like England could do if its blood was up. The harbour was bright with ships. The officers were correspondingly tough and competent. Bronzed, bearded, wrinkled, scarred, it was as notable a gallery of naval talent as could have been found anywhere on the Seven Seas.

Drake flew his flag in the *Elizabeth Bonaventure*, the biggest vessel contributed by the Navy. Martin Frobisher, the vice-admiral, sailed in the *Primrose*. Then there were Tom Fenner; Francis Knollys, cousin of the Queen and, according to Mendoza, a pirate of some distinction; and Edward Wynter, son of old Sir William. Tom Drake was there in a ship belonging to his brother, Sir Francis. Tom Moone, the carpenter who scuttled the *Swan*, and had sailed round the world in the *Golden Hind*, was now captain of a vessel of Drake's. Present too, were other shipmates of the voyage which encompassed the world: George Fortescue, John Martyn, Edward Careless and Richard Hawkins.

Under such energetic leaders, the work of preparing the fleet for sea went forward with all speed. For this there was good reason. Nobody could be sure how long it would be before the Queen, having given her approval to the expedition, would forbid it. Burghley, for once in favour of aggression, was plagued with nervous irritability even more tormenting than the gout that was his most assiduous enemy. He wrote to Drake that he hoped the reply to his letter would come from Cape Finisterre rather than Plymouth. It came from Plymouth. Burghley sent a sharp message to be off before it was too late.

There followed an odd incident illustrating the interplay in Elizabethan England of Court intrigue, personal pique and the grave business of state. Sir Philip Sidney, the handsome, the gallant, the poetic, the indulged favourite of the Queen, son-in-law of Walsingham, turned up in Plymouth. Ostensibly, he had come to welcome to England that unhappy waif of power politics, the Portuguese pretender, Dom Antonio, who after the collapse of his cause in the Azores had come ashore with hardly a ducat or a diamond. But, on arrival at the port, Sidney announced that he would sail with the fleet as a volunteer.

The offer was, no doubt, flattering to Drake but it was also embarrassing. He knew that the Queen was likely to be displeased when good-looking young men ran away from her side without leave. She was likely to be even less pleased with the reason behind Sidney's impulse: his annoyance over her hesitation to make him Governor of Flushing. On the other hand, Sir Philip was Master of the Ordnance, an exalted military office, and a son-in-law of Walsingham. Drake could not lightly turn him away. Characteristic of the age as Sidney's arrival was, equally characteristic was Drake's response. He entertained the distinguished visitor at a splendid banquet in the course of which the irritation and embarrassment beneath his joviality was detected only by Sidney's bosom friend, Fulke Greville. At the same time, Drake sent an express messenger galloping up to Whitehall so that his friends at Court would know what had happened.

He awaited the reply which came in three thunderclaps from the Queen: one forbade Drake to receive Sidney; the second ordered Sidney to come back to London at once; the third instructed the Mayor of Plymouth to see to it that Her Majesty was obeyed. Four miles from the town an accident befell the royal courier in which, surely, can be detected the hand of an old freebooter. Four seamen – or men dressed like seamen – pulled him from his horse, ripped open his bag and read the letters he was carrying. Then they dusted him off, and allowed him to remount and resume his journey. The outrage is quite in Drake's style.[14]

On the other hand, Sidney had the insouciance and audacity of a spoilt darling of the Court. He might easily have organised the attack on the royal mail, as his faithful friend, Fulke Greville, later alleged that he did. The most important clue to the incident is that the Queen's orders to Sidney to return at once to London duly reached Plymouth. Would they have done so if the Queen's messenger had been waylaid by bravoes in Sidney's pay? It may be doubted. On balance, it seems likely that the business was engineered in the fleet during the time it was riding at anchor in Plymouth Sound. On board there was many a mariner handy with a cudgel.

Immediately after this affair, the port was thrown into wild confusion as ships hurried to be off. Water-butts were left unfilled; important stores remained on the quay. Even fleet orders were left unissued. For, terror of terrors to her dutiful captains, the Queen might change her mind again, and order a stay on the whole enterprise. Under St Andrew's Church the trumpets blew, the drums beat and the quartermasters and corporals went round the taverns of Plymouth in search of the drunk and the dilatory. Drake was putting to sea.[15]

In a wind somewhat scant and sometimes calm, he was making for Vigo Bay. On the way there, he took a French salt barque, a good-looking craft which, on the approach of the English, was hurriedly abandoned by her crew. He named her the *Drake*, and announced that he meant to pay for her on his return to England. Remarkably enough, he kept his word. From another capture, a Spanish vessel, owned in St Sebastian, he removed her cargo of dried Newfoundland fish, poor John, as it was called, which was not only excellent eating but also lawful prize.

In shelter, off Vigo, the fleet reassembled so that stores could be distributed, water could be taken in, and each captain could be assigned his task in the business that lay ahead. It was true that these were Spanish waters, but the King of Spain was far away and his governor in Bayona was quite willing to take a realistic view of Drake's demands, transmitted by an Irish captain who had a natural aptitude for Drake's sabre-rattling brand of diplomacy. 'Is it peace or war?' asked Captain Sampson. 'Peace,' said the Governor. 'In that case, be good enough to supply water and fresh victuals.' The Governor professed himself delighted to oblige, all the more so as he could see the English troops disembarking on an island in the bay. But the suspicion grew in the fleet that this compliant Spanish official could not be trusted.

At that moment, a violent storm broke and raged during three days. Ships were dismasted or forced from their moorings and were blown out to sea. In the midst of it all, heavily laden boats were seen on the move in the inshore waters, as if the Spaniards were hurrying with their belongings to some safer place. Drake sent Carleill and some light craft in pursuit. They came back with plunder worth a few thousand ducats as well as the Vigo cathedral plate, including a handsome big silver-gilt cross. Then the rumour spread that some luckless English sailors were being held prisoner in the town. Captain Sampson went ashore and not only freed them but came back with 30,000 ducats of loot (Spanish valuation).* A truce was now patched up with the Governor and hostages were exchanged. But, on the eve of departure, there were fresh difficulties about returning the English hostages. Worse still, the Spaniards were reported to be confident that, very soon, they would be washing their hands in English blood. However, everything was patched up and the nor'-nor'-west wind came. After a week's stay in Vigo Bay, the fleet headed for the Canaries.

More than twenty vessels and more than two thousand able-bodied men; the force was too big for a plundering raid yet hardly big enough for a voyage of conquest and settlement. It

* £225,000 in modern values.

was a punitive expedition, an insolent trailing of the English coat along King Philip's shores, a calculated affront to Hapsburg obstinacy and Spanish pride. It had one more precise objective. Drake meant, if he could, to intercept and plunder the Spanish treasure fleet. His ships were powerful and numerous enough to defeat the galleons of the Indian Guard and the convoy they would be protecting on the four-month voyage home from Vera Cruz. Were he to bring off the coup, Philip's credit with the Genoa banks would be shattered, and Spanish prestige would be brought low; her unpaid armies would be sure to mutiny, and the London capitalists who had backed Drake's venture would be richly rewarded. So, with his ships spread like a fan over a wide expanse of sea, Drake sailed southwards along the coast of Portugal. But he missed the Flota, which had, in fact, arrived at San Lucar on 8 October. He went on to the Cape Verde Islands. There, on the evening of 16 November, he dropped anchor off the Portuguese settlement of Santiago and put ashore a thousand soldiers under Carleill's command. Marching through the night, by dawn next day they were about two miles from the defences of the town which, as it chanced, were unmanned. This did not prevent Carleill from staging a copybook exercise in the art of war.

Advancing over hilly country with a pedantic regard for military conventions, he arrived at the edge of a cliff from which he looked down on the town. It was laid out as a narrow triangle of stone-built houses on either side of a stream, and had been abandoned by its inhabitants. Carleill displayed his flag as a signal to the fleet and moved down into the town. It happened that 17 November was a day of national rejoicing in England, the anniversary of Queen Elizabeth's coronation. In consequence, when Carleill, looking down on Santiago from the hills above it, observed that fifty loaded cannon defending it from landward attack had been deserted by their gunners, he decided to celebrate the day suitably by putting a match to one gun after another. Drake's fleet in the roads took up the salute. There was a prolonged and reverberant cannonade after which the soldiers marched in and occupied the town. They found plenty to eat and drink but, to their chagrin, no bullion. Hearing that the Governor and the Bishop had fled twelve miles inland to Santo Domingo, Drake marched there with six hundred soldiers. Once again, he was unlucky. Not a soul was in sight. He set fire to the place and departed.

The general disappointment seems to have affected discipline. At this point, Drake met the situation with his usual trenchancy. Parading the soldiers, he made each of them take an oath of allegiance to the Queen and, in addition, give a promise to obey him and his officers. Santiago was then burnt to the ground, as was the nearby town of Porto Prayo, after treasure which was said to be buried there could not be found. Taking with him the captured guns which were his only loot, Drake sailed for the Indies.

As it chanced, however, he had not finished with the Cape Verde Islands. A week out at sea, the force was attacked by a malignant fever picked up in their stay ashore. In a few days, it killed three hundred men and affected the minds of some others. After making his landfall at Dominica, last stronghold of the warlike Caribs, he put in at St Kitts, to spend Christmas and clean the ships. Drake announced to a council of war that he meant to attack Santo Domingo, allured by the stories and fame of this, the most ancient and chief inhabited place in the Indies, the capital of Hispaniola, now somewhat in decline. His captains heartily approved.

The enterprise, however, presented many problems. They learnt from a captured frigate with a Greek pilot that the city was well defended, with a chain across the entrance of the harbour and a castle above it, bristling with artillery. There was a heavy surf on all the adjacent beaches and no suitable landing place nearer than ten miles west of the town. At that time, the English fleet was twenty miles from Santo Domingo, which had received no warning of its coming.

For three days, Drake teased the garrison with false alarms while he waited for the return of an emissary he had sent to the

Cimarrons who held the mountains behind the town. Their part in his plan of campaign was an important one. The beach on which he intended to make his landing was overlooked by guard-posts manned every night by pickets. The Cimarrons assured him that they would deal with the pickets. This promise they carried out. Drake put the assault force into boats and saw it land safely through the surf. Then he returned to the *Bonaventure* and left the conduct of land operations to Carleill.

At eight o'clock in the morning of New Year's Day, the advance began; it was four hours before the defenders realised what was happening. Until then they had been expecting a frontal attack from the sea, where Drake had in the meantime deployed his fleet. Glistening in the morning sunshine which sparkled on its towers and belfries, Santo Domingo, third city in the Spanish empire, was a stately place of broad streets laid out in a gridiron pattern on the west bank of the river Ozana. Opening out as it approached the sea, this stream made a fine harbour which the Spaniards had improved and defended. Fifty cannon were mounted to command the entrance. To the English fleet, Santo Domingo offered the promise of good living and rich booty. But to capture it set the assailants a serious military problem.

In one respect they were fortunate. The Spaniards were taken by surprise. They had sunk two vessels in the mouth of the harbour; otherwise they had done nothing. Preparations for the marriage of the President's niece to a local gentleman had, for days, taken up the attention of the authorities with banquets, bullfights and other festivities. In consequence, when fishermen came ashore with the news that a formidable fleet was in the offing, the Governor had difficulty in mustering three companies of soldiers.

The wedding feast was suspended. Captain Mendez, sent out to reconnoitre during the hours of night, returned without having detected Carleill's force, who at that time were lying low, waiting for the dawn. The Governor, nervous because no pinnaces had been reported as approaching the shore – thanks to the handy knife-work of Drake's Cimarron allies at the guard-posts – sent out Tristan de Leguizamo on a new reconnaisance. Tristan caught sight of the English advancing on the town and galloped back to raise the alarm. Thereupon the three Santo Domingo companies marched boldly along the seafront under Captain Melchior de Ochoa de Villanueva to meet the invaders. At the end of the Causeway of the Horses Captain Melchior paused, leaving the task of watching the enemy to Don Juan de Villandrando, who went forward with the cavalry. Don Juan returned with distressing news: the English were advancing in great strength.

These tidings produced frightful scenes in the city, as the women fled precipitately to the woods where they proposed to support themselves on wild fruit. The nuns of two convents did likewise and so, 'to the dishonour of their Spanish blood' – as Fray Pedro Simon[15] alleges – did many of the male inhabitants. Probably they were concerned to protect their womenfolk against the Cimarrons. On the other hand, the monks in three monasteries, along with the archbishop and priests, were willing to be martyred by the heretics. Had everyone followed this example, then certainly they would have repulsed the enemy for 'the sun was at their backs while its scorching rays struck full in the eyes of the advancing English'.[16]

Carleill divided his force into two, ordering Captain Anthony Powell to attack the town gate that was nearer the sea while he, at the head of the 'main battle', entered by the gate immediately to the north. The Spaniards drove herds of cattle against the advancing infantry, harassed them ineffectively with cavalry and laid an ambush of musketeers which failed. The English advance continued. In front were the city walls and Spanish artillery. When men began falling around him, Carleill quickened the pace so that he and his pikemen rushed through the gates along with the retreating Spaniards.

Meanwhile Drake, lying offshore, had kept up an enfilading fire along the streets of the town, thereby causing the only Spanish casualty of the day, that of the Bachelor Tostado, who was killed when a cannon ball hit him. Now, seeing that Carleill and Powell were inside the walls, Drake ordered the cease-fire. From the flagship, he could see the Spaniards tumbling into boats and rowing madly across the harbour to safety. Better still, he could see the red cross of St George broken from a tower in the city. Carleill and Powell had kept their rendezvous in the Plaza Mayor of Santo Domingo.

The fleet saluted the victory with its guns and Drake put ashore a party which quickly took possession of the deserted Palace and the government buildings. On the grand staircase of the Palace they found painted an escutcheon – a horse with one foot on the globe and the other in the air. The motto ran: *Non sufficit orbis* – the world is not enough. Boastful or pious? In any case, it was the cause of some merriment among the English.

Carleill made the Plaza secure with barricades, in building which he made use of church images (as Fray Pedro reports), knowing that the Spaniards would be reluctant to fire on them. Protestant feeling being what it was at the time, the report is probably true. The castle was still holding out but, before the assault on it began, its garrison had made off across the harbour. It was, by that time, a little after midnight. 'Thus the Spaniards gave us the town for a New Year's gift.'

The whole operation had gone off like clockwork. If Carleill was mainly responsible for its execution, the planning and the speed of the business have the marks of Drake's imagination. The most illustrious city in the Indies had fallen – God's punishment, as Fray Pedro wrote, on the Spaniards for their atrocious cruelty to the natives. There had been 1,600,000 of them on the island when the Spaniards arrived;[17] forty years had passed since one of them had been seen alive. And whether the friar's figures are correct or not, the ghastly fact of genocide is as he described it.

Drake and his men settled down in the abandoned city behind entrenchments which they strengthened with captured guns. And, being the practical warriors they were, they made a systematic search of the city for hidden treasure. In vain, as the accepted narrative says, although Fray Pedro speaks of ropes of pearls, bars of gold, etc., taken from their hiding-places in wells and cellars. The Governor of Santo Domingo, who had found refuge in the hills near by, opened negotiations for ransom with the commander of the occupying forces. At first, these talks went badly. A Spanish officer from the royal galley which lay in the harbour rode up to the English outpost with a flag of truce. Drake sent out his black servant to receive the message but the Spaniard, regarding this as an insult, ran the boy through. Drake at once demanded that the Spaniard be executed. When no action followed, he strung up two friars on the scene of the murder and informed the Governor that two more would be executed every day at the same time until the murderer was surrendered. Next morning, the Spanish officer was duly brought to the lines. But Drake's indignation was not appeased until the Spaniards themselves had executed him.

While he waited for the Governor to take a reasonable view about the ransom for the town, he put a party of seamen to work destroying it systematically. It was a hard task, for the buildings were substantial, and at the end of a month of burning and demolition, two-thirds of Santo Domingo was still intact. Was it worth waiting for the remainder to be destroyed? Especially since Drake had a great deal still to do elsewhere; and he was far behind with his programme. After a month's stay, then, he accepted the Governor's offer of 25,000 ducats and re-embarked his men.[18] In addition to the ransom, he had taken two hundred and forty cannon, burnt the royal galley and all the other vessels he found in the port, with the exception of an unusually fine galleon of French construction. This he carried off, along with a great many slaves liberated from the benches of the galley. He was on his way to Cartagena on the mainland of New Granada.

XIII

The Damage Done by this Corsair

'It seems as if Nature had destined [the Spaniards] to occupy the West Indies to enrich the industrious who could not live there.'

Thomas Jefferys

Cartagena, lying on the eastward side of the Gulf of Darien, was one of the richest prizes on the coast of Spanish South America. The city was an important commercial centre, although lacking the historical prestige of Santo Domingo. It was correspondingly hard to attack. This was due, not so much to the fortifications which the Spanish had built, as to the natural strength which geography had conferred.

Cartagena was built on a sandbank between a steamy mangrove swamp which enclosed two sides of the town and a long lagoon which covered the third side. The fourth side faced the open sea but could not be approached by ships. The lagoon was divided into an outer basin and an inner harbour by a spit of land which thrust southwards to within two ship's lengths of the mainland. At this point, where a narrow channel joined the two basins of the lagoon, a fort stood on guard with sixteen guns. When danger threatened, a chain could be drawn across. At the closed end of the lagoon to the north the promontory which formed it was joined to the town by a causeway, the Caleta, a hundred and fifty yards wide.

Unless there was a surprise attack, or an overwhelming preponderance of force on the English side, Cartagena should have been held easily enough. There was no surprise and, in numbers at least, the two sides were evenly matched. The Governor of the city, Don Piero Fernandez de Busto, had three weeks' warning that Drake was on his way. Thereupon the Governor ordered military exercises to be carried out every day and sowed the foreshore with poisoned stakes. Across the Caleta he built a breast-high stone barricade in which a gap was left open for mounted patrols to go in and out. Heavy guns were brought up into position here. At its seaward end, this barrier degenerated into a mere line of wine-butts filled with earth. Other preparations for defence were made. For instance, the women retired to the hills outside the town and all images were hidden from 'the bestial fury of the heretics'.

In the inner harbour were stationed an armed galleass and two galleys, the *Occasion* and *La Napolitana*, which could bring an enfilading fire to bear should the English attempt an attack along the causeway. These ships had a hundred and fifty professional arquebusiers on board under a distinguished soldier, Don Pedro Vique Manrique, general in command of all the coastal defence of the Spanish Main. Apart from these regular troops, the Governor had at his disposal 50 lancers, 450 arquebusiers, 100 pikemen, 20 Negro musketeers and 400 Indian archers.

Against these defenders, Drake could not expect to land an assault force numbering as many as a thousand. Battle casualties and, far more, disease, had cut down the numbers of combatants available to him. And, in fact, sickness was still at work in the fleet. Hardly a day passed but the burial service was to be heard on the deck of one vessel or another. Flags were dipped and a new small scratch was made on morale. For that reason alone, Drake was in a hurry.

The ships sailed along the coast, within range of the Cartagena guns. It was 9 February, Ash Wednesday, and the Governor had just received a new warning of the impending onslaught. It came by a vessel fresh from Spain which also brought the good news that, in a week's time, the latest galleon to reinforce the Indies Squadron would arrive. This news heartened the local population at the time when Drake's show of force gave them a chance to estimate, and even over-estimate, the strength that was coming against them. Drake, ignoring two shots from the land batteries, was rowed at his leisure along the seafront in a small boat. What impressed the spectators most, however, was that he was dressed all in black. The English ships were draped in the same funereal colour. What was the reason for this? Mourning? It is possible, although no personage of note is known to have died. More likely, the black emblems were a signal to the Cimarrons. If so, the signal was seen and answered.[1]

The English ships anchored at the Jews' Cape in the outer basin a mile from the entrance to the inner harbour. That same evening Drake put his infantry ashore on a beach from which they could march through wooded country to the Caleta. Meanwhile he kept the defence in a fever of doubt about what he meant to do. His fleet was placed as if it was about to break through into the inner harbour, and Frobisher was detached, with the pinnaces, to carry out a diversion against the fort covering the entrance.

Drake had heard an important piece of news. Two Negro fishermen, heirs of the old Cimarron alliance, had slipped aboard the *Bonaventure* to warn him about the poisoned stakes on the foreshore. He passed the information on to Carleill and the other leaders of the attack. As dusk closed in the soldiers on the beach formed up, waist-deep in the water. Command of the vanguard was divided between the Irishman Sampson, who led the pikes, and Goring (English), who led the musketeers. The main battle was under the Sergeant-Major, Anthony Powell, and the rear was commanded by another Welshman, Captain Morgan.

Captain Wynter, although a sea officer, had joined the landing party. In his eagerness for a fight he had bartered his ship for Captain Cecil's company of foot. He marched with the rest. Overall command was assigned to Carleill.

Among the defenders of the city there was something that fell short of unanimous enthusiasm for the battle. Complaints were heard that the rich were looking after their own safety. The soldiers wanted a rise in pay. Don Pedro Vique heard with disgust of one citizen who, after boasting of his courage, had fled disguised as a woman. When Governor Busto addressed the soldiers he was greeted with disloyal murmurs. Finally, however, the defenders of the city marched out to do battle with colours displayed and drums and fifes making music. To this martial incitement was added the support of the spiritual arm. The bishop, Don Fray Juan de Montalvo, whose sermons were much admired, marched with all his prebendaries and priests, armed with rapiers and halberds. So, too, did Fray Bartolomé de Sierra, prior of the Dominican monastery, and Fray Sebastian de Garibay, of the Franciscan friary. There was thus no lack of reminders, brown-robed or black, that the Church militant was involved in this business. Encouraging as this may have been, it was somewhat less so to men who believed, as the defending force seems to have done, that they were about to meet nine thousand English infantry – or just ten times as many as Carleill had under his orders.

His soldiers marched in the darkness towards the town holding to the seaward shore of the Caleta, knee-deep in the water. Thus they were clear of the poisoned stakes, while they were hidden by the ridge of the Caleta from the guns of the two galleys in the harbour.

Just two miles short of the town, the English infantry had a brush with Spanish horsemen. Frobisher, in his pinnace, a mile and a half farther south, may have heard the sounds of this clash, for at that moment he opened fire on the fort. It was hot work, at close range. The pinnace of the *Primrose* had her rudder shot away. The top of her mainmast was hit and oars were struck out of men's hands as they rowed.

About this time, the main action was going briskly forward in the first light of dawn. Carleill, carrying a partisan, put himself at the head of the vanguard and led the onrush against the line of wine-butts on the shore. His musketeers fired a volley. As the smoke cleared, pikemen passed through their ranks and ran, stumbling, cursing and cheering, along the beach towards the defences. There was a scrambling, vicious little skirmish in which the English had the advantage of longer pikes and heavier armour, the Spaniards being accustomed in hot climates to fight in quilted cotton jackets. Even so, casualties were heavier among the English owing to the effectiveness of the Spanish guns. For a moment, indeed, the attack wavered. Then the wine-butts were overturned and the Spanish seaward flank was broken. Among the defenders the alarming rumour spread that the town had already fallen and that they should flee to avoid being surrounded and massacred.

One Spaniard stood his ground, Cosme de Blas, the standard-bearer, a stout fighter who killed two Englishmen with the spearhead of his banner. Then Carleill felled him with a stroke of his partisan and snatched the standard. All the English officers were bloodily in the thick of the business. Sampson, brandishing his sword at the head of his pikemen, was wounded. Goring met in single combat the Spanish commander of the section, wounded him and made the man his prisoner. Wynter, who had apparently become separated from his company, fought at Carleill's side. Now that the main defence line had been broken there was nothing between the English and Cartagena but routed Spaniards. Already, says a Spanish authority, the Indian bowmen had fled.

One attempt was made, however, to rally the defence. Don Pedro Vique, commander of the galleys, rode forward with twenty lancers. 'Fight for your Spanish blood and Catholic faith!' he shouted. But the appeal came too late to save the day. The cavalry galloped off to the town and from that moment Don Pedro devoted himself to the fate of his galleys, which he ordered to be removed to safety. Here again misfortune fell on the Spaniards. A soldier, distributing gunpowder on the *Ocasion*, was careless in his work. A powder barrel exploded and the *Ocasion* caught fire. The slaves abandoned their oars and escaped, those of them who were Turks giving themselves up to the English. In the meantime, the chain across the harbour mouth had been removed so the second galley, *La Napolitana*, could escape. In their haste to be off, however, the crew ran the galley ashore and the soldiers aboard leapt on to the land and disappeared. In disgust, Don Pedro gave orders that *La Napolitana* should have her cargo unloaded and be burnt.

Fighting from one barricade to another, the English came at

length to the main square of the town, where they met a desperate resistance in front of a new and still unfinished church. The firing of a big cannon shook down part of the church wall. Its collapse seems to have induced a wave of defeatism The garrison fled southwards out of the city over a bridge and into the country beyond. About the same time the Governor, who had retired to a village near by, ordered Pedro Mejia, holding out in the fort against Frobisher's guns, to withdraw.

Cartagena had fallen at a cost in English lives which, in the circumstances, was not excessive. Perhaps thirty were killed. The worst blow to Drake came soon after the fall of the town. His old comrade-in-arms, Captain Tom Moone, was killed. Moone had heard a sentry posted in a church tower in Cartagena call out that two small craft were entering the inner harbour. At once, he, along with Captain Varney, and John Grant, master of the *Tiger*, went off in two pinnaces to investigate. The Spaniards ran their boats aground and made off into the bushes. While the English were taking over the abandoned boats, a blast of musket fire came from the snipers hidden among the trees. Moone and Varney fell dead.

On the second day, the city was given over to the looters. The official English story is that, as at Santo Domingo, the booty fell far short of the men's expectations. The Spaniards say that treacherous Negroes betrayed to Drake where they had hidden their valuables and that the plunder amounted to about 250,000 ducats. On the whole, the picture of crestfallen British soldiers and seamen baulked of their prey, in this prosperous colonial city, can be looked on with some scepticism. It is not in the least likely that, on this occasion or any other, the amount of the loot declared on the returns to the Customs bore any relation to the real value of the 'import'. Human nature is what it is.[2]

What is certain is that the hope of plunder, illusory or otherwise, helped to give special bite to the English onset. Long afterwards, Raleigh, comparing the poor performance of English troops in the bogs of Ireland with their verve and pertinacity in the Caribbean fighting, ascribed the difference to the profit motive lacking in the former: 'No man makes haste to the market where there is nothing to be bought but blows.'[3]

Thanks to his Negro allies, Drake's intelligence was good. Thanks to his own talent, the attack was shrewdly planned so as to divide the Spanish defence effort. It may be admitted, too, that the Cartagena defence was ill-organised. It was plainly absurd to keep the two royal galleys immobile in harbour. This was pointed out in a sharp memorandum written next year by no less a personage than the Duke of Medina Sidonia, first grandee of Spain. Some years later, after a far greater disaster to Spanish arms, the Duke himself was to be the target of criticism. In the meantime, he enjoyed all the advantages of the untested critic.

After the Cartagena failure, Don Pedro Vique was arrested and sentenced to death. This was later commuted to life imprisonment. To the general accusation of incompetence were added allegations of fraud. Don Pedro's private life was far from spotless. But he had one advantage. His brother was the Bishop of Majorca who employed his influence successfully to free Don Pedro from his cell in the Castle of Peniscola, on the Valencian coast. In fact, Don Pedro could not fairly be blamed for the poor display made by his galleys. He had wanted to go out and meet the enemy in the open sea but had been overborne by the population, who felt that he was proposing to desert them.

While the occupying troops busied themselves with digging for hidden jewellery, insulting church images or – most horrifying of all to the Spanish clergy – listening to 'the tenets of Luther' being preached on the terraces of the Governor's residence, Drake settled down to the serious business of war. When Bishop Tristan de Oribe, at the head of a delegation, arrived to discuss the matter of ransom he found the Englishman in a furious temper. Drake had just come upon a letter from the King of Spain in which he was described as 'a corsair'.

The English commander refused even to talk about money until the bishop had apologised for this insult to one whose flagship flew the royal standard of England. At length, simmering down, he demanded 600,000 ducats.* The bishop made an offer of 100,000 which Drake dismissed as derisory. Negotiations continued in the usual dilatory way until Drake, losing patience, gave orders for the systematic destruction of the town. He had one good reason for haste.

He has been criticised by historians for not holding Cartagena once it was in his hands. On the map, it seems to be just the base he needed in the Caribbean. But Cartagena had allies stronger than the galleons of King Philip: the anopheles mosquito and the bacillus of yellow fever. Set amidst its swamps, it was an unhealthy city on an unhealthy coast, much troubled by the Calenture, an infection which the inhabitants attributed to the evening air, La Serena. Two centuries later, an English author sombrely remarked that 'a person of a humane disposition' considering the dire effects of the climate of the Indies, especially on the English, 'cannot help deploring the insatiable desire that carries such crowds to these countries'.[4] The steady drain by sickness on the strength and morale of the expeditionary force induced Drake to settle for a ransom only ten per cent above the first Spanish offer. In addition, he claimed 1,000 crowns as the price of sparing a monastery situated a quarter of a mile outside the town. The fort at the harbour mouth he blew up.

Before agreeing to these terms he had asked his officers if they thought they could hold the town. The soldiers' answer was a reluctant 'Yes', conditional on the Navy guaranteeing to give protection against the fleet which was known to be on its way from Spain. What the sea officers believed can be deduced from the fact that the English fleet departed soon afterwards. They returned, however, when 'the New Year's gift', the galleon Drake had taken at Santo Domingo, was found to be sinking.

This return caused a renewed panic among the townspeople. But Drake wanted only the use of their ovens to bake biscuit. A few days after he sailed, the Spanish rescue fleet arrived at Cartagena, greeted by bitter sarcasm from the inhabitants, who

* Roughly £150,000 at that time.

sneered at 'Spanish help – an old ass laden with lances lacking steel heads'.

The whole of the Caribbean area was by this time in a state of nervous hubbub in which the wildest rumours gained credence: twenty thousand Englishmen were coming to conquer the New Kingdom of Granada! The entire black population had joined the invaders, who had later massacred them, lest they should again change sides! The Indians in Santa Marta had risen in revolt! Horrific stories like that kept nerves on edge.

But Drake had by this time so few men fit to fight that any idea of an attack on Panama was perforce abandoned. This was discouraging, for it meant giving up all thought of 'the stroke for the treasure and full recompense of our tedious travails'. But there was no alternative. Havana was another possible objective.

With the Negroes, Indians and liberated galley slaves, of whom he had gathered in all five hundred of both sexes aboard the ships, he contemplated establishing a settlement in the area with a fortified harbour which could serve as a base for later English operations. But this project, too, was reluctantly given up because of a strong, persistent and adverse wind.

He had one more task to attempt before sailing for England. He would pay a visit to the English settlement which, under Raleigh's inspiration, had been founded at Roanoke in Virginia.[5] Perhaps – it is by no means unlikely – he intended to reinforce it with the ex-slaves and Negroes he had taken aboard at Cartagena. By the middle of May, then, the fleet was skirting the coast of Florida sniffing out, on its way to the north, any Spanish forts from which attack on the young English colony might be launched.

From a Portuguese pilot, faithless to the Spaniards as were so many of his kind, he picked up useful information: the Spaniards had established a base at San Agustin in Florida at the place where Jean Ribault's Huguenots had been massacred. Drake resolved to find it and attack it. The first clue to its position was given when a beacon was seen from the sea standing high on four masts. Drake put a party ashore and marched inland with them along the bank of a river. Carleill, Morgan and Sampson went on reconnaissance in a rowing skiff. They could find no trace of the Spaniards. Then they heard a sound which arrested every movement and caught every breath short. Someone was playing on a fife a tune they knew, the tune which every good Protestant in Europe called 'William of Nassau' – the Prince of Orange's song.[6] Solemn and heavily charged with emotion, the notes, to which Sainte Aldegonde's poem of patriotic defiance of Spain had been set, were eerily arresting and meaningful beside that creek in Florida. It was the most anti-Spanish air in the world . . . Somewhere close by was a friend.

Following the sound, they tracked the fife-player down. He was Nicholas Borgoignon, a French prisoner, who had spent six years in Spanish hands. He had exciting tales to tell of the gold, rubies and diamonds which could be found in the Appalachian mountains by those who, at the price of hatchets presented to the Indians, were permitted to look for them. With the Frenchman as their guide, Drake and Frobisher, along with Carleill and some captains of foot, advanced in skiffs and pinnaces to San Agustin.

They found a newly built fort, built of massive tree-trunks set upright. On top was a platform on which fourteen brass cannon were ranged side by side. In a chest they came upon the garrison's pay, amounting to £2,000. But although the fort was deserted, the enemy was close at hand. When snipers fired from the trees, Anthony Powell, second-in-command of the English infantry, leapt on a horse the Spaniards had left, saddled and bridled, and rode off in pursuit. The pursuit did not last long. Powell was shot in the head and when he fell, was stabbed to death. After that, the English took fewer risks. They demolished the settlement and the fort. Tools and implements which might be of use to colonists were carried off.

Drake was now on his way to Virginia. Anchors were dropped at the entrance to Charleston Harbour, six hundred miles north of San Agustin, and search parties were sent out to look for the

English colony. In the end, it was found that Ralph Lane, the Governor, had built a fort on Roanoke Island. It seemed, however, that Lane had no great confidence in the future of the colony. When Drake realised this, he offered Lane a choice between being taken home by ship along with his colonists and having his needs supplied. Lane chose the latter and was sent a 70-ton ship and two pinnaces. They were apparently not enough to restore morale and, when the new ship was lost in a hurricane, Lane insisted on being shipped home. Thus, rather tamely, ended the first English attempt to settle in the New World.

Drake's fleet arrived in Portsmouth on 28 July 1586. It had been absent just ten months and it had achieved moral and political results out of all proportion to its material consequences. Only in one respect had it fallen short of the hopes of its backers. Money. After a careful audit of the spoils, it was found that the shareholders must be content with a dividend of 15 shillings in the pound. The expedition had cost just under £60,000 to send out. It came back with valuables worth about that sum, including two hundred and forty brass cannon. It had released many galley slaves, a hundred of whom, Turks, the Queen sent to the Grand Signior, whom she was cultivating for military and commercial reasons. Of the declared plunder, the ships' companies, as was their due, took a third – £6 a head, plus anything that might have found its way into their sea-chests.

Looked on as a commercial enterprise, then, the raid on the Indies was hardly a triumph. The only hope that it might be one had vanished when Drake missed the treasure fleet – 'the cause best known to God'[7] – by twelve hours, a misfortune which he bemoaned to the Lord Treasurer on his return. But, without some extraordinary stroke of luck, an expeditionary force of 2,300 men and more than twenty ships could not be expected to pay its way. Only in the dreams of Elizabethan Treasury officials can war be conducted as a business.

Drake's voyage of 1585–6 was conceived as a stroke of policy, an act of war. Its ultimate purpose – in which it failed – was to bring Philip to the negotiating table. What it accomplished was to expose the weaknesses inherent in the imposing but over-extended Spanish power and to do so at a time when its might seemed most overwhelming. With insolent ease, four of Spain's colonial settlements had been taken and pillaged. 'We have neither artillery nor powder, neither arquebuses nor men experienced in war.' The complaint of Santo Domingo was echoed by Cartagena: 'The damage done by this corsair amounts to more than 400,000 ducats. The English have left this city completely destroyed and desolate.'[8] The Venetian ambassador in Madrid, Gradenigo, reported that Lisbon and Castile were in an uproar over Drake's depredations, and that the King, in a panic, had, on Easter Monday, called the Marquis de Santa Cruz into secret consultations at the Escorial. The Seville fleet of fourteen ships was to reinforce the men already at Lisbon. The trouble was, said the ambassador, that the Seville troops were the mere dregs of the population, released convicts and the like, many of whom had already deserted.[9] In Spain, it seemed, the ranks were filled by much the same types as in England.*

The King irresolute, finances embarrassed, Drake – a humane man it appeared, on the testimony of men he had taken prisoner – at large again, bound for God knows where! Was it any wonder that the bankers on whom Philip depended for his flow of cash showed a disagreeable lethargy in the matter of fresh loans. For how credit-worthy was a monarch who had been unable to defend his most important overseas possessions? About this time Gritti, the Venetian ambassador in Rome, heard that the Pope had been impressed by Drake's successes in the Caribbean. He thought the King of Spain would do well to hurry up. Was Philip's health all right? His Holiness was worried about it. The King's gout was apparently troublesome. Well, well, he was entering on his sixtieth year and it was notorious that the House of Austria died young.[10]

Drake now moved in a haze of glory. Gossips in the London

* 'We disburden the prisons of thieves, we rob the taverns and alehouses of tosspots and ruffians, we scour both town and country for rogues and vagabonds.' Barnaby Rich.

taverns said that the Queen meant to make him a peer. The French Ambassador sent copies of his portrait to the dukes of Joyeuse and Epernon and other favourites of Henri III.[11] From Paris, where Mendoza had established his listening post, a stream of anti-Drake rumours was directed towards King Philip. The Queen, he was told, had not received a groat from the proceeds of the voyage; the soldiers had taken all the booty. On the other hand, the sailors were said to be discontented with results because Drake had kept everything to himself – apart from 50,000 ducats which he had sent to Leicester. The truth was that Mendoza's intelligence service was no longer quite as accurate as it had been when he lived in London.

In one respect, the raid on the Indies had been costly. Seven hundred and fifty men had lost their lives in it, most of them as a result of disease. It was more than thirty per cent of the force that had sailed from Plymouth and it included distinguished captains like Anthony Powell, Tom Moone, Fortescue, Bigges, Cecil, Hannam and Grenville.

A fortnight after Drake's return to England, Anthony Babington was arrested. The long-drawn-out and perilous drama of Mary Stuart's life had entered its ultimate crisis and with her execution, which followed six months later, the final obstacle was removed to a full-scale attack upon England by the King of Spain. Already commercial and financial interests were urging war on the Catholic monarch as the only way of ending the insulting and troublesome forays which were undermining the pride, peace and power of his empire. Now a victory over the island freebooters and their perfidious queen, if it were gained, would not be for the profit of the Scottish queen who was, after all, a Frenchwoman, a Guise princess. In making herself a martyr for the Catholic faith, Mary did something else which won Philip's approval. She bequeathed to him her most precious heirloom, the succession to the English throne. For months he had been adding galleon to galleon and gun to gun in the hope that the mere rumour of his growing strength would bring Elizabeth to reason. In much the same way, the Queen had thought that her undeclared war might induce a mood of accommodation in the stiff-necked Hapsburg. Instead, the drift towards war had become a current of growing power and speed.

With lamenting Spanish colonists and burning cities behind him and the cheers of the Portsmouth mob in his ears, Drake can hardly have expected in that late summer of 1586 to spend a long time in idleness ashore. The great clash was at hand, to which, as an instinctive man of action, he looked forward with supreme confidence. In the meantime, he was to write, in blood and fire, on Philip's own coast, a new preface to the main theme.

XIV

The Wind Commands Me Away

'Drak est en mer vers la coste de Hespaigne.'
('Drake is at sea on his way to the coast of Spain.')
Claude de l'Aubespine, French Ambassador in London, March 1587[1]

On 2 April 1587 Drake put to sea anew. He had been just eight months at home. They had been eight months of plans and counter-plans, projects that had been prepared and then abandoned, alarms and calms. During that time, he had crossed to Holland to try to persuade the Dutch to take part in a new assault on Portugal in aid of Dom Antonio, that eternal Pretender. But the Dutch did not trust the steadfastness of Queen Elizabeth's resolution far enough to fall in with an English scheme. Nothing came of the proposal.

Where all was confusion and frustration, where the Queen seemed to have raised indecision to a principle of statecraft, one grim certainty rose out of the swirl: Mary Stuart was dead, with all that implied for Spanish policy and Catholic propaganda. The first news of the Scottish queen's execution had arrived from Mendoza at the Escorial on 23 March, just thirty-three days after the event it reported – and just a week before Sir Francis Drake sailed out of Plymouth Sound.

All controversies were now resolved or, if not resolved, evaded. His orders were clear, or clear enough. He was to distress Spanish ships within their harbours, capture their sea-borne supplies and do all he could to 'impeach the drawing together of the King of Spain's fleets out of their several ports'[2] to the main base of Lisbon, where the ships were to assemble under the Marquis of Santa Cruz. No assignment could be plainer. It is true that, a week after Drake departed, the Privy Council in London drafted a fresh set of instructions based on the Queen's alleged belief that she could detect in the King of

Spain a new spirit of conciliation. Drake was therefore not to force his way into any Spanish harbour, attack any Spanish town or 'do any act of hostility upon the land'. However, a pinnace, sent from Plymouth with the revised orders, failed to overtake Drake's fleet, which was hardly surprising since he had nine days' start.

Whether the new instructions were ever seriously intended to reach the Queen's admiral may be doubted. The episode is too reminiscent of Elizabeth's tortuous behaviour over the execution of Mary Stuart. On that occasion, Secretary Davidson was threatened with the gallows and Lord Treasurer Burghley was pursued with 'marvellous cruel speeches, calling him traitor, false dissembler and wicked wretch', and all because they had arranged for the execution of a woman whose death sentence the Queen had signed! The belated dispatch might help to clear her of responsibility should Drake go too far and King Philip lose his temper. And, since it could not arrive in time, it would not frustrate any practical benefits from the expedition.

Drake was, all through that period of international crisis, in an exalted frame of mind, aware of a sense of mission, touched as he thought by divine approval and, with the meek arrogance of the religious, liable to view opposition to his will as akin to apostasy. He was on the brink of his most brilliant campaign and what shone out before long as an inspired audacity in action is to be seen already in the fervour of his letter to Walsingham on the day he sailed:

> 'The wind commands me away. Our ship is under sail. God grant we may so live in His fear as the enemy may have cause to say that God doth fight for Her Majesty as well abroad as at home . . . Pray unto God for us that He will direct us the right way; then we shall not doubt our enemies, for they are the sons of men.'[3]

Here, obviously, was the religious enthusiasm that belonged to the age. But was there not something else, too, older and even more profound? 'The wind commands me away. Our ship is under sail.' In the joyous lilt of these sentences there is something that Drake shared with all the sea rovers: Columbus, Leif Erikson, Ulysses himself. The thrill of escape from queens, statesmen, domestic concerns, and the cramping letter of the law, into the infectious anarchy of the sea. He knew that he was at the height of his powers; he did not doubt of success.

Considering the task ahead, a challenge to King Philip in his own waters, the fleet which Drake led out of Plymouth was none too numerous. But it was powerful: four ships of the Queen's, including Drake's old flagship, the *Elizabeth Bonaventure*; four other ships which he and his business associates had contributed; a ship of the Lord Admiral's; and eight which nineteen London merchants, prominent in the privateering business, had supplied. There were, also, six pinnaces, likely to be useful in any inshore work. It was, then, a composite fleet partly owned by the state, partly private, as in the case of most naval adventures of that period. Drake had as his second-in-command William Borough, a Devon man like himself, a regular naval officer with a gallant record at sea in the Baltic; Borough was respected among the graver navigators for his *Discourse of the Variation of the Compass*. He was six years older than his admiral. Captain Robert Flick, member of the Drapers' Company, nominee of the City of London, was vice-admiral of the fleet. Aboard were ten companies of infantry under Captain Anthony Platt. These soldiers were to carry out one of the most gallant exploits of the campaign that lay ahead.

Somewhere off Lisbon, Drake picked up the news from Flemish merchantmen that Cadiz harbour was packed with ships. On 19 April he called a council of war at which he gave perfunctory attention to the views of the others, having already made up his mind what he was going to do. William Borough, in particular, was shocked by this unconventional way of conducting a war, 'wherein', as he complained by letter to Drake at the time, 'we have served but as witnesses to the words you have delivered; or else you have used us well by entertaining us with your good cheer . . . and we have departed as wise as we came.' He was even more dismayed by the outcome of these 'assemblies', as he called them. Drake announced that he was going into Cadiz Bay at once; they were all to follow him and destroy what shipping they found there. The scheme had a splendid simplicity more appealing to one who had known the results of surprise onsets in the Pacific than to a prim naval technician like Borough.

The harbour defences of Cadiz were reasonably strong. The topographical lay-out of the port resembled a funnel which first narrowed and then opened out again into a basin shaped like a retort and roughly four miles across. This was the inner harbour. The city of Cadiz straddled a detached spit of land, an island, although joined to the mainland by a bridge. This protected the harbour from the open water. On its seaward side it rose cliff-like out of the water. In order to make their way into the harbour, ships must sail through a narrow channel, skirting dangerous shoals and coming under the gunfire of a castle which had been built fifty years earlier as a protection against the Algerine corsair, Barbarossa. (This fortress was less dangerous than it looked.) In addition, there was in attendance a pack of galleys under an experienced officer, Don Pedro de Acuña, which had been detained in port by high winds. Among the shoals of confined waters like this, the oar-driven, shallow-draught galley, with its complete command over speed and direction, should enter into its own. Coming in under the land, Drake might lose the wind and would then be at the mercy of the galleys' rams. On the other hand, he had more gun-power in the *Elizabeth Bonaventure* than there was in the whole galley fleet.

He went in to attack at four o'clock in the afternoon, his ships flying French or Flemish colours. As he did so, two galleys put out from Port St Mary on the distant side of the bay. They wanted to know his business. The *Bonaventure* made towards them at once, her guns blazing. At the same time, she and her consorts hoisted the Cross of St George. The galleys sheered off out of range. Drake ordered his helmsman to bring the ship's head round so that it was pointing towards the harbour. He could see, to his satisfaction, that sixty sail of merchant ships were alongside the quays.

They had been loading or unloading. Many of them lacked their sails, which had been removed because these were foreign ships which had been commandeered by the Spanish authorities and, if given the opportunity, might desert King Philip's service. Most of them were waiting for their artillery, at that moment on its way by sea from Italy. At the sound of Drake's guns, all this mass of shipping was thrown into the wildest confusion. Everything that could move on the water cut its cables and bolted for safety. The smaller boats hurried across the shoal water to Port St Mary. Half a dozen Flemish cargo boats made for the inner harbour.

To the citizens the invasion of their harbour came as a complete surprise. They had been passing the afternoon agreeably, and now there were these unknown ships suddenly crowding into the bay – for what purpose had they come to Cadiz? The noise of the guns, rolling across the water and echoing back from the farther shore, made that only too plain. The Governor sent the women, children and old people to the citadel. But the citadel gates were firmly shut in the faces of the refugees, and more than a score of them were crushed to death before the commander of the fortress relented. Citizens picked up what arms they could find, forgetting in their haste to lock their doors against looters. Soldiers were dispatched to the point of rock where the channel between the outer and the inner harbour is narrowest. And a message was sent across the bay to the Duke of Medina Sidonia who, as the most important magnate in the province, was expected to organise the rescue of the city. As soon as he received it, the Duke dispatched fast couriers to Seville and Jerez, ordering those towns to send reinforcements to Cadiz. Then he set off for the scene of action.

Meanwhile, in Cadiz Bay, ten galleys of Pedro de Acuña's command rowed out, as was their duty, and launched themselves at the beam of the incoming English fleet. They ran into the broadsides of four Royal Navy warships, sailing across their bows. The English shot struck them before their own bow guns were within range of the invading ships. With all decent speed, the galleys left the scene either for the inner harbour or for the shelter of the guns of Cadiz fortress. The shipping in the outer harbour could now be pillaged or destroyed at the convenience of the English. There was one exception, a Genoese argosy of 700 tons, loaded with cochineal and logwood and, since it carried forty guns, a match for any two ships in Drake's flotilla. What is more, it was willing to fight.

Naval gunfire in the sixteenth century was notable for noise and smoke rather than for accuracy. '*Il fait plus de peur que du mal*' ('It causes more fear than damage'), as Montluc said, scornfully. And even if that remark is put aside as exaggerated, guns were certainly inaccurate and the effective range was modest. Beyond two hundred yards – the range of a musket – a cannon was useless.* As for accuracy, the windage of a gun, i.e. the difference between the diameters of the bore and the bullet, was by no means uniform. For those reasons, there was more banging than blasting in the average sea-fight of the time. Besides, a wooden ship is very hard to sink.

However, a close-up duel in a sheltered harbour provided ideal conditions for the naval gunners of the time. After a good deal of pounding, the obstinate Genoese, firing her brass guns to the last, went down. She was mourned by the victors, who hated to see forty good cannon lost. Meanwhile, the English ships that were not involved in this main engagement were busy with those other cargo boats that had not been able to reach the inner harbour. Burning some and towing off others – it was a congenial task which the guns of the coastal batteries hardly disturbed. When night fell, the outer port of Cadiz was under a heavy pall of smoke through which ships, burning like torches, reeled crackling towards the shoals.

Drake ordered Captain Flick in the *Merchant Royal* to anchor

* 'Fighting farther off [than pistol shot] is like a Smithfield fray, nothing but wasting and consuming of powder.' Sir William Monson.

with the London squadron out of reach of the Cadiz guns, near the entrance to the inner harbour. He himself with the Queen's ships kept a watch on the galleys. Borough urged that the fleet should now clear out. But Drake would have none of it. He had not finished with Cadiz yet. Apart from anything else, he had still nothing to take home to the shareholders. The ships spent the hours of darkness uneasily at anchor, where they lay.

On the Spanish side the alarm went up after midnight that an English landing was imminent near the bastion of St Philip. It was low tide; a cold, damp night. The sentries strung out along the shore depended on the light given by blazing tar barrels. One of Acuña's galleys had run aground and the noise made by her crew as they worked to get her off was mistaken on shore for the coming of an English assault party. However, good news came: at the bridge that joined Cadiz to the mainland a guard of arquebusiers was in position, while a relief force was hurrying on its way from Jerez

The people who had taken refuge in the citadel recovered their courage and went to church to give thanks for their deliverance. Those who had left their houses unlocked went back, expecting the worst. But nothing had been touched. This, in a town teeming with Moors, slaves and suchlike untrustworthy elements, was thought to be indeed miraculous.

At daybreak, Drake took his flagship closer to the inner harbour, where he knew there lay a fine galleon belonging to the Marquis of Santa Cruz, commander-designate of the fleet with which King Philip was proposing to invade England. This ship had lately arrived in Cadiz from the shipyards on the Biscay coast to take on her cannon; she was laden with wine. Two galleys were on guard over her and the other merchantmen which had taken refuge from the attack of the previous evening. Drake collected a flotilla of pinnaces and boats and led them into the attack.

Before long, Santa Cruz's galleon was surrounded by a swarm of little craft and her decks were overrun by English boarders. Resistance was soon at an end. Having taken the ship, they looted it thoroughly; having looted it, they set it on fire. Other ships that could be reached were similarly treated. There was a ship about to take on spices, nails, horseshoes, etc., for a voyage to the Indies. Four ships were loaded with victuals for the King of Spain's armada at Lisbon. Some of these were sunk; some were fired; some were towed away.

When Drake went back to his flagship he left the inner basin of Cadiz harbour filled with the reek of burning ships. In the *Bonaventure* he found Borough, his second-in-command, shaking his head over the recklessness of the morning's work. After a time Borough set off in his boat to return to his own ship. What followed is in some doubt. Borough's story is that, while he was absent looking for Drake, his ship, the *Golden Lion*, came under fire from a shore gun, and the master began to warp it out towards the open sea. At this point, seeing the *Lion* dangerously isolated, the galleys darted out from their sheltered position behind the shoals of Port St Mary. Drake, who observed that his vice-admiral was in some danger, moved seven ships to his support. Borough then anchored in the harbour mouth. (Drake's opinion was that his vice-admiral, who had taken no pains to hide his disapproval of the whole operation, was keeping his ships out of trouble.) Borough claimed later that he posted them there to beat off the galleys should they attack the main fleet. What is certain is that there was a clash of temperament between the two men and the Drake became convinced that Borough was disloyal to him.

But now the work was finished. Twenty-four ships, perhaps as many as thirty, had been taken or destroyed. Considerable damage had been done and little had been suffered. Five unlucky sailors whose craft had trailed too far behind the main fleet on the way in had been snapped up by galleys. The master gunner of the *Golden Lion* had his leg broken by a shot from a shore cannon. And that was all. But now it was time to leave, with drums beating and trumpets sounding in strident derision from the English ships. At that point, one of those dangerous situations arose to which sailing-ships were subject when they operated in closed waters. Hardly had Drake hoisted the signal to withdraw than the wind died.

This was a possibility against which Borough had all the time been warning Drake. His ships were now immobile, in a landlocked harbour. And Cadiz had been reinforced. At the moment when the calm fell on the sea, the Duke of Medina Sidonia, answering frantic appeals for help, marched into the town with three hundred horse and three thousand foot. Encouraged by the arrival of this nobleman, Cadiz prepared to avenge itself for the affront it had suffered. Culverins were brought down to the foreshore. Fireships were made ready and sent out on the ebbing tide to annoy the invaders.

And there were the galleys. Now, if ever, was their opportunity. But they could do nothing. Again and again they darted into the attack but were beaten off by the English broadsides. Watchful officers and experienced crews had hauled the ships into the right alignment for firing. 'I assure your honour there is no account to be made of his galleys,' wrote Thomas Fenner to Walsingham. 'Twelve of her Majesty's ships will make account of all his galleys in Spain, Portugal and all his dominions within the straits.'

The fireships likewise were coolly fended off by longboats and sent on their way towards the shoals, where they ran aground and burned out. Drake remarked jovially, 'The Spaniards are doing our work for us by burning their own ships.' The shore guns did no damage. About two o'clock in the morning, the weather changed. The cheeks of Drake and his captains were freshened by a wind that had blown up from the land and, in a few minutes, was filling the sails of the fleet. He stood out to sea, past the Cadiz fortifications, unharmed by the fire of their batteries. He beat off the galleys, which, dogged but ineffective, sought to embarrass his escape and, in the open sea, at a moment when the wind had died once again, darted in with a last futile onslaught.

After that attack, too, had been beaten off, Drake and his ships lay at anchor outside the town. He tried to negotiate with the galley commander an exchange of his prisoners against English galley slaves. But although there were courteous talks, on a matter of this kind no Spanish officer was prepared to do business. There was, in any case, no lack of other and more urgent things to think about. Drake wrote an exultant dispatch home. Then he set sail for Cape St Vincent, shadowed as he went by two caravels, acting on instructions from Medina Sidonia.

On the first Sunday after the departure of the English, the people of Cadiz held a solemn procession of gratitude to the convent church of San Francisco. They had good reason to be thankful: the English had not killed one civilian in the town.

One reason why Drake went to Cape St Vincent was that he had just heard that one of the most redoubtable of Spanish admirals, Juan Martinez de Recalde, marked down to be second-in-command of the Enterprise of England, was to be found in those waters. But, apart from that incentive, the Cape had a strategic importance clear to anyone from a glance at a map. There it was, a hundred and fifty miles west of Cadiz, a pivot as it were where the Portuguese coastline, which had been running east and west, suddenly turned due north. All the Spanish shipping coming from the Mediterranean to reinforce or to supply the Armada assembling in Lisbon must sail round the Cape. No more convenient station, therefore, could be found for an English fleet charged, as Drake's was, with the task of impeding Spain's war preparations. So, although as it turned out Recalde with his squadron had been warned in time and had fled to the security of Lisbon, Drake found enough to occupy him at Cape St Vincent. So long as he was on station there, with his powerful fleet, only a major formation of heavily armed galleons could fight its way past him from Cadiz or the Mediterranean to the main Spanish base at Lisbon.

About this time, King Philip, who had been confined to bed with gout which had gone to his knee, and who had been bled twice, felt well enough to get up. He was much distressed by the news from Cadiz, especially as he knew that all Spain expected some counter-action from him. 'The Spanish say that the King thinks and plans while the Queen of England acts,' the Venetian ambassador reported. 'These injuries inflicted by Drake will raise many considerations in the minds of other princes . . .' But what was Philip to do? And what, if there was truth in this rumour that a second English fleet was waiting for the troopships that were bringing to Spain the Sicilian *tercio*? What a relief to hear that Medina Sidonia had arrived at Cadiz and had taken a grip of the business there! Now he ordered the Duke to leave the city and raise troops to be ready to meet the new attack that was expected at any moment. 'I should be more worried about the situation,' he wrote, 'if you were not in charge.'

At sea, Drake had decided that it was not enough to cruise about off Cape St Vincent. It was necessary to establish a shore base where ships could be cleaned and watered. And there, a few miles south and east of Cape St Vincent, at Sagres on the Algarve coast, was a natural harbour, protected by a castle on the cliffs above it. Drake resolved to attack the castle and lay hands on the anchorage.

He had been painfully impressed by what he had seen and what he had picked up from talkative prisoners about the scale of King Philip's preparations. 'Prepare in England,' he wrote to Walsingham, 'strongly and most by sea. Stop him now and stop him ever.'[4] To John Woolley, the Latin Secretary, he wrote a letter on the same day, scrawling in haste a postscript, 'Cease not to pray continually and provide strongly to prevent the worst.'

Ships were being built in Mediterranean ports; guns were being shipped from Italy; Don Diego de Pimentel's Sicilian *tercio*, the fortune of which had been such an anxiety to King Philip, had now arrived at Cartagena, within the Straits. So long as Drake's ships remained on station off Cape St Vincent, Philip's galleons could not be concentrated and Pimentel's soldiers, ear-marked to be a spearhead of the invasion of England, would be compelled to make their way overland to Lisbon. This, in due course, they did, by forced marches.

After hovering about off the Algarve coast and snapping up two Dunkirk flyboats laden with Spanish goods, Drake had tried and failed to surprise the fortified port of Lagos.

Now he resolved to attack the redoubtable castle at Sagres, famous in the history of the sea as the hermitage of Henry the Navigator, the Portuguese prince who more, perhaps, than any man, launched the age of discovery. It was over this attack that Drake broke finally with his restive second-in-command, William Borough, who considered the whole operation crazy, contrary to the instructions which the Lord Admiral had given them and launched by the commander-in-chief without proper consultation with his senior officers. Drake dealt with the dissident officer with his usual vigour. In the heat and sweep of action, Drake was a dangerous man to cross; suspicious, despotic, intolerant and unjust. But if that was Drake at his worst, the assault on Sagres, like the dash and fury of the Cadiz raid, showed him at the top of his form. Borough was unlucky to collide with him at such an hour. Perhaps – indeed, it is likely – Borough meant only to recall the proprieties of the naval service, to offer the sound advice which had not been invited. But he had shared his misgivings with his subordinates; his doubting spirit had infected his ship and to that extent Drake's passionate charge of disloyalty against this veteran naval officer was justified. Borough was deprived of his command and made a prisoner in his own ship, 'expecting daily when the admiral would have executed upon me his bloodthirsty desire as he did upon Doughty'. And Drake landed with eight hundred men at Cape Sagres. His purpose was to storm the castle, a task which, on the face of it, seemed incredible. On three sides cliffs fell a sheer two hundred feet to the sea; on the fourth side, a wall forty feet high and surmounted by battlements impeded the advance of an attacking force.

Through the scattered fig trees, bowed by the wind that always blows up there, past the almond trees with their ash-coloured branches, up to the heights where rare juniper bushes raised their dark pylons. After that climb the sweating English could look down on windmills and the sea that stretches out towards Africa.

Drake took command of the assault. After the failure at Lagos, he had little confidence in the spirit of his subordinates. He had infinite confidence in himself. In helmet and corselet, with targe and sword, he climbed at the head of the troops up the steep slope to the castle gate. There, after a preliminary exchange of musket fire, he demanded the surrender of the garrison. When this was rejected, he called up the pitch and faggots which, in the absence of cannon or explosives, were his only hope of destroying the gate. Under fire from four flanking towers in the wall, he took part in piling and firing the faggots. It was hot work: two of the storming party were killed, many were wounded. But Drake's musketeers kept up a steady covering fire which had miraculous good fortune.

After two hours a trumpet sounded from the castle. A parley! The commander had been badly wounded by two musket balls. The garrison of a hundred and ten men asked terms of surrender, which Drake conceded, generously. He had won a victory which astonished everybody – except himself. For in his mood just then, it is probable that only a repulse would have surprised him. He was now master of the Sagres anchorage, from which a fleet could command the exit from the Mediterranean. This he meant to use as his shore base while denying it to the Spanish ships that were accustomed to call there on the way to and from Gibraltar. He set about dismantling the castle, tumbling its eight cannon over the cliffs into the sea, from which they were salvaged by his longboats and carried off. Neighbouring strong-points were treated in the same way.

While these demolitions were taking place ashore, the rest of the fleet had been carrying out savage destructive raids against the local shipping and fisheries. Nets were taken and burnt; forty-seven caravels taking barrel-hoops and such-like stores to the Armada at Lisbon were seized. In the evening, the ships came back to Sagres and took off the infantry who had been finishing their task of demolition at the castle. One of the captured flyboats, an exceptionally fast sailer, was sent off to England with dispatches for the Queen and Walsingham; two other flyboats were sent home with the sick. Drake suggested to Walsingham that he should be reinforced. Six more of the Queen's ships 'of the second sort' would, he said, enable him to prevent the Spanish forces from uniting and, 'in my poor judgment, will bring this great monarchy to those conditions which are meet'.[5] A great matter had begun but 'the continuing unto the end until it be thoroughly finished yields the true glory . . . Haste!' Having sent this message home, Drake set sail for the mouth of the Tagus where, behind powerful shore batteries, Santa Cruz was waiting for supplies of every kind, guns, ammunition, biscuits, men, to reach him, and plagued by a stream of orders from his gout-stricken master.

Having inspected the situation, and reflected, Drake decided that Lisbon, the second richest city in Europe, was too hard a nut to crack. Not only was the estuary lined by impressive forts, but the approach along the narrow, winding fairway of the Tagus was an operation for which special pilots were normally required. And Santa Cruz, supervising the defence of the port from St Julian's Castle, had a squadron of galleys at his orders. Drake, coming to anchor on 10 May outside the river bar, could see them, their oars out, ready to strike the water. He sent a message to Santa Cruz by two Hamburg merchantmen bound for the port to say that he was waiting for the galleys to come out. The galleys did not budge. Then he suggested an exchange of prisoners to Santa Cruz. When the Marquis replied that he had no English prisoners, Drake, who did not believe him, said that in that case he would sell his prisoners to the Moors and use the money to buy the release of Englishmen held in slavery by the Moslem. There being nothing for him to do outside Lisbon, he sailed back to Sagres to clean his ships and give his men shore leave.

Meanwhile, King Philip from his sickroom at Aranjuez was trying to control the situation. His doctors, who disagreed among themselves about the treatment for his gout, were unanimous in thinking that he should not be encouraged to work. It was useless. Philip insisted in grappling with a crisis which, changing hour by hour, usually made nonsense of his orders. First, Medina Sidonia, in command at Cadiz, was to embark the soldiers of Pimentel's *tercio* in galleys and dispatch them to Lisbon. Then, hearing that Drake was no longer hovering outside the Tagus bar, the King issued new orders. He decided that the Englishman must have sailed off to attack the infinitely precious treasure fleet due to arrive from the Indies. That being the most likely peril, Santa Cruz, Recalde and Medina Sidonia were to make rendezvous at Cape St Vincent and, acting together, save the treasure from the pirate.

Then the news reached Philip that Drake had turned up again off Cape St Vincent. Santa Cruz was brought into consultation and gave it as his opinion that Drake's purpose could only be to prevent a junction of the Cadiz and the Lisbon fleets. Philip agreed, and ordered Pimentel's troops to make for Lisbon overland by forced marches. At this juncture, however, the authorities in Cadiz announced that they would be ready in a week's time to attack Drake with sixty ships. In his perplexity, the King fell in with this idea. But, to be sure that Cadiz was capable of carrying out its plan, he sent Don Alonso de Leyva to report. Leyva, an exceptionally brilliant soldier, who had charmed the King into making him Captain-General of the Sicilian galleys and then Captain-General of the Milanese Cavalry, sent back gloomy news. Cadiz was quite incapable of dealing with Drake. Philip was recasting his plan once more when a new presage of disaster reached him.

Drake, as if on a sudden impulse, had set off westwards into the ocean. Watchers on the coast saw his ships disappear, one by one, below the horizon. This made no kind of strategic sense at all but, then, the Cadiz expedition, like other episodes in this strange half-war between England and Spain, was only in part a military undertaking. It was business, too. Very much so, as Drake knew better than most men. He remembered how, only a year earlier, his prestigious raid on the Indies had been followed by complaints: the speculators had been paid a dividend of only 15 shillings in the pound. As one who was himself an investor both in the Indies expedition and in this new one, he had a personal interest in the commercial side of the venture.[6]

So, when he picked up the information, probably somewhere on the Portuguese coast, that an immensely valuable cargo boat was on its way home from Goa, he set off to snatch it. A whole year's harvest of the Portuguese settlements in Asia was expected to reach the Azores in the carrack *San Felipe*. With luck, he should be able to intercept it, thus winning favour in the eyes of the Queen, the City merchants and the poor mariners to whom one prize was worth many weeks of vigil off Cape St Vincent. And so it fell out.

Although he lost contact with the London squadron in a heavy gale, and with the *Golden Lion* in which Borough was held prisoner, Drake, with the Queen's ships and three others, one of which was his own, met the *San Felipe* off the Azores. By that time he had been sixteen days on the way from Cape St Vincent. The big Portuguese carrack, on the last leg of her voyage from India, invited Drake's flagship to declare her nationality, but this she declined to do until the *San Felipe* was within range of her guns. After that, there was a brisk exchange of fire between the *Elizabeth Bonaventure*, a flyboat and a pinnace on the one hand, and the *San Felipe* on the other. In this engagement, the Portuguese had the worst of it; with six dead and many wounded and with the English ready to send boarders at any moment, the captain of the *San Felipe* struck his colours.

In all the records of privateering down to that June day, there had never been such a prize. The pride of the Portuguese merchant marine, laden with all the spices, silks, china, jewels and gold she could conveniently carry! Sir Horatio Pallavicino, a Genoese who had settled in London, was said to have offered £100,000 for her cargo, as was sourly reported by Mendoza to King Philip. Mendoza was probably not far wrong because he had a spy in Plymouth that year, a Fleming, who brought the news over by fishing boat to the French coast. The official valuation of the *San Felipe* and her cargo was £114,000.* What it was in reality, heaven knows.

A fortnight after taking her, Drake sailed triumphantly into Plymouth Sound. He had been at sea for less than three months, in which time he had done a great deal of damage to Spanish shipping, more to Spanish credit and most of all to Spanish pride. The Portuguese mourned the loss of their best merchant ship and swore that they were worse off now than they had ever been under kings of their own. Among the Spanish public the conviction grew that Drake worked in collaboration with a familiar spirit who told him where and when to strike. It is, indeed, clear that he had excellent intelligence about Spanish shipping movements, probably obtained from disaffected Portuguese.

While Drake was on his way home with £40,000 of prize money for the Queen and £17,000 for himself, Santa Cruz had been able to find crews to man a punitive fleet, which was now scouring the seas round the Azores for signs of Drake. When at last the old Spanish admiral gave up the hunt, and came fuming back to Lisbon, he had made up his mind on one important question: there would be no attack on England that year.

The Cadiz raid had a sequel which Drake found less than satisfactory. Not long before the capture of the *San Felipe*, he had been enraged to hear that the crew of Borough's ship, the *Golden Lion*, had mutinied and, defying Captain Marchant, whom Drake had put over them, had stood away before the wind for England. Rather risk the anger of the Queen than certain death in the company of this madman, Drake! Marchant had left the ship, convinced, as he told Drake, that the real source of the trouble was to be found in Borough, then a nominal prisoner on his own ship. Drake, who probably did not need much convincing on the score, called a court-martial which duly passed sentence of death, *in absentia*, on the officers of the runaway ship, chief of whom was, of course, Borough. On his

* Say £3,000,000 today.

return to England, Drake presented the case against his vice-admiral before the Council, then in session at Lord Burghley's country house. To the Queen, who was staying there at the time, he brought a fine casket of jewels which had been turned up when the *San Felipe* was being searched at Saltash.

Drake had, as usual, no doubt at all that right was on his side. And, indeed, the *prima facie* case against Borough was a substantial one. Out of vanity and pique, as it seemed, he had dragged a foot in the crisis of battle. Later, when he had been deprived of his command, he had allowed himself to be brought back to England as a passenger by mutineers who shared his lack of confidence in the fleet commander. However it was regarded, the episode lacked the dignity expected of a member of the Navy Board and Clerk of the Ships. But, as it proved, Borough was in luck. He returned to England at a time when the Queen and Burghley were inclined to think or, at least, to hope that war after all could be avoided or postponed. Walsingham wrote despondently to Leicester: he had never seen the Queen so little inclined to war. The Duke of Parma, who was encouraging this mood of optimism among the Queen and her councillors, let it be known that he greatly disliked Drake's actions, which might turn King Philip from thoughts of peace.[7]

In the same week as Borough's case came before the Council, Burghley wrote to Parma's London agent, explaining that only contrary winds had prevented Drake from receiving later instructions which would have kept him off Spanish soil.[8] As it was, the Queen was very much annoyed with him. The case of the stolen carrack was, however, on quite a different footing. There could be no question of disgorging any of the prize money which Drake had brought home. He pointed out that it would go only a small part of the way to recompensing the Queen and her subjects for the losses they had suffered at Spanish hands.

From Borough's point of view the important thing was that the Queen, while taking her share of the loot from the *San Felipe*, was blaming Drake for the landing at Cape Sagres which

Borough had criticised. So Borough, favoured by a change of wind in the Council chamber, was not hanged as his admiral had proposed; he even received his share of the *San Felipe* money and, in due course, was promoted. And this during days when a grave view was being taken of mutiny by the Council! Recently it had ordered the Lord Mayor of London to deal severely with some conscripts who had refused to obey Captain Sampson's orders. They were to be tied to carts and flogged through the streets from Cheapside to Tower Hill. There they were to be set on a pillory and have each an ear cut off. But a more tolerant attitude was taken towards the supposed offence of a distinguished naval officer.

Drake may well have resented it that the decision of his court-martial was overturned by Burghley. He persisted in his belief that Borough had, by his behaviour in the crisis at Cadiz, endangered the whole operation. He told the Queen so when she sought his advice during the tense months before the Armada came. But whatever Drake's inner feelings, he swallowed his annoyance. He had more important things to think of than his quarrel with an elderly and pedantic sailor. As for Borough, he did not suffer too severely in career or reputation as a result of his quarrel with Drake. During the Armada campaign of the following summer he commanded the *Bonavolio*, the only galley in the English fleet. His service was confined, however, to the Thames estuary at a distance from his enemy; when it was all over, he busied himself with handling another matter, 'getting a good wife', in which apparently he was successful.[9]

XV

It is Enough to be Duke of Medina

'For the love of Jesus Christ, madam, awake and see the villainous treasons round about you.'

Lord Howard of Effingham, to Queen Elizabeth I[1]

Sir James Crofts wrote to the Queen, 'Those who recommend war, recommend it for sundry respects; some for war's sake, as I should do, perhaps, if I were young and a soldier; others for religion; others for spoil and robbery.'[2] Elizabeth had no higher opinion of Crofts than Parma had ('a weak old man of seventy with little or no sagacity')[3] but, as the months of 1587 rolled past, her natural inclination towards the party and the hopes of peace grew stronger. She was more conscious of the grass roots of England than most people. She knew that the cloth trade was in deep trouble.[4] Its Spanish, Portuguese and Flemish markets were closed. The passage of goods into Germany was blocked because Parma commanded the middle Rhine and because Spanish diplomacy was active in Hamburg. The merchant adventurers, unable to sell on the Continent, ceased to buy from the middlemen (the clothiers), who ceased to buy from the weavers, who began to starve. Before long, the wool growers would feel the pinch on their pastures. 'The extreme cry of the poor for lack of work' might not sound loudly in Whitehall but, let it grow only a little more, and it would drown the thunder of Drake's culverins and even the soft, enticing chink of his plundered ducats.

Elizabeth had been queen of a poor land and had seen it grow to riches through frugality. She had no intention of throwing away the gains of those twenty-nine extraordinary years in the pursuit of some phantom of glory, prestige or empire or, even, at the behest of religion. So at times she was irritated with Drake. 'He has never fought yet and has only scandalised the enemy at considerable loss to me.'[5] Maybe she did not fling these angry words at Leicester. Maybe, if she did, they were only meant to be carried through Mendoza to Philip, as they were. But she sometimes rebelled against the counsellors of war and those gallant exploits which seemed only to bring war nearer, and which limited her freedom of manoeuvre.

The trouble was, however, that gathering evidence which she could not ignore was on the side of the warmongers. Parma, while negotiating with her along four different channels, was methodically extending his grip on the Low Countries. Three months after Drake's spectacular coup in Cadiz Harbour, the Duke had compelled the surrender of Sluys, a fortified town, on the south bank of the Scheldt. 'God be praised!' he wrote joyfully to the King. 'Sluys is taken.'[6] Philip echoed the cry, recognising that with the port in his hands, it would be easier to dispatch an invasion force against England. For Elizabeth it was small consolation to know that the English garrison of the town had made a stubborn resistance much to their own credit and that of their commander, a redoubtable Welsh professional soldier named Sir Roger Williams. Williams, who had learned his trade under Alva, declined Parma's invitation to change sides again. It was particularly galling for the Queen to suspect that, with a little more skill and resolution, Leicester could have relieved the town. 'Never,' wrote Sir Roger bitterly, 'were brave soldiers thus lost for want of easy succours.' The English cause in the Low Countries, on which the Queen was spending half her ordinary revenue every year, had suffered a serious set-back.

Then there was the news out of Spain, brought to her by Drake and by Walsingham, who had his own sources of information. Walsingham was able and assiduous, a natural spymaster. On a secret fund of £3,300 a year, he gave his mistress as good an intelligence service as any in Europe. Sometimes, when he exceeded his budget, he paid for information out of his own purse: 'knowledge is never too dear.'[7] It was a foible Walsingham could afford to indulge, having a farm of the customs which brought him, in a good year, nearly £7,000.

One of his most useful agents had the cover name of Pompeo Pellegrini.[8] Twenty years earlier, under his real name of Antony Standen, this man had been an associate of Mary Stuart's husband, Lord Darnley. An Englishman and a Catholic, he had fled to the Continent when Darnley was murdered. Standen entered the service of the Grand Duke of Tuscany, whose ambassador in Madrid kept him well posted about Spanish affairs. And at some time, Standen had come on Walsingham's pay-roll. Thus, when Drake with his fleet was making provocative noises off the mouth of the Tagus, Standen had planted a Fleming in Lisbon, a man whose brother was a servant of the Marquis of Santa Cruz. Thanks to this source, Standen was able to assure Walsingham that there would be no attempt to invade England that year (1587). Obviously this was news of supreme military importance.

In the spring of the following year, when the Anglo-Spanish crisis had become even more acute, Pompeo Pellegrini went to Spain in person. The time had come when Walsingham was no longer satisfied with news that came to him at second-hand, whether from Santa Cruz's kitchen or from the Governor of Guernsey's reports of the gossip on Breton ships or in Rouen taverns. He needed an accurate and detailed stream of information about the number of Philip's ships, their tonnage, the sailors who would man them and the soldiers they would carry. Thanks above all to Standen, he got what he wanted, plus some illuminating facts about Philip's finances: for instance, that the Genoese bankers were refusing to lend the King any more money: everything depended on the safe arrival of the Plate Fleet that year. To the King's enormous relief, it arrived in August with bullion aboard worth 16,000,000 ducats.*

Drake's coup at Cadiz has been thought important because it postponed by a year the attack on England. But it had another important consequence. Drake had made the Spanish people critical of their government. He had shamed the King in the

* Worth, at that time, £4,000,000.

eyes of his subjects.[8] He had wakened in Philip a passionate desire to wipe out this humiliation, although the King had, at first, no precise idea about how he would take his revenge. At one moment, Parma was to surprise England with a landing at Margate; at the next, he was to wait for the Armada, so that both he and Santa Cruz could cross the Channel together. According to a third variation of the plan, Parma was to attack through Kent while the soldiers whom the Armada had brought over were to seize the Isle of Wight. But whatever form the plan took, Philip was determined on one thing, the Enterprise of England must go on.

Parma had favoured the first scheme; he had dreamed of a sudden, unexpected attack on England by an army crossing the Straits of Dover in flat-bottomed boats, and had considered that the Armada would be needed to cover this invasion only if the English discovered the secret. But the English *had* discovered the secret. Burghley hinted as much to Parma's agent and Parma sent the news by letter to Philip, who scribbled in the margin 'Oho!'[9] Already worried about money to pay his soldiers, worried about the safety of his base in the Low Countries, pessimistic about the help he might expect from Catholics in Britain, Parma thought that the chance had been missed.

Santa Cruz, too, had lost some of the enthusiasm he had felt for the Enterprise after his victory in the Azores in 1583: 'Victories as complete as those which God has deigned to give your Majesty might normally encourage princes to make other enterprises,' he wrote at that time. By the autumn of 1587, the Marquis was decidedly more cautious. In the meantime, goaded by Drake's outrages, the King had become the soul of belligerency. The Venetian ambassador in Madrid reported that Philip had offered a free pardon to bandits and outlaws if they entered his service.[10] Parma became steadily more despondent, reporting that, although the Italian infantry which had reached Flanders were of excellent quality and would enable him to release Walloons and Germans for the invasion force, the Spanish reinforcements were a poor lot, almost without arms and clothing. Eight hundred of these new arrivals had been struck down with a sickness which quickly spread to their Italian and Corsican comrades. The hospitals at Namur were filled to capacity. Then there were the autumn gales to consider. 'Everything depends on the will of God,' the Duke decided gloomily, 'for the zeal and activity of men cannot be enough.'[11]

Such pessimism had no power over Philip's mind. He wrote in exasperation to Parma about the Duke's change of tune: 'In the beginning you did not speak about the Spanish fleet: you had worked out a plan that did not require its intervention. It was I who drew your attention to the help the Armada could give you.' If the Enterprise was delayed, Philip pointed out, the chance might be lost – the chance which Parma thought had already vanished. The Grand Turk might make peace with the Shah, and launch his galleys against Italy. The heretic Elizabeth had an ambassador in Constantinople who was working to that end, and had already been given an encouraging reception by the Sultan.[12] Very soon, these English manoeuvres were supplemented by a gift of silver vases sent by Drake to the Capudan-Pasha, the admiral commanding the Turkish fleet.

There was enough in those activities in Constantinople to give Philip cause for concern. As he pointed out to Parma, if the Turks moved against him, other enemies of Spain would join in the game. As the King saw the problem in the late summer of 1587, the decisive hour had arrived. Every obstacle, if its existence was admitted at all, must be swept away. The Armada must sail.

Sail, yes. But sail whither and when? Perhaps, Philip thought, it ought not to arrive until Parma had marched into London; before then it should be content to seize the Isle of Wight. This was one out of several propositions which he considered and, in the end, rejected.

Elizabeth, for her part, was snatching at the straws of peace, then, when some new evidence of Spain's malevolent purpose was provided, turning to John Hawkins or Drake for advice on how she should ward off the two-headed dragon that threatened from beyond the Bay of Biscay and beyond the Narrow Seas. The sailors did not lack ideas. Hawkins urged that a standing naval patrol should be set up off the Azores which would stand between Philip and his American treasure. This was known as the 'Silver Policy', which would have brought Philip's finances down in ruins. If it succeeded! But, in the vastness of the Atlantic, a strongly escorted convoy of two dozen galleons was only a tiny speck and the search for it would have swallowed up half of England's Navy. And, while Elizabeth's ships watched for the Flota in the ocean, Philip might strike at England directly. Drake's conception was a simpler one: to seek out the Spanish fleet in its home ports and either destroy or cripple it. In other words, to bring off the stroke at Lisbon of which, during the Cadiz expedition, he had not felt himself capable.

In Christmas week, 1587, Drake was given the command of a squadron of thirty ships to be based on Plymouth with the secret duty of harassing Spanish ships wherever he should find them. The momentous year 1588 was only a few days old when he arrived in Plymouth and, from his house in Looe Street, set about the congenial task of fitting out and manning the ships that were gathering in the familiar old harbour at the foot of the hill. Seamen poured in, looking for berths in the new expedition which, as a skilfully planted rumour ran, would take them back to the Indies, to the fine Spanish towns, to the source of the gold, silver and pearls that they or their brothers had plundered before. There were soon enough of them to man two hundred ships. So, at least, a Spanish prisoner reported, who had been allowed to go home, no doubt to spread among his fellow-countrymen this alarming, erroneous report on El Draque's intentions.

All this time Dom Antonio, the pretender to the Portuguese throne, was watching over his shrinking store of jewels in Drake's brother's house in Devon. Perhaps the time had come to make use of him? Drake seems to have thought so. But no sooner had he made his Plymouth squadron ready for action than the wind that blew in Whitehall changed yet once more.

An event had occurred which gave statesmen and monarchs reason to pause and reflect. The Marquis of Santa Cruz, Commander-in-Chief of the Armada, died at Lisbon on 9 February 1588, weighed down by the endless worries of a task in which it is probable that he no longer believed, and the nagging of a taskmaster who would not give him a day's peace.

From this heavy blow, King Philip made a rapid recovery. 'God has shown me a favour,' he wrote a week after the death, 'by removing the Marquis now rather than when the Armada is at sea.'[13] It was a singularly chilly farewell to his most famous sailor, suggesting that Philip was relieved that the Enterprise should be led by a younger and more amenable commander. He nominated the Duke of Medina Sidonia as Admiral-in-Chief of the Armada, Captain-General of the Ocean Sea. Elizabeth, for her part, decided that, with Santa Cruz gone, peace had a better chance. In the month of February, she sent negotiators to Ostend to discuss with Parma the possibilities of peace. One of the mission was Sir James Crofts, who was not only a fool but also a traitor in Spanish pay.

In the meantime, Drake was kicking his heels in Plymouth. An admiral, eager to be actively employed. A strategist with a natural bent towards attack. And commander of a fleet which could certainly do damage to the force Philip was massing in his ports. Two English scouting vessels, the *Spy* and the *Makeshift*, had loitered off the Spanish coast.[14] One of them had even slipped over the Tagus bar and, between the forts of Belem and St Julian, had kidnapped the master of a fishing boat, gaining valuable intelligence, which Drake was able to confirm when he seized two Swedish cargo boats off Plymouth. They had just left Lisbon and the pale-blue Scandinavian eyes of their crews were full of wonder at the scale, the energy, the determination of the Spanish build-up.

The Queen released more royal ships to her impetuous Admiral, but did not let him off the leash. William Hawkins, brother of John, worked by night and day on these vessels while torches and cressets burned along the Cattewater at

9 Sir Francis Drake aged 53, by Marcus Gheeraerts the Younger
(reproduced by kind permission of Lieutenant-Colonel Sir George Tapps-Gervis-Meyrick)

10 A map of Cartagena by Baptista Boazio, from Walter Bigges' *A Summary and Tr*
Discourse of Sir Francis Drake's West India Voyage, published simultaneously
in London, Leyden and Cologne in 1589 (*British Museum*)

K
N
A
O
S
G
X
X
C
C
B
B
D
V

11 Sir John Norreys (*British Museum*)

12 Dr John Dee (*British Museum*)

13 The Earl of Essex (*National Portrait Gallery*)

14 Christopher Carleill (*British Museum*)

Plymouth. Foul as they had been, inside and out, the ships would be ready in time to meet the Spanish galleons when they came. Perhaps, while waiting, Drake could raid Lisbon . . . But the Queen said, No. It was a frustrating time for a prayerful, patriotic English sailor.

It is not surprising then to find Drake writing, one February day, to his new friend at Court, Robert, Earl of Essex, whose father had given him the letter of recommendation to Walsingham which had opened the door to the great circumnavigation voyage, and to fame. This young earl was handsome, spirited and rich. Most important of all, he was the Queen's newest favourite. 'The employment of your lordship's crowns and mine shall be in victual, powder, small ammunition, spades, shovels, pickaxes, baskets, ropes, twine and such like. If this arrow fail us for a time, it cannot be long ere there be as good . . . God hath much honour to lend your lordship.'[15] What was this enterprise, so plainly hinted at, yet so secret that it should not be put down on paper? 'Pardon my pen, not so much for that I write ill, as for the danger thereof . . . Good my lord, tear my letter.' Perhaps these two adventurers, the young and the not-so-young, were dreaming of some pre-emptive strike against the Spanish fleet gathering in Lisbon. Perhaps they had in mind a new attempt to inflame Portuguese nationalism into armed support of Dom Antonio.

Either project would have agreed with Drake's impatient nature, his burning conviction that he knew how and where to hit the Spaniards. That he, the man of Santo Domingo, Cartagena and Cadiz, whose name had become a terror in Spanish minds, should be idle at such an hour of supreme national peril, was intolerable! Why not slip off to sea one day, with like-minded comrades? Success would, as it had done so often before, obtain forgiveness for the disobedience.

This is all a matter of conjecture. Before long, the two principals were busy in other ways. Essex was raising at his own charge a troop of light horse to defend the Queen in the event of a Spanish landing. They would be a pretty spectacle in the orange uniforms he was buying for them. And Drake was beseeching the Queen again to let him loose to fight off the Spanish coast. He had no plan, at least no plan he could divulge. The occasion would inspire the plan, as it had done at Cadiz, although he admitted the danger that 'one flying now, as Borough did, will put the whole in peril'. Spanish strength was greater now than it had been a year before. But he had no doubt, and every phrase of his barely articulate prose urged the message home. The time was now. The place was the magnificent harbour at Lisbon, where Philip was assembling the fleet which, under that reluctant crusader, the Duke of Medina Sidonia, would restore the Catholic faith to a lapsed member of the Church. 'Give me fifty ships and the task is done!' That was Drake's argument to which Elizabeth was bound to give the attention due to the opinion of her most famous admiral. Was Drake right? True, he spoke with the authority of repeated victory and profit. But the question was not at all so easy to decide. Elizabeth's instinct was to keep her watchdog at home. Drake, as it chanced, was not the only English admiral who fretted in idleness.

The Lord Admiral himself, Lord Howard of Effingham, who had the bulk of the Queen's ships under his command, lay off Margate in the month of April, worried by bad weather and the short commons which the Navy Board inflicted on his crews. Lack of food and shortage of money to pay the men – at that time these were the trials of every commander whether he was Lord Admiral of England, tossing in the rough seas off the mouth of the Thames, or Alexander Farnese, Duke of Parma, Philip's Captain-General in the Netherlands, and reduced, at times, to eating the same ammunition bread as his soldiers. Howard had a temperamental preference for activity and aggression. He, like other men, was feeling the strain of the long waiting for this mighty fleet which, one day, would surge up across the Bay of Biscay and fall upon the coasts of little England. How many hundred ships? How many thousand soldiers, who would link up with Parma's terrible professionals, sixty thousand strong?

The last figure was roughly correct, but Parma had many commitments on his hands besides the invasion of England. He must provide against the rebels in Holland, against the Germans on the Rhine and against the danger from France, where, at any moment, the treacherous king might make his peace with the Huguenots and march into Flanders. In consequence, Parma could spare only sixteen thousand troops for the flat-bottomed boats of his invasion fleet lying in Dunkirk harbour and in the canals behind it. But sixteen thousand of Parma's veterans, plus the troops that Medina Sidonia would bring from Lisbon, were together a powerful argument for preventing a junction of the two Spanish armies.[16]

The Lord Admiral was converted to the offensive strategy which had its most vehement advocate in Drake. Never before, Drake told the Queen, had there been so terrible a threat to 'your majesty and true religion'. He proposed that his western squadron, the ships based on Plymouth, should be strengthened so that it could strike at the Lisbon Armada and prevent it from preparing the way for Parma's 'better entrance'. 'My very good lords,' he told the Council on 30 March,[17] 'with fifty sail of shipping we shall do more good upon their own coast than a great many more will do here at home; and the sooner we are gone, the better.' In the same letter, he complained that his ships were short of gunpowder, although he had been attentive that none of it should be used unnecessarily on target practice. He had barely enough for one day's battle. In answer to Drake's expostulations, the Council opened the gunpowder store in the Tower of London, grudgingly enough. But the signal that would launch his squadron on a new and marauding expedition to the Spanish coast was not given. Indeed, by keeping Drake's ships and Howard's short of provisions, the Council effectively pinned both squadrons of the English fleet to home waters.

When the Queen asked Drake what he had in mind to do on the Spanish coast, he asked for four more of the Queen's galleons, plus sixteen of the ships that were being prepared in London. With these ships, added to those already in his command, he would propose to lie in wait for the Armada outside Lisbon and harry it all the way to England. But – 'I have order but for two months' victuals,' one month of which would probably be consumed before he could reach Spain. Drake was summoned from Plymouth to attend the Council. By that time, it seemed that he had won his case. The Navy Board was convinced. John Hawkins had probably needed no convincing. Lord Admiral Howard, weary of being 'a bear tied to a stake', seemed to have joined the partisans of attack. But one authority remained sceptical, and that the highest. The Queen could still not bring herself to dispatch into distant waters the ships on which so much of her people's technical skill and her own housekeeping money had been staked. She has been greatly blamed for it, the fickle, stingy Tudor woman. But was she so wrong?

In his study at San Lorenzo, Philip Hapsburg pondered the strategic problem before him. It was not at all a simple one. He might try to make a base in Scotland from which to attack England, as Captain Sempill kept urging. Sempill was a professional soldier; a Scots Catholic with all the optimism natural to one who felt that his cause had been unfairly beaten in a civil war and might, by a fresh turn in events, regain all that it had lost. It was true also that the Scots, no matter what their religion, had a cause for furious resentment against England in the execution of their queen. When Captain Robert Keble of Harwich brought to England from Havre alarming news of the strength of the Armada – between four hundred and five hundred ships! – he also reported that he had been fined 30 crowns by the Governor of the French port for brawling with Scottish seamen. The Scots had sworn that, if they caught him at sea, they would heave him overboard. What is more, they would do the same to all other 'English dogs' in vengeance for the blood of their queen.

It was possible, too, although not so likely, that the King of Scots, Mary's son, was at heart a Catholic, as Lord Morton had told Philip in secret conference in Madrid.[18] Said Morton, King James waited only for a convincing demonstration of Spain's will to fight. Then he would appear in his true colours and lead his people – who surely would need no leading – across the border into England. There may have been a grain of truth in the story. But Philip was bound to reflect that James would be more likely to imitate his brother sovereigns: he would wish Philip well, do nothing to help him and rush to his aid in the hour of victory! Besides, Scotland was far away; it was cold, hungry and inhabited by tribes who might be warlike but, alas, were unreliable.

Ireland? That was another possibility. It was nearer than Scotland, Catholic, and nourished in dislike of the English. Its claims as a theatre for Spanish action were urged upon Philip by Sir William Stanley, an English turncoat who, in 1585, had betrayed Deventer in the Low Countries to Parma. A traitor to his Queen? In the heat of an ideological war, 'traitor' is not a word to be used too lightly. But Stanley's honour as a Catholic soldier of Elizabeth would shine more brightly if he had gone over alone to Parma and had not given up the Sconce at Deventer as well. Philip detailed a staff officer, Juan de Ortiz, to look into the Irish project. Ortiz rejected it, which was undoubtedly a correct decision for, even if a Spanish army were established in Ireland, it would still be separated by sixty miles of sea from England. And Spain would be six hundred miles away. England might be – as she later was – dragged into a long and wasting war in Ireland. But Philip needed a quick decision. He could not afford to leave Cadiz for long unavenged.

Which brought him back to plans for a direct assault on the English coast. The troops in Parma's command were the best infantry in the world, and certainly superior to the raw militia they were likely to meet in England. Once landed in Kent, in country ill-suited to the English cavalry, they would have little difficulty in marching on London, sweeping the English levies before them. Even if Parma could spare only sixteen thousand men for the English venture, a figure which seemed absurdly low to Philip, the joint operation seemed the best strategy.

Knowing all the ponderables almost as well as Philip himself, thanks to her secret service, Elizabeth could look at the question through his eyes. What she could not know was which of the courses open to him he or his commanders would finally take. She might have an opinion, she could guess – but to guess wrongly would bring irredeemable ruin to England and to her. Danger might come from one of several quarters and England must be covered against all of these threats. At first glance, Drake's plan seemed the more hopeful, since the scene of the decisive clash would be as far as might be from English shores. But what if Drake's ships ran into bad weather on the enemy coast, far from a friendly port? That could be a source of disaster. Crews kept too long at sea were not only expensive to the Treasury for beef, biscuit, beer and pay, but were deplorably liable to various deadly forms of sickness. It was cheaper, healthier, wiser to keep those brave hearts in English waters where they could be paid off immediately there was the faintest glimmer of a peace settlement with Parma.

To what extent the Queen took her negotiations with the Duke seriously is not certain. Seriously enough, in appearance, to drive to distraction a leader of the war party like Walsingham. But the Queen was not likely to ignore the warnings of Burghley against one who 'offers to treat of peace in words and uses all the actions of a bloody war at the same instant'. Or the pleadings of Drake, 'Pardon my boldness in the discharge of my conscience . . . the promise of peace from the Prince of Parma and those mighty preparations in Spain agree not well together.' In fact, the Queen did not take the negotiations so seriously as to dismantle any of the main preparations for defence. Parma, for his part, did not take them seriously at all. They were an overture to be played until the curtain rose with the arrival of the Armada off the Lizard.

The Duke of Parma expressed his own doubts about the Enterprise with ironic malice, in a letter of 5 April to his uncle, the King: 'Since God has been pleased to defer for so long the sailing of the Armada from Lisbon we are bound to conclude that it is for His greater glory and the more perfect success of the business . . . The enemy have thereby been forewarned and acquainted with our plans.'[19] He would have preferred to clear up the troublesome rebellion in Holland before undertaking this English adventure. What a pity that the King was now in such a hurry! Meanwhile, in Spain, the Duke of Medina Sidonia was showing a similar lack of enthusiasm for his task.

Philip's choice of Commander-in-Chief was an unexpected one, but it was by no means absurd. In the first place, there were objections to promoting any one of the subordinate commanders of the fleet. Recalde (who asked for the job); Oquendo (who proposed Alva's bastard son, Hernando de Toledo); Martin de Padilla, a dashing galley commander; Alonso de Bazan, brother of Santa Cruz; and the flower of chivalry (and ambition), Alonso de Leyva – to each there was some weighty objection of jealousy or age.

In favour of Medina-Sidonia[20] were powerful arguments: He was the first grandee of Spain, a Knight of the Golden Fleece, and head of the illustrious house of Guzman. In his veins flowed (through two bastardies) the blood of Ferdinand the Catholic. He was the traditional leader in battle of the host of Andalusia, able to raise in his own estates ten thousand armed men. He was closely associated with the work of the Council of the Indies. Socially and historically, the Duke would possess an inborn pre-eminence among the officers of the fleet. Besides, his loyalty to the King was beyond doubt. When Philip threw into prison the Duke's mother-in-law, that one-eyed beauty, the Princess of Eboli, the Duke had approved. As for his character, at the time of the Cadiz disaster he had taken command of a critical situation with energy and resolution. Had it not been for his prompt action, it was thought the town might have been seized and pillaged by the English raiders. Plainly, he was a man likely to choose wisely among the counsels given him by his naval experts and to show courage in an emergency.

The trouble was that the Duke did not want the job: when the King's secretary wrote to tell him that Philip 'has fixed his eye on your lordship', he was appalled. He wrote explaining why he would be a bad choice. He easily became sea-sick, had no experience whatever of naval war and was burdened by a family debt of 900,000 ducats. The King brushed all objections aside. And, bowing to his sovereign's will, the Duke commended himself to God and hurried obediently to Lisbon, leaving the Duchess to tell her friends what a fool he was to accept the post. She made it clear, too, that this came as no surprise to her. The glory of it? 'It is enough,' said the Duchess, 'to be Duke of Medina.'[21] In Lisbon, the Duke found that the dying Santa Cruz had left the work of preparing the fleet in a lamentable confusion. With zeal and ability, he began to put things right, so that by mid-May the Armada was ready to sail. All that was lacking in the Duke was confidence in his mission. He was not alone in his scepticism.

'Although his Majesty is justly provoked, it is thought he will not, for the sake of revenge, hazard upon a doubtful and uncertain battle the peace and liberty of his many States and Kingdoms.' So wrote the ambassador of Venice to the Serene Republic that employed him. And certainly the King was sending his ships on one of the wildest escapades in all history: an attack on a great maritime power in its own home waters, at a distance of eight hundred miles from the main base at Lisbon. It could be justified only if he were confident of possessing an overwhelming preponderance in fighting power, or the special favour of Heaven. Otherwise it was a gamble such as no monarch should take. But upon that enormous, breathtaking venture King Philip was embarking, implacable, undeviating, the instrument or the victim of destiny, and with a reluctant coadjutor on either hand.

Meanwhile, on 10 May, the Council met in London to listen to Drake. In letters which might be short in grammar but were plain enough in meaning, he had urged his plan: 'The advantage of time and place in all martial actions is half a victory: which being lost is irrecoverable. Wherefore if your Majesty will command me away with those ships . . .'[22] If it were all as simple as that! If it were only a question of another plundering raid, with the proceeds split between Crown and raider and all political responsibility indignantly disclaimed! But the hour was graver and the scale of things was greater. Besides, there was that tiresome, nagging problem of cost.

Those vehement, forceful sailors, urging their case in a whirr of West Country voices, could ignore money. But Elizabeth was hard put to it to keep her head above water financially. The stoppage of trade had hit the revenue from customs; already the war in the Low Countries was eating up half of her ordinary revenue. She could exact forced loans from the well-to-do; raise money in the City at ten per cent. Reminders came from Burghley that the people were in no mood to stomach new taxes. The Queen had to watch the pennies. Not for her did the Flota sail in from the Indies. Not for her the hope of a 1,000,000-ducat[23] loan from Pope Sixtus! She was in the mood where, even at a small but convincing sign of peace, or postponement of war, she would order crews to be disbanded and ships to be paid off. If, in the end, no measure of economy was put into force which did fatal damage to defence, it was because, behind all the flashes of hope, there was a steady drift towards the storm. There were warning signals which Elizabeth could not ignore.

The Council ended its long sitting. Drake took his leave and ordered his horse for the ride to Plymouth. Howard, a few days later, made his way to Margate to board his ship. Elizabeth had commanded her Lord Admiral to join Drake at Plymouth, where from that time onwards, Howard was to be Commander-in-Chief of the combined fleet with Drake as Second-in-Command.

XVI

The Force and Flower of a Kingdom

'Men muster now in every place,
And soldiers are pressed forth apace.
Faint not, spend blood
To do your Queen and country good.'
A Posie of Gilliflowers – *Humphrey Gifford, Gent.*

Howard sailed in the *Ark Royal* for Plymouth with a fleet of thirty-four ships and eight pinnaces. He was met off Plymouth Sound at daybreak by Drake, who had by this time gathered forty ships which the western ports had provided, some willingly enough and others with groans and protests that intolerable burdens were being laid on impoverished communities. The meeting of the two fleets was conducted with pomp and dignity.

Drake in the *Revenge* led out of the Sound a line of thirty ships, three abreast, which dipped their flags and fired a salute as they met the incoming ships. Howard flew the royal standard, the Lord Admiral of England's flag and a rear-admiral's flag. Drake hauled down the admiral's flag he had been flying and hoisted in its place the rear-admiral's flag which Howard sent him by pinnace. Then the combined fleet sailed back into the Sound, Howard's ships in the lead.

Tactically, the movement of Howard's ships to the western station was wise, for the prevailing wind in the Channel is west or south-west and, if Howard's fleet had been left to patrol the eastern area, it would not have been able to intervene in aid of Drake should he become embroiled with the Spaniards in the western approaches to the Channel. One Admiralty official, however, was embarrassed by the change in the centre of gravity of the fleet. Marmaduke Darell, who was responsible for victualling the ships, found that, suddenly, he had to supply twice as many men as he had bargained for.[1] He scoured the Devon countryside desperately, looking for provisions; he swooped thankfully upon a Hamburg merchantman homeward bound with a cargo of rice. Rice was not the ordinary fare of the English seamen, but a godsend to a perplexed victualler. Darell paid cash for the German rice. On the ships the strictest economy was practised. Men were five or six to a mess instead of four; that is to say, four rations had to do for five or six. Worse trouble lay ahead. The beer, brewed in Sandwich, was universally denounced as sour, undrinkable, an insult to the palates of honest seamen.[2] The brewers alleged that the fault lay in a failure in the harvest of hops. But, whatever the explanation, no disaster could well be graver than this one in the English fleet, where the ration of beer was a gallon a day per man. In a situation so critical, Darell tried to brew the sour beer again and mix it with fresh. What success he had with that expedient is not known. But by the time the experiment was completed, the battle with the Armada was over.

When Howard had met Drake at Plymouth, the Armada was already at sea. Medina Sidonia had signed the fleet orders in Belem Roads in the cabin of his flagship, the *San Martin*. The tone was appropriately grave and religious, such as Drake himself, with a few necessary doctrinal alterations, would have approved. In conformity with their sacred mission, crews were enjoined to take the sacrament before embarking. They were to avoid blasphemy, gambling and quarrels. Prayers were to be said morning and evening by the mainmast. And no common women were to be carried.[3] When thirty of the trulls, wearing men's clothing, were detected in the fleet, they were sternly put back on the quay. But even that was not Satan's final ruse in his efforts to besmirch the crusade. A band of loose women hired a ship and put to sea in the wake of the Armada; eventually, the vessel of these enterprising harpies ran aground on the French coast, where, no doubt, they found customers.

At last the great day arrived. The Duke of Medina Sidonia took from the altar of Lisbon cathedral the standard given by the ladies of Portugal which showed the cross on one side and the Madonna on the other, with the motto, '*Exsurge Domine et vindica causam tuam.*' This was borne in solemn procession to the ships. Bells pealed. Cannon fired salvoes and King Philip was reported by the watchful Venetian Ambassador to be on his knees two or three times a day. The Duke embarked on St Mark's Day. To the sound of hymns and prayers, the chanting of friars and the blare of trumpets, the Armada nosed its way over the Tagus Bar, past the Rock of Lisbon and so into the ocean, where for days it was lost to sight. In fact, misfortune had befallen it almost at once. A great gale which blew up scattered the ships over leagues of sea. The Armada had for a time ceased to exist as a coherent fleet. But the gale was experienced by English commanders, too, on whom it had a depressing effect. They had lost sight of their enemy. They did not know where the Armada was and they feared the worst. It might have established a base in the Scillies or among the bays of Southern Ireland. At any moment, the Spanish galleons might loom up out of the mist in the Channel. And there they were, Howard, Drake and all their captains, shut into Plymouth Sound by the wild seas outside, with idle ship's companies grumbling about short commons and with the threat poised all the time over the fleet that for one reason or another, whether economy or starvation, it might be dispersed on orders from the Council.

Another of the principal actors in the drama was also in the dark about what was happening to the Spanish fleet. The Duke of Parma had not been idle during those last months. He had mobilised an army of workmen to dig a canal joining Sluys to Dunkirk and Nieuport. Thus, although the Dutch commanded the estuary of the Scheldt with a hundred and thirty armed vessels of shallow draught, he expected to be able to assemble the two hundred boats and hoys he had laboriously collected at Sluys with the seventy ships he had at Dunkirk. But matters did not work out so simply. The Dutch fleet, commanded by Justin of Nassau, a bastard son of William of Orange, extended its blockade so that Dunkirk as well as the Scheldt was under its surveillance. A dozen of these little warships maintained a constant patrol of the Flemish ports.

Parma, without warships of his own, must wait until the Armada had arrived and had driven off those Dutch mosquito craft. He busied himself in the meantime with preparations for the invasion of England: filling three hundred small boats with stores; and fitting out seventy flat-bottomed boats designated for the transport of horses with ramps that could be lowered to enable the animals to be put ashore. He collected twenty thousand empty casks at Gravelines which would come in useful in making temporary piers on English beaches. And he sent his recruiting agents to the north German seaports to engage seamen capable of handling his flotilla of boats. Experienced men were hard to come by and, it seems, when they were engaged, showed some resistance to the idea of a Channel crossing.[4] For over there, to the west, lurking behind the mists that hid the English coast, was the appalling Drake, scourge of the Seven Seas, master of every devilish device. At the thought of this monster, the pious crossed themselves, and the prudent sought the consolations of dry land. In fact, Drake was hundreds of miles away to the south-west. The nearest English squadron to Dunkirk was commanded by a hot-tempered nobleman named Lord Henry Seymour, son of the Duke of Somerset. Lord Henry passed on to London the good news which he had picked up from a French merchant recently returned from Cadiz: Spanish seamen[5] were much alarmed if they but heard the name of Drake.

In such stories there was, no doubt, an element of propaganda similar to reports reaching England about the same time, which told how Antonio de Tasso[6] was confidently praying to God to assign him the house of some rich English merchant when the hour came to divide up among the crusaders the spoils of the conquered heretics. Young Spanish aristocrats were casting lots as to which of them could have what in the great carve-up of English estates and offices. In the last days before sailing, it seems that morale in the Armada had somewhat improved.

Cupidity had usefully abetted religious zeal. The mere spectacle of so many gorgeous and powerful ships with so many thousands of tough Spanish soldiers on board, following the *San Martin* one after the other down the Tagus, answered all doubts. The Armada began to be called Invincible.

One or two important personages did not share this last-minute glow of optimism. One of them was Parma. His was a polyglot army, Spaniards, Italians, mustered not long before in the States of the Church, Flemings, Germans and a few hundred renegade English. A patchy host – but Parma counted on being able to leave the worst of them behind, so that, with a stiffening of the first-class troops who were coming in the Armada, they would keep the Low Countries quiet in his absence. As the weeks of summer passed, he brought his soldiers closer to the points of embarkation and inspected his boat-fleet at its moorings – not thoroughly enough, as later appeared. But, perhaps, at this point, a residual scepticism in Parma about the whole operation played its part. How else can one account for his failure to detect shortcomings that soon appeared? Some of his boats were not adequately caulked. Stores were defective. Some of his subordinates had been neglectful or dishonest – a common enough occurrence in those days when armies were led by great noblemen. But Parma, although his blood was certainly of the bluest, was not one of those aristocratic amateur generals who were an easy prey for careless officers or fraudulent contractors. He was a professional – the great professional of his age. He should have made sure that all was well with his boat fleet.

The Pope, too, remained steadfast in prayerful defeatism and distrust of Philip. 'The King of Spain is old,' remarked His Holiness with a charitable smile. 'We must put up with him as he is.' Needless to say, a Venetian diplomat was within earshot who repeated the remark and added with something like enthusiasm what the Pope said about the English sailor, the ubiquitous Drake: 'What audacity! And what luck!'[7] Meanwhile, the gale in the Atlantic had blown itself out and Medina Sidonia's scattered flock had gathered together again at Corunna, somewhat knocked about by the weather, short of food and greatly in need of fresh water. It was just three weeks since they had left the Tagus.

Medina Sidonia was so alarmed by the weaknesses which that short ocean trip had revealed in his fleet that he wrote a reasoned letter to the King, urging that the expedition should be postponed for a year. Philip would have none of it. Already he had fought off the misgivings of Parma and the advice of the Grand Commander of Castile, who had argued that he must establish a main base in northern waters before launching the attack on England. Philip had probably heard that the Pope had said he should have sent his fleet out in September of the year before. No doubt gossip brought the Holy Father's exact words into Philip's study. They were echoed with a touch of mockery in the Doge's Palace in the Most Serene Republic. (How much of the flavour of those electric days can be caught in the sardonic dispatches of the Venetian diplomatic service! Hieronimo Lippomano, Giovanni Gritti, Vicenzo Gradenigo, Matheo Zane, Lorenzo Priuli – they were ambassadors, spies and gossip-writers all in one; patricians of Venice and journalists in an age before journalism. Without the reports of these tireless eavesdroppers a great deal of the enlivening details of the time would have been lost for ever.)

Having urged the Armada almost half-way on its voyage to the English coast, King Philip was not prepared to see it turn back. The political planets were in a favourable conjunction which might not be repeated. And somewhere beneath that phlegmatic exterior of his, a sensitive nerve had been touched: Nombre de Dios, Santo Domingo, Cartagena, Cadiz. Each like a knot on a scourge. That woman and her pirate must be punished . . . Besides, the cause was holy. He wrote to assure his Admiral of the Ocean Sea that deficiencies would and could be made good and that the Enterprise would go on. Philip proved to be right. The Duke's fears were exaggerated. The Armada left Corunna for England on 22 July.

Not before anxious debate was the decision taken to sail!

On the 20th, Medina Sidonia had consulted his admirals in council: to set out or not? What was the weather forecast? Six of them said, Sail. Three said, Wait. Francisco de Bobadilla, the soldier in command of the *tercios*, would give no advice, but he stressed that the fleet must leave as soon as possible. Time pressed. The Duke then called his pilots to the *San Martin*. These experts told him that if the fleet were ready to go to sea by dawn next morning it could probably sail. He said that if he fired a gun after midnight, the ships were to begin to weigh anchor. Midnight came: the night passed: no cannon was heard from the flagship. The Duke had considered that the seas were running too high.

Next day (21 July) the weather abated somewhat and, after midnight, Medina Sidonia ordered the signal to be given. After that, every ship rode out the remainder of the night to a single anchor. When the first streak of daylight showed, a second cannon boomed out from the flagship. Then anchor chains groaned, sheets creaked through the blocks, the big painted sails fell and tautened. The Armada, with the *San Martin* in the van, was putting to sea.

The wind was marvellously favourable and on the 23rd the Duke sent a dispatch to his sovereign that the Armada was on its way. Operations against England had at last begun. Three days later, when the ships were due west of Ushant, the weather changed: there was half a gale blowing from the north, unprecedented for the month of July. This was more than the Armada's four galleys could endure. They had a low freeboard and no deck; it was not possible for the slaves to man the oars with the Atlantic waves breaking over them. The galleys turned away to the south-east and took no further part in the Enterprise.

The Armada, with the loss of one galleon which sought refuge in a French port, ploughed on northwards through the storm. On the 28th, the wind eased. By this time the Spanish fleet was in the Sleeve, the entrance to the English Channel and, during the next twenty-four hours, its scattered units came together. On Friday evening (29 July), the Duke's pilots pointed out a headland to him that, they said, was the Lizard. England. It was the Duke's first sight of the land in which he was to restore the Faith. He ordered three cannon shots to be fired, while to the head of the mainmast, amid prayers from the assembled clergy, rose the standard on which the ladies of Portugal had worked.

The wind, which had encouraged Medina Sidonia at last to launch the great assault on English sea-power, had by no means been favourable to Lord Admiral Howard and his aggressive second-in-command, Sir Francis Drake. Authorised, at last, by the Queen to leave their anchorage, they had set out to do what harm they could to the Armada where it lay in Corunna harbour. They were ill-provided with essential stores, as Howard grumbled to Burghley, but 'God send us a wind to put us out, for go we will though we starve' and – consoling thought – 'there is good fishing in the sea'.[8] Half-way across the Bay of Biscay, the wind swung round to the south and freshened. There was nothing to do but turn about and make for home.

Once more into Plymouth Sound crowded the cream of the Queen's Navy, those well-found, fighting galleons with their surprising turn of speed and their gratifying ability to sail a point or two nearer the wind than any ship they were likely to meet. Children of John Hawkins's brain, they were the themes of lyrical praise by Howard, Wynter and Seymour for their gallantry and seaworthy qualities.[9] Drake flew his flag in one of the best of them, The *Revenge*, and dropped anchor under St Nicholas' Island, where he had lain all those years before when he returned in the *Golden Hind* and was waiting for the courier from Whitehall to bring the news on which so much depended.

Somewhere near him was John Hawkins in the *Victory*[10] – a galleon already twenty-seven years old and destined to serve Queen, King and Commonwealth in succession during another seventy-eight.* The main fighting units, royal ships and big

* The *Victory*, after serving as Blake's flagship, was at last burnt by the Dutch in 1666.

armed merchantmen on which the state had laid its pre-emptive hand, came to anchor in the Sound. The rest found shelter in the Cattewater. Some of the merchantmen were as powerful as any ships of the regular fleet, others had already revealed minor weaknesses. Repair and recruitment went forward with feverish speed. After all, the battle for England would be fought in home waters. And it would be fought soon.

At the last minute, the English, unmilitary, slovenly and inclined to be lazy, discovered that they had a taste for war. There was a flurry of preparations on land to match the energy at sea. The training of potential officers for the militia had for years been dogged by discouraging circumstances. 'The sacred profession of perfect men of war is now, by ill-training, grown to mis-order and mischief.'[11] The long bow had fallen into abeyance. English archery was a forgotten art. William Harrison mourned that the French and the Germans would 'turn up their tails and cry "Shoot English"' in derision. If Edward III's archers were alive, the picture would be different indeed. 'The breech of such a varlet would have been nailed to his bum with one arrow and another feathered in his bowels!'[12]

Counting by his old-world Roman methods – for the new Arabic figuring was something he never got used to – Burghley thought that the nobility and gentry could supply sixty men fit to be captains on hand and another forty-five for naval commands. Suitable commoners were still harder to find: Captain Turberville (Dorset) was not only inexperienced but boorish; Mr Hutton (Cambridge) was old and, by an issue in his leg, unable. True, the fighting in the Low Countries had thrown up two hundred captains of proved quality but, at this point as elsewhere, old social prejudices arose. The Earl of Leicester was recalled from the Low Countries, as were a thousand of his men. The Earl, whose task was to command the defence force encamped at Tilbury, found that the London trained bands would serve under their own captains or not at all.[13] Their officers were rich merchants like Sam Saltonstall, but Leicester expected no good from these Cockneys when – which God forbid! – they met the enemy. But, by the middle of June, the Londoners were drilling twice a week. There were six thousand of them, armed and trained, in four regiments. And with uniforms – officers in black velvet, other ranks in white – almost as fine as any in the force whose task was to serve as a bodyguard for the Queen. Walsingham offered the Londoners corselets from Norfolk but they preferred to buy their own from Mr Hopkins of the Minories, paying him 3 shillings for working through the night. Expense was, of course, a difficulty – 'insupportable', Burghley thought. He ordered that only at the last minute should the county militia march to Tilbury, because as soon as they arrived there, they became chargeable to the Queen's account. In fact, the first troops arrived there in July 1588, which was cutting it rather fine.

At the same time, the royal bodyguard began to assemble on the outskirts of London under the command of Lord Hunsdon, a relation of the Queen's.[14] In theory at least, it numbered 12,500 infantry and a thousand horse, uniformed, caparisoned and paid by the great nobles. Needless to say, it was stylishly turned out. Sir Henry Cromwell's horsemen were in straw colour and the Huntingdon infantry in light popinjay green – although all these were outclassed by the young Earl of Essex's lances, in orange. But what would they be worth in action, all these glorious warriors, swaggering about the countryside, thirsting for battle? Opinions differed. The question was put by the Queen to Sir John Norreys – 'Black Jack' – a professional soldier hardened in the wars of Flanders, who had just been inspecting the troops guarding the South Coast. 'They all want the Spaniards to land,' he told her. 'Every man is telling what feats he will do. I am the only man who is trembling for the fear of it.'[15] A more cheerful opinion about the quality of the militia was that of Sir Christopher Hatton:[16] 'In truth, they were young gentlemen, yeomen and yeomen's sons and artificers of the most brave sort such as went as voluntary to serve of gaiety and joyalty of mind. All which kind of people are the force and flower of a kingdom.'

In addition to the Tilbury army and the Queen's bodyguard, there was an army to watch the Scots border and, it seems, a large mobile force which was to shadow the Armada as it passed along the coast. All told, there were maybe two hundred thousand Englishmen with arms of one kind or another. Maybe half of them were half-trained. Few of them had heard a shot fired in war. All were supremely confident that, when the day came, they would drive the Spaniards into the sea. When the hour of danger came, the warlike fury of the people impressed one observer (Digges), 'every man violently running down to the seaside'. But another authority (Sir Thomas Wilford) thought that 'a few orderly soldiers would chase great numbers of these furious, inflamed, savage flock.'[17] Happily, the issue was never put to the test, although it is possible that the outcome would have surprised Sir Thomas. After all, it was English soldiers who inflicted the first real defeat on the Spanish regulars in the Low Countries.

The war fever of that summer infected the nation at every level of society. The Earl of Shrewsbury, crippled by gout, assured the Queen of his devotion. Three years before he had thanked her for saving him from two devils, the Queen of Scots and his wife. Now he wrote that 'lame of body yet lusty in heart' he hoped to strike one blow for her.[18] Walsingham, a sick man near to death, was shopping in Middelburg for a suit of armour.[19] And, in every town, little boys drilled with home-made St George's flags and staves, a game they were still playing in the next reign when they caught the benevolent eye of James I, who was normally not an enthusiast for military matters.

Apart from the mobilising of the militia, there were other measures of defence. The coast was heavily fortified. A boom was built across the Thames at Tilbury to the design of an Italian engineer. Above all, there was a system of beacons to give warning of the enemy's approach.[20] This cost money for wages (8*d*. a day – and no dogs allowed lest the watchers be distracted from their duties). Fuel, too, was provided, three trees per beacon. The beacon was usually built on top of a church tower or a prominent hill. It was the job of the Justices of the Peace to keep the system under close inspection and ensure, for instance, that when a hut was built to shelter the watchers in bad weather, it did not have a seat which might tempt them to sleep. At the Isle of Wight, rightly regarded as one of the most vulnerable strategic areas, an elaborate system of signalling existed to indicate the size of the approaching fleet. Having hoisted the signal, one watcher was to run to the church and clash the bells while his companion rushed to tell the local Justice of the Peace. Soldiers were then ferried to the island in thirty-seven boats capable of conveying 1,186 men at a crossing. Local magnates were ordered to stay on the coast. The Marquis of Winchester, who had one quarrel with the Earl of Sussex and another (on a question of military protocol) with the Bishop of Winchester, was to his irritation forbidden to go up to London, where he had some interesting lawsuits pending.[21]

And while in England the warlike excitement boiled up, a strange hush fell upon Europe. The Continent settled down to await the outcome of a collision which would determine the fate of some and the policy of all. The Pope was observed to be in a notably bad temper during those days, which the English ambassador in Paris, when he heard of it, attributed to the difficulty a poor monk had in accustoming himself to his exalted station. It might be, however, that His Holiness was irritated by the thought that if Philip were to force a landing in England, he would be able to demand 1,000,000 ducats promised him by the Pope; on the other hand, should he fail, it would be bad for the Catholic cause in general. The French Queen-Mother was profuse in goodwill for Spain, but nobody believed her.

The King of Navarre's Huguenots, on the other hand, waged an annoying campaign in the Landes of Bordeaux against King Philip's couriers passing on their way to and from Flanders. In consequence, Philip was compelled to order his messengers to travel by the long route through Provence and Languedoc.[22]

Two large deeds on parchment sealed with lead, on their way to the Venetian ambassador in Madrid, were captured by those Protestant highwaymen, who used the lead to make bullets. Against all the hopes of the Scottish Catholic exiles, their king was bought by Elizabeth with the promise of a permanent guard of gentlemen for his person, an English dukedom and a pension of £5,000. It was not a high price for closing the back door into England, especially as the promises were not kept.

XVII

Great Expense of Powder and Bullet

> 'This great Galeazzo which was so huge and hye;
> That like a bulwark on the sea
> Did seem to each man's eye.
> There was it taken unto our great relief
> And divers Nobles in which traine
> Don Pietro was the chief.'
>
> *Thomas Deloney*

The news that the Armada was off the Lizard arrived in Plymouth on the same day that Medina Sidonia saluted his first glimpse of the English coast by hoisting the sacred standard of the Enterprise on his flagship, the *San Martin*. In the early afternoon of that day* the *Golden Hind*, a pinnace belonging to the English covering screen, came into port and her captain, Thomas Fleming, reported that he had made contact after a long wait and many false alarms. Immediately Drake dispatched William Page to take the news to the Queen.† Fleming's news came as an unpleasant surprise to the English admirals. For if the Spaniards had been off the Lizard, sixty miles away, at the time Fleming saw them that morning, where might they be now?

The situation was all the more alarming because of the hour, the state of the tide and the direction of the wind. It was three o'clock in the afternoon and only an hour was left of the ebb-tide. The wind was blowing from the south-west into the Sound. For that reason, if the galleons were to be brought out of harbour, they must be warped out – towed by sailors rowing hard against the wind in pinnaces and longboats. And that could be done only when the tide was on the ebb. But there was only an hour of the ebb to go – it was not long enough. High water

* 29 July by the New Style, 19 by the Old.

† Cost to the Queen, according to Drake's account books, £5.

was due at half-past ten. Some time after that, say, at eleven o'clock, the English fleet could begin to move. And not until then. 'We have time to finish the game and beat the Spaniards afterwards.' Drake's legendary remark on the bowling green of Plymouth Hoe may well be authentic, although the first record of it in print occurs a generation later. It is certainly in the style of the man and true to the mood of jocose fatalism in which he faced this vast crisis. More important, it was an accurate description of the situation in Plymouth Sound that July afternoon. Seven or eight hours must pass before the English fleet could move and the main enemy force was probably forty – maybe no more than thirty – miles away. Moreover, the wind was in the south-west, favouring the attack. The Spaniards had a magnificent opportunity.

If their fastest ships were sent ahead of the main body of the Armada so that they reached the entrance to Plymouth Sound, they could sail in when the tide turned and damage the English galleons, which at that time were being towed out. The Armada had the advantage in heavier, short-range guns, just the armament for a fight in narrow waters. If there was hand-to-hand work, as was likely, the Spaniards had not only ships which rode higher in the water, but an abundance of trained soldiers – nearly ten times as many as were in the English fleet. Finally, it was a perfect tactical situation for the use of fireships by the Spaniards on a crowded English fleet struggling out of port against the wind. Waiting for the tide to turn, adding the final touches that would make their ships battle-worthy, and warping them laboriously out of the embrace of land, the English look-out men peered anxiously seawards: patches of mist; visibility variable. But no sign of the enemy. They were lucky, luckier than they had reason to expect. The flowing tide brought no Spanish ships into the Sound and when, on the ebb-tide in early morning, some units of the English fleet led by the Queen's galleons had reached the open sea there was still no interference from the Spaniards.

In the half-light of a cloudy morning, the main portion of

Howard's squadron, fifty-four ships in all, sailed across the bows of the oncoming Armada. The Lord Admiral's aim was to work to windward of the Spanish fleet. Drake, with eight ships, probably took an independent course. As a Plymouth man, he knew that, while with an ebbing tide a current set up-channel, there was a back-current which set westwards round Rame Head. Six hours would suffice to bring the ships round the promontory; another six hours and the inshore current would take them west of Looe.[1]

While the English fleet was working out of Plymouth during those early hours of 30 July, the enemy was still loitering off the Lizard waiting for the stragglers to catch up. Medina Sidonia summoned another council of war. At that time, the Spaniards did not know that Howard and Drake had united their squadrons at Plymouth.

One account of the meeting has it that Oquendo, Leyva and Recalde urged that Plymouth should be attacked at once. The wind was in the right quarter for an incoming fleet. The narrow approach channels of the Sound were ideal for a close action in which the Spaniards would have the advantage. Some sailors objected that, in entering the Sound, the Armada would advance under a heavy enfilading fire. But, according to this account, the Council in numbers and professional authority, was in favour of attack. The Duke, however, imposed his veto. His instructions from the King were to continue up-Channel until he linked with Parma. To attack Plymouth would be a plain deviation from this royal command. But, said the partisans of attack, if the king were here, with this situation – this golden opportunity – before him, he would think otherwise. These protests were brushed aside. The chilly hand of the crowned bureaucrat reached out from his study in the Escorial to the tumbling seas within sight of the Lizard.

Whether this report is accurate or not, it is clearly possible that an attack on Plymouth was discussed. On the other hand, it is unlikely that Medina Sidonia would act against the weight of expert advice in his council. Immediately afterwards, he sent off

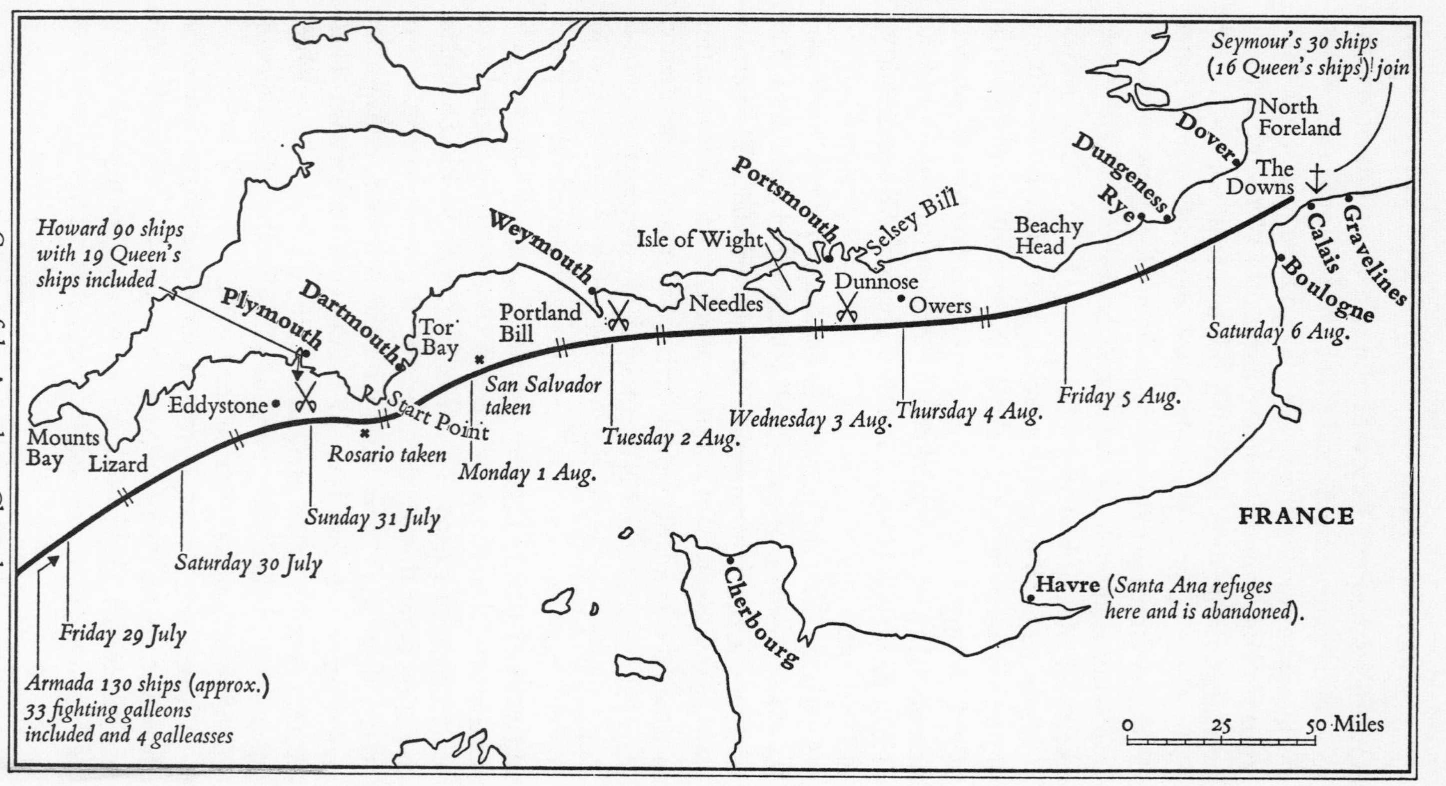

5 Course of the Armada up-Channel

a dispatch to the King, in which he did not mention any project for an attack on Plymouth but said simply that the council had decided the Armada should not sail farther east than the Isle of Wight until Parma had sent word that he was ready to put his soldiers on shipboard. When the Council was dispersing, news came which made it clear that there was no longer a golden opportunity in Plymouth Sound. One of the Spanish scouting vessels had captured an English fishing boat and brought in its crew who reported that the English fleet – Drake's squadron and Howard's, too – was coming out of Plymouth Sound.

By sunset, the Armada was somewhere between Fowey and Plymouth, sailing eastwards in good order and close formation at the pace of the slowest sailer. And, sometime that evening, in the bursts of light that came between the scudding rainclouds and the drifting sea mists, top-men in the English fleet caught their first glimpse of the Spanish Armada. It was as imposing a spectacle as anything the most alarmist English rumour had imagined. It seemed that the gloomy predictions of Drake were amply realised.

Over miles of grey sea a vast and orderly congregation of warships, their painted sails swelling with the wind of attack, moved up-Channel. How many were they? In the shifting weather it was impossible to be sure. But it is unlikely that those who watched from the mastheads of the English ships under-estimated the numbers of the hostile array, or that they failed to be impressed by the height and majesty of the Spanish galleons, qualities which would be emphasised by the light dying behind them, and which, as the events of the next few days were to show, had their corresponding defects. There was, too, magnificence as well as scale. The ships might be corpulent and top-heavy, incredibly clumsy sailing machines by modern standards. But as works of art of the Renaissance, how fantastic, how elaborate, brilliantly painted and lavishly gilded, gay with the banners of all the provinces of Philip's empire! Each vessel wore the ragged red saltire on a white ground of the Burgundian flag.

A hundred and thirty ships, 8,000 seamen, 18,000 soldiers – five *tercios* of infantry, thirty-two companies of light troops and 2,000 Portuguese – such was the army of invasion that had set sail from Lisbon. Now the numbers were fewer by the complement of four galleys and the flagship of the Biscay squadron which had fallen by the way and taken refuge in Havre. Even so, the spectacle was majestic and, to those of weaker fibre, daunting. The Happy Armada of the King of Spain was a major national effort worthy of the leading military power in Europe. It was a tribute to the resources of Spain and to the dour resolution of her King. Philip had sent to crush the island heretics the most powerful fleet that had until that hour sailed the Ocean Sea. To beat off its onslaught would call for a corresponding effort by England.

To Drake, second-in-command of the English fleet, that first sight of the enemy in the late hours of a Saturday night, might have been the occasion for a grim exercise in 'I told you so'. For here, imminent on the threshold of England, was the danger he had hoped to smother in its own harbours. It is quite likely, indeed, that, being the kind of man he was, an extrovert with no gift for reticence, he did exhibit such a weakness, even if by nothing more than a shrug of the shoulders to his captain, Jonas Bodenham, a trusted companion, who had been with him in the Cadiz affair the year before and was the nephew of his first wife. But there was a great deal to do, and it was work he revelled in, a task vastly greater in scale than anything he had ever experienced. But which commander, in either fleet, had ever faced a conflict like this one? They were about to take part, all of them, in the first great naval battle of a new era, the first in which the darting manoeuvres of oar-driven galley squadrons were supplanted by the movements of sailing-ships, clumsily dependent on the fickle wind. Instead of the rams of the galleys, fleets would rely on their broadsides to sink or cripple an enemy.

The new age of naval war opened with chivalric ceremony when Howard sent out the pinnace *Disdain* to deliver his defiance to the Spanish duke by firing her gun at him.

It was early on Sunday morning, and by this time the English warning system had sprung into life on land. Smoke by day and flame by dark, the beacons on hill and church tower passed the message along the coast to Dover and inland to London and the north. In the towns and villages drums beat. The trained bands prepared to march. The village armour came off its hook in the village church. Cheerful and bellicose, the reinforcements poured southwards to the coast down the country lanes of Devon, Dorset, Hampshire and Sussex. The war was a lark, as war often is at that stage. Laggards whom the justices had so far overlooked took out their arms from the dusty cupboards where they had been stowed. Women went to church. Lord Burghley was crippled by gout. The Queen heard the news at Richmond.

During the early hours of daylight, an important and, as it proved, decisive change occurred in the conditions in which the sea battle was to be fought. Six miles west of the Eddystone Rock, the English ships had gained the weather gauge of the enemy. From that moment they did not lose it, so long as the wind stayed in the west, which it did during the greater part of this week to come. The English could select for a battering any Spanish straggler, any weakling, or outlying vessel, while it would be hard for a Spanish rescuing party, working its way against the wind, to come to the aid of an endangered comrade. Until the wind changed or died the English captains could fight or break off action as they chose.

Along with Frobisher in the *Triumph* and Hawkins in the *Victory*, Drake took the *Revenge* into action against the Spanish rearguard. The trio concentrated its attack on a Portuguese galleon, the *San Juan de Portugal*, flying Recalde's flag as vice-admiral. Under the stress of the artillery duel, Recalde sheered off, causing another galleon, the *Nuestra Señora del Rosario*, commanded by Don Pedro de Valdes, to foul a nearby ship. With his foremast and bowsprit overboard in a confusion of splintered wood and tangled rigging, Valdes fell out of station.

A few minutes later, there was a sudden sheet of flame

followed by a detonation echoing along the water. The *San Salvador*, vice-flagship of the Biscay squadron, a ship of 800 tons or more, had her innards blown out by the explosion of a powder barrel. A week later, survivors of the disaster alleged that a Dutch master-gunner had put a match to the barrel in a fit of pique. The Armada story, like most historical epics, has attracted its share of legends. By evening the *San Salvador*, still burning, had been towed into the shelter provided by her consorts.

With the light failing and the wind rising, the Duke still had one task to perform: to bring Don Pedro de Valdes' damaged ship, the *Rosario*, under control. In this, perhaps, he would have succeeded had he not given in to vehement protests from his chief of staff, Diego Flores de Valdes. This experienced officer argued that there must be no waiting to pick up stragglers or rescue casualties. The Armada must press on. The Duke submitted. The galleons resumed their course. And, some time after dark, Drake pounced on the *Rosario* – which, by that time, had drifted far behind her companions.

Later on, there was trouble in the English fleet about this incident. Drake, it was said, had been carrying the lantern in his poop which the other ships were to follow. In consequence, when he went aside to snatch the *Rosario*, the ships that followed him were at a loss and, when daylight came, the Lord Admiral found himself too near the Spaniards for his liking, especially as, at that time, the wind had swung round, giving the Spaniards the weather gauge. Martin Frobisher, an envious Yorkshireman, who had no love for Drake, was particularly indignant over his conduct, which he deemed selfish and disloyal.

Drake's account of the business was given to Howard on the following afternoon when the *Revenge* had caught up with the *Ark Royal* once more. He explained that in the dark he had seen ships passing to seaward. Were they Spaniards who were, perhaps trying to regain the weather gauge which the English had snatched from them? The matter must be looked into. He put over the helm of the *Revenge* and ordered the poop lantern to be extinguished so that the whole English fleet should not follow him in what might turn out to be a wild-goose chase. And so, at first, it seemed to be. For, when challenged, the mysterious strangers proved to be peaceful German cargo ships.

On his way back to rejoin the fleet, Drake fell in with the *Rosario*, and summoned her to surrender. There was a considerable element of bluff in this, for the *Rosario* had forty-six guns, and three hundred soldiers aboard, which was more than Drake could muster in the *Revenge* and the *Roebuck*, a Plymouth privateer he had brought along with him. However, a man's name may have a power of its own. At any rate, the impudence succeeded. Don Pedro de Valdes thought it no dishonour to strike his flag to so celebrated an admiral as Drake and the *Rosario* was taken under escort into Tor Bay. Don Pedro and his chief officers were put aboard the *Revenge*, where they were given the hospitality due to distinguished captives.

By a happy chance, in the passenger list of the *Revenge* was Nicholas Ouseley, an English merchant, who had been one of Walsingham's leading agents in Spain. Don Pedro spoke frankly about naval matters in the admiral's cabin of the *Revenge*. He spoke to men who could understand. If he said more about Spanish plans and hopes than he should have done, it should be remembered that Don Pedro was a very angry man at that time. The Duke, as he later complained to the King, had left him comfortless in the sight of the whole fleet, although the *San Martin* could easily have relieved the *Rosario*. After the fight was over, Don Pedro spent agreeable years as Drake's nominal prisoner until his ransom of £3,000 was paid. Then he was given a farewell banquet by the Lord Mayor of London and was exchanged for one of the Wynter family, Edward, who had been captured by the Spaniards.

The *Rosario*'s crew had not such a pleasant time among the Dorset country people who, simple peasants, were shocked that they had to support, at 2*d*. a day, men who had come to their coast for the purpose of enslaving England. They said that they would have preferred it if the Spaniards had been pitched overboard as soon as they were captured. The maintenance of these Spanish prisoners of war brought about a bitter quarrel between two local gentlemen, Sir George Carey and Sir John Gilberte.[2] Carey said Gilberte put two hundred and twenty-six Spaniards in a Bridewell* sixteen miles from Carey's house, so that he could get no service from them, while the prisoners were kept hard by Gilberte's estate and laboured in his garden. And where, Sir George wished to know, is 'all the wine I left with him?'

Drake's behaviour over the *Rosario* has scandalised the staider kind of naval historian. He had deserted his post, they argue, and he deserved a court-martial and, probably, as the more censorious allege, a firing squad. And the explanation he gave of his truancy has been doubted on the ground that nobody else reported German merchantmen in the Channel mists that night. But it is hard to see why Drake should have invented these ships. They did not really strengthen his defence against the charge that he had left his station. The truth is that we are dealing with the year of the Armada and not, say, that of Trafalgar, not with Nelson's Royal Navy but with a fleet manned for the most part by hard-bitten merchant skippers, brought up in the privateering trade. To ask a captain to let a rich prize slip through his hands was asking a great deal.

Too much need not be made of the extinguishing of the poop lantern. It was surely reasonable for Drake to assume that his fellow-captains could be trusted to look after their ships. There was, in any case, no court-martial for him. And any doubts about the morals of the business were finally laid to rest when, a few days later, the Lord Admiral of England himself left his place in the line of battle to make sure of a prize.

Meanwhile, the battle was moving up-Channel. The day (1 August) that Drake rejoined Howard and made his explanations to his commander-in-chief was marked by an intense and noisy artillery duel off Portland Bill, which Spanish veterans swore was fiercer by far than anything at the battle of Lepanto

* A gaol.

itself. The wind veered from east to south and the fortunes of battle veered like it. Martin Frobisher was beset under Portland Bill by four Spanish galleasses – ships with oars as well as sails – and was saved when once more the wind changed, allowing Howard to bring English galleons to the rescue. Then Recalde's *San Juan* was set upon by a swarm of English ships at a time when only Medina Sidonia's ship could come to her aid. In consequence, the Spanish flagship, caught in isolation for an hour, was raked by repeated broadsides from Howard's ships without suffering any mortal wound. The action was broken off and the Armada sailed on.

By the end of the second day's fighting it was plain to the English admirals that their tactical plan was not likely to yield a swift, decisive victory. An enormous quantity of powder and shot had been squandered, the Channel had resounded for hours with the thunder of cannon, culverin and lesser artillery, but no Spanish ships had been taken or sunk, save two that had fallen into English hands as a result of accidents. While practically no English lives had been lost in the battle, it was all too probable that casualties in the Duke's galleons had been far from crippling. It was, of course, gratifying that the English vessels were faster than those of their rivals, that they answered the helm more promptly and that they were, as the sailors said, more 'weatherly'. These were solid assets, especially when added to the general tactical advantage of the weather gauge, seized on the eve of battle. Drake was satisfied with the way things had gone and distributed £100 among the crew of the *Revenge*, as a reward, no doubt, for the capture of the *Rosario*.[3]

But the ugly fact remained that the Armada had maintained its close formation unbroken and that, with a sinister air of calm and discipline, it was pursuing eastwards a settled plan of campaign, whatever that might be. And Parma, with his redoubtable army, was lurking behind the sand dunes of Dunkirk. The English had relied on better ships and defter seamanship to keep them out of range of the heavy Spanish guns and on their own culverins to batter life – or, at least, order – out of the Armada.

And the culverins had apparently failed. It was a great disappointment.

It seems to have been the case that English culverins discharged too light a projectile – 17 pounds or less – to sink a ship, and that English galleons were out of the range of the Spanish cannon, firing a 90-pound shot. The Spaniards fired a heavier broadside while the English had a greater number of guns (1,900 pieces firing a 4-pound shot or heavier, against 1,100). Naval gunnery in that age was a chancy business. Sir George Carey, Captain of the Isle of Wight, said of the battle fought on 3 August that although it went on from five in the morning until ten at night 'with great expense of powder and bullet, there hath not been two of our men hurt'.[4] What were the casualties among the Spaniards, even if the most charitable assumptions are made about the superior accuracy of English gunnery? The English were inclined to blame the gunners and themselves for the disappointing results of the Channel fighting. But good ships could survive an inordinate amount of the gunfire of those days. Seven years after the Armada, and in Drake's flagship, *Revenge*, Sir Richard Grenville fought a whole Spanish fleet for fifteen hours and had sixteen feet of water in the hold before he surrendered. The *Revenge* sank days later in a full Atlantic gale. Sir Richard Hawkins, captain of the *Swallow* in the Armada fighting, survived a sixty-hour battle in the Pacific against a large number of Spanish ships. He had fourteen holes under the water-line when he asked for terms. Still, his ship did not sink.[5] Something more than gunfire was needed. Sir William Wynter, talking to the Lord Admiral, in the cabin of the *Ark Royal*, thought that, in a crisis so grave, fireships might soon be useful.

Out on the seaward wing of the action in the Channel, Drake closed the range when the *Gran Grifon*, a powerful converted merchant ship of 650 tons* mounting thirty-eight guns, began to drop out of the close Spanish formation. Drake led his wing of the fleet into action and a savage gun battle followed in

* By Spanish measurements, equivalent to about 500 English tons.

which the *Revenge* took some risks with Spanish cannon-fire so that she could bring her culverins into more effective play. Before the action was broken off, the *Gran Grifon*, badly damaged, was taken in tow by a galleon which brought her into the shelter of her companions. By that time the wind had fallen and the two fleets spent the rest of the day in idleness. So far, fighting had been desultory, bringing no great glory to either side and no spectacular disaster.

An English council of war decided on a major reorganisation of the command system in accordance with which the fleet was divided into four squadrons of a manageable size, about twenty-five ships apiece, under the leadership of Frobisher, Howard, Hawkins and Drake, proceeding from north to south of the fleet formation. It was the first recognition that in an engagement on such a scale, with naval tactics in so primitive a state, centralised control meant no control at all.

Next morning, in a calm, Hawkins had his squadron towed within range of two Spanish stragglers. It was a rash move. Medina Sidonia, who must have regretted at that moment that he had been deserted by his galleys, ordered three galleasses to row to the relief of the threatened ships. The *Ark Royal* and the *Golden Lion* were towed into the fight and there was an exchange of rowdy broadsides. But once again there was no decisive end to the fight. The Spanish stragglers were towed out of danger.

Next morning (4 August) the two fleets had reached a point in the Channel of which the strategic importance was obvious to all – the entrance to the Solent, the approaches to the Isle of Wight. 'Wait there on Parma if you must,' Philip had said. 'Beyond the Isle we will not sail until we are sure that Parma is ready to come out,' the Spanish Council of war had decided on that morning of 30 July off the Lizard. Without knowing anything of these opinions among the enemy, the Lord Admiral saw real danger to England from an attempt to establish a base on the island.

With the movements of wind, now swelling and now fading

away, and the changes of current in one of the most deceptive stretches of water on the whole coastline of Western Europe, the two fleets had drifted this way and that off the Isle of Wight. Frobisher's squadron, covering the entry to the Solent, was caught between the land and the Spaniards and for a time his flagship, the *Triumph*, was in danger from a Spanish boarding party. On the other wing, Drake had nosed into an attack on the Spanish seaward flank, which had the effect of crowding the whole Armada northwards towards dangerous reefs from which it was saved only by the orders which Medina Sidonia sent out in time. There must have been a heavy swell running also, for Thomas Fenner thought that the enemy would be 'touched very near because of the great seagate' and their shipping 'so light as in fair weather would hardly bear their topsails'.[6]

By the end of the day both fleets were desperately short of ammunition. Medina Sidonia had, from the beginning, been better supplied than the English. He had set off with almost as much gunpowder in his magazines as was to be found in all the arsenals in England. But, in compensation for that handicap, the English were fighting in their own home waters. They could summon additional stores with the knowledge that, if they were available, they would be quickly alongside. The battle in the Channel was gobbling up roundshot and powder on a scale which neither side had bargained for. In addition to these worries about ammunition, Medina Sidonia was deeply anxious because he had not heard what his fellow-duke and senior coadjutor in the Enterprise against England, Alexander Farnese, Duke of Parma, was doing. It was time, it was past time, for the two grand components of the Spanish campaign to co-ordinate their efforts.

Two days later, Medina Sidonia dropped anchor off Calais. That night he sent Captain Pedro de Leon with an urgent plea to Parma for ammunition. This message was followed immediately by one carried by one of the Duke's pilots, Domingo de Ochoa, who arrived at Bruges having sailed in a fast dispatch boat.[7] He reported that, in the last three days, Medina Sidonia had progressed only twelve leagues (thirty-six miles) owing to the constant need to round on the harrassing enemy and beat off his attacks. Could not Parma send him forty or fifty flyboats so that he could attack the English? On the tail of this message went a third one: at Calais there was no shelter for the Armada. The English bombardment was pitiless and unending. And he, Medina Sidonia, could make no effective reply. Flyboats, those handy tough mosquito craft of the northern inshore waters, were what Midonia Sidonia wanted. But Parma had none to spare. Next morning (8 August) he left Bruges for Nieuport to supervise the embarkation of sixteen thousand troops of the expeditionary force. The supreme moment had arrived.

When the Armada came to anchor in Calais Roads, Howard's fleet was not far off, an unfriendly, assiduous presence to windward which from time to time belched flame and smoke when some unwary Spaniard strayed too far out of station. At this moment in the battle, the Lord Admiral was joined by Lord Henry Seymour's squadron of observation, which all this while had been watching the Flemish coast. Thirty-five ships strong, it had been on patrol off Dunkirk lest Parma's army in its flat-bottomed boats might take advantage of calm seas and suitable tides to slip over the straits to Kent. Now only twenty-three miles of coastal waters separated Medina Sidonia at Calais from Parma at Dunkirk. Soon, unless there was some extraordinary flaw in King Philip's conception, the two would join and, together, launch the attempt on England. At this moment, then, the English Navy must be gathered into a single force.

But, ignored by the Spaniards and distrusted by the English, there was a fatal obstacle to the junction of Parma's troops and Medina Sidonia's galleons. The fleet that had come all the way from Lisbon, all the way up the Channel, hammered and chivvied but unbroken, could not enter Dunkirk. And Parma could not come out.[8] Outside Dunkirk were sandbanks stretching for thirteen miles out to sea and dangerous to ships drawing more than five feet of water. The Spanish ships drew twenty-five or more. As for Parma's crowded boat-fleet, it could not emerge from the canal at Dunkirk without being set upon and sunk, one boat after another, by the flyboats of Justin of Nassau, Admiral of Zeeland, which could operate freely among the Flemish shoals without fear of interference from the Spaniards.

When this simple but calamitous truth at last dawned on the Spaniards is not clear. Almost up to the end, Medina Sidonia expected Parma to emerge from his shelter so that his boats could be escorted to England. Almost up to the end, Parma was waiting for the fleet from Spain to bring him the naval answer to Justin. Parma did not know that in the Armada were no ships able to fight among the Banks of Zeeland. Medina Sidonia had assumed that his business was with the English and deep water, and not with the Dutch and sand.

The English, of course, should not have overlooked this Dutch factor. But the Dutch were their allies and often tiresome, and the English share with other nations an aptitude for distrusting an ally and underrating him. So they did not believe that Justin would or could blockade Parma or – better still – drown his soldiers in their boats. This was a failure in understanding. The Dutch were far more passionately and bitterly committed to the war against Philip than the English were. They had reason to be. Justin of Nassau had a hundred and thirty flyboats at his disposal in the Scheldt, and Medina Sidonia had no light craft to help Parma and, on the contrary, was begging Parma to send him some.

In the early days of August, when everything still hung in the balance, neither side could relax an iota of effort or anxiety. Parma, having seen his soldiers embarked in Nieuport, rode to Dunkirk (9 August) where he found the sea so rough that he could not even send the Armada the powder and cannon balls for which Medina Sidonia was imploring him. When Veedor-General Jorge Manrique, the Duke's latest envoy, came in from the sea, distraught and insistent, he refused to accept Parma's explanations. Parma called in his experts, Flemish skippers who knew that coast as well as Drake knew Plymouth Sound.

They assured Manrique that the thing could not be done. In

that wind, with those seas running and with those Dutch fly-boats always in the offing, it would be suicide. If the wind fell, as it might do at any moment, and if there were no English or Dutch ships in the way, of course there would then be nothing to prevent Parma's veterans with all their equipment sailing straight over to the mouth of the Thames. While the debate and the expostulations went on, vehement and anguished, there came a peremptory rapping at the door of the council room. A new messenger had arrived from the Armada, a young man of high rank, the Prince of Ascoli, natural son of the King. He came ashore at Dunkirk accompanied by an equerry, three servants and a chaplain. He brought momentous tidings.[9]

XVIII

The Devil Ships

> 'We have the army of Spain before us . . . never anything pleased me better than to see the enemy flying with a Southerly wind to the northwards.'
>
> *Francis Drake, at Gravelines*

The English admirals, lying off Calais, had not been prepared to stake their country's safety on any chance of weather or connivance of the Dutch. They faced across the water, only two musket shots away, a fleet that was still unbroken in order and unbeaten in battle. The Armada might have been punished, how badly they did not know, but, since the accidents of the first day's engagement, it had not lost a single ship. And this, after a squandering of ammunition such as nobody – Drake alone excepted – had foreseen, was deeply discouraging.

On Sunday morning (7 August) the commanders met in Howard's stately cabin in the *Ark Royal*. It was clear to all of them that, short of some extraneous help, a tactical device was needed to break up the close defensive order of the Armada. It was now or never, for at any hour the two Dukes might join forces. What was to be done? Fireships might be used, as Sir William Wynter had mentioned five days earlier[1] and for which, at that moment, the provident Walsingham was collecting pitch and faggots at Dover. But there was no time to wait for fuel from England. The fleet must improvise its own fireships. Drake at once offered a ship of his own, the *Thomas*[2] (200 tons); Hawkins put in the *Bark Bond* (150 tons); another two ships were taken from Drake's westward squadron – altogether there were eight vessels totalling 1,240 tons which during one feverish day were crammed with every kind of combustible. During the afternoon, Drake changed the position of his squadron so that its new anchorage was directly to windward of the Spanish fleet. That night when the ships and the crews of volunteers were ready, the weather became the ally of the English Navy. The tide at midnight set towards the Spanish anchorage and a fresh wind sprang up from the west. The eight fireships were set off on their course together, with results that surpassed all reasonable expectations.

Drake, who had been one of the protagonists of the scheme, had seen in Cadiz Bay the year before how easy it was for cool-headed seamen to deal with a menace of this kind. But Calais Roadstead is not Cadiz Bay. It is an exposed anchorage the dangers of which had already been stressed to Medina Sidonia by the Governor of the town, a Frenchman friendly to the Spanish cause. More important, however, there was a horrid memory which oppressed many stout-hearted Spaniards of the 'devil ships', brainchildren of an Italian engineer named Federigo Giambelli of Mantua. These monstrous engines of war had been launched in the Scheldt against a bridge built across the river by the Duke of Parma, then besieging Antwerp. Each ship had carried a cargo of 3½ tons of gunpowder under a canopy of 'blue gravestones'. The bridge had been destroyed by the explosion; eight hundred men were killed. And Giambelli was known to be now in England.*

The Spanish look-out men in Calais Road saw eight black shapes approaching on the wind; each shape showed a spark of red fire which, in a matter of minutes,[3] swelled into a mass of flames so that eight floating furnaces were bearing down on the anchored galleons. Worse still, the loaded cannon aboard these mysterious vessels fired their shot as the flames reached their charges. Instantly, a frenzy seized on the Spaniards. The fireships had a mile and a half to cover and wind and current to help them. The Armada had ten minutes to get clear. Cables were cut. A hundred and fifty anchors were abandoned in Calais Sands. Sails were set to catch the wind. Every ship made off as best she could, so as to put as much sea-room as possible between her and the dreaded mine machines (*maquinas de minas*)

* He was helping to build the boom across the Thames at Tilbury.

which a malignant spirit among the English – and could it be any other man than the arch-demon himself, El Draque? – had conjured up out of the night to destroy the Invicible Armada and bring the Enterprise to ruin.

In short, the Armada panicked.

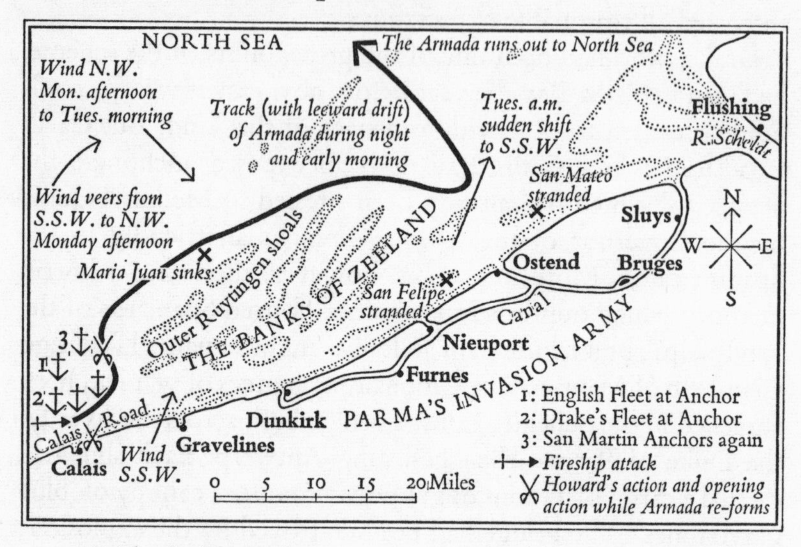

6 The fireship attack
The battle off Gravelines, and the peril of The Armada on the Banks of Zeeland

Medina Sidonia was the first to recover his nerve. His officers begged him, as the fireships approached, to take to a pinnace and reach the safety of the French coast. The Duke shook them off and, with the sangfroid of his race and rank, watched the fireships as they drifted past on their way to the sandbanks, where they guttered out harmlessly. Then he ordered the *San Martin* to drop anchor once more and fired a gun as a signal for the rest of the fleet to do likewise. At the same time, he sent the Prince of Ascoli to take more detailed instructions to some of the captains. From this mission, the Prince did not return. Feeling, perhaps, that he was too valuable a hostage to fall into enemy hands, or for some other reason, he went ashore and made his way to Dunkirk with the disastrous news. No doubt the Duke was relieved that responsibility for so precious a life was no longer on his shoulders.

Alas, not all the Spanish ships could obey their commander-in-chief. Most of them were making eastwards as fast and as far as they could from the danger. The *San Lorenzo*, flagship of the galleasses, had already had trouble with her rudder off the Lizard. Now she lost it in a near-collision with one of the merchantmen and ran hard ashore on the sands in front of Calais Castle. Her commander, Don Hugo de Moncada, prepared to sell his life dearly, as a gentleman should, but he was grievously incommoded by the fact that the *San Lorenzo* lay over on her side, her guns looking either up to heaven or downwards into Calais Sands.

The dawn light of Monday (8 August) brought the English a spectacle such as can rarely have rejoiced the eyes of seamen at the end of a week of hard and indecisive fighting. A fine galleass, the *San Lorenzo*, disabled and aground on the bar outside Calais harbour. The flagship, the *San Martin*, and four other galleons at anchor some distance to the east. And the rest of the Great Armada? Scattered far and wide on the grey seas to the north-east, in no kind of order and apparently unable to anchor. And the wind was steady in the south-west, dead in the right quarter for the attack. Medina Sidonia had been, once again, unlucky with the weather. Howard gave the signal to attack. While he marked out the crippled *San Lorenzo* as his own particular prey, he unleashed Drake and his squadron on the Duke's *San Martin* and its attendant galleons. The *Revenge* led the way followed by the *Nonpareil* and after that by ship upon ship of the western squadron. Each in turn poured its broadside into the *San Martin* and veered off to the north-west. Frobisher's squadron, which followed Drake's, stayed to fight it out with the *San Martin*. All of this was work at close range, a hundred yards or so between the fleets. Wynter's culverins fired five hundred rounds; he was never out of range of the enemy's arquebus fire and 'most time within speech of each other'.[4]

To Drake it was obvious that the time had come to close

with the disordered enemy and deal him the blows which his heavy cannon had so far warded off. While Frobisher pounded the *San Martin* and her gallant consort, the *San Marco de Portugal*, and Hawkins came up in the *Victory* to share in the fight, Drake and his squadron had moved on to spread the terror of English gunfire among the galleons of Castile and Portugal. Under the stress of battle the Spanish ships had recovered something like a defensive formation.

Overwhelmed as he might be with his task, the Duke bore himself as one who had inborn qualities of leadership. All around was the unrest of the sea and the confusion of battle, smoke, gunflashes, noise, ships heeling this way or that. How to make sense of it all? The Duke – it is his own story, but he was a modest and a truthful man – climbed up into the top of the *San Martin* to survey the scene above its shroud of smoke. What he saw brought him little comfort: his galleons were being worried like bears at the stake by dozens of English ships. He could see the *San Felipe*, of the Portugal squadron, in trouble with Frobisher's *Triumph*; Hawkins, too, was taking his revenge for that day, all those years ago, in the anchorage at San Juan de Ulua. To the rescue came the *San Mateo*, commanded by Don Diego de Pimentel, colonel of a crack infantry regiment and now eager to get to grips with these elusive English. Once his grappling irons had secured one of them, his soldiers would swarm on to her decks and – Don Diego had no doubt what the outcome would be! But, although the English gunners were ready enough to exchange broadsides, although some of the time not more than a pike-length separated the ships, they would not come to hand-to-hand work. And having the nimbler ships and the handier seamen, they could choose the kind of battle they were going to fight. So the *San Mateo*, which was running out of shot, very soon leaked like a sieve; her gundecks ran with blood; her sails were in shreds, her rigging cut to pieces. From the top of the *San Martin* the masts of the two stricken galleons were descried above the clouds of gunsmoke when Medina Sidonia brought up his flagship, herself crippled, with blood on her decks and salt water in her hold, and the Spanish ships were saved.

In the meantime, the Lord Admiral of England had decided that he could not make a prize of the *San Lorenzo*. The *Ark Royal* drew too much water for the inshore operations that were needed. He left the task to a lieutenant, a Margate man named Richard Thomson, who mustered fifty or sixty men in a long-boat along with as many musketeers in a pinnace. The storming party was none too strong, for the *San Lorenzo* had a crew of 124 in addition to 244 soldiers, and 300 galley slaves who need not, however, be reckoned as units in the combat strength. But, as it turned out, Thomson was in luck. Hugo de Moncada was killed by a bullet in the head and the Spanish resistance crumbled. The agreeable work of looting then went forward, until some of the rougher elements among the boarders began to rob a French deputation sent by the Governor of Calais, tearing the very earrings from the Frenchman's ears. At that, the guns of Calais Castle protested loudly and to some purpose. Thomson and his band of thieves made off with all possible haste.

By this time, the Lord Admiral, putting behind him the thoughts of private gain, had joined the main actions being fought ten miles farther east outside the sandbanks at Gravelines – where Medina Sidonia had brought together more and more of the vessels scattered in that access of panic when the fireships bore down on his anchored fleet. After seven hours, when the battle drew to a close (about four in the afternoon) as many as fifty Spanish ships had rejoined their Admiral. Then the sky darkened, the wind rose and veered to the north-west and a fierce squall struck both fleets. The cannons stopped barking. Amid shouts from ship's masters, crews swarmed up the rigging to shorten sail. The English fleet stood away.

The storm was especially cruel to the Spanish ships which had taken the worst punishment in the battle. The *Maria Juan* of the Biscay squadron overturned and went down. The *San Mateo* and the *San Felipe* were kept afloat until sunset by strenuous work at the pumps. But it was a losing game and, by sunset, the Duke had given orders that both ships should be abandoned. Last seen, the two galleons were drifting eastwards towards the sandbanks at Ostend, where next day Justin of Nassau's flyboats gratefully gobbled them up. This incident was not noticed by the English. Such was the lack of liaison between the allied navies that the English Lord Admiral wrote to Whitehall, 'There is not a Hollander or Zeelander at sea.'

At the end of the fighting that day Sir Francis Drake sat down in his cabin in the *Revenge* amid his officers and the distinguished prisoners he had taken in the *Rosario*, and wrote a letter to Walsingham. 'God hath given us so good a day in forcing the enemy so far to leeward as I hope to God the Prince of Parma and the Duke of Medina Sidonia shall not shake hands these few days . . . Send us munition and victual whithersoever the enemy goeth.' The letter ended with a phrase that is half a yawn and tells more than pages of description could do of the strain of those momentous days. 'Your honour's most ready to be commanded,' he said, 'but now half sleeping, Fra. Drake.'[5]

Strung out along the Flemish coast, the Armada was now in danger of total destruction. Anchors lost, seamen killed, guns silenced for want of ammunition, and the heretic wind steadily in the north-west, ominously nudging Medina Sidonia's galleons towards the Banks of Zeeland. As for the junction with Parma's invasion flotilla, on which the whole Enterprise had been planned, it was out of the question. The Armada was already to leeward of Dunkirk where, on that very morning (9 August), Parma was hearing from the fugitive Prince of Ascoli the gloomy news of the fireship attack and its sequel.

The Italian duke's Flemish pilots told him that the boats in which his pikemen and musketeers were sitting in serried ranks, disciplined but restless, could not leave the canal in which they were lurking and take to the open sea. The Spanish duke's pilots gave him the warning that, in spite of all their efforts to keep the *San Martin* close to the wind, the flagship was drifting ominously, implacably, towards the shoals.

Medina Sidonia probably did not need any telling. He had only to use his eyes. Each time he gazed to leeward, he could see that the yellowish tongue of foam which marked the line of sandbanks had come a little nearer. His officers begged him to take a pinnace and row to the coast with the standard which the pious ladies of Portugal had worked and the Patriarch of Lisbon had blessed. The Duke would have none of it. He confessed and received absolution. Only God could rescue them. The *San Martin*'s leadsman called seven fathoms below. Six! . . . A galleon near by, closer to the shore than the *San Martin*, found five fathoms. The *San Martin* drew five. The Armada was within minutes of catastrophe, edging ever nearer to the breakers that would pound its ships to pieces, and the vengeful Dutchmen who would cut their throats. The English, down to their last few rounds of ammunition and kegs of powder, watched in pious resentment for the completion of the task which the Lord had taken out of their hands. It seemed that they would not have long to watch.

The Duke, whose nerve had held admirably until then, seems to have known a moment of weakness. 'Señor Oquendo,' he shouted across the waves, for the commander of the Guipuscoan squadron had come within hail during those critical minutes, 'what shall we do? We are lost!' Oquendo, a hot-tempered fighting sailor from San Sebastian, who had an intense dislike for the Duke's Chief of Staff, shouted back, 'Ask Diego Valdes! I am going to fight.'

Then, without warning, the wind changed its direction.

It backed all the way from north-west to south-east. The Armada was reprieved! Prayers of thanksgiving rose in Spanish and Latin from the throats of weary men who had known so long a companionship with despair. One by one, the galleons edged away northwards towards darker water and deeper sea. The English watched, followed, but could do nothing to prevent the escape. For to fight called for ammunition and they had barely any. 'Many of those great guns,' wrote Raleigh, who was not there but talked to many men who had been, 'stood but as cyphers and scarecrows.' Nor could the English believe that the Spanish fleet would not make a new attempt to carry out its royal master's design, just as the Spaniards thought that only some strange failure of strategic vision prevented the English from launching a new attack. The Spanish admirals, in council, resolved that, at the first chance, they would return to the Channel. The English council had a livelier session. Lord Henry Seymour was ordered to take his squadron back to the Narrow Seas to resume the tedious watch on Parma. Drake, who at that time was the man most alarmed over the continuing danger from those crowded transports, seems to have been the leader in urging this step. This can be safely inferred from what followed.

Seymour felt that already he had been cheated of the glory of the Channel fighting – but had he not won some credit in the more furious engagement at Gravelines? Why then should he be sent back, as he put it bitterly, to fish off the Flemish coast while the others were more glamorously engaged in worrying the Armada to death? He obeyed sulkily and wrote a letter to the Queen to say that, if there were any more fighting in the Channel and Sir Francis Drake were there, as vice-admiral, could he, please, be excused?[6] Once more, Drake's imperious temper and impetuous tongue had brought him into trouble. It was certain that Parma must be watched, for if the wind died and the sea fell, those three hundred boats of his bristling with pikes and arquebuses in the hands of grim, experienced soldiers, might slip across to Kent. In these circumstances, what was more natural than to return to the original disposition of the fleet and allow the indignant Lord Henry to resume his independent command? Besides, his ships had only one day's rations and who was to say how long the North Sea chase would last? As it turned out, there was no new glory to be won in shadowing the northbound Armada. It never turned back. King Philip's whole enterprise petered out in futility, which bad weather and crippled ships converted into disaster before many days were over. Howard, Drake and the other captains followed the Spaniards as far as the Firth of Forth. There they gave up the hunt.

Drake, Drake, Drake – over all Europe spread the news that the arch-enemy of Catholic Christendom had been captured while boarding the *San Martin*; that he had been drowned; that the *Revenge* had been sunk in an engagement off the Isle of Wight in which fifteen English ships had gone down; that he had lost one leg; that he had fled from the scene of the disaster in a ship's boat. It appeared that the great naval duel between the Catholic King and this low-born heretic corsair had, under the providence of God, ended in a victory for the King. But could anything else have been expected by good Christian people?

If, here and there, a tinge of regret accompanied the chorus of delight, it was only because the fascination which the bold law-breaker exerts over timid people can be more safely indulged when at last he is brought to justice. And surely there could be no doubt, in the face of such a multitude of reports, varied but all tending to the same conclusion, that Drake really had been defeated. No doubt at all, said the Spanish diplomats, Mendoza in Paris, Olivares in Rome and San Clemente in Prague. No doubt at all, thought Cardinal Allen, impatient to set foot on English soil and begin his stern missionary task. Henri III of France was reluctant to believe, Rudolph the Emperor would not order a *Te Deum* and the Holy Father himself, effusive in admiration of Drake ('What courage! A great captain')[7] showed no haste to hand over the 1,000,000 ducats he had promised King Philip as a reward for victory. But then Sixtus had always been hostile to Philip; Rudolph was mad; and Henri was French.

Meanwhile, the subject of these dire exultant reports had taken refuge from a westerly gale in an east coast harbour. Looking at the weather, he was now less anxious about the situation than he had been. He sensed that Medina Sidonia could not return and knew that, so long as the wind blew strongly from the west, Parma could not come. Admittedly, one had to be watchful but Drake was by nature an optimist. 'The uncertainty of these reports,' he wrote to Walsingham, 'make me rather to rest upon mine own conjecture,' and so he believed that, if Medina Sidonia really were coming back through the North Sea, as an alarming report stated on 11 August, it was because bad weather had prevented him making the voyage back to Spain round Ireland. But if he were to join forces with Parma, weather, wind and tide must all be in a favouring conjunction. It was not likely to happen.[8]

The Lord Admiral, who had come ashore at Margate, galloped all the way to Canterbury, where he met the Commissioners who had been negotiating for peace with Parma up to the day the Armada was sighted off the Lizard. Having just landed from Ostend, they reported to Howard that, in their opinion, the Duke was not yet ready to invade. In fact, by that time, Parma had ordered his soldiers ashore and had begun to disperse his boat-fleet.

Drake was confident that, in the state to which the Armada had been reduced by the fighting, it would be sure to suffer losses on the long voyage back to Spain. Even so, he can hardly have counted on the toll being as grievous as in fact it was. In time, news of the sufferings of those Spaniards leaked back to Madrid and was seized on avidly by the Venetian ambassador – 'I am very hungry and thirsty,' wrote one unfortunate from Scalloway in Shetland. 'One pint of wine a day. You cannot drink the water. It stinks.'[9] Three ships were lost on the Scottish coast and seventeen on the Irish. There are doubts about some items in the casualty list; but on the whole it seems that the reefs and shoals of western Ireland accounted for most of King Philip's losses, 'dissevered on the high seas and to a great number of them driven into divers dangerous bays and upon rocks and there cast away'. Some were driven to seek succour among the 'wild Irish'; others, even less fortunate, fell into the clutches of the Lord Deputy and his minions and without any ado had their throats cut, saving only those who, 'by their apparel, seemed to be persons of great distinction' and good for a profitable ransom.

Don Alonzo de Leyva, who held in Spanish eyes a position comparable with that of Sir Philip Sidney in English, the flower of the nation's youth and chivalry, adored by king and people alike, lost his ship off Achill Island and seized a deserted galleon, the *Gerona*, which he found in Donegal Bay. With him was an adventurous company of young men recruited from the best families in Spain. These bright paladins patched up the *Gerona* as best they could and set sail for home. Alas, the galleon struck a rock and went down with all of them. In the respect that death came quickly, they were not the least fortunate of the victims of that homeward voyage. Sir Richard Bingham, Governor of Connaught, and only a shade less bloodthirsty than the Lord Deputy in Dublin, reported complacently to the Queen that 'the cruel and bloody hands of Your Highness's enemies, overthrown through the wonderful handiwork of Almighty God, by great and horrible shipwrecks upon the coasts of this realm . . . did all perish in the sea save the number of 1,100 or upwards which we put to the sword.'[10]

Not all those Spaniards who survived the seven weeks' voyage with 'never good night or day' while it lasted, found happiness at the end of it. The Duke of Florence's galleon, which had been in the thick of the fighting, crawled into port, unfit for repair. The *Santa Ana* reached San Sebastian. There she was burnt, on the same day that her admiral, Oquendo, died – of shame, as they said. Soon, too, Recalde, sick and sorrowful, would be dead.

On the whole, the Spanish royal navy came out of the ordeal better than the auxiliary vessels – only seven King's ships were lost while the Armada as a whole had lost fifty-one.* The *Gran Grifon*, flagship of the transports, had remained afloat after her duel with Drake's *Revenge*. She made the perilous passage between the Orkneys and Fair Isle and, on two separate occasions, reached the Hebrides before the changeful wind drove her back

* Some say sixty-four.

to the east and she was wrecked on the rocks of Fair Isle. A handful of her crew, thirsty, famished and suffering terribly from cold, were given a little food by the poor fishermen who lived on the island. More luckily still, after six weeks, a passing fisherboat took them to Anstruther in Fife, where they were charitably received by the Presbyterians in the town. Eventually they made their way back to Spain. Not so happy was the fate of those in a ship with a similar name. The *Gran Grin* hit the rocks of Clare Island in Clew Bay. There an improvident Irish chieftain massacred all who crawled ashore from the wreck, sparing not even Don Pedro de Mendoza, who should have been worth a decent ransom.

How many Spanish lives had been lost in the Enterprise of England? Twenty thousand? Where no figure can be certain, it seems a reasonable guess; some by drowning, some by massacre, some by sickness and the rest, maybe two thousand, in battle, above all, during those final hours when the English closed in at Gravelines.

The Duke of Medina Sidonia, grey-haired and physically exhausted by the time he reached home waters, remained with the remnants of his ship's companies until the King released him from his duties. Then he returned to his house among the orange-groves at San Lucar. It is said that, on that melancholy journey from San Sebastian he spent a night at Valladolid while, beneath his windows, the crowd shouted, 'Here comes Drake.' If so, the taunt was grossly unfair, although it shows the extraordinary power of the Drake legend over the popular imagination. In truth, the Duke had been defeated by an impossible plan, by better ships and by more skilful seamanship. He was doubly punished for his obedience to his sovereign. He drove homewards through Spain, followed by the open or covert contempt of his fellow-countrymen. And, at the end of the journey, there was waiting his duchess, who was a termagant.

After Parma had sent his invasion force back to their billets, he was annoyed by reports of grumbling among his officers, some of whom, now that the crisis was over, thought that the

Army should have done more to help the Armada. The ugly word 'cowardice' was used. Parma issued a challenge, not as Captain-General but as Alexander Farnese, to any man who doubted his courage. He spent a day in the Grand Place of Dunkirk, rapier in hand, but had no takers.[11]

Meanwhile, the condition of the English fleet was causing alarm to its commanders. It had come through the fighting with only the lightest of losses: not one ship sunk and fewer than a hundred men killed, and only one of them an officer, a brave man named William Coxe serving in a pinnace of Sir William Wynter's. When the intensity of the fighting between two main fleets is considered, these casualties were modest indeed. But, now that it was all over, the seamen were being denied their pay, the lack of which, said Howard, temperately enough, 'breeds a marvellous alteration' among the mariners. He met the pay claims of his officers out of his own pocket. 'It were pitiful to have men starve after such a service.' The Council, incited by the Queen, was more interested to know why so few of the Spanish ships had been boarded and although Sir Walter Raleigh made a defence of the Navy's tactics, it was only half-accepted.

But worse was to come. The ships were swept by an epidemic so much more devastating than the normal outbreaks of ship fever that modern authorities have been driven to believe that it was some form of food poisoning. In the hygienic conditions prevailing in Elizabeth's ships, in which food was cooked directly over the bilges, an outbreak of this kind was only too likely. What is certain is that crews which had come through the Channel battle almost unscathed were now mown down by a deadly sickness.

The Lord Admiral told Burghley, 'It is a most pitiful sight to see, here at Margate, how the men die in the streets . . . Sir Roger Townshend, of all the men he brought out with him, hath but one left.'[12] Twelve days later, he wrote to the Queen from Dover, 'Those that come in fresh are soonest infected; they sicken one day and die the next.' The only clinical evidence on the subject is provided by Robert Carey, who, like so many young gentlemen of spirit, had found his own means to reach the fleet and join in the fight as a volunteer. He left it after the Gravelines battle and hurried to join Leicester at Tilbury. There he was prostrated suddenly with a high fever and was taken by litter to London. This, for what it is worth, seems to suggest that the epidemic was not, as some have supposed, a form of food poisoning but a virulent outbreak of ship fever.

The general opinion among the sailors was that sour beer was the cause of it all. Whatever the reason, it seems certain that four or five thousand of the crews that fought the Armada perished miserably after the battle was over. It was a ghastly sequel to the victory. Yet it may be noted, that in spite of all these tribulations – disease as well as a stingy Treasury and an overwhelmed commissariat – not one breach of discipline was reported all that summer. Morale in the English fleet was as high as that.

One English sailor had been denied any share in the engagement. Thomas Cavendish, a Suffolk gentleman, had left Plymouth two years before with three ships. On 3 September 1588, having circumnavigated the world, he hailed a Flemish hulk off the Azores and heard of the defeat of the Armada, 'to the singular rejoicing and comfort of us all'. Six days later, all but overwhelmed in the interval by a terrible storm, Cavendish entered Plymouth Harbour and heard more about the great deliverance.

XIX

The Pay You Give Soldiers

'From shires and townes too long to name
To serve the Queen of England
Her Grace to glad their harts againe
In princely person took the paine
To honour the troupe and martialle traine
In Tilburie camp in England.'

Contemporary Ballad

'We untied our anchor and so we sailed away,
Where the sun do shine most glorious,
To Lisbon we are bound.'

English Folk Song[1]

The Queen addressed her troops at Tilbury in words which ring like trumpets down the centuries. She was enough of an artist to savour the drama of the occasion, and enough Harry's daughter to respond to the nearness of danger and the simulacrum of war. So to the joy of her amateur army she spoke her defiance of Parma and departed by barge to London. By that time the Armada was beaten and in flight.

On another day she made a triumphant progress through London to St Paul's. Passing along Fleet Street she heard a choir sing the verses she herself had written:

'He made the winds and water rise
To scatter all mine Enemies.'

At the Cathedral a *Te Deum* was sung and eleven captured Spanish standards were displayed. It had been a spectacular victory which all Europe would acknowledge, led by the Pope, the Venetian Republic and the French. But the English were not satisfied. Their naval gunnery, it was thought, had been below expectation in destructive power. There breathes through the letters of Drake, of Howard, a faint note of apology. 'If I have not performed as much as was looked for,' wrote Drake, 'yet I persuade myself his good lordship will confess I have been dutiful.' Although they had driven the Armada off, the English had been somewhat taken aback by the scale and determination of the Spanish onslaught. And they were aware that there had been an element of good fortune in their success. If the execution of the Spanish plan had not been so wooden, if there had been a touch of imagination to enliven the scale and majesty of the attack, if Medina Sidonia, that most unlucky duke, had been a leader as well as an administrator – the business might have turned out differently.

Good fortune – that is to say, the hand of God – having been with the English, was it not meet, wise and the duty of Christian men to complete the task which had been so happily begun in those summer days of 1588?

From one interested party abroad came war-like counsel. The French King's minister, Philippe Duplessis-Mornay, wrote in October to the French ambassador in London, 'It is important that the Queen keep her foot upon the neck of the Spaniards. We have no certainty of a similar success a second time.'[2] The Venetian ambassador in Madrid reported about the same time that if Drake went to Spain he would find no obstacles. Drake was very much of that opinion himself.

He had done rather well out of the Armada. His claim against the government for the vessel he had contributed to the fireship attack was satisfactorily settled for £900. His claim to the prize money for the *Rosario* and the ransom of her officers was disputed by some. Some, like Sir Martin Frobisher, said he had no claim at all. There was even the possibility that the Queen would take the ship's treasure (25,200 pistoles*), her cargo of wine and the ransom money. In the end, however, Drake got the prize money and was able to buy a seventy-one years' lease of a substantial house in the City of London, the Herbery, on the river in Dowgate.[3]

Drake was by nature one of those who believed in an active strategy. By the middle of September he and Sir John Norreys

* About 3 pistoles to £1.

put before the Queen proposals for an attack on Lisbon. Drake and Norreys were a formidable team in authority and competence: the former, one of the most famous of English admirals, the latter, a professional soldier of high distinction, a veteran officer in the war against Parma in the Low Countries, the man who had commanded English troops in the first successful action against Spanish infantry. Norreys had been brought back from Holland to act as Leicester's chief-of-staff at the time of the invasion scare. He and Drake lost no time in agreeing on a plan of campaign. Their temperaments were alike, the one as forceful and aggressive as the other, a similarity which suggested that their co-operation might be stormy. They now proposed a large-scale expedition against the Portuguese capital by a joint naval and military force which would be in part an affair of state, in part a private venture. In tempting the City of London to come into the consortium with capital and ships, Drake could put forward strong arguments.

If a friendly ruler like that depressed little man, Dom Antonio, were set on the throne of Portugal, then English ships and merchants would gain entry to the enormously lucrative Portuguese trade with the Far East. The spices, the silks, the gold and precious stones – the very thought of them was calculated to make mouths water in the London counting-houses. There was also the fact that harbour facilities for English warships in the Tagus would be a direct threat to Spanish trade with the Indies. The regular, twice-a-year shuttling of the Flota and the Galeones between Seville and the Caribbean would be subject to interference by a hostile fleet based a mere two hundred miles to the north.

If Lisbon fell, Philip would be compelled to make a major military effort to win it back. If that effort failed – so ran the thinking of Drake and his like – Spain would be forced to seek peace. And in the immediate aftermath of the Armada disaster, Spanish military strength was at a low ebb. Crack troops like the Sicily *tercio* and the Portugal *tercio* had suffered terrible losses. Everybody – even the Queen – saw the advantage of an instant English counter-attack. The plan was for a private joint-stock company in which the Queen was, as usual, to be the chief shareholder in recognition of the fact that she was to provide six naval vessels and two pinnaces, a siege train, arms and armour for soldiers, three months' victuals and £20,000 in cash.

The City found £10,000 in ten days and Drake's firm £5,000. Norreys went over to bargain with the States-General of Holland for the loan of ships and English troops hardened in the Dutch wars. The conditions for such a deal were favourable because, by this time, Parma had switched his main military effort to France, where, after Navarre's victory at Coutras and the assassination of the Duke of Guise, it seemed that the Catholic cause was in danger. Norreys was promised six hundred English cavalry, thirteen companies of English foot and ten companies of Walloons.

Then the chief shareholder took fright, probably realising that she was committing herself too deeply to an expedition which in the end she could not control. Among other clauses in the agreement, Drake had inserted one which declared that, if the Queen countermanded the order to depart, she would pay all the costs. This can hardly have been to Elizabeth's liking. Even less so was the tendency of the estimated costs to rise until they had reached a total of £64,000. Sniffing the wind of disapproval blowing from Whitehall, some of the noble subscribers to the project drew in their financial skirts. However, news of fresh Spanish preparations for war kept the enterprise alive.

When Parliament met in February 1589, the Chancellor of the Exchequer made an appeal for funds to be voted, which touched the patriotic Protestant heart of the House of Commons. And the Queen designated a clerk of the Council to accompany the commanders and make sure that they used her money providently. There were some disappointments, one of which proved to be fatal: the promised siege-train was not furnished. Half of the troops from the Low Countries failed to turn up. But the matter went forward. George Peele, an industrious poet of the day, wrote a set of stanzas:

To arms, to arms, to glorious arms!
You fight for Christ and England's peerless queen!

and to these heartening strains of farewell Drake sailed from Dover to Plymouth in March 1589 as the commander of a substantial fleet.

By that time, Spanish spies at work in London had sent to King Philip an account of Drake's doings. It was obvious that he had returned to his old Portuguese obsession. The point on the coast where the invasion was planned to take place was supplied to the King by a Portuguese informer, Antonio de Veico, a treacherous member of Dom Antonio's household. From this source Philip knew all the details of the enterprise – its strength, its allies in Portugal, the operational plans of its leaders.

On the way down Channel, Drake had one piece of good fortune: he fell in with sixty Dutch flyboats sailing in ballast to fetch salt at La Rochelle and, with irresistible arguments, persuaded them to join him. He was short of transports and the flyboats would be invaluable. At Plymouth he was joined by West Country vessels and by an embarrassing number of volunteers, gentlemen adventurers out for the fun and the profit of war under the most famous captain of the age.

In the end he sailed out of Plymouth with a fleet comparable in numbers to that which had fought the Armada and carrying far more soldiers. There were 8 ships of the Navy, 77 armed merchantmen and 60 Dutch flyboats. They had on board 3,000 English and 900 Dutch sailors. In addition, they carried 11,000 soldiers of whom a thousand were volunteers. These adventurous souls might have only a modest experience of war but they were expected to make up for it in spirit. Among them were the Norwich city waits, whose services Drake had begged from the Mayor. These musicians, five in number, unanimously volunteered to go. They were fitted out with stannel cloaks and given a wagon to carry themselves and their instruments to the ships. Three new hautbois and a treble recorder were bought

(£5) and Peter Spratt needed a new case for his sackbut (10*s*.). Alas, only two of these gallant minstrels returned to Norwich.

But there was no lack of veteran campaigners in the expedition, many who had fought against Parma, and many ships, half of the English contingent, that had exchanged broadsides with the Armada. Every day before the fleet sailed the soldiers were drilled for battle, and a court-martial was held in Plymouth market-place to deal with breaches of discipline. There were financial difficulties, there were troubles about victuals, but in the end the fleet sailed in five squadrons. Although it was short of food, Drake told the Council that 'by the end of the month, harvest will begin both in Spain and Portugal, which doth put us in good hope of relief . . .

'P.S. God bless us and give us grace to live in His fear.'

At the last minute and, happily, after the fleet had sailed, there occurred an incident which was calculated to arouse the Queen's anger and suspicion. The young Earl of Essex, thirsting for glory, fled secretly from Whitehall to join the ships. The Queen had forbidden him to go, but Essex had disobeyed. He was the handsome, brilliant, vainglorious favourite, the sun who shone in her Court where Leicester had shone before him, the beams of whose radiance were beginning to outshine those of Sir Walter Raleigh, Captain of the Guard. The young man had already tried the Queen's tolerance; he thought that he could go further.

There were times when the silken strands that bound him to the Court seemed unworthy of youth and courage and a proved aptitude for martial exploits. Had he not already shown his courage at Zutphen, in the mad charge in which Philip Sidney got his death-wound? Had he not contrived with Drake, in secret, an enterprise of just such a kind as that which the admiral was about to embark on? It was vexatious, galling, intolerable, that he, Robert Devereux, of an ancient line, should be tied to Court and women's company when the trumpets were sounding and the ships were about to weigh anchor in Plymouth Sound. To make it more insufferable, he had persuaded friends to take the risk and – 'I am not of the number, nor humour which like to wager upon other men's hands.'

Essex wrote forty letters, in which he excused what he was about to do on the grounds of debt and idleness: 'If I speed well, I will adventure to be rich. If not, I will never live to see the end of my poverty.'[4] It was true that his debts totalled £22,000 and that half of the burden was the result of patriotic spending – £4,000 when he went soldiering in the Low Countries, £3,500 when he raised a troop of cavalry in the expectations of a Spanish landing; and now £7,000 for the adventure in Portugal. The letters he left in his desk at Essex House. Then one evening he took his way surreptitiously to St James's Park where two of his servants were waiting with horses. After that, it was a matter of hard riding down the Plymouth road, two hundred and twenty miles in two nights and a day, with all the speed that good horseflesh could provide when it was urged on by a young man who knew that the wrath of England's sovereign lady was certainly following close on his heels. At Plymouth, he found that Drake's fleet had put back into port to escape adverse weather. But Sir Roger William's *Swiftsure* was ready to sail and willing to carry the eager young warrior without delay, while Drake and the other leaders who stayed behind were ready to deny that they knew anything about the escape when the Queen's messengers arrived from London. Perhaps they did not know and perhaps the Queen believed their denials, but in the circumstances neither conjecture seems very probable.

One who did know and, to his great annoyance, was left behind in London by Essex, was young Robert Carey, in whom the restless spirit of the age was awake. Once before, the Queen had sent him posting after Essex to bring him back from an escapade in the Low Countries. During the Armada battle he and his friend, Lord Cumberland, had ridden to Portsmouth, chartered a frigate and sailed after the two fleets. When night came they had found themselves surrounded by Spanish galleons. By daylight they had escaped and joined the Lord Admiral. Now, deserted by Essex, Carey suffered all the pangs of frustration. In this state he took – and won – a bet of £2,000 that he could walk to Berwick in twelve days.[5] Such were the young men, rich and usually loaded with debts, idle and fretting at idleness, eager to command and hating obedience, who adorned the Queen's Court, seduced her maids of honour and fought her battles. Essex was only the most spectacular of them.

In the Channel the bad weather persisted, so that the fleet was stayed in harbour for a fortnight – at the Queen's expense. That was provided for in the contract. For the Queen, the alternative to paying up was to abandon the expedition altogether. But that would have been more expensive still. When at length Drake set sail (18 April) he left behind £6,000 in cash, which had arrived too late from London to pay the troops, and also a resentful monarch, who demanded that her lost young man should be returned to her and that Sir Robert Williams, his accomplice, should be arrested. But the *Swiftsure*, Williams and Essex had vanished into the sunny waters of the Bay of Biscay.

Six days after leaving Plymouth, Drake arrived in Corunna Bay. This was in obedience to his instructions, which said, 'Before you shall attempt either Portugal or the Azores, our express pleasure and commandment is that you distress the ships of war in Guipuzcoa, Biscay and Galicia.' After so clear a directive, failure to look into Corunna would have been inexcusable. It was the port from which the Armada had sailed ten months earlier. How many of the survivors had returned there to lick their wounds?

Corunna Bay was formed by a curving spit of rock joined to the mainland by a stretch of lower land. It resembled an open right hand of which the thumb consisted of a fortified lower town, leading to a more strongly fortified upper town, represented by the tip of the thumb, while the farther side of the bay took the place of the grasping fingers of the hand. The town was an important administrative centre, seat of the Governor and Council of Galicia, to whom the sudden appearance of the English came as an unpleasant surprise. In the harbour, when

Drake arrived, was the *San Juan*, flagship of the Portugal Squadron of the Armada, and two galleys. This was a disappointing quarry, although, no doubt, it was worth seizing.

Without loss of time, Drake sent parties in boats to seize landing points on the seafront directly across the bay from the town. They picked their way over the rocky ground, working all the time nearer to the defences of the lower town, which however they did not attack on the first day. Rain came on; a wind sprang up. The soldiers spent the night in cottages which they had seized. They were in a position where they could stave off any attempt by the garrison of Corunna to prevent further landings unless the landing parties were dislodged by gunfire from the Spanish ships in the Bay. Sir John Norreys, in command of the assault, sent to the fleet for artillery with which he drove off the Spanish galleys.

Drake and Norreys now worked out a plan for the attack on the fortified neck of land separating them from the town. It resembled very much the tactics which had been successful at Cartagena three years before. Captain Richard Wingfield and that redoubtable Irish veteran of Cartagena, Captain Sampson, were sent with five hundred skirmishers to work round the western end of the defences at low tide. This was exactly the same manoeuvre as had succeeded against the line of wine-casks on Cartagena beach. There was to be a simultaneous attack on the eastern harbour end of the wall. It was to be out-flanked by a sea-borne force under the command of Tom Fenner, who had served with Frobisher at Cartagena.

At midnight the signal for the attack was given: two shots were fired by the cannon Norreys had brought ashore. Under covering fire from the boats, landings were made on the harbour front. The eastern end of the fortified line was carried without loss. Only at the western end, facing the open sea, was there trouble. There, the water was too deep to allow wading men to pass round the wall. They must storm it. This they did at the third attempt and with some help from the parties which, in the meantime, the boats had landed in the harbour. The

Lower Town of Corunna was now in English hands. Five hundred of the garrison were slaughtered, according to the custom of war. Men of rank were made prisoners, among them Don Juan de Luna, the military commander of the town. The defenders who had evaded capture made their way through the twisting alleys of the fishing village to the High Town, where they were protected by impressive ramparts. Next morning, the Spaniards set fire to the galleon in the harbour. Expert English looters stripped the other vessels. The countryside was scoured for cattle and other eatables. Troops broke into a wine store full of local produce. Everything, it seemed, had gone well. 'We trust in God,' wrote Tom Fenner to Burghley, 'the like shall befall them in other places.'[6]

However, the English commanders allowed themselves to be diverted from their main task – finding and destroying Spanish warships. They were annoyed by gunfire from the High Town of Corunna; they resolved to storm it. This was very much a problem for Sir John Norreys, as an old professional hand trained in the siege warfare of the Low Countries. He had no siege-train but he brought up four of the heaviest cannon he could spare to breach the wall at a southern sector. In the north he found a tower that his engineers could mine. After five days' work – including one failure when the gunpowder, insufficiently bedded in, blew back – gunners and engineers had completed their task.

While Drake made threatening noises with his ships' culverins against a fort in the harbour, San Antonio, the engineers fired the charge in the mine and the tower came tumbling down. This was the moment for the assault troops to go forward, with sword, pike, buckler and an English cheer. They were in two parties of picked men, one against the breach made by the cannon, and the other against the ruined tower. But how rarely do manoeuvres in war go exactly according to plan! When the smoke and the dust cleared, it was seen that only half the tower had collapsed. Seen too late! Already the assault troops were clambering over the fallen masonry. At that instant, the other half came down with a horrible roar, burying more than a score of them. One of the assailants, Captain Sydenham, was pinned down by four or five heavy fragments. The English standards fell but were rescued and carried back to safety. Next day, ten men at least lost their lives trying to rescue Sydenham.

Those who had the task of breaking in at the breach made by the cannon had no better luck. As they scrambled over the rubble, it gave way under their feet, falling outwards. It revealed that half of the wall was still intact. In the dust and confusion, they took to their heels. Both of the assault parties now retreated to their starting lines in the lower town, running, stumbling, huddled together in a narrow lane, shot at all the way. Many of them were wounded. So ended, in total failure, the first attempt to capture the High Town of Corunna.

It also proved to be the last. For now a fresh danger diverted the attention of the English chiefs. A few miles to the south of Corunna, a narrow stone bridge crossed a creek at a point not far from the sea. Across this bridge any attack on the English invaders from the Spanish hinterland must come. A prisoner, taken in the fighting for the town, suggested that such an attack was imminent. Eight thousand Spanish troops had been assembling beyond the bridge and would soon launch an attack. Norreys with seven thousand men set off next morning to deal with the threat.

They found that the Spaniards had established themselves in a fortified camp on the far side of the bridge with a bridgehead at El Burgo on the nearer end. Sir John Norreys' brother, Sir Edward, charged the bridge, pike in hand, at the head of the English infantry. In a sharp fight for the barricade at the far end of the bridge, Sir Edward fell, bleeding from a sword slash on the head. His brother, Sir John, snatched up a pike and, without helmet or cuirass, rushed into the fight. At his heels, running across the bridge three by three, came the pick of the English and Dutch foot. In a few minutes the Spanish camp was overrun, and its defenders were fleeing in four different directions. As many as a thousand of them were slaughtered in the pursuit in their hiding-places in the vineyards and hedgerows. The Dutch captain, Nicolas van Meetkerke, discovered two hundred of them sheltering in a monastery and killed them all. Ah! sighed the English generals, if only we had had some cavalry or a few companies of Irish kerns, none of the enemy would have escaped! The victors marched back to Corunna carrying at their head a captured Spanish standard, on which were the royal arms of Spain. The English had lost two men killed in the skirmish.

Next day, there was a change of wind and the troops re-embarked with their plunder, which included fifty bronze cannon and three thousand pikes. The Lower Town of Corunna was set on fire and, in the light of its burning houses, Drake, Norreys and the other leaders, naval and military, met to consider their next move. At Santander, three hundred and fifty miles farther east along the coast, were forty of the surviving ships of the Great Armada. To destroy them by cannon, flames or capture would be the most obvious way to carry out the Queen's directive. The trouble was that Santander was a strongly fortified harbour. To approach it, attacking vessels must run the gauntlet of powerful shore batteries. Those guns must first be silenced, said Drake. Could Norreys storm the batteries? Not without siege artillery, replied the soldier. The ball was then passed to the ships' masters, who swore that nothing in the world could persuade them to take their ships through the tortuous channel leading into Santander, unless they were sure of an anchorage safe from westerly and northerly gales. Consequently, an attack on Santander was not feasible. Drake sent an optimistic message home on 8 May, 'Great happiness is fallen to our Queen and country by our coming thither'; coupled with a warning, 'The King of Spain sleepeth not.' Next day the fleet set sail, with the Berlengas off the coast of Portugal as its rendezvous. The decision of the Council of War at Corunna had perhaps been a correct one, yet there is something strangely perfunctory about the debate as it is reported, something inadequate about the reasons given for the failure to carry out the

Queen's orders. Were the real motives being disclosed? Critics were likely to doubt it.

Four days later, as the fleet made its way slowly southwards, much troubled by a strong westerly wind, the look-out men sighted a sail, then other sails. They turned out to be the missing *Swiftsure* with six other ships in attendance. Here were the absconding Earl of Essex and Sir Roger Williams, who, it was plain, had not been wasting their time while seeking the main fleet. On a marauding expedition of their own they had captured, off Cape St Vincent, three well-laden merchant ships and three pinnaces. Whether Drake was altogether pleased to be joined by the glamorous, overbearing and temporarily disgraced young nobleman may be doubted. But there he was, brave as a lion and thirsting for battle. There could be no question of packing him off home again. Nor was there any lack of work for a gallant young man to do. The time had come to attempt the second part of the grand design, the capture of Lisbon.

The operational plan for the attack followed the general pattern of Drake's earlier seaborne assaults, although it was on a much bigger scale and the initial landing was farther from the main objective. On the Atlantic coast of Portugal, fifty miles north of Lisbon, was the seaport of Peniche, in a sheltered bay commanded by a strongly garrisoned castle. The fleet dropped anchor in the bay just out of range of the castle guns, which were capable of sweeping the shore that was the obvious place to land. On the other side of the bay, under a cliff, was a beach broken up by rocks on which a heavy surf was running. To attempt a landing there was, if not impossible, perilous to the point of madness. But there seemed to be no alternative.

Sir Roger Williams and Essex led a flotilla of boats towards it. One boat was overturned in the attempt to reach the shore. For a few minutes, the bay was a confused mass of boiling surf and struggling men, twenty-five of whom were drowned. Essex leapt into the water up to his shoulders, kept his footing and struggled up to the dry sand. Williams and others were soon at his side. Then the cliff was scaled and they found themselves on a stretch of sand beyond which lay the town. Pike in hand, Williams led a charge against a Spanish force that barred the way and, after a fierce little battle, in which there were losses on both sides, put it to flight. The people of Peniche fled and, in due course, the castle surrendered.

Good so far, but only the beginning of an ambitious operation. And Drake seems to have thought, reasonably enough, that they had begun in the wrong place. He urged that a new landing should be made farther down the coast, nearer the mouth of the Tagus, so that the soldiers and the ships could co-operate in an advance on Lisbon. But he was only one of two equal generals and, when it was a question of operations on land, out of reach of the fleet, Sir John Norreys had the primacy.

Who can doubt also in what direction the influence of Essex was thrown? He was a soldier rather than a sailor and naturally would be eager that the capture of Lisbon should be a purely military exploit. He had no defined position in the expedition but enough self-assurance and force of personality to press his opinions vehemently at the councils of war. He was already busily intriguing to promote the fortunes of his associates. As he cynically wrote later on, 'Though I had no charge, I made my brother general of the horse and my faithful friend, Sir Roger Williams, Colonel-General of the infantry, seven or eight of my fast friends colonels and twenty at least of my domestics captains, so that I might have authority and party enough when I wanted.' There would be more 'authority' for Essex ashore than afloat.[7]

Overborne in debate, Drake landed the main body of the troops at Peniche and took the salute as the army marched past in three divisions under Norreys, Essex and Dom Antonio. His last instructions were that they should be circumspect in their espousal of the Pretender's cause until it was clear what the Portuguese really thought about him. And they were to attack Lisbon only if they found that there was no large Spanish force in the neighbourhood. After promising that, if possible, he would meet them again in the river at Lisbon, he embarked once more on the *Revenge* and sailed south to the mouth of the Tagus, there to await events. He had misgivings about the advance on Lisbon by a force which had little discipline, no siege guns and only one troop of horse, but he had plenty of worries of his own in the fleet. The Dutch skippers who had been pressed into transporting soldiers were loud in complaints about the behaviour of their passengers. More serious, sickness was developing in the ships, on a scale reminiscent of the terrible days after the battle with the Armada. Very soon, if it continued, the ships would not have crews able to work them. Very soon, Fenner was reporting to Walsingham that of three hundred men on board his ship, the *Dreadnought*, a hundred and fourteen were dead and only eighteen were fit for work.

On 22 May, Drake cast anchor at the little port of Cascaes at the mouth of the Tagus. He found the town deserted. The population had fled, having noticed with foreboding that it was a year to a day since the Invincible Armada had passed down the river, guns booming, trumpets sounding and banners displayed, on the way to conquer England. And now the Armada was shattered and the English were here. Drake waited for news of Norreys and his army. Until that came, he was not prepared to risk a crippled fleet in an attempt to batter his way past the Tagus forts into Lisbon harbour. The news when it came was bad.

Norreys marched to Lisbon, losing men on the way by disease and desertion. The Spaniards had given way and had not risked a pitched battle. And the walls of Lisbon were an obstacle which Norreys was not prepared to storm without siege guns. Before the English withdrew, Essex broke his spear on the wood of the city gate and hung his chain on it as a symbol of defiance. It was a fine gesture, which made no impression on the enemy. The Spaniards followed the retreating English army and a collision seemed in prospect. As might have been expected, Essex had sent a challenge to Count Fuentes, a Spanish nobleman of rank equal to his own, saying that he would be found in the centre of the vanguard with a red scarf over his left arm and a plume of feathers in his helmet. But for the second time it was proved that the age of chivalry was over. There was no duel and no battle. The Spaniards withdrew and Norreys resumed his dejected march to the ships. Sickness was growing among the soldiers. Ammunition was running out. And, worst of all, there had been no sign of that patriotic uprising of the Portuguese people which Dom Antonio had promised.

Whatever prospect of one there had been was effectively stifled by Philip's Viceroy in Portugal, the Cardinal-Archduke Albert. Henry of Navarre said later, 'Three things are true, but nobody believes them: that the Queen of England is a virgin, that I am a good Catholic, and that the Cardinal-Archduke is a good general.' The Cardinal-Archduke had been kept informed by the traitor in Dom Antonio's entourage of what was likely to happen. He had acted with all the ruthlessness that was needed. Some of the Portuguese nationalists had been garrotted, others had been carried off into Spanish prisons. Left without their natural leaders among the nobles, the Portuguese had no heart for the fight; they were, as the Venetian ambassador unkindly reported, 'too stupid to act well and too cowardly to act ill'. It seemed that only the friars and the aged were bold enough to come out for Dom Antonio, although the Spaniards reported that the businessmen of Lisbon, mainly 'new Christians' (i.e. Jews), tried hard to stir up the people.

Drake was still at the mouth of the river when the retreating army arrived there. For six days he had been preparing to advance upstream with as many of his best ships as he could man but had failed to complete the work. Sickness among the crews was severe: 2,791 men were infected. But the decisive factor must have been the discovery that the Portuguese were not willing to fight for Dom Antonio. Without some degree of local co-operation there was no chance whatever of the great design succeeding. And even if Drake and Norreys had been able to seize Lisbon they could hardly expect to hold the city with a purely English garrison.

Meanwhile, a stream of sharp inquisitive letters arrived

from London: Why had they failed to destroy the Armada galleons being refitted in the Biscay ports? Why were expenses running so far above the amount the Queen had agreed to contribute? And let them send the Earl of Essex home without delay. 'If ye do not ye shall look to answer at your smart.' By this time, the young Earl was quite willing to return. Seeing that there was no chance of winning fame or glory on the expedition, he took the first occasion to make his way back to London carrying an explanation from the commanders that until then they had not been able to spare the *Swiftsure* to carry him back. He was greeted on his arrival in England with a poem of welcome from George Peele. He had a frostier greeting from his indulgent but not deluded sovereign.

Neither Norreys nor Drake could expect so happy a return. They found some consolation when they seized eighty French and Hanseatic cargo vessels laden with grain and naval stores from the Baltic. The invalids were sent home in several of those ships. The Dutch flyboats were offered the grain if they would take it back to England. But their skippers thought that they had suited English convenience for long enough. They preferred to set sail for La Rochelle where they could fill up with cargoes of salt as they had originally set out to do. Drake and Norreys, glumly digesting a tart refusal from the Queen to send a siege-train and infantry reinforcements, decided that an attack on Lisbon was out of the question and that they would do better to seize a base in the Azores. From that they would perhaps, with a little luck, be able to intercept the homeward-bound treasure fleet. Their decision to leave was strengthened by a misfortune that befell them. During a sudden calm that fell outside the Tagus, twenty-one Spanish galleys darted out to intercept some of the less powerful English ships. Three of these were lost.

But the wind was too uncertain for the Azores voyage. The ships were blown here and there about the coast of Portugal by pitilessly adverse weather; the crews and the soldiers were weakened by sickness and wounds. Even so, Drake was not ready to give up the fight. Landing at Vigo a force of two thousand men – all who could bear arms – he attacked the town. If anyone had thought that Drake's conduct outside Lisbon indicated some abating of his aggressive spirit, they now had their answer. For he, the Admiral of the fleet, led one wing of the assault in person while Sir Roger Williams led the other. The Vigo defences were carried and the town occupied and burnt. In the hand-to-hand fighting, Drake showed that he was still the man of Nombre de Dios and Sagres, more at home in a hot action at close quarters than in the cool planning of a campaign.

He and Norreys now decided to part company, the latter taking the bulk of the fleet home while Drake with twenty ships proposed to make a dash for the Azores. But once more luck was against him. The worst storm they had so far experienced now struck the ships. The *Revenge* sprang a leak and could scarcely be kept afloat. When Drake brought her into Plymouth Sound, she – a major unit of the Queen's Navy – was on the point of sinking. The other ships found their way back to port as and where they could. Many of the captains had good reason to wish their return to be inconspicuous. They had prizes on which the officials of the Admiralty Court and similar busybodies would cast an all-too-inquisitive eye.

With the homecoming of the last straggler, the Portuguese Expedition of 1589 was at an end.

Strategically it had been a failure. Not one of the main objectives had been achieved. Lisbon had not been taken, as the two generals, those 'so overweening spirits', had wished.[8] The returned ships of the Armada had not been destroyed, which had been the Queen's chief interest. Half a dozen ships had been lost and of the 12,000 men* who set out, 3,000 were forced to quit the expedition at one time or another and only 3,700 had come back. Assuming that the balance represents the death-roll, a casualty rate in excess of forty per cent is high for an operation that lasted a little over two months. It should be remembered, though, that most of them died by disease, which was a risk in

* An estimate.

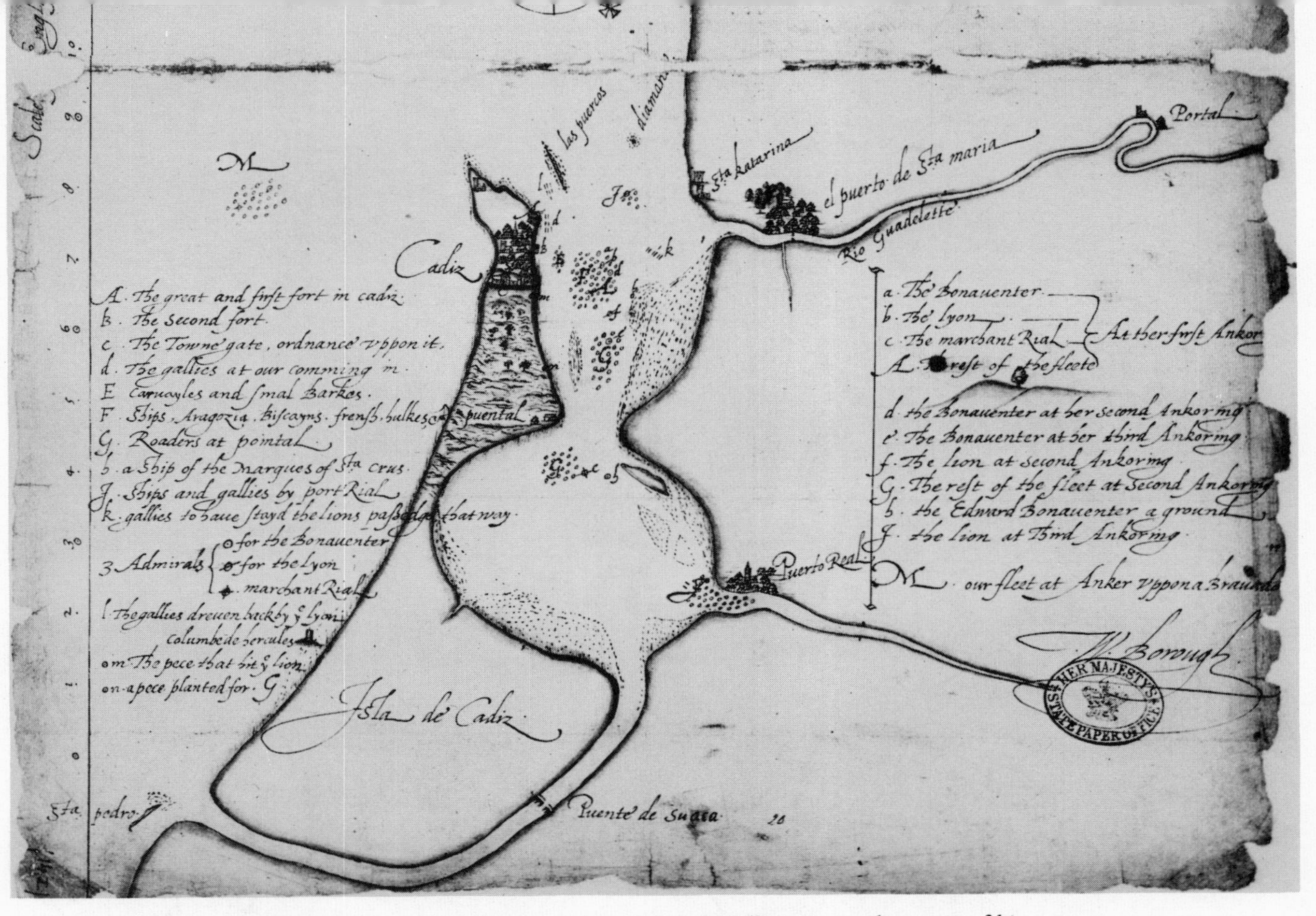

15 Chart of Cadiz prepared by Admiral William Borough as part of his defence before the Council (*Public Record Office*)

16 The *Golden Lion*, from an engraving by C. J. Visscher (*National Maritime Museum*)

civil as well as military life. In 1593, plague killed 10,662 people in London.[9]

Everyone blamed everyone else, although naturally most of the blame fell on Drake, who, it seems, was less to blame than anyone. The Queen had not kept her promise to provide siege guns. The Dutch had not kept their promise to send a substantial force of experienced soldiers. They had wasted a month in futile negotiations. They could, no doubt, be excused since they had reason to fear a new military threat from Parma, burning to wipe out the shame of the Armada; and they did not trust the English. The Dutch and bad weather, between them, had delayed the departure of the ships, thus giving King Philip time to prepare his defences against the blow to Lisbon, the precise form of which, thanks to his intelligence service, he knew. At the same time the delay increased the cost of victualling the expedition.

Another factor had helped to swell the expenses. Drake, famous as a lucky plundering commander, was an irresistible magnet for adventurous young Englishmen with light purses and roving dispositions. Whether he lacked the heart or the will to rebuff these eager volunteers, the truth is that they flocked to Plymouth in numbers far exceeding his power to provide rations, pay or adequate shiproom for them. The Queen was invited, implored, finally blackmailed, into supplying funds. The net result was that her share of the cost, which was to have been £20,000, exceeded £50,000. It did not improve her temper.

Yet the expedition was not without fruit. Philip's prestige and pride were damaged by the insult inflicted on him by 'a woman, mistress of only half an island, with the help of a corsair and a common soldier'.[10] There were also material injuries. The invading force had intercepted naval stores earmarked for a new Armada. It had compelled Philip to pull some of his regiments out of the Low Countries. Most important of all, it postponed the arrival of the treasure fleet. Spanish credit was damaged and Parma's troops, unpaid, broke out in mutiny. Resenting the criticism which the enterprise had aroused among the home-staying public, Norreys retorted, 'If as much had been done by the Queen's enemies against England, there would be bonfires through Christendom.' And, surely, there was some justification for his annoyance.[11]

The Portugal Expedition of 1589 exposed a weakness inherent in the system of financing war which was imposed on Elizabeth by the poverty of the English crown. It occurred at a time when that poverty was particularly acute owing to the need to bribe the Scots, restrain the Dutch, mobilise against the Armada, hold Ireland in check and find some money for that penniless but promising adventurer, Henry of Navarre. All this at a time when trade was bad, the customs revenues were at a low ebb and unemployment was rife. The Crown had not the resources to launch alone a counter-offensive against Spain, so that the Queen, who lent six of her ships and subscribed £50,000 of her money to the expedition, has been unfairly accused of lacking either the vision to see the dazzling opportunity which was offered to her or the resolution to grasp it. She was driven to seek a partnership, and the partnership foundered in a confusion of purposes: strategic advantage against mercantile gain; the plan to waylay the treasure fleet against the plan to set a Pretender on the throne of Portugal; the sailors' notions of how the war should be fought against the soldiers', jealous always of the 'idolatry of Neptune'; the appetite for plunder against the need to remember that, in theory at least, Portugal was Dom Antonio's kingdom 'in which property must be respected by his allies'.

Sir Roger Williams, who had taken no part in the operations at Corunna, told Burghley that if the fleet had gone direct to Lisbon they would have taken the city without a blow and returned laden with treasure. They would have escaped the infection, brought on by decaying clothes and baggage left at Corunna by the ships of the Armada. 'Some will say, How could you have kept Lisbon? Believe it or not, with six thousand we would have kept it against all Spain and Portugal.'

The Queen spoke her mind on the matter with her customary vehemence, annoyed, as the biggest shareholder that the dividends were so disappointing. Those who had taken possession of the captured German cargo boats had been at pains to bring them into home ports where Drake would not easily find them. The prizes were sold for £30,000, a proportion of which would, no doubt, reach the Queen. In addition, a hundred and fifty guns were brought home and added to naval stores. How much Drake was able to claim as a return on his capital and a modest reward for his exertions cannot be told. It is unlikely, however, that he brought nothing home.

The loudest complaints rose from the soldiers. Most of them were disbanded on their return, each being given 5 shillings in cash and permission to keep his arms. To men who had just been forbidden to plunder Lisbon, this reward seemed less than adequate. Five hundred of them made their way to London and threatened to sack Bartholomew Fair. In alarm, the Lord Mayor called out two thousand men of the train bands. After disorderly scenes, four of the ringleaders were duly hanged. 'This,' cried one of them to the crowd, 'is the pay you give soldiers for going to the wars!'

XX

Seville is Illuminated

'The wings of man's life are plumed with the feathers of death.'

Sir Humphrey Gilbert, 1577

The years after the Lisbon expedition were the quietest in Drake's life. No new adventures. No cities looted, no ships captured, no treasure brought home. And this at a time when privateering activity by English seamen was at its peak, and when in the years between 1589 and 1591 two hundred and thirty-six English ships went out in search of plunder. They took three hundred prizes and their plunder was believed to equal a tenth of the country's total imports. Naturally enough, then, it has been supposed that the half-failure of Lisbon had cost him the Queen's favour, in short, that he was 'in disgrace'. It may be so, but the evidence for it is slight. He was wealthy enough to let other adventurers have the pains and profits of a life on the edge of piracy. His life had been hard and dangerous; he carried its scars, especially the old leg-wound which was probably troubling him a great deal. And at home he had many things to occupy his mind.

In the House of Commons he spoke quite often, with that natural eloquence of his which amazed those who knew how simple had been his schooling. He had plenty to say. In Plymouth he carried out a project which had been in his mind for years – the improvement of the town's water supply. Now there was time to put his ideas into practice. There was also money, £200 voted to him by Parliament, plus £100 to compensate the landowners (one of them himself) whose property might be affected. Water was drawn from the River Meavy some miles above the town. It was fed into a leat or channel, which followed the contours carefully and was carried to Plymouth on a course about twenty-seven miles long. The work was begun in December 1590 and finished on 24 April of the following year. When the water flowed for the first time Drake rode alongside it, accompanied by trumpets. For years afterwards, the last day of April was celebrated in the town as the Leat Feast. A goblet of water was passed round the councillors, 'to the pious memory of Sir Francis Drake', followed by a goblet of wine. 'May the descendants of him who gave us water never want for wine.' After which, the council feasted on trout from the leat.[1]

At the same time, Drake took over the proprietorship of the town mills from the Hawkins family, and added six new mills with his own capital. Most important of all, he was made responsible for fortifying the port, contributing £100 from his own pocket,* and taking the first spell of sentry duty when a fort was established on St Nicholas' (now Drake) Island in the Sound. When there was a scare over an expected Spanish invasion, Drake and his wife came into his town house from their country seat at Buckland so as to steady the nerves of the Plymouth people.

In 1592, a huge East India carrack, the *Madre de Dios*, crammed on all its seven tiers with the riches of the Orient, had been seized off the Azores by Robert Crosse, an officer in Raleigh's service, and brought into Dartmouth. With good reason, Her Majesty's Customs came to suspect that a fair accounting of the ship's contents was not being given. The ship's purser had been set free and his bills of lading had mysteriously disappeared. The customs officers, who were thought to be too inquisitive, went in peril of their lives. Soon the Privy Council was distressed by stories of tipsy mariners who sold valuable goods to merchants who, on the same day, resold for many times the money they had paid. A naval officer named Broadbent, while searching for stolen goods, bought eighteen hundred diamonds and two hundred rubies from a seaman, paying £130 for the lot. He sold again at a reasonable profit. Captain Thompson, who had

* The government had already imposed a duty on the export of pilchards, the proceeds to be ear-marked for the forts at Plymouth.

stowed away part of the loot aboard his ship, prudently sailed to Harwich where he thought the search would be less severe. He explained later that it was impossible for him to interfere with the seamen lest he lose their goodwill. The searchers of the carrack came upon one find of more than commercial interest: in a case of sweet cedar wood, 'lapped in almost a hundredfold of fine calicut cloth', was a Latin treatise on China. It was sent to Richard Hakluyt, who was fascinated by every kind of geographical information.

Lord Burghley dispatched to the West Country his clever son, Sir Robert Cecil, who reported that, as he approached Exeter along the Devon lanes, he could almost smell the spices. With a vast sum of money at stake, the Council ordered Drake to go down to Dartmouth to sort things out. He found the task a thankless one; he was accused of favouring the looters and retorted that, on the contrary, they thought he was too severe with them. Raleigh, who had financed the ship that captured the carrack, was at that time doing a spell in the Tower for daring to marry one of the Queen's maids of honour. Now he was released and went with all speed to Dartmouth, where the seamen greeted him as their champion. Perhaps he was. But in the end the investors did not come so badly out of this business. The Queen, who had put in £3,000, was paid a dividend in excess of £60,000. The total value of the prize after the unauthorised looters had done their worst was £150,000.

Sometime in 1594 it became clear in England that the unfinished business of 1588 would need to be taken up once more. The catastrophe of the Invincible Armada had been for Spain what the outcome of Lepanto had been for Turkey, a terrible blow to the country's naval prestige. But it had not broken Spanish power. Nor had it stemmed the flow of bullion from the Indies which was the ultimate source of that power. Spain was still the mistress of the richest and closest trade monopoly in the world. And Philip, her King, was still inflexibly resolved on revenge on England. He had sworn to turn his silver candlesticks into money, if necessary, to pay for a new Armada. He kept his word. He built better ships, closer in design and performance to the ships that had outsailed the first Armada. And he reorganised the carriage of the Caribbean treasure with the help of an inspired naval constructor, Pedro Menendez Marques, son of a famous Spanish admiral.

Menendez invented a new type of ship which he called the *gallizabra*, because it could use oars like a galley, and was small and fast, like a *zabra* (frigate). It was long in the keel and low in the water, and it carried twenty guns. In the year Drake was engaged in the expedition to Lisbon, Menendez completed the first *gallizabras* in his shipyard at Havana. His idea was that they should carry the bullion to Spain without any need to sail in convoy under the protection of the Indian Guard. They would be fast enough to escape from any ship heavy enough to sink them. They proved a resounding success. They were not, however, the only improvement made in the Spanish system. Communications with the overseas empire were speeded up by the employment of *avisos*, fast dispatch boats capable of conveying news and orders from Spain to Havana in twenty-eight days. Fortifications at colonial key points, like Cartagena and San Juan de Puerto Rico, were modernised. Garrisons were reinforced. In consequence, an attack on the Spanish empire would now be a more formidable undertaking than it had been in the old carefree days when Drake had led his robber band to the Treasure House of the world at Nombre de Dios. But it was precisely an enterprise of this kind that Drake embarked on at the end of August 1595.

After endless haggling and chaffering, Drake and Hawkins had, in January 1595, persuaded the Queen to commission them to 'offend our capital enemy the King of Spain' by making a large-scale raid on the Caribbean. The germ of this was an idea which had haunted Drake for twenty years – to seize and hold Panama.

But as the months passed, the aim of the expedition altered and, indeed, doubts grew as to whether it would take place at all. By adroit diplomacy, Drake did what he could to strengthen the Queen's interest in the project. For instance, he presented her with his own account of the circumnavigation voyage, a priceless document, long since lost to sight. But events were working to make the Queen even more fickle than usual. England was now on the defensive. The Spaniards had seized a base on the Breton coast at Blavet 'for the better invading of England'; in July their galleys had appeared at St Evall in Cornwall and had sent men ashore to damage various Cornish ports. Only the fear of Drake's fleet at Plymouth prevented them from staying longer and doing more. It appeared that they would soon launch a new major attack on England – and perhaps on Ireland, too. When Elizabeth had suggested to Henry of Navarre, now King of France since the assassination of Henri III and the Battle of Ivry, that he should cede her a French port, Henry had replied, 'Why not take Blavet?' If Henry's humour failed to amuse her, his realism shocked her. Having failed to storm Paris, he entered it by becoming a Catholic. If this meant that France must in future be numbered among the friends of Spain, England's plight was indeed grim. As matters turned out, it meant nothing of the sort but, in the anxious months of 1594 and 1595, who was to know that?

Elizabeth felt her realm to be in danger as it had never been since the perilous spring of 1588. To allow good ships and experienced admirals to leave home waters at such a time was a risk she shrank from taking. Three Spanish fleets, she told them, were getting ready in Cadiz, Lisbon and Corunna for the invasion of Ireland. The preparations were on a greater scale than those of 1588 had been. In these circumstances, the project of seizing Panama and holding it indefinitely was dismissed.

The two entrepreneurs were told that they had already wasted so much time that the Spaniards had ample warning of their intentions. The Queen's orders were that they were, first of all to sail to the Spanish coast, destroying what enemy shipping they could; in particular, they were to keep a sharp lookout for the incoming Flota. After that, they might proceed to the Indies, on condition that they were back in England by May 1596. Drake and Hawkins did not always agree with one another but, when these instructions reached them in Devon, they exploded in unison.

Their fleet had been assembled with amphibious operations in mind. They had transports, landing craft, and soldiers; they had spent, between them, £30,000 on victualling the ships – and now the Queen was talking in terms of naval battles and cruising in search of prizes. Worst of all, she was insisting on an absurd time-limit, as if God did not decide when sailors came home from sea!

With such ideas prevailing, such fluctuations, such contradictions of interest, they vowed they could foresee that the disappointments of the Portugal expedition would be repeated. No! If the Queen insisted on her terms, on an operation of that kind, let her bear all the expenses. Then they would be happy to oblige her. They sent a salvo of protest to their friend at Court, young Essex, ardent for every bold enterprise and already deep in this one. 'We beseech your lordship that, if Her Majesty do alter our just agreement, you stand strongly for us.' But while Essex might plead the cause, it was the Queen who gave the verdict. She conceded that the admirals might omit the visit to the Spanish Coast but, at all costs, they must be back by May of the following year. The argument that this depended on God's will was exactly the kind of pious sophistry which the Queen thought downright frivolous and she told them as much.

Was the enterprise still worth while? Could it be carried out? While Drake and Hawkins were pondering the problem down in Plymouth there came into their possession a piece of evidence which seemed relevant and exciting. A disabled Spanish galleon, vice-admiral of the Mexican treasure fleet, with 2,500,000 ducats of gold and silver aboard, had been forced by bad weather into San Juan de Puerto Rico. At this news, the old piratical fire in both men flared up: 'It lieth in our way and will in no way impeach us.' The Queen, when told of the discovery, remembered the *Golden Hind*, the *San Felipe*, the *Madre de Dios*. She, too, was tempted. The fleet was given permission to sail.

It was a decision reached on the flimsiest of grounds: news of a possible prize which had taken refuge in a well-defended enemy harbour four thousand miles away, news which, by the time it reached Plymouth, was already three months old. When an English fleet could reach Puerto Rico, at least another two months would have passed. Who would believe that the Spaniards would allow the treasure to remain in the crippled ship all that time when they had no lack of strongholds ashore in which to hide it? But, after all these weeks of frustration, Drake and Hawkins were too eager to step back on the stage again to look at the thing coolly and sceptically. These were vivid, tumultuous and heroic years for England at sea: Grenville's mad, immortal fight of 1591 in the *Revenge* which had been Drake's ship in the Armada battle. The profitable activities of John Watt, merchant of London, arch-financier of freebooters. In the cargo ship *Centurion*, Robert Bradshaw of Limehouse had met six Spanish galleys off Gibraltar and, while her trumpet blew defiance, had beaten off repeated waves of Spanish boarders. Drake's old rival, Frobisher, who detested him, had died covered with glory when the Spanish fort at Blavet was stormed at last. Then there were the exploits of Lord Cumberland, resembling in their bold opportunism those of Drake twenty years earlier. It was hard to listen to these stories with patience if you were a sea captain, living in retirement, rich, famous and remembering, as if they were scenes in some paradise lost, the tropical seas, the landfalls on the Spanish Main, the aroma of spices born by the wind from the Moluccas.

On 29 August 1595 the fleet sailed from Plymouth. The ships were sternly admonished by Drake to hold divine service twice a day, to eschew gambling, to show no lights except the light in the binnacle, to keep company, to speak with the Admiral twice a day, and so forth. In fact, the fleet orders were closely similar to those the Duke of Medina had promulgated seven years before when the Armada was about to weigh anchor in the Tagus.

The ships sailed in two squadrons. They consisted of six galleons of the Queen's and twenty-one armed merchantmen. In addition to her ships, the Queen had invested £30,000 in the venture; the two admirals and their City backers about twice as much. Aboard were 2,500 men, of whom about a thousand were soldiers, under the command of Sir Thomas Baskerville, an experienced officer. Even before the fleet sailed, it bore ominous presages.

First, the command was divided between two men of opposed temperaments. Could Hawkins, elderly and cautious, ever make an amiable working arrangement with his headstrong colleague? The task would have been hard. But it was made vastly harder since it was known that the older man had been appointed for the purpose of restraining the younger. He was a symbol of the distrust that Whitehall felt for Francis Drake. The strain would have been felt by a duo of archangels. Inevitably the opinions and actions of Hawkins were likely to be suspected, disputed and resented by his co-equal commander.

Secondly, the purpose of the fleet was known to the King of Spain three weeks before it sailed. A Fleming who had seen the preparations in London passed the news on. The whole of Spain was shivering with apprehension over a new pounce by Drake, whose name was, as one English spy reported, more dreaded by Spaniards than Talbot's had ever been by the French. Before long, the Spanish intelligence was to be even more exactly informed.

Just a month after the ships left Plymouth Sound, standing away south-west by south, they sighted the Canaries. Drake's first idea, which he pressed in council almost to a point of breach with Hawkins, was to land troops in a sandy bay close to Grand Canary. But, having reconnoitred the position in his barge, he decided that the swell was too heavy and the Spanish cannon too many. At the west end of the island, a party that went on land in search of water was set on by mountaineers.

Seven men were killed and a surgeon was captured. Unfortunately he knew the destination of the ships, which Hawkins had foolishly discussed in the hearing of his crew. Now the surgeon betrayed the plans to the Spaniards, and the Governor of the island without delay sent off a fast dispatch boat to the Indies with the warning that trouble was on the way. This warning reached Puerto Rico a week before the English fleet came over the horizon.

At the same time, word was sent to Spain, where a strong fleet was being made ready to go out and bring Drake to battle when he appeared in the Caribbean. The Spanish admiral, Delgadillo de Avellaneda, now knew where he would be most likely to meet the English, if he hurried. He did not hurry. Seven weeks passed before his ships (twenty-one in all) put to sea from the Tagus. The English were, however, even more dilatory. They avoided Dominica and went to seek fresh water at Guadeloupe. While they lay at anchor there on 30 October, bad news came. The *Francis*, a small barque, which had parted company with the others four days earlier, had been set upon and captured by five *gallizabras*, each of which was six times bigger than the English vessel. These vessels were on their way to collect the silver from the disabled galleon at Puerto Rico and carry it to Spain. Now they took the news to Puerto Rico that the English fleet, long awaited and much feared, had arrived in the Antilles.

Drake urged that the *gallizabras* be pursued. He thought they could be overtaken before they were able to give the alarm. Hawkins would have none of it. There was to be no action, he said, until the last gun was mounted on the last pinnace! And Hawkins had the one great advantage in the dispute: he was a sick man whom it would be cruel to thwart. Thus the last chance of surprising Puerto Rico was lost. The commander of the Spanish frigates not only brought the city exact information. He was also carrying a mass of artillery, three hundred trained soldiers and his own energetic and resolute character. His name was Don Pedro Tello.

While Baskerville was training his soldiers for the coming assault, Drake went on reconnaissance in his ship's boat to seek a new sailing route through the dangerous shoals of the Virgin Islands. It was work in which he excelled and, in consequence, he was able to conduct the fleet along a navigable channel unsuspected by the Spaniards. At dawn on 12 November, the leading English ships appeared off San Juan de Puerto Rico, having evaded the Spanish screen of scouts. They found a city ready to receive them.

It was built on high ground at the western end of an island joined by a bridge to the mainland of Puerto Rico and enclosing an excellent natural harbour. The tactical advantages of the place had been enhanced during recent years, ever since the Spanish government had woken up to the perils of naval attack on their colonies and their treasure. Forts had been built, especially, and a strong castle, the Morro, at the harbour mouth. Cannon had been installed and a permanent garrison of professional troops had been brought in. As it chanced, Puerto Rico was exceptionally able to resist an attack at the time the English fleet was sighted.

Sancho Pardo, the officer in command of the disabled galleon, summoned Don Pedro Tello, the governor, the bishop, the captains of the frigates and the officers of the garrison to meet him in council. It was decided that, since the *gallizabras* would need eight days to make ready for their return voyage to Spain with the treasure, their guns and crews should be brought ashore and employed in the defence of the harbour. Two ships were sunk to block the entrance while the frigates were lined up behind them. The bullion was to be stored in an old fort on the waterfront so that, if the worse came to the worst, it could be thrown into the sea. Seventy guns were sited and seven hundred and fifty soldiers distributed at different points where an attack might be expected; the remainder (probably about the same number) were held in reserve. Women, children and slaves were sent inland. The bishop in a sermon exhorted the citizens to do their Christian duty. Priests were assigned to each defence post to keep up the fighting spirit of the garrison. When the English fleet was descried, approaching slowly, its sails barely filled in a light wind, Puerto Rico was in excellent moral and military state to beat off an attack. The General was confident. Very different was the mood among the English.

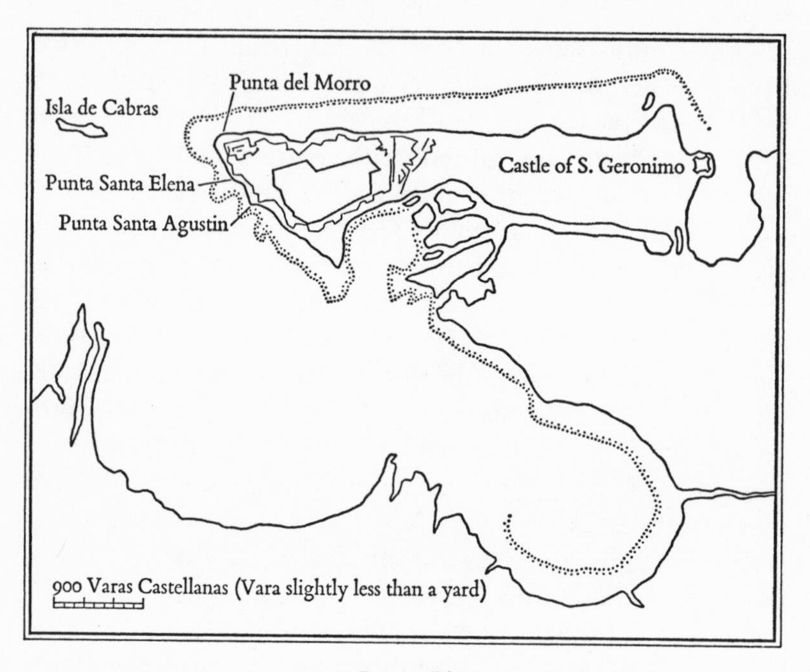

7 Puerto Rico

From the day of its departure from Plymouth, things had gone badly with the expedition. In the Canaries, frustration; at Guadeloupe, the loss of the *Francis*, a small but irritating defeat. On each occasion the enemy had been sent a warning, one more exact than its predecessor, of the coming attack. Now came an event of a different kind which was even more damaging to English morale. On the afternoon that the fleet dropped anchor off the north shore of Puerto Rico Sir John Hawkins died. He was a man of sixty-three, old then, as age went at that time, and worn out by a life spent at sea or among the endless worries of naval administration. His time had come. No doubt. But he had been one of the glories of an age in which England had challenged and worsted the King of Spain and, breaking its shell, had emerged as the fledgling of an eagle. He, more than any other man, had shaped and built the fleet that had beaten off the Armada. And, now that he was dead, every Englishman felt himself diminished. The fleet off Puerto Rico became a funeral procession, with foreboding in every heart, especially as the news went round that, while he lay dying, Hawkins had despaired of the enterprise and, in his will, had bequeathed £2,000 to the Queen in token of his regret for having wheedled her into something that he saw as doomed to failure. To 'my very good cousin, Sir Francis Drake', he left 'my best jewel, a cross of emerald'. It seems, then, that the old bitterness of the San Juan de Ulua days had long since been forgotten and that the recent disagreements between the two men did not exclude affection. But, with the death of Hawkins, the assault on San Juan de Puerto Rico was opening with the most sombre auguries. Drake must have been affected by all this. He had owed the dead man his first command. He had rivalled him, outstripped him and bickered with him down the years. With Hawkins had departed a severe, familiar presence at his elbow.

The attack on the city went forward as it had been planned. Boats displaying white marker flags passed along in front of the port, taking soundings as they went to show the way to the men-of-war. They anchored to the east of the town. But the coast defence guns proved to be much stronger and more accurate than had been expected, and one round shot went through Drake's cabin in his flagship, the *Defiance*, while he sat drinking a mug of beer. It knocked the stool from under him and killed two of his companions, one of whom was a much-loved friend. Drake made a signal to the fleet to move out of range of the shore batteries. At dawn next morning the Spaniards found the English at anchor to the west of the harbour and protected from the coastal guns by two small islands named Goat Island and the Kid. There, the ships lay all day without sign of life, while Drake made his plan to attack the Spanish frigates where they were drawn up under the guns of the forts at the harbour entrance. After dark, the attack was delivered by twenty-five boats and pinnaces. The frigates were deluged with incendiary devices, a form of naval weapon in which the English specialised.

Drake himself led the attack, which was at first concentrated on the flagship of the frigates. This caught fire along with three of her consorts. While the crew were fighting the flames, the artillery of the land defences came into play. After an hour of stubborn fighting, three of the frigates were saved. The fourth was burnt to the waterline but, as it burned, lit up the battle area enabling the gunners to improve their aim. By the time Drake gave the order to withdraw, several boats had been sunk and fifty men had lost their lives.

On the following day, he planned to bring off a still more daring stroke by sailing into the harbour along the narrow channel between the sunken ships and the shore. It would have been a gamble because it meant braving the guns of the Morro at point-blank range. But Don Pedro Tello guessed what the English admiral's next move would be and, in the nick of time, sank two cargo boats and a frigate in the path of the incoming fleet. Seeing this, Drake gave up what had now become a hopeless enterprise.

What to do next? It was a question which Drake alone could not answer. Sir Thomas Baskerville, in command of the soldiers with the expedition, had taken Hawkins' place and was, therefore, co-equal with Drake. He must be consulted. Drake called a council of war in his cabin in the flagship, at which he proposed that the town should be attacked by the soldiers, who would approach it on the landward side, thus avoiding the permanent fortifications. In other words, he proposed to repeat the tactics which had been so successful long ago at Cartagena. The situation was different now, however. The Spaniards had more trained soldiers at Puerto Rico than Baskerville had. The time was past when an English landing force had nothing more formidable to meet than colonial militia. Baskerville rejected

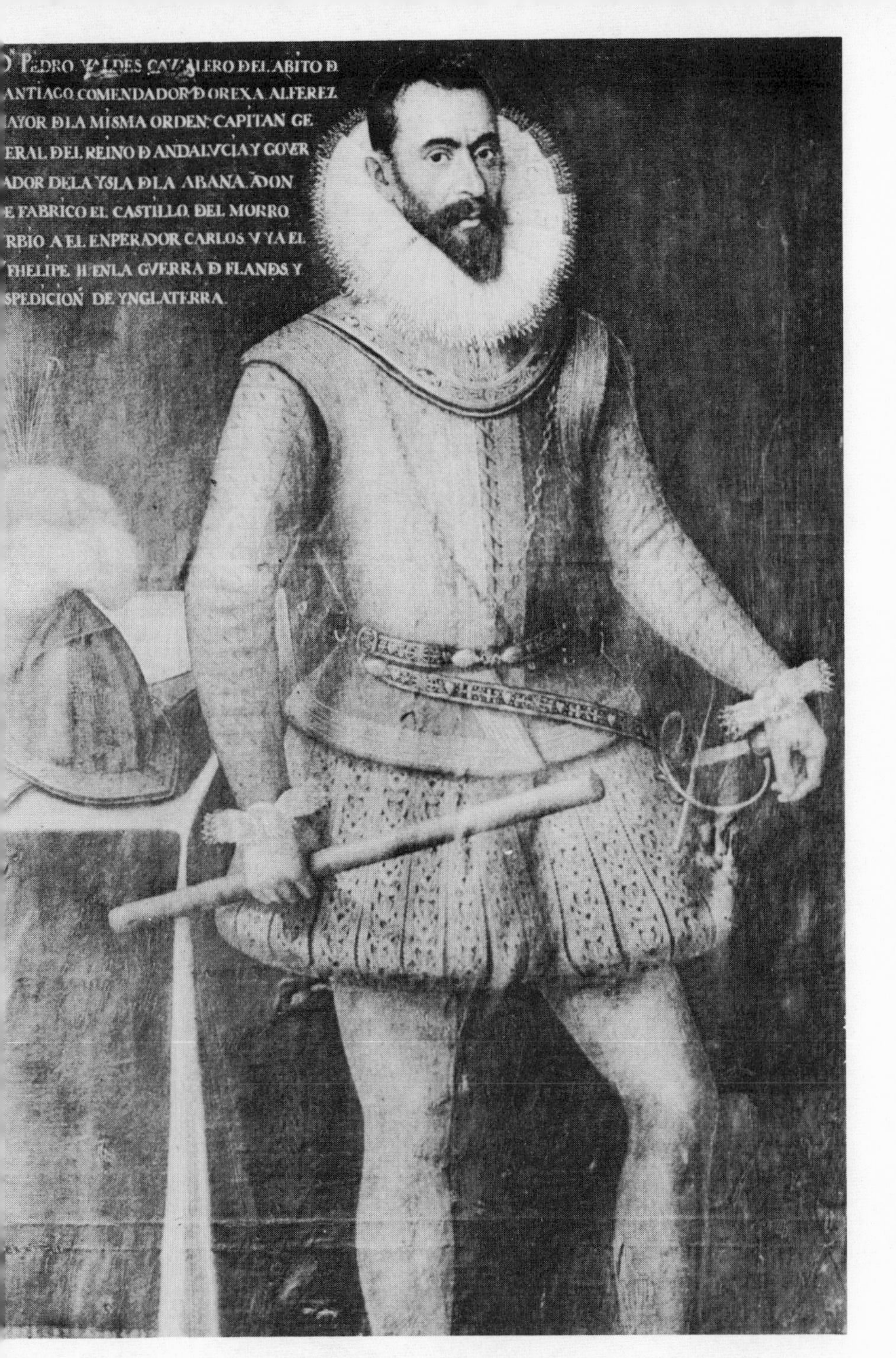

17 Vice-Admiral Don Pedro Valdes, Knight of the Order of Santiago, Captain-General of the Kingdom of Andalusia, and Governor of Havana (*British Museum*)

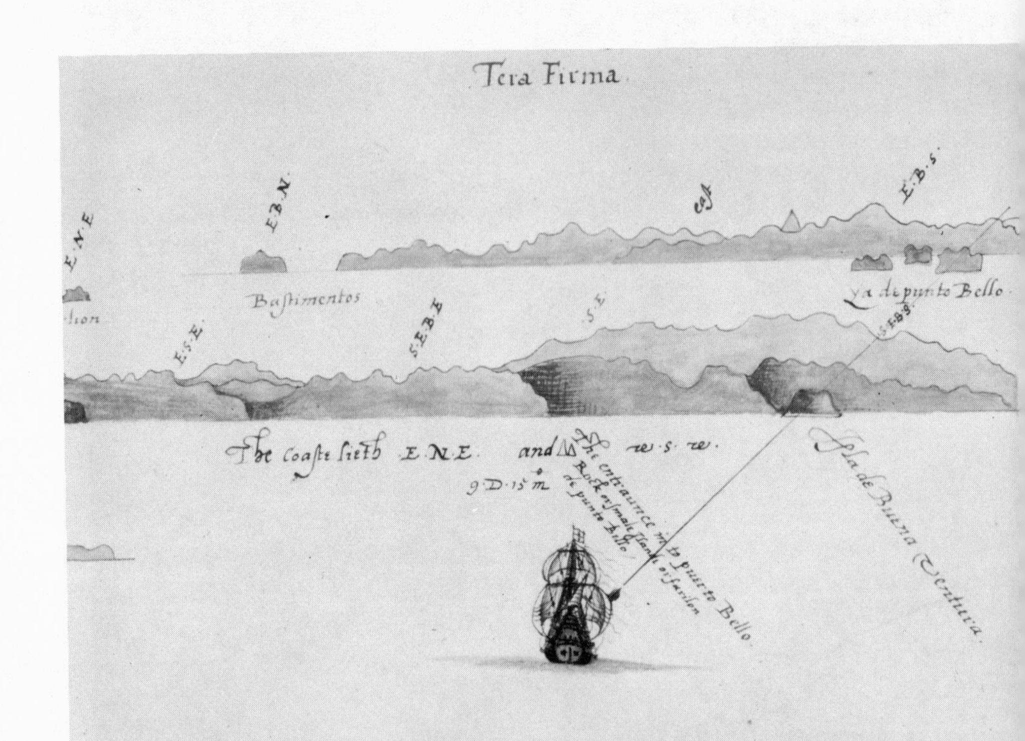

This lande heare presentid shewith the firme or runinge of parte of the neck an
from Nombre de Dios or I meane from the weste Cape of Nombre de Dios Cauli
Bastimentes untill you com to the westwarde unto the Ilandes of Laies Min
Viesas de Discribinge the rocks and Ilandes betweene thes too placis also the entr
in to the good harburo calid Puerto Bello note hou the corraunte setith heare to
N.E. The variasion of the Compas 2 pointes to the west and all what someue
I haue heare in this place notid I haue notid it plainelie with our Englis
Compas as it hathe shewid with respecte of the variasion /

This Morninge when the discription notid or taken of this lande beinge
28. of Januarie 1595 beinge wedens daie in the morninge Sr Francis D
Died of the bludie flix righte of the Ilande de Buena ventura som
Leagues at see whom now restith with the Lorde

18 Prospect of Nombre de Dios drawn on the day of Drake's death
(*Bibliothèque Nationale*)

the plan and Drake did not insist. Some of the younger officers were reluctant to lose the rich prize which they knew was waiting in Puerto Rico. But Drake consoled them. 'I will bring you,' he said, 'to twenty places far more wealthy and easier to be gotten.' Crossing to the Spanish Main, he paused at Curaçao and Aruba. After that, he took the pearl village of Rio de la Hacha, where, as a young man, he had had his first encounter with the Spaniards. Escaped slaves showed the English where their masters had hidden their treasure. At Rancheria, not far away, the plunder was still richer – enough to cover the whole costs of the expedition. Here the Governor, Don Francisco Manso, spun out negotiations for the ransom of houses, slaves and prisoners, until warning of Drake's presence had reached neighbouring settlements. When he confessed his duplicity Drake gave him two hours to clear out and then set fire to the town – sparing the church and the house of a lady who had asked him to be merciful. At Santa Marta the marauders had no luck and, a week later, the fleet dropped anchor in Nombre de Dios.

In retracing the course of his first raid, Drake had now returned to the town he had once called the Treasure House of the World. Now he came, not with a handful of desperadoes, but with two thousand men and six galleons of the Queen's. The town was deserted and, this time, there was no gold in the King's House. Fever-stricken Nombre de Dios had been demoted from its status as the Caribbean terminus of the gold route from Panama, and Puerto Bello had taken its place. While Drake, with the help of communicative and resentful slaves, dug up jewellery and plate which the population had hidden away in the neighbouring forests, Sir Thomas Baskerville made ready for the attack on Panama. When Drake had first set eyes on the city, he had been guided by his allies, the Cimarrons. This time there were no Cimarrons. Soon after John Oxenham's attempt to mobilise them against the Spaniards in 1576, they had been the victims of a brutal punitive campaign which beat the spirit out of them.

But Baskerville faced a still greater handicap. From Puerto Rico, Don Pedro Tello had sent word that Drake was on his way. In consequence, Panama had an interval of three weeks in which it could get its defences into good order. The main crossing of the mountain range had been fortified by an Italian expert, engaged by King Philip to strengthen his treasure route. The Viceroy of Peru, in answer to cries for help from Panama, had sent a frigate from Lima with arms and seasoned troops. Finally, the weather was against the English. Incessant rain turned the mountain paths into torrents and the hills into muddy slopes on which it was impossible for a man to find a foothold. On the first day Baskerville's force covered nine miles, and on the second eighteen. By that time, they had reached the half-way mark, the point in their journey where there were stables for five hundred mules of the *recuas*. These buildings they burned to the ground.

On the third day, a couple of miles farther on they approached the main ridge of the Cordillera, where in the Capira Pass the Italian engineer, Juan Bautista Antonelli, had established a strongpoint held by a hundred musketeers. Seven hundred English advanced in single file uphill along a deep gully cleft in the mountains until they reached a line of trees which the Spaniards had slashed and bent over to form a barrier. Here the English assault troops were pinned to the ground by musket-fire from a Spanish blockhouse. The rain had spoilt their powder, match and biscuit. They were wet and ill-shod. Their leader, Baskerville, saw no prospect of being able to overrun the Spanish position. Worst of all, he heard that there were two similar forts between him and Panama. He listened to the enemy pioneers at work ahead of him, chopping down the trees, preparing new barricades.

Once again, the English were paying dear for the slow pace of their operations. Panama had been given the alarm by Puerto Rico and Rio de la Hacha, as Puerto Rico had been warned from the Canaries and Guadaloupe. By chance, reinforcements had arrived from Lima which could be mustered for the battle.

The decision to hold the Capira Pass was taken just ten days before Baskerville delivered his attack. By so narrow a margin of time was the Pacific terminus of the treasure route saved from a coup that would have brought down King Philip's credit and might well have shaken his empire.

The garrison in the pass was commanded by Juan Enriques Conabut, a resolute officer. The defence held fast, and Baskerville, with death in his heart, gave the order to retreat. He knew that on the outcome of this foray turned the whole purpose of the expedition as it was conceived in the first place. Those of the wounded who could ride he put on horseback: the others he left optimistically to the compassion of the enemy. Then he and his men made their way back to the coast down the treacherous, streaming mountain paths. A messenger went on ahead bearing the bad news. Soon the beaches near Nombre de Dios were strewn with the dead bodies of English soldiers, most of whom had been drowned in the torrents of the Cordillera.

On the return of the footsore and dejected troops, Drake summoned a council of war. Now that it was clear the Spaniards were fully informed about their intentions, what should be the next move? He suggested that they might attack either the settlements on the Lagoon of Nicaragua or those in the Bay of Honduras. Attack both, said Baskerville who had apparently made a rapid recovery from his disappointment on the way to Panama. So they set sail for the Lagoon of Nicaragua, after burning Nombre de Dios to the ground and taking what silver they could find there, a mere twenty bars. Drake did not encourage this petty pilfering. 'Why', he asked, 'gather the harvest grain by grain when at Panama we are likely to thrust our hands into the whole heap?'

The setbacks had been wretched but neither he nor Baskerville was disheartened. It is quite possible, indeed, that Drake had not given up hope of the grand coup against Panama which would reward all their pains. There were two difficulties, however. He had given his word that he would be home in May. It was already the middle of January. More ominous, the fleet was being swept by sickness. Captain after captain took to his hammock and died. The deck above the ballast, the only sick-bay in a ship of that time, stank with sickness.

Finally, Drake himself, who over the years had escaped death in so many fever-stricken ships, took ill. At first he did not lose heart, although confessing that the Indies were hardly recognisable as the delicious arbour he had known as a young captain – now they were a desert, with blustering winds and not a sail worth giving chase to. To Thomas Maynarde, who spoke with him while the fleet lay for twelve days at anchor off an island named Escudo de Veragua, 'counted the sickliest place of the Indies', he kept up a brave front: 'It matters not, man. God hath things in store for us and I know many means to do Her Majesty good service and make us rich. For we must have gold before we see England.' Maynarde thought this was so much bravado but, then, Maynarde seems to have been a poor-spirited soldier.

Drake's might have been the utterance of one whose spirit, battered as it might be, was still unbroken, one who still felt equal to preparing fresh audacities as, only a few weeks before, he had astounded the Spaniards in their own waters with proofs of his undiminished cunning as a sailor. Or it might have been the talk of one passing into the clouds of fever, already touched by the hand of death and harking back in thought or fantasy, the poison encroaching on his reason, to the forays of youth, to the mule bells on the King's Highway, to the one glimpse of Panama which haunted him all his days, to the gold of Peru. And what was no longer attainable became all the more poignantly desirable to the sick man for whom, although he knew it not, the circle of life was already closing.

The treasure of the Indies was guarded by invisible dragons one of the most terrible of which, dysentery, now fastened on him. Before long, Drake, a dying admiral of ships crowded with dying men, was in no state to think of battle or treasure. All about him was the odour of disease and the presence of death. He had made his will before leaving England: 'Forasmuch as all men are born to die, that the time of our departure out of this mortal life is most uncertain and that we are here but as stewards for the time to dispose of such things as God hath lent us . . .' He entailed all his estates on his brother Thomas so that his property should remain in his own name and blood to the good pleasure of Almighty God. His wife, Elizabeth, a rich woman in her own right, was left furniture and property; including the Plymouth mills; Thomas Drake, the house in Plymouth he was then occupying, while £100 was to go to Jonas Bodenham, his first wife's nephew, the captain of his ship and his lieutenant in many a sea fight. Now, in a second will made at sea, he left a manor to Bodenham and another manor to Francis Drake of Esher. Trouble arose through both of these bequests.* His officers had farewell gifts while William Whitlocke, a tall, flaxen-haired young man who had looked after him in the final days, received plate and jewels.[2]

It is said that Thomas Drake intercepted those bequests on their way to Whitlocke, thinking perhaps that the youth had taken undue advantage of Drake's weakness. But Whitlocke had the reputation of being a spendthrift and Thomas may have judged it reasonable to keep temptation out of his way. The poor of Plymouth were left £40 by their most famous burgher. He signed the will on 27 January. That night he raved in delirium, bidding Whitlocke put his armour on him so that he might die like a soldier. Then he quietened down and was persuaded to go back to his bunk. An hour later, he died.

By that time the fleet lay at anchor off Puerto Bello on the isthmus of Panama. Next day, Baskerville who was now in command of the expedition, took the ships three miles from the shore. Cannon boomed; trumpets wailed; and the Master Thief of the Unknown World, housed in a lead coffin, vanished below the waters on which all these years ago his legend had been born. 'Fortune's child was dead, things would not fall into our mouths, nor riches be our portion how dearly soever we adventured for them.' There was only one thing to do.

* See Appendix I.

Baskerville set off for home. There was no time to lose because, just three months earlier, a Spanish fleet of twenty-three galleons and a number of smaller craft had left Spain with orders to intercept Drake and destroy his ships. The admiral to whom this task was assigned had been refitting his ships at Cartagena, three hundred miles east of Puerto Bello. He set out to intercept Baskerville as soon as he heard that Drake was dead. The two fleets met off the Isle of Pines to the south of Cuba and the English, although by far the weaker force of the two, had the better of the three hours' engagement. They were able to continue on their homeward voyage. The ships had all returned to English waters by the end of April or the early days of May. The promise Drake gave to the Queen had been kept.

From one settlement to another the news sped round the Spanish empire, bringing the end of a nightmare. Seville was illuminated. And King Philip showed more pleasure than he had done on any day since he heard of the Massacre of St Bartholomew.[3]

The joy in Spain was soon over. Before Baskerville's ships had reached England, a powerful new fleet had left for Spain and by the end of June it was hammering at the gates of Cadiz. The war was going on.

XXI

Farewell, the Phoenix of Our Age

'Proud Spain, although our dragon be bereft us
We, rampant lions, have enough for thee.'
Sir Francis Drake, his honourable life's commendation – *Chas. FitzGeoffrey*

Francis Drake, in many respects a typical Englishman of his time, acquired a unique position both then and in later history. He did so because of an altogether special assortment of gifts.

Like most other English boys, born into a poor, large family, at that time, he was ill-educated, although not illiterate, so far as can be judged from the remarks of those who wished to denigrate him and those, more patronising, who were astounded that one who started with so few advantages should have his readiness of address, fertility of ideas and native eloquence. He may have been conscious of this himself. It seems the best explanation that can be offered of his insistence on the quality of the stock he sprang from. Clarencieux Herald declared, 'Sir Francis Drake may by privilege of his birth and right descent from his ancestors bear the arms and surname of his family . . . with the difference of a third brother.' Perhaps Clarencieux was right. What is more significant is that Drake thought the matter important enough to seek an official ruling. He, a man of the new kind – the supreme example of the new man – wished to make sure of his place in the old establishment. He was also a pious Protestant, a Puritan, with the prickly, proselytising zeal of one whose family had been persecuted for their faith and who was warily conscious that the shiversome terrors depicted in his friend John Foxe's *Book of Martyrs* were not necessarily abolished for ever. But all this could have been said of a hundred English sea officers of the time. Why was Drake picked out from among them so that the reign of Queen Elizabeth I is almost synonymous with the age of Drake?

The answer can surely not be in doubt. Because of personal qualities which exerted a strong influence upon the youth of the time. A youth which was unusually restless, acquisitive and ungovernable, but which was also filled with wild and – as we should say – romantic dreams of discovery and adventure. And plunder, too. Wealth won by running dreadful dangers but involving no tedious labour. That, of course, was an element in Drake's appeal. He was the most spectacular freebooter of his time. And if the name 'pirate' was one that he himself resented, it carried a lighter weight of moral obloquy than it might have done with many of his contemporaries. He was, as he insisted, a privateer. And that was – what exactly? A pirate with a licence more or less valid, or a patriot fighting his country's battles while sparing his sovereign any embarrassment his deeds might bring? But there were scores of privateering captains sailing out of Plymouth, Weymouth and the Thames. Drake was neither the first nor the last of them. True, he worked on a bigger scale than most. There was an element of the thunderclap about his exploits. But this was true of Hawkins, Frobisher, Cavendish, Cumberland and, in later years, the dazzling Essex. Yet Drake possessed in a singular degree the power to stamp his image on the time and draw its young men to his ships. In what did that power lie?

There was a magic of personality in the man marking him out from the thousands of God-fearing Englishmen, gentry, merchants, shopkeepers, sailors and the footloose workless artisans to whom his ships wore the same golden hues of hope and opportunity as America, Canada and Australia wore for later generations of their kind. He thought as those men did, but he had a magnetic power which made him their natural leader. Men chose him as Napoleon chose his generals, because he was lucky. They stayed with him because they loved him. He was apt to be overbearing to his rivals and irritating to his social betters; but it is plain that he radiated a genial warmth captivating to those on whom he exerted it.

Sharp in focus and lucid in colour as a miniature by Hilliard is the picture of Drake painted in verse by Robert Hayman, a Devon man who became Governor of Britaniola (Newfoundland). The incident he described occurred when Hayman was a child, and one day met Drake walking up the long street of Totnes.

> *He asked me whose I was. I answered him.*
> *He asked if his good friend were within.*
> *A fair red orange in his hand he had.*
> *He gave it me, whereof I was right glad.*
> *Takes and kissed me and prays, God bless my boy,*
> *Which I recall in comfort to this day.*[1]

Hayman's lines may limp but how touching is his account of the meeting of the little boy and the famous corsair, whose name was used by Spanish mothers, then as now, to frighten their children into obedience! And how far it goes to explain the irresistible appeal he made to the seamen and adventurers of England. According to Spanish witnesses discipline in his ships was strict, orders were given imperiously and obeyed at once. But the mariners who went in awe of him worshipped the deck he trod. When he was about to set sail on that last expedition, his final throw with Philip, nothing embarrassed him more than the importunate horde of young men clamouring to be taken aboard his ships, and this in spite of the fact that the Lisbon operation, five years earlier, had turned out badly for the serving soldiers. Only two other leaders of the age, Henry of Navarre and Essex, seem to have had a comparable power to command men's hearts. But Henry was a king, Essex a great nobleman. In truth, Drake, who was neither the one nor the other, may have owed the special quality of his magnetism to his origins among the Thames-side people, the mudlarks.

He had defied one entrenched power and elbowed his way into another, and they felt in a confused way that he had done so as their representative. He had sailed round the world, a heroic feat, and had plundered the rich, a praiseworthy form of crime in the eyes of the poor. And, if he had become rich himself, with results that were there for all to see – showy clothes, plate, jewels and fine estates – these were outward signs of wealth that men understood and approved. He was good-natured, with a nice gift of ironical wit; humane to a degree extraordinary in that rough age; fond of hearing his own voice, listening politely to the advice of others and then going his own way. His 'self-willed and peremptory command' had its value on the quarter-deck of a galleon at sea, but in Whitehall it aroused distrust. Drake was, in other words, a 'card', that is to say, a man of character whom a touch of eccentricity redeemed from the commonplace. It would be a mistake to think that there was no more to him than affability, professional skill and an eye to the main chance. Drake was not merely a bluff sea-dog. There was in him a vein of ruthless enquiry (the autopsy on his brother); a resolve that could become steel when it was threatened (the execution of Doughty); and a profound secretive cunning (the scuttling of the *Swan*). In short, he was a man for lonely enterprises and solitary decisions. A born explorer with a touch of the missionary thrown in. Drake founding New Albion is like Brigham Young at Salt Lake City, and those wild doings outside Nombre de Dios suggest that other marauding knight, Henry Morgan.

Was he, as some have thought, a strategist prefiguring Chatham or a pioneer of naval tactics in the class of Nelson? Was he denied the full flowering of his genius by the Queen's avarice or by Burghley's timidity? The answers are surely these: it was one thing – a brilliant flash of insight – to see that Panama was Spain's jugular vein, that if the Isthmus could be seized and held, then Spanish military supremacy in Europe would collapse as the unpaid *tercios* dissolved into bands of mutinous brigands plundering the countryside. It was possible, too, that England could best be defended off the Spanish coast. But, naval hygiene being what it was, large fleets could not be maintained in distant waters without having their efficiency for battle destroyed by disease. Elizabeth's finances being in the state they were, the Navy was compelled to earn its living in partnership with business. War could not be fought on military principles alone. As for naval tactics, they were not even in their infancy. The Armada battle was the first tentative skirmish in a new kind of war. The ships were clumsy; the guns were inadequate; the ammunition ran out.

It is best to think of Drake as an inspired guerrilla leader. In a series of amphibious operations, mostly quite modest in scale, he administered a succession of shocks to the Spanish system which disturbed the aim of Philip's policy, damaged his prestige and, in the end, changed the course of history. In this sense, indeed, Drake had stumbled upon one of the keys to naval strategy – the power to produce a major result by exerting a small force at a critical place. Certainly he did not bring the Spanish empire down or build the British. But he baited Philip into the disastrous Enterprise of England. Requesens was right: in order to invade England, Philip needed a base on the North Sea. Parma was right in wishing to go on with his Dutch campaign, tedious, inglorious, but promising to be crowned with success. He sought to free the Scheldt and open Antwerp to the sea. That estuary was only two miles across where it met the sea but until the northern bank was in Spanish hands, Antwerp was blockaded and England was safe. Two miles! The margin of English and Protestant freedom was as narrow as that. But Hapsburg pride could not tolerate the repeated minor outrages which Drake and his like inflicted on it. And, after Cadiz, Philip could not wait. The object of Cadiz was to delay the Armada. That it did, but it also made certain that it would sail at a time when it should not have sailed.

The full consequences of the defeat of the Armada were not immediately visible but they were in the end decisive. And so Drake, after all, played his part in one of the great mutations in history. His cause has sometimes been championed for the wrong reasons: for example, that he was wilfully denied scope for his ideas by a jealous government. He was criticised, in his time, on grounds that seem equally mistaken. Thus Maynarde, who sailed with him on the last voyage, said that he was 'better able to conduct forces to places where service was to be done than to command in the execution thereof'. But this is to misunderstand the nature of the man's talent, which was not to be the officer commanding a fleet of transports, as at Lisbon, but to be the general of a raiding force. Drake's is one of the glorious names in England's naval history but the truth is that the greater part of his fighting was done either in harbours or ashore. It was, however, fighting in the course of which he had stumbled on one of the essential secrets of seapower and exhibited it to his successors.

Had Norreys not failed before Lisbon and Baskerville not been beaten back on the way to Panama, Drake's glory would not have been dimmed at the finish. The first venture was betrayed by a spy and the second, with more resolute leadership, might have succeeded. Drake has received too much blame for them. But he, on whom fortune smiled so often, could not reasonably have complained if for once she was unkind.

With Drake there vanished – and more fittingly in a ship of war off Puerto Bello than at home in bed – the only being who could dispute with the Queen the title of the age. It is likely that they understood one another tolerably well, those two, different as they might be in temperament, different as might be their outlook on policy. But the policy was hers and hers alone. Drake was no more than the executant. And in the end, it was her strategy, with all its twists and turns, its second – and third – thoughts and false economies, that was victorious. 'Though beset by divers nations her mortal enemies,' wrote one chronicler long after the Queen was dead, 'she held the most stout and warlike nation of the English four and forty years and upwards, not only in awe and duty but even in peace also. Insomuch as in all England for so many years never any mortal man heard the trumpet sound the charge to battle.'[2] Drake, who heard that sound many times, was one of those who by their exploits in distant waters kept its harsh music from the ears of his countrymen. At the same time, he created and named a legend of boldness and confidence which was more fruitful than any of his deeds.

The imperial idea had its prophets, publicists and poets – Dee, Hakluyt, Gilbert, Raleigh and the rest. Drake's contribution was at a different level – that of a man who fused the ideas of adventure, exploring, conquest and gain into one glittering mass and held it up before the hungry, ambitious and spirited youth of England. No longer did they feel themselves confined to an offshore island. They stood on the verge of the Ocean, and the oceanic age had arrived. This they might have learnt from the maps, even the maps of those days, but Drake and his like, Drake above all, turned geography into a passionate desire to emulate. This he did by achievement, by success, measured in captured ships and plundered cities, in handfuls of ducats and sacks of softly glistening pearls.

When the coffin was let down into the sea off Puerto Bello, 'the trumpets in doleful manner echoing out this lamentation for so great a loss, and all the cannons in the fleet were discharged', it was the end of a life and the preface to a history.[3]

Notes on Sources

A good, modern account of the age Drake lived in and which he helped to change is to be found in J. H. Parry's *The Age of Reconnaissance* which, in conjunction with the third volume of the *Cambridge Modern History*, sketches in the background of the story. In Fernand Braudel's monumental and inspiring *La Méditerranée à l'époque de Philippe II*, the centre of gravity of the world may be seen moving from the Mediterranean to the Atlantic. This process may be studied, too, in Volume II of Jacques Pirenne's *The Tides of History*.

For Spain and the Spanish empire the following are of value: C. H. Haring's *The Spanish Empire*, R. B. Merriman's *The Rise of the Spanish Empire* (vol IV), A. P. Newton's *The European Nations in the West Indies* and John Lynch's *Spain under the Hapsburgs*. The organisation of trade between Spain and her American colonies is the subject of the exhaustive statistical study of H. and P. Chaunu, *Séville et l'Atlantique*.

To turn to England at the time, there is A. L. Rowse's *The Expansion of Elizabethan England*, a luminous and imaginative book; the essays by various hands which S. T. Bindoff collected in *Elizabethan Society and Government*; Conyers Read's biographies of Cecil and Walsingham; Sir John Neale's superb biography of the Queen, and Elizabeth Jenkin's *Elizabeth the Great*. On the narrower, but important, front of finance, W. R. Scott's three-volume work on *English, Scottish and Irish Companies* is indispensable. The thirteen volumes of E. M. Tenison's *Elizabethan England* provide a vast quantity of document and illustration relating to the age.

On maritime life and enterprise, the student is indeed fortunate in the wealth of collected and edited material at his disposal. He has, first of all, the twelve volumes of Hakluyt's *Principal Navigations* and the twenty volumes of Samuel Purchas *His Pilgrims*. There is also a near-contemporary work, the *Naval Tracts* of Sir William Monson, edited by Oppenheim. To these have now been added the collections of Spanish and English documents edited by Irene A. Wright, Zelia Nuttall, D. B. Quinn and others. These give a picture of events from the Spanish point of view.

Of the contemporary narratives, which are mentioned below where they are most relevant, the most interesting is *Sir Francis Drake Revived*, since it was probably dictated and certainly revised by Drake himself and is, in that case, the only piece of autobiography he left. Published in the reign of Charles I, its foreword by Drake's nephew makes an appeal to a predatory, nationalist spirit, 'calling upon this dull and effeminate age to follow his noble steps for gold and silver'.

Later works which should be mentioned include J. A. Williamson's *The Age of Drake* and his *Sir John Hawkins*. There is also of course the magisterial work of Sir Julian Corbett, *Drake and the Tudor Navy*. K. R. Andrews has contributed two valuable studies of *Elizabethan Privateering*.

For the ships, the guns and the naval battles, Michael Lewis, Sir William Clowes, Sir Julian Corbett, Sir John Laughton, Gregory Robinson; de la Roncière (French) and Duro (Spanish) should be mentioned.

The sumptuous volume *Sir Francis Drake*, compiled by Hans P. Kraus, contains some useful new material and a large number of contemporary maps and illustrations.

The Calendars of State Papers of the reign of Elizabeth, Domestic, Spanish, Venetian and Foreign, are of incomparable interest and value. I have used those sources with enthusiasm.

CHAPTER I

No Peace Beyond the Line

1 Spanish couplet, quoted Wright, *Spanish Documents*.
2 Text of Papal Bull and Treaty of Tordesillas, F. G. Davenport, *European Treaties*.
3 Thomas Jefferys, *The West-India Atlas*, 1775.
4 Peru had mercury at Huancavelica; Mexico depended on imports. Chaunu, *Séville*, vol 3.
5 Haring, *Spanish Empire*.
6 De la Roncière, *Histoire de la marine française*, vol. III.
7 Terra Australis Incognita still appears on a map of Mercator's published ten years after Drake's voyage.
8 Lynch, *Spain under the Hapsburgs*, which also gives a concise description of Spanish social structure.
9 Licence to import was not, however, the only obstacle. Slaves were expensive to ship; they must be fed during a voyage of six to eight weeks (Chaunu). For Herrera's report, see D. P. Mannix, *Black Cargoes*.
10 French corsairs: de la Roncière, *Histoire de la marine française* (vols III and IV); Gabriel A. Marcel, *Les Corsaires français*, and Leon Lemonnier, *La Grande Légende de la mer* (*Sir Francis Drake*). 'No peace beyond

the line.' Treaty of Cateau Cambrésis (1559) and accompanying oral agreement (Lynch, *Spain under the Hapsburgs*).

11 De la Roncière, *Histoire de la marine française*, vol. III.

12 J. A. Williamson, *Hawkins of Plymouth*, and *Sir John Hawkins: The Time and the Man*. Michael Lewis, *The Hawkins Dynasty*; I. A. Wright, *Spanish Documents*.

CHAPTER II

A Permit to Trade

General sources for this chapter include *The Third Troublesome Voyage of Sir John Hawkins*, 'A Discourse of one Miles Philips' (Hakluyt); Robert Barrett's narrative in Wright's *Spanish Documents*. A vivid account of the voyage by an anonymous officer is to be found in a (mutilated) manuscript in the British Museum, Cotton MSS Otho E pp. 17–41b.

Among modern authorities, Andrews, *Elizabethan Privateering*.

For Drake, Lady Eliott-Drake, 'The Family and Heirs of Sir Francis Drake'; *The Western Antiquary* (vol. 5).

1 A reasonable inference from his inclination to spell his name 'Frauncis'.
2 Braudel, *La Mediterranée*.
3 Wright, *Spanish Documents*.
4 Monson's *Naval Tracts*. The cartographer was Pedro de Sarmiento.
5 Braudel.
6 Lynch, *Spain under the Hapsburgs*.
7 Wright, *Spanish Documents*.
8 Cotton MSS, Otho E ff. 17–41b.

CHAPTER III

Echo Beyond the Mexique Bay

For the San Juan de Ulua incident, see *The Third Troublesome Voyage of the Right Worshipful Sir John Hawkins* (Hakluyt, X). The incident is thoroughly studied in Rayner Unwin's *The Defeat of John Hawkins*. Contributions by Michael Lewis to the *Mariner's Mirror*, July 1936 and July 1937, give additional Spanish accounts of the battle.

Arber, *An English Garland*; reprisals proposed by William Hawkins.

For the composition of the *flota* encountered by Hawkins, Chaunu, *Séville*. Spanish accounts by Luis Zegri, etc., in Wright, *Spanish Documents*. Robert Tomson describes the fort (Hakluyt).

CHAPTER IV

The Duke of Alva's Silver

Conyers Read, *Lord Burghley and Queen Elizabeth;* see, too, his article, 'Queen Elizabeth's seizure of Alva's pay ship' (*Journal of Modern History*, pp. 443–64, 1933). State Papers (Domestic) Elizabeth, xlix. Van Meteren (*Histoire des Pays Bas*) and J. L. Motley (*The Rise of the Dutch Republic*) for the background of events in Low Countries. Haring and Merriman are, as before, essential to an understanding of the situation in the Indies, and inflation caused by inflow of Peruvian bullion.

Events in Caribbean, Wright's *Spanish Documents.*

1 'The Distresses of the Commonwealth with the meanes to remedy them.' State paper of December 1558, evidently addressed to Cecil. P.R.O. State Papers (Domestic) Elizabeth, p. 145.
2 Philip to the Pope. Braudel, *Méditerranée.*
3 'The best of his secretaries'; quoted in Braudel.
4 Heredity of Philip II. See Michael de Ferdinandy, *Karl V.*
5 Philip's *Lettres à ses filles*, edited M. Gachard.
6 Spanish postal services. Lynch, *Spain under the Hapsburgs*; Braudel, *Méditerranée.*
7 Colonial revenues. Merriman, *Rise of Spanish Empire.*
8 Campaign by a *tercio* cost 1,200,000 ducats. President of Spanish Royal Revenues tells Lippomano, Venetian ambassador; Philip has 108,000 soldiers. Cal. S. P. (Venetian) 5 November 1587.
9 Alava; quoted in Braudel.
10 Perez, *L'Art de gouverner.*
11 Braudel.
12 Wright, *Spanish Documents.* Cal. S.P. (Dom.), August 1586.
13 Fulke Greville, *Life of Sir Philip Sidney.*
14 From Archives of Indies, Wright, *Documents concerning English Voyages.*

CHAPTER V

The Treasure House of the World

The documentation of Drake's expedition to Nombre de Dios will for for the most part be found in I. A. Wright's *Documents concerning English Voyages* and *Spanish Documents concerning English Voyages.* See too, Hakluyt, X, 'The first voyage,' etc. Later authorities, Sir Julian Corbett's *Drake and the Tudor Navy* and the excellent modern account in K. R. Andrews' *Elizabethan Privateering* and *English Privateering and Voyages.* Andrews is notably cool towards this phase of English maritime genius and provides, for that reason, a useful corrective to the heroics of some earlier historians.

Sir Francis Drake Revived, published by Drake's nephew, gives a brilliant eye-witness account of this expedition. The Spanish documents translated and printed by I. A. Wright agree closely with the English account of the Nombre de Dios affair.

1 Richard Eden, *A Treatise of the New India.*
2 Bishop of Panama. See Wright's *Documents.*
3 Depositions of Jorge Nuñez de Prado in Wright's *Documents*; also accounts printed there by Martin de Mendoza, Diego Flores de Valdes, Pedro de Ortega Valencia.

CHAPTER VI

Thank God, Our Voyage is Made!

Main authorities are as for the previous chapter.

Lionel Wafer's *Description of the Isthmus of America*, although not contemporary, gives a detailed, convincing account of the vegetation, animal life and inhabitants as they probably were in Drake's time. Antonio Vazquez de Espinosa, *Compendium of the West Indies.* David Howarth's *Panama.*

1 Philip's excommunication. Martin Hume, *Philip II.*
2 'I found this coast.' Document 11 in Wright's *Spanish Documents*; 'This place is as good as lost' (Document 20). For fear of English settlement in Panama, see dispatch from Municipal Council of Panama to King. 24 February 1573.
3 Diego Calderon's report. Wright, Document 30.
4 'It is a sad thing to contemplate.' Wright, Document 26.

CHAPTER VII

To the Great South Sea

For this chapter, Crispin Gill, *Plymouth*, and Jewitt, *History of Plymouth.*

1 Grand Signior, Cal. S.P. (Venetian) 7 July 1587.
2 Scottish incursions. G. A. Hayes McCoy, *Scots Mercenary Forces in Ireland.*
3 John Dee: Fulke Greville, *Life of Sidney;* J. A. Williamson, *Age of Drake*; E. G. R. Taylor, *Tudor Geography* and 'Master John Dee, Drake and the Straits of Anian', *Mariner's Mirror*, 1929. John Dee's 'Petty Navy Royal' and *Famous and Rich Discoveries.*
4 Hakluyt, *Discourse of Western Planting*, Chap. 4.

5 Dee, *Famous and Rich Discoveries*.
6 Cal. S.P. (Spain). This seems to be the earliest mention of Drake in Spanish diplomatic correspondence.
7 Camden.
8 'The Missing Draft Project'. E. G. R. Taylor, *Geographical Journal*, 1930.

CHAPTER VIII

The Bay of Crisis

So resounding an exploit as the voyage of circumnavigation has naturally a rich sheaf of sources. *The World Encompassed by Sir Francis Drake* (1628), is edited by Vaux (1854) who includes a narrative by John Cooke (Harl. MSS. 540) and material on Doughty's trial. Zelia Nuttall in *New Light on Drake* translates a mass of relevant Spanish documents, e.g. John Drake's two accounts of the voyage (given to the Inquisition), one in Sante Fé, River Plate, 1584, the second at Lima, 1587. For Francis Fletcher's account of the voyage, see N. M. Penzer *The World Encompassed* (1926). There is also E. G. R. Taylor, 'More Light on Drake' (*Mariner's Mirror*, 1930). Greville's *Life of Sidney*, for Queen's gift of perfumes.

1 The Doughty affair: Gregory Robinson, 'Forgotten Life of Sir Francis Drake' (*Mariner's Mirror*, 1921); Fletcher's notes in B. M. Sloane MSS. No. 61, 'Indictment of Doughty', B. M. Harl. MS. 6221. f. 9; Minority report by Doughty's brother, imprisoned in the Marshalsea, 'When the Queen did knight Drake she did then knight the arrantest knave, the vilest villain, the falsest thief and the cruellest murderer that ever was born.' Corbett, *Drake and the Tudor Navy*, vol. II, p. 341, and State Papers (Domestic) Elizabeth, clxiii, 19.
2 Unified command at sea, essential as it seems to us, was difficult to accept. Some consequences of the failure to do so can be studied in C. R. Boxer's *Tragic History of the Sea*.

CHAPTER IX

The Boldness of this Low Man

Authorities as for previous chapter; Zelia Nuttall's texts from the Spanish (*New Light on Drake*) are most valuable; Espinosa Vazquez, *West Indies*, describes the South American coast as it was a little after Drake's time. For the Oxenham expedition Hakluyt, X and XI, also Wright, *Documents*, Nuttall, *New Light*.

1 Chapter heading. Don Miguel de Eraso y Aguilar to the King.

2 Oxenham was caught by the Spaniards through the carelessness of his companions who left a trail of broken biscuit behind them as they passed through the woods.
3 'Fluent and vigorous Spanish.' It is clear from this incident and others during the voyage that Drake could express himself in Spanish. See, however, the note (Chap. XII) on Torrequemada who negotiated with Drake at Santo Domingo.
4 'This very strange affair.' The King to Bernardino de Mendoza, Cal. S.P. (Spain) 10 August 1579.

CHAPTER X

Spill or Save

Main sources as before.
1 Hakluyt, *Discourse of Western Planting.*
2 The Indians, see Kroeber's *Handbook of Indians of California.*
3 Until the arrival at New Albion, there was no sickness in the *Golden Hind*, a remarkable achievement for that time. Keevil, *Medicine and the Navy.*
4 'Enough to break the heart of a miser.' *The World Encompassed*, Vaux.

CHAPTER XI

New Year's Day at Court

1 Sir Philip Sidney, quoted in A. H. Bill, *Astrophel*, p. 234.
2 The thirteen change points. Robinson, *British Post Office.*
3 Cal. S.P. (Spain) 16 Oct 1580.
4 Among other proposals, it was suggested that the adventurers should get their money back plus one hundred per cent on condition that Philip stopped interfering in Ireland. Cal. S.P. (Spain) 1580–6, pp. 59 and 63.
5 Mendoza to the King. Cal. S.P. (Spain) 5 September 1579.
6 The master thief. Quoted in Stow.
7 Mendoza's interview. Cal. S.P. (Spain) III. 9 October 1581.
8 £10,000. John Drake told Inquisition it was 40,000 pesos.
9 Cal. S.P. (Spain) June 1581.
10 The value of the loot is fully discussed in W. R. Scott's *English Scottish and Irish Companies.*
11 J. M. Keynes, *A Treatise on Money*, pp. 156–7.
12 Cal. S.P. (Spain) 1580–6, pp. 8 and 9.
13 Search among the manuscripts at the Bibliothèque Nationale has failed

to find the 'richly ornamented map of the circumnavigation' last catalogued as MS. fr. 15454. fol. 133 and sent to Henri after he had written to Walsingham (12 March 1585) and asked for one.

14 Quoted in Kraus, *Sir Francis Drake.*

15 Dealings with pirates, K. R. Andrews, *Elizabethan Privateering.*

16 Stendhal. *Abbesse de Castro.*

17 Cal. S.P. (Spain) 1578. 'Apart from the fruit of her robberies, England is poor.' Antonio Perez, *L'Art de gouverner.* 'Nothing is thought to have enriched the English more than the war with the Spaniards,' Venetian Ambassador, quoted in Andrews, *Elizabethan Privateering.*

18 Mendoza's report. Cal. S.P. (Spain) January 1581.

CHAPTER XII

War for the Atlantic

For a general account of the West Indies Raid, Corbett, *Navy During the Spanish War*; Bigges, *Sir Francis Drake's West India Voyage*; Fray Pedro Simon, *Noticias Historiales* (trans. *A Spanish Account of Drake's Voyage*) is useful for the attacks on Santo Domingo and Cartagena.

1 The Queen at Deptford – Corbett, *Drake*; Jenkins, *Elizabeth the Great.*

2 The slipper incident, Cal. S.P. (Spain) 1580–86, p. 573.

3 John Drake – see Nuttall, *New Light.*

4 'They must have found very wealthy regions.' Mercator to Ortelius. Letter translated in Kraus, *Sir Francis Drake*, p. 86.

5 Dom Antonio's jewel. Corbett's *Drake and the Tudor Navy*, vol 1, p. 348 et seq.

6 The Elizabethan social system. Bindoff, *Elizabethan Society and Government.*

7 Crispin Gill, *Buckland Abbey.*

8 The naval war in Mediterranean. Braudel.

9 Mendoza warns Philip, 'They are building ships.' Cal. S.P. (Spain) 1581, p. 72.

10 Walsingham's plan. Conyers Read, *Mr Secretary Walsingham.*

11 R. B. Wernham, *Elizabethan War Aims.*

12 Carleill, *D.N.B.* article.

13 Fleet seen off at Woolwich: Lord Talbot's letter to Earl of Rutland, 14 July 1585 (Hist. MSS. Comm. xii. iv 178).

14 The attack on Queen's courier. (Hist. MSS. Comm. xii. iv. 178).

15 Fray Pedro Simon. *Noticias Historiales de la Conquesta de Tierra Firma.* Fray Simon was a theology professor at Bogota who talked to many who had witnessed these events.

16 Spanish accounts of Santo Domingo attack. Documents 11–20 in Wright, *Further English Voyages*; A. K. Jameson, *New Spanish Documents*.

17 'There had been 1,600,000 of them on the island when the Spaniards arrived.' Fray Pedro Simon. For comparable decline in Mexican population, Cook and Borah, *Population of Central Mexico*.

18 Drake negotiated ransom with Garcia Fernandez de Torrequemada, H. M. Factor for Hispaniola, who sent this word portrait to the King: 'Drake is a man of medium stature, blond, rather heavy than slender, merry, careful. He commands and governs imperiously. He is feared and obeyed by his men. He punishes resolutely. Sharp, restless, well-spoken, inclined to liberality and to ambition, vainglorious, boastful, not very cruel.'

Torrequemada's sketch agrees closely with that of Zarate. But, he says, Drake spoke no Spanish, which is at variance with the testimony of those Spaniards who met him during the Circumnavigation. No doubt, Drake was astute enough to negotiate in his own language and feign ignorance of Spanish. (Document 56, in Wright's *Further English Voyages*.)

CHAPTER XIII

The Damage Done by this Corsair

Sources for Cartagena attack as for Santo Domingo. In addition, Spanish narratives, Documents in Wright, *Further English Voyages*.

1 'More likely, the black emblems.' Oxenham had shown a black flag as a signal to the Cimarrons.

2 One Spanish estimate is that the damage to the town amounted to 400,000 ducats. Wright, *Further English Voyages*. In September 1586, the Venetian ambassador in Madrid reported that Drake had returned with a million (ducats) in gold and 300 cannon. Cal. S.P. (Ven.) 12 September 1586.

3 Raleigh: 'No man makes haste to the market,' Monson, *Naval Tracts* (vol 2); quoted Quinn's *Roanoke Voyages*.

4 'This climate, at all times dangerous to Europeans, deadly during six months of the year, infectious to strangers accustomed to a temperate air, to a convenient way of living and to a wholesome nourishment, becomes soon their grave. The most moderate computations make the loss of the English amount to four-tenths . . . It is very remarkable that the Spaniards do not lose more than one-tenth.' Introduction to Thomas Jefferys' atlas *The West-India Atlas* 1775.

5 The Roanoke settlement. D. B. Quinn, *The Roanoke Voyages*.

6 'William of Nassau.' C. V. Wedgwood, *William the Silent.*
7 'The cause best known to God.' Drake to Burghley. Lansdowne MSS. 51. art. 14.
8 The English estimate of the plunder was £60,000. Bigges; Corbett, *Spanish War.*
9 Gradenigo's report, 12 April 1586, Cal. S.P. (Ven.) vol 8.
10 The Pope's anxiety about Philip's health – Gritti's dispatch, 10 May 1856. Cal. S.P. (Ven.) vol 8.
11 Portraits to Joyeuse and Epernon, Mendoza from Paris. Cal. S.P. (Dom.) 26 September 1586.

CHAPTER XIV

The Wind Commands Me Away

General sources for the Cadiz Raid are Corbett, *Papers relating to Navy during the Spanish War*; C. Hopper, 'Sir Francis Drake's memorable service'. Hakluyt, *Principal Navigations,* VI. A valuable and handsome contribution to understanding of the action is William Borough's map (Public Records Office, S.P. 12. Eliz. 202, f. 20); Fernandez Spanish accounts in Duro.
1 'Drak est en mer.' Quoted Conyers Read, *Walsingham.*
2 Walsingham to English ambassador, Paris.
3 Corbett, *Spanish War.*
4 Drake to Walsingham, 27 April 1587. Corbett, *Spanish War.*
5 'Six more Queen's ships of the second sort.' Monson, *Naval Tracts,* vol. 1; Corbett, *Spanish War,* p. 133.
6 The commercial side of the venture. Monson's *Naval Tracts,* vol 1.
7 Walsingham despondent, see Conyers Read. *Walsingham,* vol 3.
8 Burghley to Parma's agent in Corbett, *Spanish War* p. 148.
9 Borough, 'a good wife'. *D.N.B.*

CHAPTER XV

It is Enough to be Duke of Medina

Main Sources: Corbett and Laughton are now of increasing interest. For Parma, van der Essen, *Farnese,* vol. 5.
1 Howard. Cal. S.P. (Dom.), 1581–90, p. 492.
2 Crofts to the Queen, Conyers Read, *Walsingham.*
3 Parma on Crofts.
4 Trouble in the Cloth trade. Conyers Read, *Mr Secretary Cecil.*
5 'He has never fought yet.' Advices from London in Cal. S.P. (Spain). Was the Queen play-acting so as to separate herself from Drake in Spanish eyes?

6 Parma on Sluys. van der Essen, *Farnese.*
7 'Knowledge is never too dear.' Conyers Read, *Walsingham.*
8 Antony Standen's career. Birch, *Memoirs of reign of Elizabeth.*
9 'Oho!' van der Essen, *Farnese.*
10 Bandits and outlaws. Cal. S.P. (Ven.) 27 June 1587.
11 For Parma's growing pessimism, see van der Essen, *Farnese*, vol 5.
12 English ambassador, Constantinople, William Harbone. Best account of his mission in Cal. S.P. (Ven.) 1581–90 p. xxix.
13 'God has shown me a favour.' Cal. S.P. (Ven.) February 1587.
14 The English scouts Cal. S.P. (Spain).
15 Drake to Essex. 'The employment of your lordship's crowns,' Corbett, *Drake and the Tudor Navy.* vol II. pp. 129–31.
16 Parma's army. van der Essen, *Farnese*, vol 5, and his boat-fleet, seen by English observer. Cal. S.P. (Foreign) 1588.
17 Drake to Council, 30 March 1588, 'my very good lords . . .' Corbett, *Drake*, vol II, pp. 140–1.
18 James's religion. Cal. S.P. (Ven.) 2 July 1587.
19 'Since God has been pleased.' Cal. S.P. (Foreign) 5 April 1588.
20 Medina Sidonia. Fernandez Duro; O'Malley Pierson, 'A Commander for the Armada', *Mariner's Mirror*, November 1969.
21 'It is enough to be Duke of Medina.' O'Malley Pierson.
22 'The advantage of time and place.' Laughton, *Armada Papers.*

CHAPTER XVI

The Force and Flower of a Kingdom

The military preparations in England: Boynton, *Elizabethan Militia*; Cruickshank, *Elizabeth's Army.* Conyers Read, *Walsingham.*

1 Laughton, *Armada Papers.* Darell's task was to feed eighteen thousand men in two hundred ships strung out along the South Coast.
2 Laughton, *Armada Papers.* The beer ration may seem excessive, but the diet of the fleet was likely to promote thirst: three days a week of dried fish; three of salt beef or pork; one of bacon and pease, *Armada Papers.*
3 Medina Sidonia's fleet orders, translated and published in London, 11 May 1588, Cal. S.P. (Domestic).
4 Parma's preparations, van der Essen, *Farnese.*
5 Cal. S.P. (Domestic) 1581–1590, 16 May.
6 Antonio de Tasso, Cal. S.P. (Domestic) 1581–1590 (18 May 1588).
7 Cal. S.P. (Ven.) 9 July 1588.

8 'God send us a wind.' *Armada Papers*. 8 May 1588.

9 The English ships, William Hawkins (18 February 1587); Lord Henry Seymour; Howard to Burghley (21 February 1588); William Wynter (28 February); Laughton, *Armada Papers*.

10 The *Victory*; Gill, *Plymouth*.

11 'The sacred profession.' Captain Edward Turnor, quoted, Boynton, *Elizabethan Militia*.

12 'The breech of such a varlet.' William Harrison in *Elizabethan Militia*.

13 London train bands; Murdin, *State Papers*.

14 The royal bodyguard; Murdin.

15 Norreys, 'They all want the Spaniards to land.' See Norreys' biography in *D.N.B.*

16 Brooks, *Sir Christopher Hatton*.

17 Digges, Wilford in Boynton, *Elizabethan Militia*.

18 Shrewsbury. Cal. S.P. (Domestic) 9 August 1588.

19 Walsingham, suffering from 'tympany and carnosity', a carbuncle or tumour. He paid 25*s*. for a corselet.

20 The beacons. Brooks, *Hatton*; and Boynton.

21 Marquis of Winchester, Boynton, *Elizabethan Militia*.

22 Huguenot highwaymen. Cal. S.P. (Ven.) 28 August 1588.

CHAPTER XVII

Great Expense of Powder and Bullet

Authorities for the Armada campaign: Fernandez Duro, *La Armada Invencible*; Laughton, *Armada Papers*, Michael Lewis, *The Spanish Armada*, *Armada Guns*; Corbett, *Papers relating to the Spanish War*; van der Essen, *Farnese*; J. R. Hale, *Great Armada*; Laughton, *Armada Papers*; Mattingley, *The Defeat of the Spanish Armada* (an outstanding modern account), Ubaldino, *Narration*.

1 The up-channel current. Crispin Gill, *Plymouth*.

2 The quarrel of Carey and Gilberte. Laughton, *Armada Papers*.

3 Drake's Accounts for the year of the Armada. MS. in private hands.

4 'An enormous quantity of powder and shot.' Sir George Carey, quoted Lewis, *Armada Guns*.

5 The battle of the *Revenge*. Lewis, *Hawkins Dynasty*.

6 Fenner, 'the great seagate'. Laughton, *Armada*, vol II.

7 Medina Sidonia's messengers, van der Essen. *Farnese*.

8 Parma could not come out. Essen and van Meteren.

9 The Prince of Ascoli. van der Essen, *Farnese* (vol 5), and Cal. S.P. (Ven.) vol 8, p. 383.

CHAPTER XVIII

The Devil Ships

General sources, as for previous chapter.

1 Wynter suggests fireships. Cal. S.P. (Domestic) 1 August 1588; written from Harwich.
2 Drake's Accounts for the Armada Year. MS.
3 'The fireships had a mile and a half to cover.' Waters, 'The Elizabethan Navy'.
4 Wynter: 'Most time within speech.' Lewis, *Armada Guns.* Wynter was wounded in this action, not seriously, it appears.
5 'Your honour's most ready to be commanded.' 8 August, Drake to Walsingham, quoted Gill, *Plymouth.*
6 Seymour's annoyance. Letter of 12 August; Laughton, *Defeat of Armada*, vol 2.
7 'What courage.' Cal. S.P. (Ven.) 3 September 1588.
8 Drake, 'The uncertainty of these reports.' Quoted, Corbett, *Drake*, vol II, p. 302. After mid-August, the spring tides were past and there was no more to fear from Parma.
9 'I am very hungry.' A friend of the Venetian Ambassador Lippomano. Cal. S.P. (Ven.) vol 8, p. 394.
10 'The cruel and bloody hands.' Laughton, *Spanish Armada*, vol 2, p. 299.
11 Parma in Grand Place of Dunkirk. van der Essen, *Farnese.*
12 'It is a most pitiful sight.' Keevil, *Medicine and the Navy.*

CHAPTER XIX

The Pay you Give Soldiers

General sources for Portugal Expedition: Corbett, *Drake*; Monson, *Naval Tracts*; Cheyney, *History of England*; Andrews, *Drake's Voyages*; R. B. Wernham, 'Queen Elizabeth and the Portugal Expedition'; Hakluyt, *Principal Navigations* vol VI; Purchas, *His Pilgrims* vol XIX.

1 *Penguin English Folk Songs*, eds. R. Vaughan Williams and A. L. Lloyd.
2 Duplessis-Mornay. Cheyney, *History of England.*
3 The Herbery. Stow, *London*: Elliot-Drake, *Family of Drake.*
4 Essex, 'If I speed well.' Tenison, *Elizabethan England.*
5 Carey. *Memoirs.*
6 Fenner to Burghley, 'We trust in God.' Cal. S.P. (Domestic) ccxxiv. 13.
7 'Though I had no charge.' For Essex at Lisbon, Monson, *Naval Tracts.*
8 'So overweening spirits.' Ralph Lane, Muster Master of the expedition. See Monson, *Naval Tracts.*

9 'More men died in London in six months than twice our army.' Col. Anthony Wingfield and *Cambridge Modern History*, vol III.

10 'A woman, mistress of only half an island.' Dispatch to Venice of Tomaso Contarini, Cal. S.P. (Ven.) 1589.

11 'If so much had been done by the Queen's enemies.' Norreys in Cheyney, *History of England*; see too, Col. Wingfield and Sir Roger Williams, Corbett, *Drake*, vol II, pp. 349–50.

Oppenheim in his *Naval Tracts of Sir William Monson* (vol 1, p. 223) considers that if Drake had lost his touch in this operation, as he thought, it was due to bad health. It may be so, but the only evidence is a letter of 23 January 1589 (Add. MSS. 12507, f. 17) B.M. from Drake to Sir Julius Caesar excusing himself from attendance at the Admiralty Court, 'being touched with some grief before my coming out of London, with a strain I took in quenching the fire . . . and notwithstanding I have and do use all possible good means by physic following the advice of Doctor French' (spelt Fraunch) 'I do yet find little ease, for that my pain, not tarrying in one place, is fallen now into my legs and maketh me very unable to stand without much grief.' This seems to suggest some injury (a slipped disc?) rather than ill-health.

CHAPTER XX

Seville is Illuminated

General sources for the last voyage: Thomas Maynarde, *Sir Francis Drake and his voyage*; Anon, *The voyage truly discovered*; John Troughton, *Journal*; W. Bigges, *A Summary and True Discourse.*

1 The leat at Plymouth, and fortifying the port. Gill, *Plymouth.* Murdin, *State Papers*, January 1592 and August 1593.

2 Drake's Will. See Appendix I.

3 Seville was illuminated. Chaunu, *Séville.* Venetian ambassador's report to Doge. 'His Majesty shows the keenest delight and declares that this good news will help him to get well rapidly.' Cal. S.P. (Ven.) 14 May 1596.

CHAPTER XXI

Farewell, the Phoenix of our Age

1 Robert Hayman. *D.N.B.* and Hayman's *Quolibets.*

2 Norton's translation of Camden, *History.*

3 'The trumpet in doleful manner.' W. Bigges, *A Summary and True Discourse.*

Appendix I

Drake made two wills. The second, which supplemented and amended the first, was made on 27 January 1596 when he was 'now in service for the West Indies, being perfect of mind and memory thanks be therefor unto God, although sick in body'. The main difference between the two documents is that, by the second will, he bequeathed his manor of Yarcombe in Devon to his cousin Francis Drake of Esher, one of the Queen's equerries, on condition that his cousin paid £2,000 to his brother Thomas Drake of Plymouth. Further, he left his manor of Sampford Spiney to Jonas Bodenham. As for the rest, the earlier will was to stand.

There was very soon trouble in the Chancery Court over the second will, which Thomas Drake alleged was 'imperfect'. However, Francis Drake having produced the money at Plymouth Parish Church on the last day of 1597, the Court ordered that he was to have quiet possession of Yarcombe.

Against Jonas Bodenham, Thomas Drake was more successful. His argument can be seen in a mutilated bill of complaint presented to the Lord Keeper, Sir Thomas Egerton. Thomas Drake alleged that Bodenham not only wasted money Drake had put into his keeping 'at cards, dice and other like games playing away sometimes many hundred pounds at once', but would never give Drake an account of his outgoings. When matters came to a crisis Bodenham announced that his chamber had taken fire and the records had been destroyed. Drake believed this story.

After that, Bodenham secretly acquired a property in Ireland as 'a place of refuge in time to come' while he continued to fob his master off with the argument that to examine the accounts would be 'intricate and tedious' and that Drake should spare himself 'so infinite a labour'. In short, to the day of his death, Drake did not look at the books. Yet in the ship in which he and Bodenham sailed on that last voyage were important documents belonging to Drake. These Bodenham violently seized as soon as Drake was dead. The result was that Thomas Drake, his brother's executor, did not know how matters stood financially between the Queen and Sir Francis. Thomas Drake asked the Lord Keeper to order Bodenham to hand over the books or make good the money he had embezzled.

Bodenham in his answer denied that he had taken anything belonging to the late Sir Francis Drake; any papers in his possession related wholly to the business of the ship, which was Her Majesty's. On the contrary, before the breath was out of Sir Francis Drake's body, his brother, Thomas, fell to rifling the dead admiral's belongings so that there was nothing left for Drake's gentlemen. Bodenham had not, he said, kept the account books of the various voyages; had not gambled with Sir Francis Drake's money; had not set any papers on fire; and had bought the Irish property with his own money. Bodenham asked the Court to award him costs.

Thomas Drake, in his reply, stuck to his story of the fire and insisted that Bodenham had used £1,500 of Drake's money on the 'great purchase' in Ireland; he denied that he did 'fall a-riffling and gathering together' chests containing documents on the ship.

When the case came before the Court in November 1599, Bodenham did not appear and the Sheriff of Middlesex directed a commission of rebellion to Alderman Paul Banning to apprehend him. However that legal action may have ended, the fact is that Bodenham sold the Sampford Spiney estate to Thomas Drake in 1601. This may have been because the claim against Bodenham had been made good in Court. The legal tangle makes a sorry footnote to a tempestuous career.

Being wealthy and handsome, Lady Drake did not remain long in widowed solitude. In 1597, she married Sir William Courtenay, a widower with a large family.

(Drake's will is found in the Public Records Office, PROB/11/87 f.1. The Depositions in the case of Francis Drake *v*. Thomas Drake are at C 21/20/9, and those in Drake *v*. Bodenham at C2/ Eliz. D. I. The records of the proceedings in the latter case are at C33/93; C33/95; C33/97, and f. 769.

Appendix II

The Quest for Port Pheasant

But where was – or is – the hidden harbour that Drake called 'Port Pheasant'? Most writers have been content to say that it was on the Acla coast and to leave it at that. The Acla coast stretches for some distance on the west side of the Gulf of Darien. Sir Julian Corbett goes further. He describes it as 'a romantic natural harbour . . . in the silent recesses of the Gulf of Darien, an ideal pirate's lair. It was probably Puerto Escondido or "Secret Harbour" which lies some four leagues to the South-West of Caledonian Bay.'

This is confusing, even if it may be assumed that 'South-West' is a slip for which 'South-East' should be read. For the name Puerto Escondido occurs twice on the charts, each time at a distance of many miles from the Acla and neither looks secluded enough to be suitable as a hiding-place.

Port Pheasant is described thus in the account of the voyage which, probably, Drake himself corrected:

> 'A fine round bay, of verie safe harbour for all winds, lying between two high points, not past halfe a cables length over at the month, but within eight or ten cables length everie way, having ten or twelve fadome water, more or lesse, full of good fish, the soile also verie fruitfull.'

There are several claimants for the title and in each case there is some objection to acceptance:

(1) Puerto Escoces is certainly secluded and is approached between two 'high points'. But its approach channel is about a mile across and the harbour is two miles across. To enter it, a ship must pass to one side or the other of a rock planted directly in the fairway. The depth of water in the inner reach of the harbour is five or six fathoms, not eight or ten.

(2) Ten miles to the south-west of Puerto Escoces is another tempting cove, Puerto Carreto – between two high points, not so well sheltered as Puerto Escoces but almost perfectly circular. It has a depth of eight or nine fathoms. But its entrance is wider and the expanse of its harbour, larger than that of 'Port Pheasant'.

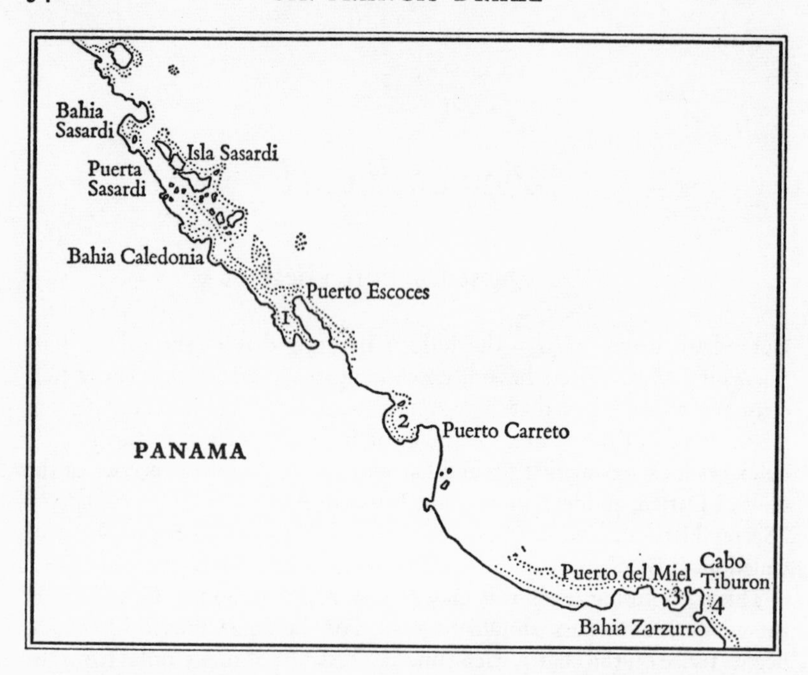

Twenty miles further east is Cape Tiburon, a high point which marks the boundary between Panama and Colombia. It shelters two coves, (3) Puerto del Miel to the west and (4) Bahia Zarzurro to the east. The first of these is too open to fit the description in the narrative.

Bahia Zarzurro is small, a mere crevice in the coast which rises steeply behind it in hills covered with tropical forest. Its entrance channel is about a hundred yards wide; its basin is about twice as wide. It is big enough to take a seventy-ton ship; it is deep enough – ten fathoms lessening to seven. But it has not the area attributed to 'Port Pheasant'. And, should the wind blow from the east, it would not provide shelter.

But it seems that the choice lies between this modest cleft in the Colombian Coast and Puerto Escoces. The latter has already a place in history. A century and a half later the ill-fated Scots expedition to Darien came to grief in its harbour. In spite of all the discrepancies I think Puerto Escoces was 'Port Pheasant'.

Bibliography

ANDREWS, K. R.: *Elizabethan Privateering*, Cambridge University Press, 1964.
ANDREWS, K. R.: *English Privateering & Voyages*, London, Hakluyt Society, 1959.
ANDREWS, K. R.: *Drake's Voyages*, London, Weidenfeld & Nicolson, 1967.

BESANT, Sir Walter: *London in the Time of the Tudors*, London, A. & C. Black, 1904.
BIGGES, Walter: *A Summary and True Discourse*, London, R. Field, 1589.
BINDOFF, S. T. *et al.*: *Elizabethan and Government Society*, London, Athlone Press, 1961.
BIRCH, Thomas: *Memoirs of the Reign of Queen Elizabeth*, 2 vols, London, 1751.
BOXER, C. R.: *The Tragic History of the Sea*, London, Hakluyt Society, 1959.
BOYNTON, Lindsay: *The Elizabethan Militia*, London, Routledge and Kegan Paul, 1967.
BRAUDEL, Fernand: *La Méditerranée à l'époque de Philippe II*, Paris, Armand Colin, 1949.
BROOKS, Eric St John: *Sir Christopher Hatton*, London, Routledge and Kegan Paul, 1967.

CALLENDER, Sir Geoffrey: 'Drake and his Detractors', in *Mariner's Mirror*, 1921.
CALLENDER, Sir Geoffrey: 'Fresh Light on Drake', *Mariner's Mirror*, 1923.
Cambridge Modern History, vol III (The Economy of Europe, 1559–1609; P. C. Spooner), Cambridge University Press, 1968.
CAMDEN, William: *The History of the most renowned and victorious princess Elizabeth, late Queen of England*, translated Norton, London, Fisher, 1630.
CHAUNU, H. and P.: *Séville et l'Atlantique*, Paris, Armand Colin, 1955–1957.

CHEYNEY, E. P.: *History of England from the defeat of the Armada*, London, Longmans, Green, 1914.

CLOWES, Sir William Laird: *The Royal Navy*, London, Sampson Low, 1899–1903.

COOLEY, W. D. (ed.): *Sir Francis Drake. His Voyage 1595 by Thomas Maynard*, London, Hakluyt Society, 1849.

COOK, S. F. and BORAH, W.: *The Population of Central Mexico 1531–1610*, Berkeley, 1960.

CORBETT, Sir Julian S.: *Papers relating to Navy during Spanish War*, London, Navy Records Society, 1898.

CORBETT, Sir Julian S.: *Drake and the Tudor Navy*, 2 vols, London, Longmans, Green, 1892.

CRUICKSHANK, C. G.: *Elizabeth's Army*, London, Oxford University Press, 1946.

DARBY, C. H. (ed.): *Historical Geography of England before 1800*, Cambridge University Press, 1951.

DAVENPORT, F. G.: *European Treaties bearing on the history of the United States*, Washington, vol 1, 1917.

DRAKE, Sir Francis, Bart.: *Sir Francis Drake Revived*, London, Nicholas Bourne, 1626. (Reprinted in I. A. Wright's *English Voyages*, 1932.)

DRAKE, Sir Francis, Bart.: *The World Encompassed*, London, Nicholas Bourne, 1628.

DEACON, Richard: *John Dee*, London, Muller, 1968.

DEE, John: 'The Petty Navy Royal' (in Edward Arber's *An English Garner*, vol 2), London, 1879.

ELIOTT-DRAKE, Lady: *The Family and Heirs of Sir Francis Drake*, London, Smith, Elder, 1911.

ESSEN, J. P. van der: *Alexandre Farnese*, Bruxelles, 1933–7.

EDEN, Richard: *A Treatise of the New India*, London, Sutton, 1553.

FERDINANDY, Michael de: *Karl V*, Tubingen, Verlag Hermann Leins, 1970.

FLETCHER, Francis: 'The World Encompassed', in John D. Upcott's *Three Voyages of Drake*, London, Ginn, 1936.

FERNANDEZ DURO, Cesareo: *La Armada Invencible*, Madrid, 1884–5.

GILL, Crispin: *Buckland Abbey* (A guide to the house), 1968.

GILL, Crispin: *Plymouth*, Newton Abbot, David & Charles, 1966.

GLASGOW, Tom: 'The Shape of the Ships that Defeated the Spanish Armada', London, *Mariner's Mirror*, 1964.

GREVILLE, Sir Fulke: *The Life of the Renowned Sir Philip Sidney*, Oxford, Clarendon Press, 1907.

HAYMAN, Robert: *Quolibets*, London, E. All-de. 1628.

HAKLUYT, Richard: 'Discourse of Western Planting', in *Original writings of the two Richard Hakluyts*, London, Hakluyt Society, 1955.

HAKLUYT, Richard: *The Principal Navigations*, 12 volumes, Glasgow, Maclehose, 1903–5.

Vol. VI. 'The Voyage of Sir Francis Drake to Cadiz.' 'A brief relation of the notable service performed by Sir Francis Drake upon the Spanish fleet prepared in the Gulf of Cadiz.'

'A true discourse written as it is thought by Colonel Anthony Wingfield employed in the voyage to Spain and Portugal, 1588.'

Vol. VII. 'The taking of the mighty and rich carrack called the Madre de Dios.'

Vol. IX. 'The relation of Nicolas Burgoignon alias Holy.'

'The voyage and course which Sir Francis Drake held from the haven of Guatulco . . . to the northwest of California.'

Vol. X. 'The third troublesome voyage of the right worshipful Sir John Hawkins.'

'The first voyage attempted and set forth by the valiant and expert captain Sir Francis Drake . . . about the year 1572.'

'The opinion of Don Alvaro Bazan, marquis of Santa Cruz . . . touching the fleet of Sir Francis Drake.'

'The famous expedition of Sir Francis Drake to the West Indies wherein were taken the cities of Santiago, etc.'

'The last voyage of Sir Francis Drake and Sir John Hawkins.'

Vol. XI. 'The famous voyage of Sir Francis Drake into the South Sea.'

'The voyage of Nuno de Silva, a Portugal pilot taken by Sir Francis Drake.'

'A letter written in the South Sea by Sir Francis Drake unto Mr John Wynter.'

'The voyage of Mr John Wynter into the South Sea.'

HALE, J. R.: *The Great Armada*, London, Nelson, 1913.

HALL, A. R.: *Ballistics in the 17th century*, Cambridge University Press, 1952.

HARING, C. H.: *The Spanish Empire*, New York, Oxford University Press, 1941.

HAWKINS, Sir Richard: *Observations in his voyage into the South Sea*, London, John Jaggard, 1622.

HAYES MCCOY, G. A.: *Scots Mercenary Forces in Ireland*, Dublin and London, Burns, Oates, 1937.

HOWARTH, David: *Panama*, New York, McGraw-Hill, 1966.

JAMESON, A. K.: 'Some New Spanish Documents dealing with Drake', London, *English Historical Review*, 1939.

JEFFERYS, Thomas: *The West-India Atlas*, London, 1775.

JENKINS, Elizabeth: *Elizabeth the Great*, London, Gollancz, 1958.

KEEVIL, J. J.: *Medicine and the Navy* (vol. 1), Edinburgh and London, E. and S. Livingstone, 1957–63.

KEYNES, J. M.: *A Treatise on Money*, London, Macmillan, 1930.

KRAUS, Hans P.: *Sir Francis Drake*, Amsterdam, N. Israel, 1970.

KROEBER, A. L.: *The Handbook of the Indians of California*, Smithsonian Institute, Bureau of American Ethnology, Washington, Government Printing Office, 1925.

LANDSTROM, Bjørn: *Sailing Ships*, London, Allen & Unwin, 1969.

LAUGHTON, Sir John K.: *State Papers relating to the Defeat of the Spanish Armada*, London, Navy Records Society, 1894.

LEMONNIER, Leon: 'Sir Francis Drake', in *La Grande Légende de la mer*, Paris, Le Renaissance du Livre, 1932.

LENG, Robert: 'Sir Francis Drake's Memorable Service', ed. Hopper, London, Camden Miscellany, V, 1863.

LEWIS, Michael: *The Hawkins Dynasty*, London, Allen & Unwin, 1969.

LEWIS, Michael: *Armada Guns*, London, Allen & Unwin, 1961.

LEWIS, Michael: *The Spanish Armada*, London, Batsford, 1960.

LYNCH, John: *Spain under the Hapsburgs*, Oxford, Blackwell, 1964.

McFEE, William: *Sir Martin Frobisher*, London, John Lane, The Bodley Head, 1928.

MARCEL, Gabriel A.: *Les Corsaires Français*, Paris, Ernest Levoux, 1902.

MATTINGLY, Garrett: *The Defeat of the Spanish Armada*, London, Cape, 1959.

MAYNARDE, Thomas: *Sir Francis Drake and his voyage*, London, Hakluyt Society, 1949.

MERRIMAN, R. B.: *The Rise of the Spanish Empire*, New York, Macmillan, 1918.

METEREN, E. van: *Histoire des Pays Bas*, La Haye, 1816.

MONSON, Sir W.: *Naval Tracts*, ed. P. Oppenheim, 5 vols, Navy Records Society, 1902–14.

MORYSON, Fynes: *An Itinerary*, London, 1617.

MOTLEY, J. L.: *History of the United Netherlands*, vol. II, London, 1860.

MURDIN, William: *A Collection of State Papers*, London, Bowyer, 1759.

NEALE, Sir John E.: *Queen Elizabeth*, London, Cape, 1934.

NEWTON, A. P.: *The European Nations in the West Indies*, London, A. and C. Black, 1966.

NUTTALL, Zelia: *New Light on Drake*, London, Hakluyt Society, 1914.

NUTTALL, Zelia: 'Communications on H. R. Wagner's criticisms' [reprinted from *Hispanic American Historical Review*], 1928.

OMAN, Sir Charles: *A History of the Art of War in the sixteenth century*, London, 1937.

PARRY, J. H.: *The Age of Reconnaissance*, London, Weidenfeld & Nicolson, 1963.

PEREZ, Antonio: *L'Art de gouverner*, Paris, Plon, 1867.

PHILIP II, King of Spain: *Lettres à ses filles*, ed. M. Gachard, Paris. Plon., 1884.

PIERSON, Peter O'Malley. 'A Commander for the Armada', *Mariner's Mirror*, November 1969.

PIGAFETTA, A.: *A Journal of Magellan's Journey*, ed. George Sanderlin, London, H. Hamilton, 1960.

PIRENNE, Jacques: *The Tides of History*, vol. II, London, Allen and Unwin, 1963.

PURCHAS, Samuel: *His Pilgrims*, Glasgow, Maclehose (20 vols), 1905–6.

Vol II. 'The second circumnavigation of the earth.' 'The renowned voyage of Sir Francis Drake.' 'The third circumnavigation . . . of Master Thomas Cavendish.'

Vol XVI. 'A brief history of Sir Francis Drake's Voyages. By R.M.'

Vol XIX. 'A Discourse of the Portugal Voyage . . . written it is thought by Col. Anthony Wingfield.'

QUINN, D. B.: 'Some Spanish Reactions to Elizabethan Colonial Enterprises', *Transactions Royal Historical Society*, 5th series, vol. 1, 1951.

QUINN, D. B.: *The Roanoke Voyages*, London, Hakluyt Society, 1955.

READ, Conyers: *Sir Francis Walsingham*, Oxford, Clarendon Press, 1925.

READ, Conyers: *Mr Secretary Cecil and Queen Elizabeth*, London, Cape, 1955.

READ, Conyers: *Lord Burghley and Queen Elizabeth*, London, Cape, 1960.

READ, Conyers: 'Queen Elizabeth's Seizure of Alva's pay ship', *Journal of Modern History*, pp. 443–64, 1933.

ROBINSON, Gregory: *Elizabethan Ship*, London, Longmans, 1956.

ROBINSON, Gregory: 'Forgotten Life of Sir Francis Drake', *Mariner's Mirror*, 1921.

ROBINSON, Howard: *The British Post Office*, London, Oxford University Press, 1948.

RONCIERE, C. G. Bourel de la: *Histoire de la marine française*, vols III and IV, Paris, 1899.

RONCIERE, C. G. Bourel de la: *Un Atlas inconnu*, Paris, Imprimerie Nationale, 1909.

ROWSE, A. L.: *The Expansion of Elizabethan England*, London, Macmillan, 1955.

ROWSE, A. L.: *Sir Richard Grenville*, London, Cape, 1937.

SCOTT, W. R.: *Constitution and Finance of English, Scottish and Irish Companies*, 3 vols, Cambridge University Press, 1910–12.

SMITH, Captain John: *Seaman's Grammar*, London, 1627.

SIMON, Fray Pedro: 'A Spanish Account of Drake's Voyage', *English Historical Review*, 1901.

STATE PAPERS, Public Records Office, Cal. Domestic Series, vol. CLIII.

STOW, John: *A Survey of London*, London, J. Wolf, 1598.

TAYLOR, E. G. R.: *Late Tudor and Early Stewart Geography*, London, Methuen, 1934.

TAYLOR, E. G. R.: 'The Missing Draft Project', *Geographical Journal*, London Royal Geographical Society, 1930.

TAYLOR, E. G. R.: *Tudor Geography*, London, Methuen, 1930.

TAYLOR, E. G. R.: 'Dawn of Modern Navigation', *Journal of the Institute of Navigation*, London, 1949.

TENISON, E. M.: *Elizabethan England*, 13 volumes, Royal Leamington Spa, issued for author, 1933–.

UBALDINO: *A Genuine and Most Impartial Narration*, 1740.

UNWIN, Rayner: *The Defeat of John Hawkins*, London, Allen and Unwin, 1960.

VAZQUEZ, Antonio de Espinosa: *Compendium and Description of the West Indies*, Washington, Smithsonian Miscellaneous Collections, 1942.

WAFER, Lionel: *A New Voyage and Description of the Isthmus of America*, London, 1699.

WAGNER, Henry R.: *Sir Francis Drake's Image*, San Francisco, 1926.

WATERS, D. W., R.N.: *The Art of Navigation in England in Elizabethan and early Stuart Times*, London, Hollis & Carter, 1958.

WATERS, D. W., R.N.: 'The Elizabethan Navy and the Armada Campaign', *Mariner's Mirror*, vol 35, 1949.

WEDGWOOD, C. V.: *William the Silent*, London, Cape, 1944.
WERNHAM, R. B.: 'Elizabethan War Aims and Strategy.' See S. T. Bindoff's *Elizabethan Government and Society*.
WERNHAM, R. B.: 'Queen Elizabeth and the Portugal Expedition of 1589', *English Historical Review*, 1951.
WILLIAMSON, J. A.: *The Age of Drake*, London, A. & C. Black, 1938.
WILLIAMSON, J. A.: *Hawkins of Plymouth*, London, A. & C. Black, 1949.
WILLIAMSON, J. A.: *Sir John Hawkins: The Time and the Man*, Oxford, Clarendon Press, 1927.
WRIGHT, I. A.: *Further English Voyages*, London, Hakluyt Society, 1951.
WRIGHT, I. A.: *Documents concerning English Voyages*, London, Hakluyt Society, 1932.
WRIGHT, I. A.: *Spanish Documents concerning English Voyages to the Caribbean*, London, Hakluyt Society, 1929.

XIVREY, Berger de: *Recueil de lettres missives de Henri IV*, Paris, Imprimerie Royal. 1843.

CALENDAR OF STATE PAPERS:
Domestic, Elizabeth 1547–1601. Longmans, London, 8 volumes, published between 1856 and 1857.
Foreign, 1558–1591. London, Longmans and later H.M.S.O., published between 1863 and 1969.
Venetian, 1556–1603. London, H.M.S.O., 1881–1897.
Spanish, *Calendar of Letters and State Papers . . . in Archives of Simancas. Elizabeth.* (1558–1608), 4 volumes, London, H.M.S.O., 1892–9.
Volumes of the *Dictionary of National Biography*, containing lives of Sir Thomas Baskerville, William Borough, Christopher Carleill, Sir Robert Carey, Dr John Dee, Sir John Norreys, Sir Walter Raleigh.

Index